INDISCRETIONS

Indiscretions:

Avant-Garde Film, Video, & Feminism

is Volume 12 in the series

THEORIES OF CONTEMPORARY CULTURE

Center for Twentieth Century Studies

University of Wisconsin-Milwaukee

General Editor, KATHLEEN WOODWARD

Patricia Mellencamp

INDISCRETIONS

AVANT-GARDE FILM, VIDEO, & FEMINISM

INDIANA UNIVERSITY PRESS

Bloomington and Indianapolis

"Video Politics" was published in *Discourse* 10, no. 2
(Spring–Summer 1988); another version appeared in *Global Television,* edited
by Cynthia Schneider and Brian Wallis (New York: Wedge Press, 1988).
"Postmodern TV" appeared in *Afterimage* 13, no. 5 (December 1985).
"Uncanny Feminism" was in *Afterimage* 14, no. 4 (September 1986) and
Framework (November 1986). "Images of Language and Indiscreet Dialogues"
was in *Screen* 28, no. 2 (Spring 1987). A long version of "Last Scene in the
Streets of Modernism" was published in *East-West Film Journal* 3, no. 1
(December 1988).

The paper used in this publication meets the minimum requirements of American
National Standard for Information Sciences—Permanence of Paper for Printed
Library Materials, ANSI Z39.48-1984.

Manufactured in the United States of America

Library of Congress Cataloging-in-Publication Data
Mellencamp, Patricia
Indiscretions : avant-garde film, video & feminism / Patricia
Mellencamp.
p.   cm.
Includes bibliographical references (p.   ).
ISBN 0–253–33743–7 (alk. paper).—ISBN 0–253–20587–5 (pbk. : alk. paper)
1. Experimental films—History and criticism.   2. Feminism and
motion pictures.   I. Title.
PN1995.9.E96M45   1990
791.43'0973'09047—dc20   89–45804
1 2 3 4 5 94 93 92 91 90   CIP

GRATITUDE

My friends and colleagues who have shared their knowledge, eccentricities, and friendship with me populate this book. Of my Milwaukee connections, particularly Stephen Heath, in various seminars from the late 1970s to early 1980s, has deeply influenced my thoughts about Hollywood film (whose history I teach, along with other national cinemas, in my everyday life) while Teresa de Lauretis, during her lengthy tenure in Milwaukee, existed as a feminist friend of stylish inventiveness and intellectual rigor. My colleagues in the Film Department, Bob Nelson, Dick Blau, and Rob Danielson, share my great respect for these films. My friends in the Modern Studies program, Herbert Blau and Kathleen Woodward, share my fascination with artists. Patrice Petro shares my love of cinema. Meaghan Morris is, pedagogically speaking, all of the above.

To Rob and Dae Mellencamp, extraordinary human beings, who supported me into writing a book and then left for college, and who live in fear of my sentimentality and weepy declarations of respect and love; to Peg and Bob Jewson, who gave me a happy history which included strong, working women and constant support, and who funded and upscaled my daily life; to Nancy Mooney, the best of all sisters, who shared my past and advises my present; to Marge and the women of New Day, love and gratitude. This book is dedicated to you, and to my sidekicks, B.P. and Baggins.

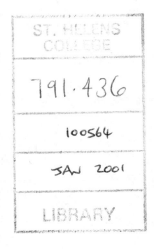

CONTENTS

PROLOGUE

Speaking Personally

During the 1960s and 1970s in the United States, the noble mission of three broad but then very marginal-to-scandalous discourses and practices—avant-garde, feminism, and theories of the text and subjectivity—was to create more aesthetically and politically satisfying cultures. But seen from the vantage point of the 1980s, the differences among them are painfully clear: the difficulty of locating any subject position for the female spectator in many U.S. avant-garde films and videotapes; the hostility of U.S. critics of avant-garde to contemporary theory; theorists' shunning of cinema and video in general as mere popular culture or avant-garde work as obscurantist or poorly/badly made; the tendency of many feminist practices to eschew avant-garde work and theory as jargonist elitism while favoring the populism of alternative "positive images"; the focus of feminist film theory (and most film theory) on the construction/use of narrative in classical movies, thereby producing "ruptures" via deconstruction with places for women in virtually any film; the banishment of both word and place of women in many theories of the text and/or subject; and the glaring absence of a social politics in avant-garde practices as well as theory. Along with these differences are the cultural divergences between film and video—recently in realignment but traversing different social and artistic paths, a separatism defended by arguments of ontology through the 1960s, 1970s, and early 1980s.

Granted these good reasons for acrimony, and with historical and cultural specificity in mind, the intense debates between these then marginal practices have been the liveliest and most fruitful intellectual/political encounters of the past decades. As Barthes remarked, "With intellectual things we produce simultaneously theory, critical combat, and pleasure."[1] And combat is an apt word, not only for avant-garde with its military etymology. There were moments at the Milwaukee film theory conferences from the mid- to late 1970s when speech contained an almost palpable violence. I envisioned a shoot-out between the "humanists" and the "theorists." The generic labels—avant-garde, theory, and feminism—had specific, oppositional meanings in the 1970s; each faction met with outright hostility or patronizing derision within the academy, although the lines of disputation were drawn differently. It is important to remember the scholastic furor triggered by "theory," vitriolically attacked by defensive humanists who had read very little of it. Avant-garde films precipitated outraged walkouts due to "senseless" boredom and "meaninglessness," usually experienced by guilty scholars who had seen few, if any, films.

A mere twelve years have passed since the first of these events and memories. Predictably, the debates have cooled down and defused, with, however, a difference that remains a symptom and a problem. Unlike the generic acceptance of theory and avant-garde as central, defining terms and accepted concepts in the mid-1980s debates, feminism's centrality and effects, while enacted in mandatory claims by intellectuals to political correctness, are still contained by denial, acts of disavowal. Yes, feminism was important, but it is over, history; feminism is now acclaimed, even victorious, but old hat, something so apparent and achieved by now that further arguments are unnecessary.

As Barthes argued, "we subject the objects of knowledge and discussion—as in any art—no longer to an instance of truth, but to a consideration of *effects*."[2] This crucial displacement of "truth," promulgated by humanities professors, from center stage by questions of reception, effectivity, subjectivity, and the conceptualization of audiences is occurring in theory and in pedagogy. In our arguments, the formerly acknowledged but artificial or illusory divisions between art and mass culture no longer cohere; the demarcations among media have been elided, just as efforts to taxonomize work into, for example, narrative or not have been abandoned.

This book will consider some effects on avant-garde film and video of the collision/collusion with contemporary theory. (One notable effect was Peter Gidal's 1978 declaration, in an impassioned debate with Jean Louis Comolli, translated/mediated by Stephen Heath, that representation of women was impossible given the sexist baggage of connotation which their images had historically accumulated.) Theoretical discourses imported into the United States during this twenty-year span—for example, those of Roland Barthes, Walter Benjamin, Michel Foucault, Jean Baudrillard, Gilles Deleuze, and Felix Guattari—will mark detours. The significant coupling in film theory of Freud with Jacques Lacan (and, minimally here, Marx with Louis Althusser) will insistently return, inflected by feminist interpretations.

Specific analyses of films and videotapes—perhaps unfamiliar and thus disengaging moments of lag—will suggest the transverse relation between theory and avant-garde, mutually inflected by context. That avant-garde works are, in themselves, theories of space, time, and culture is a primary assumption. My excursive remarks have no pretensions of being comprehensive or an overview of this complex, rich, and feisty cultural period. I merely want to analyze a few films and videotapes through and in tandem with historically coincident theories. I prefer foraging through texts, picking and choosing ideas rather than marshaling great systems, anticipating my arrival and returning later to the same issues. Like the Soviet constructivists and Sally Potter, I prefer the spiral which allows revisions rather than a straight and dogged line. Rather than the grand and pithy summary of others' writing, often a flat, dull reduction, I prefer quotations, a tactic which retains a variety of styles, intonations, and, I hope, accuracy. I try to let others speak for themselves, although I imagine myself in dialogue. Many of the scattered quotations are rich with ideas I cherish but do not dissect. Fragments have always interested me, perhaps explaining my attraction to Barthes. Partial, angled, kaleidoscopic views intrigue me while omniscient visions raise an anxiety of "truth" and "power." Questions and contradictions which continue to transform with the hindsight of history and the humility of age, unexpectedly flipping over to reveal the other side of the proposition, reveal more to me than answers, explaining my continuing interest in Freud, who argued through contradictions.

I have left out analyses of many films and videos which I have studied in detail for the simple reason of presumed unfamiliarity as well as the current fashion of criticism: metaphorical proclamation about the state of culture, supported by brief, wide-ranging citations as documented assertions, rather than detailed, textual explication is the postmodern, academic style. The list of absentees includes films by Peter Kubelka, Tony Conrad, Paul Sharits, Ernie Gehr, Barry Gerson, along with the earlier films of Rainer. Although I refer to Brakhage, I do not analyze any film in detail; P. Adams Sitney and Annette Michelson have already studied his work in depth. That I arranged encounters between avant-garde artists and scholars of theory (and history) at the Milwaukee conferences with my cohorts Stephen Heath and Teresa de Lauretis, as well as importing many filmmakers to show their work throughout a fifteen-year period, should be noted, along with the fact that many of the protagonists of these debates are my acquaintances and friends. Hence I write with some neutrality qualified by firsthand experience.

There is an argument and historical trajectory: the move, for women, from the late 1960s and 1970s paradoxes of "sexual liberation" (including being a sexual partner for the nomadic artist—permanently as wife, great mother, business manager, and general caretaker or transiently as postscreening reward, plucked from various audiences on tour) to the 1980s recognition of female subjectivity is of critical significance, a shift from being a desirable, supportive object to becoming a speaking subject, artist, or writer. Accompanying this inclusion has been an expansion(ism) of the binary model of difference to include racial, cultural, and chronological as well as sexual differences—collisions productive of knowledge. In the scholastic move to cultural studies, intertextual and contextual differences must be added to the list. As Foucault pointed out, differences, like power and pleasure, can be beneficial, productive as well as prohibitive. Contradictions can provide openings as well as functioning as containments. ("Difference" as a theoretical concept might have lost all meaning in its conclusive grasp, with its opposition, "indifference," assuming currency, gaining ascendancy; if everything is difference, then only indifference is argument.)

Other seismic cultural shifts include the moves from pop art to postmodernism, from counter- to consumer culture, from process to product, from film to video, from cinema to television, from underground to academic, from politics to therapy, and from protest to worship. The social landscape has remarkably changed to conservative, high-fashion, sports car politics.

The theoretical object beneath avant-garde, "bourgeois culture," has swerved from the left to the right. Like a lumbering behemoth, debates regarding avant-garde remain ploddingly, familially constant, the same spokespersons dragging their by now representative bodies to the podium or into the fray yet again to defend their maligned avocation, as yet unsanctioned by history or art. This ahistorical constancy of avant-garde as something you can count on, art that is "there for you," is precisely not avant-garde.

Let me parenthetically digress to the personal: from being nurturing curators, critics, and applauding fans for scholars and artists alike (functions which I, like many women behind the avant-garde and theory scenes, have performed as "hostess"—organizer, fund raiser, party giver, chauffeur, and innkeeper; I shudder when I remember how many events I arranged rather than writing), women are claiming their on- and off-screen work; this emerging shift in power has altered the edifice of independent film and video; the effects of feminism on film theory have been virtually definitive.

Indeed, it could be argued that by not heeding women and feminism (along with other oppositional marginalities, such as race and ethnicity), the male-dominated U.S. avant-garde made a critical error, losing a golden opportunity to maintain its radical impulse, eventually falling into a familiar, tired patriarchy, however marginal, nonprofitable, or artistic. In addition, the avant-garde's stated disdain toward analyzing popular culture (particularly in many artists' other role as teacher) reeked of elitism, albeit a long-haired, stoned, hippy figuration. Continental theory (which unbalanced the entrenched conventions of the classical text, along with unsettling the hierarchy of intellectual power, letting women into the debates) was ignored or disparaged. Favoring art as countercultural life-style fostered by drugs, random sex, booze, and introspective individuality, many artists seemed to be trapped in a time warp—living out the turn-of-the-century dream of romanticism rather than engaging with emergent voices, including the knowledge of mass culture held by their audiences and students. That mass culture, particularly television, has rearranged everyday life, politics, and culture in the United States, altering perception and reception, was rarely considered.

When seen historically and in relation to audiences' learned conventions of either the classical Hollywood cinema or the European narrative avant-garde, the films were, and continue to be, aesthetically, formally radical, frequently upsetting. (At the end of a screening of Snow's *La Region Centrale* at a Milwaukee conference, Jean-Francois Lyotard and I were the only people left in the audience of initially over one hundred scholars; the glass on the theater door had been shattered from the many slams of angry viewers; I have encountered glowing references to this film by writers who walked out on it in rage.) The garb and context of protest and the counterculture, including an opposition to commodity culture simply labeled "Hollywood," suggested a political radicalism as well. Thus, a paradox (comparable to the premises of the counterculture) was operative: while the work was modern or postmodern, the intellectual premises, including the enshrinement of the suffering male artist laboriously producing the precious art object, smacked of the nineteenth century and romanticism. While hanging out with scruffy student converts and smoking pot at what seemed like a twenty-year traveling party, eating health foods, wearing Birkenstock sandals, and on the road with only a knapsack and cans of 16mm films, New York, MOMA, the Whitney, and fame were ever-present goals. I love Robert Nelson's still incredulous description of his instant fame and artistic status: one review by Jonas Mekas of *Oh Dem Watermelons* and he was virtually an overnight sensation on the circuit. All of this while he was having fun with his friend William Wiley by making off-the-cuff films.

There was a star system, indeed (with a coastal bias—New York being slightly superior to San Francisco and Chicago). Although success was not measured by money, cars, houses, and designer fashion, it was embodied in famous names and landmark films, and fueled by gossip; word of new work spread in a flash via a private network of aficionados; filmmakers' reputations verbally and intimately preceded them. We knew about Owen Land's parsimonious spending habits, as well as his various spiritual conversions; Paul Sharit's courting of violence, his brushes with death, worried his friends. However, there was a significant difference from the Hollywood star system: these famous folk would travel to our classrooms and would become, at least for that visit, our close friends. But best of all, fame and status could be conferred on anyone, even after a first film, and without any formal training. Celebrity, like exhibition, was accessible and could be immediate.

Knowledge of film history or criticism was not a requirement. In fact, some filmmakers/teachers believed that the less one knew about cinema (heaven-forbid theory), the better to claim artistry via intuition. The standards for adjudging works of art and the qualifications for making avant-garde films (and, significantly, teaching them, resulting in the recent situation in which certain filmmaker/teachers are, fifteen years later, learning about narrative cinema and watching television) were unfamiliar, up for grabs. The movement and its reception were personal and idiosyncratic more than institutional, to a degree; at the same time, institutions such as the Whitney and the National Endowment for the Arts and *Film Culture* were determinate; in their own way, the cooperatives, along with critics, meted out acclaim and inclusion, based on an artistic ranking; there was definitely a pecking order, although it was denied by the new radical pluralism.

In production, distribution, and exhibition, the edict "the personal is political" was taken literally; "person" was inscribed as the quintessential value. It was not so much the Whitney as John Hanhardt's convictions and labor at the Whitney. The marks and scratches left on a print were not errors but experimental inspirations of the maker, incorporated by chance. Rough, fragmented editing did not lead to illegibility but was a sign of the humble conditions of production, of personal invention rather than a critique or revelation of the cinematic apparatus. Thus, rather than generating theoretical models other than anti-narrative, criticism was delimited to specific films (as unique) and personal testimony; to a degree, it stopped with artist recall and anecdote. As the great film would reveal the hand of the artist, so could we meet him, in person. The "personal" was both the glory and the pitfall of the movement, without a national structure of permanent exhibition (with New York, San Francisco, Chicago, and Minneapolis significant exceptions), dependent on stalwart individuals. (In one of the many ways that the 1980s rewrote the 1960s, this claim, the equation of person with truth and affect, was operative within mass culture, particularly television; proliferating "talk" shows such as Oprah Winfrey's or Phil Donahue's produced people as political positions; to disagree was to discredit a person, with "feelings" and "real experience"; or, voters liked Ronald Reagan, the charming person and husband, while aware that he was an incompetent administrator and mediocre father.)

Momentarily, it might appear that avant-garde has spoiled to retrograde, the good old days; or, it is believed to be over; or, it has abruptly shifted in the 1980s to pursue rather than unravel, overthrow, or critique narrative in frequently opaque, awkward "features"—to a degree giving up the good fight of variable duration, alternate structures of temporality. (Or, its project has been taken up and inverted by popular culture—MTV.) In cinema, as in television, time is money; a ticket still buys a feature-length narrative, a regulated, predictable economy of time and story. By and large, artists did not heed Maya Deren's oft-repeated dictum that contemporary artists needed to be in the forefront of knowledge, what she classically called philosophy; for her—a tireless proselytizer and pedagogue, arguing against romanticism, which she equated with surrealism, as well as being a filmmaker and writer—good art and advanced scholarship were inextricable. Many independent filmmakers resisted two decades of the liveliest radical (in its time and context) thought, including rhetoric and linguistics, Marxism and structuralism, semiotics and psychoanalysis, denigrating the new theory, including feminism.

Most filmmakers failed to notice that they had everything in common with, everything to gain from, these new unsettling and marginal discourses, which they avoided like the plague. Like avant-garde claims for access to the artistic means of production for so long dominated by studio commerce, which held to narrative's conventions and temporality, theories of the text, subjectivity, and particularly feminism were claims for access, participation, and equality; they were strategies of resistance, operating across the artificial divide between art and mass culture. On the other hand, the debate over narrative or not ignored or derailed the avant-garde's critique of the institutional practices of dominant cinema—the desire for an alternative economics, other conditions and venues of production, distribution, and exhibition, in tandem with a new aesthetics.

I use the term *avant-garde* advisedly, aware of the value of recent attempts to categorize and differentiate avant-garde from modernism—for example, Peter Burger, Peter Wollen, Andreas Huyssen, and Paul Willemen—and both of these concepts from postmodernism—for example, Huyssen, Lyotard, Hal Foster, Craig Owens, and Fredric Jameson (only Willemen and Wollen deal primarily with film). With film and video, aligned technologically and institutionally with precious art *and* reproducible mass culture, the assessment of borders and fault lines along a historical trajectory becomes difficult, perhaps irrelevant. The delineation and typology become even more tautological, or oxymoronic, because attributes of film (for modernism) and television (for postmodernism) exist in the above literary delineations as unargued, unstated theoretical objects or founding metaphors. It is unfathomably paradoxical that while contemporary theory is predicated on models and machines of vision, literary critics in the main still sidestep cinema and television.

The influence of early, popular U.S. cinema—for example, William Hart, Mack Sennett, Charlie Chaplin, Buster Keaton, and Cecil B. De Mille—on the surrealists and Louis Delluc in France, in turn taken up by the history of French theory, is incalculable. Invoking popular film and audiences as argument, as the formulation of film's specificity or *photogenie*, as a technology of modernity which had irrevocably altered space and time (along with rearranging the perception of reality), was shocking in 1915, a challenge to genteel aesthetics as pertinent as the anti-clerical, erotic assault of surrealist art. (There is a difference, however, in experiencing and analyzing popular culture taken from one national context to another, a cultural collision which displaces the everyday onto another terrain—a recontextualization, a defamiliarization of the familiar; watching Japanese quiz shows in the United States is not an ordinary experience.) Echoes of these early intense film debates can be heard in Barthes's euphoria over the Marx Brothers, in Godard's innumerable quotations of Hollywood films, in Christian Metz's "imaginary signifier," which is predicated on an analysis of Hollywood "continuity style" with its visual conventions established as early as 1915, and in Gilles Deleuze.

Eisenstein's study of D. W. Griffith, Douglas Fairbanks, and John Ford is common knowledge. Posters by the Stenberg brothers and Rodchenko for Buster Keaton's films suggest that Keaton's analysis of modernity, including advanced technologies—cinema, automobiles, trains, escalators, electricity, and domestic machines—in a Taylorist analysis of the body/machine relationship, and his critique of the domestic couple and do-it-yourselfism (with assembly-line production, or Fordism, continually taken into the home, for example, in *The Electric House* during a dinner party in which the food is served on a miniature train shuttling between the formally attired guests and the kitchen) were, like U.S. mass culture itself, more critical to Soviet constructivism than is usually argued. Popular or mass culture, including audiences and reproduction/conditions of mass production, has always figured centrally in film theory and avant-garde practice, albeit often not remembered.

While the U.S. eclectic period of vastly divergent styles has much in common with a romantic or Greenberg modernism, at least on the surface and in much criticism—particularly the centrality of the suffering, tormented artist, the tactic of (self)-reflexivity, the purified search for ontology, and an opposition to commercial cinema—this is not predominantly the case. Unlike modernism, video embodies the historical avant-garde's critique of the constraints and values of institutions, in particular commercial television. In simple retrospect, the premises of surrealism (and Soviet constructivism and Italian futurism), whose practices and manifestos had migrated to various New York art galleries in the 1960s, were reinvented with a backward glance by Brakhage to Georges Melies, Sergei Eisenstein, and Ezra Pound and an eye to 1960s art movements (a decade of almost frantic labeling)—abstract expressionism (Brakhage), pop art (Kenneth Anger, Owen Land), conceptual art (Hollis Framptom and Michael Snow), op and kinetic art (Tony Conrad, Paul Sharits).

At the same time, the argument can be located within reproducible mass culture, including movies (amateur, educational, professional), still photography, advertising, and network television. Mass culture, envisioned by scholars not only as the enemy but as an ahistorical constant, is itself historical, neither, as the Edsel and the automotive industry demonstrate, infinitely reproducible nor a monolithic sameness; electronic techniques and labor practices in the 1980s were qualitatively different from late-1940s mechanical industrialism. Many films and videotapes could be aptly labeled postmodern, with attributes of bricolage, an engagement with popular culture, complex systems of allusion and referencing, and the predominance of parody—for example, Robert Nelson, Bruce Conner, Kenneth Anger, and William Wegman. Crucially, unlike the historical avant-garde, which critiqued the sacred position of the artist (a questionable claim), the value of the art object, and the institutions of "art," avant-garde cinema centered artist and art, although the status of film as precious and valuable is only recently being realized under the pressure of television and computer-generated images. A market now exists for celluloid art, witnessed by the increasing prices of Disney-animated cells, an art market which Paul Sharits discerned early on as he mounted his film strips, exhibited them in galleries, and sold them as collages. Until recently set against commercial structures (which are now being courted, particularly German television and Channel 4 in England, but including the U.S. video cassette sales market), avant-garde film and video makers, like modernist painters, writers, dancers, and musicians, relished art and sought its modern, institutional imprimatur, mainly in New York but also in San Francisco and Chicago.

The significant difference is reproducibility; and unlike photography, film and video are intangible processes of light and sound waves more than material objects, dependent on being projected or transmitted, and then, still illusory objects. Unlike film, video can simply be erased, vanishing into what techs call "video vapor"; however, the tape, a pointillist process of iconoscopic scanning, of continuous particle movement unlike the static jerks of film's discontinuity, can be reused, is ecologically capable of receiving and retaining new images and sounds, like audio tape.

I chose *avant-garde*, in the end, because of the oppositional stance to institutions, and *postmodern* because of the recycling, quotation, and referencing of images and sounds (including rock 'n' roll), and the always/already positioning of film and video within mass culture, keenly aware of the vast differences between filmmakers. For example, the work of Owen Land, influenced by Brakhage, is light years away from Brakhage, while the work of Robert Nelson shares certain affinities with not only Land but also Snow. (One might even somewhat perversely argue a comparison between the editing styles of Nelson and Brakhage.) To complicate things, Brakhage's *The Act of Seeing with One's Own Eyes* is vastly different from most of his work, closer to certain films of Frampton. To make avant-garde (hetero/homosexual male) politics even more contradictory, it was a movement built on the art and writing of a powerful and beautiful woman, Maya Deren (a dancer, as are Sally Potter and Yvonne Rainer), and publicly precipitated in films about homosexuality by, for example, Kenneth Anger, who wrote *Hollywood Babylon* in the early 1960s in France (censored for years in the United States), an exposé of sex, death, and drug scandals, gossip etching a fascination with Hollywood cinema, which has been consistently disavowed by the majority of film and video artists and a relationship sometimes arduously disclaimed by most critics, arguing from the side of art rather than mass culture. (A book could be written about the influence of Anger's films, particularly *Scorpio Rising*, on segments of narrative films and rock videos; the effect of Scott Bartlett's film techniques on megabuck spectacles might also be noteworthy.)

What united the U.S. avant-garde, experimental, underground, independent film movement was (1) the privileging of the personal (as, literally, political) seen as eccentricity, experimentation; (2) the belief that aesthetic difference was radical—the restructuring of conventions of visual pleasure (what many critics see as dis- or un- pleasure/pain), including duration and legibility; (3) the critique of temporality and expectation (and also the banality of "the everyday," along with the centrality of desire and its lack in, for example, virtually all of Warhol's films) in the relentless forty-five minutes of *Wavelength*, or the three minutes of Bruce Baillie's *All My Life*, which disrupts the equation of time and money massively instituted by commercial television in the late 1940s but already in play on radio and narrative/commercial cinema, anticipating contemporary emphases on models of time and speed—for example, Felix Guattari and Paul Virilio; (4) an assault on the dominance and hold over the spectator of chronological, cause-effect logic by unraveling narrative time as well as disrupting narrative space, which is, as Heath argued, transformed by the classical text into place; and (5) the realization that the narrative had become a profitable commodity, a set of constraints.

The presentation of various and unexpected economies of time, whether abundantly plentiful (slow) or magically scarce (fast), is a serious (perhaps Eastern) challenge to the corporate, middle-class West and capitalism which equates time and money, both of which are calibrated and predicted. Avant-garde experimentation with time and its effects is an aesthetics of temporality. It critiques the way mass culture has transformed time, which has become a valuable commodity—sold by McDonald's and network television alike. The films refuse to enact predictable, exchangeable, chronological temporalities; some are very slow compared with the hyped-up everyday of 1988 in which time along with repetition has become an issue of politics, aesthetics, and economics (what the service industries sell is our valuable time). It could be conversely argued that funds influenced length, or that the films sought what Benjamin and other German critics of mass culture called contemplation, linked to art and tradition, opposed to distraction, a mode of viewing applicable to commercial film and later television.

When I show many of these films in my classes today, I remember the excitement of the first screenings in the 1960s through the late 1970s, which was an eclectic, counter(sub)cultural, intellectual, committed party. It had a great beat and urgency; we could not predict what we would see, or how long the work would be; unfortunately, except for a few intrepid, stalwart allies, most critics, scholars, and audiences found it difficult to dance to, even then and certainly now. Perhaps my memory is nostalgic, rather like Meaghan Morris's assessment of Lyotard's recent writing: "Lyotard's version of the sublime as a history of events, a tradition of happenings constituted by the invention of moves and rules, implies that actual artworks might be but the residues of such events and/or testimonials to a mission to produce new events (to keep on keeping on)."[3] That avant-garde, like conceptual art, might be aptly analyzed as a series of remembered, continually reinvented events suggests, like Renato Poggioli, that it can only be historical, disconnected from objects and tied to reception. Or, what Lyotard calls its sublimity must be immediate, instantaneous.

Within this time frame, witnessing the rewriting in scholarship and popular culture alike of the 1960s, a formative period of my life, not after I am dead or even old but merely middle-aged, is, for me, an extraordinary speeding up of history, of the notion and security of cultural time, at the very least, arguing for a breakdown of any concept of stable, stylistic periodization, making style, like genre, available, any time, any place; we must think history and our place in historical temporality differently. Television promos used to announce what we could watch next week; they gradually began to anticipate the next day; now the "Today Show" informs us of what we will see in the "next half hour" or in the next minute—counting down throughout the program until the blast-off of the segment; soon some successor of Jane Pauley will tell us what we are seeing now, collapsing the future into the present; the entire program will consist of these expectations and segmentations of time, anticipating a future which is now but perpetually promised and continually delayed—ironically enough, like *Wavelength*, where visual space is figured with aural velocity, but exactly the opposite. Television, like an airport, involves waiting more than watching, hearing and anticipating as much as viewing. This postmodern temporality of speed and expectation (the sine wave in *Wavelength* going from its lowest cycle to its highest, a question of acoustic speed) and prediction/satiation-completion, however, also has the great virtue of making the past retrievable (unlike *Wavelength*), accessible, and correctable, enabling us to go back faster and "correct things that were wrong in the first place." For example, a cultural, social, and political revision/revelation has occurred regarding the romanticism of drugs and alcohol, a myth deeply embedded in our scholarship and our thinking about art and creativity—a mythology of inspiration which functioned as one well-spring of avant-garde practice but a secret which was rarely argued directly in stylistic criticism of various "visions."

That electronic reproduction has a spatiality and temporality different from mechanical forms suggests that film and video cannot be easily equated, or that they chart divergent histories of representation and reception and hence should not be held within the same general arguments, which I do. Finally I wonder whether Walter Benjamin might be right when he claims that "the greater the decrease in the social significance of an art form, the sharper the distinction between criticism and enjoyment by the public."[4]

CHAPTER
1
HISTORICALLY SPEAKING

The seeing machine was once a sort of dark
room into which individuals spied; it has become a transparent building in which the exercise of power may be supervised by society
as a whole.

—Michel Foucault[1]

Foucault's metaphor of the "seeing machine" is applicable to U.S. avant-
garde cinema: during the 1940s, 1950s, and 1960s, it was considered illegal
or scandalous, and duly censored. To counter this, the New American Cinema Group met in New York in 1960 and issued a "First Statement." This
manifesto asserted that cinema was "indivisibly a personal expression," rejected censorship and the "high budget myth," and declared that new forms
of financing, distribution, and exhibition were to be collectively and internationally organized. Posited directly against "official cinema," which the
document argued was "morally corrupt, aesthetically obsolete," and with
allegiance to New Cinema movements in other countries, the conclusion
announced: "We don't want false, polished, slick films—we prefer them
rough, unpolished, but alive; we don't want rosy films—we want them the
color of blood."[2] The language was that of battle on an international scale.
The proponents (including a single woman, Shirley Clarke, who would
quickly shift her work to video) were cast as warriors against the enemy—
Hollywood cinema.

"A group of twenty-three independent film-makers, gathered by invitation
of Lewis Allen, stage and film producer, and Jonas Mekas, met at 156 West
46th Street (Producer's Theater) and, by unanimous vote, bound themselves
into a free open organization of the new American cinema: The Group."
Although sorely lacking in inventive names and clarity of language—bound
into free and open—"a temporary executive board was elected, consisting
of Shirley Clarke, Emile de Antonio, Edward Bland, Jonas Mekas, and Lewis

Allen" (79). (Perhaps Bland named "The Group.") It is important to point out that narrative cinema was not under siege per se; commerce, emblematized by Hollywood, was. As I argue elsewhere and frequently, the conventions of the classical style and the story of the heterosexual couple, on its way to romance with marriage or murder as the end, within the American dream of upward mobility and the family, were challenged, along with recognizing that this style had been packaged and traded for years as a profitable and standardized commodity. The initial impetus was to create alternative narrative features expressive of personal style and link up with the tradition of European art cinema, which had 16mm distribution outlets and virtually its own exhibition circuit developing in the late 1950s and 1960s, including art houses, university theaters, and, critically, student film societies.

I note that the date of the meeting was coincident with the flurry of new wave auteurism and the excited celebrity following the successes and publicity of the Cannes film festival in 1959, where Truffaut's *400 Blows* had won a prize and *Breathless* had also been shown (along with a winner by Alain Resnais). The "politique des auteurs" would soon be popularized in the United States, tenets which were endorsed by "The Group" and the manifesto—first films, made for low budgets, by first-time directors.

The document passionately asserts: "We are not joining together to make money. We are joining together to make films. We are joining together to build the New American Cinema. And we are going to do it together with the rest of America, together with the rest of our generation. . . . Our colleagues in France, Italy, Russia, Poland, or England can depend on our determination" (82). That this was a generational struggle, that it was international, and that it aligned itself with the goals of new wave directors and Italian neorealist filmmakers was clear. The goal was an alternative, U.S. narrative/feature film practice, made possible by the recognition that a market for "foreign" films was developing. Many participants had their "first feature" in preparation or production, suggesting an allegiance with the auteur policy which, among other things, was a claim to become a director, against the union-studio system of apprenticeship and nepotism—which was also a system of training, the apprenticing of the classical style, which ensured its survival and dominance.

The subsequent and quite rapid shift within New American Cinema from features and an allegiance to its European precursors to "visionary film" and opposition to European narrative is rapid and significant. Thus, between this document (and long before it) and the emergence of U.S. avant-garde film as a movement exists much additional history, missing from my account. Let's call it a dialectical leap rather than ignorance. Mekas, "The Group" cofounder and a film critic for the *Village Voice*, was initially critical of the often short, frequently unpolished films, with a posture comparable to that of Andrew Sarris and his version of auteurism. However, Mekas undergoes a radical conversion early on and becomes proselytizer, nurturing prophet, and filmmaker. An explanation more satisfying than the personal realignment, preferences, and early films of the players is the beginning of the counter-culture—a youth and generational movement with a critique of U.S. capitalism and a commitment to internationalism via the linkage of the local and the global. International cultural pluralism combined with a devaluation of money and the capitalist work ethic (a rigid instantiation of time and hierarchy) and led to the endorsement of amateur movies, a rapidly developing phenomenon which overlapped with "the personal is political." (While many filmmakers in the 1980s have returned to the narrative tradition mapped out in this document, Rainer and Potter outrun it by taking the premises of the avant-garde into narrative. By adding a third knowledge, feminism, they rewrite the rules of both games.)

To illustrate the critical paradigm that emerged after this switch of gears, a dogma influenced by and endorsing the films and arguments of Brakhage, Jacobs, and Anger, I will turn to a 1966 essay by Annette Michelson, "Film and the Radical Aspiration," an essay dedicated to Noel Burch and inspired by Walter Benjamin, in turn influenced by revolutionary Soviet filmmakers.[3] For Michelson, while the European film accepts what she calls the dissociative principle, "It is the almost categorical rejection of that principle and the aspiration to an innocence and organicity that animates the efforts of the 'independent' filmmakers who compose something of an American avant-garde" (409). She asserts, rather like de Lauretis and others later but to opposite ends, that "the crux of cinematic development lies . . . in the evaluation and redefinition of the nature and role of narrative structure." After a discussion of the historical avant-garde, then the French nouvelle vague—particularly Godard and Resnais and their "decline" due to their continuing "allegiance" "to the conventions of Hollywood's commercial cinema, and of the conversion of those conventions to the uses of advanced cinema" (412) which then become preconditions, premises—her essay moves to the "American independent film" and "its almost categorical rejection of the aesthetic grounded in the conventions hitherto discussed. The film-makers with whom we are concerned have, in fact, been led to abandon the tactics of reconciliation basic to European film as a whole. Most importantly, this rejection is in turn predicated on a negation . . . of the middle-class society that supported Hollywood . . . and that *continues* to sustain . . . the activity of most major European directors" (416).

She then argues the "militant aspect of a radical aspiration in American film. It is postulated on a conception of film as being . . . redemptive of the human condition itself . . . the radicalism . . . of Stan Brakhage, and, to some extent . . . the criticism of Jonas Mekas" (416). The linkage is made with abstract expressionism, with the artist as a "moral hero," with a quote by Harold Rosenberg who posits the contradictions of an "aesthetic-as-morality," a "certain radicalism" (418). The American cinema today is compared to the "post-Revolutionary situation in Russia." The contours—abstract expressionism, Soviet constructivism, ethical aesthetics as morally radical, and an anti-middle-class stance—have shaped the avant-garde critical imaginary and are, for Michelson, the radical aspiration. Her claims for this cinema resemble counterculture claims. Critically, she sets the U.S. avant-garde against the contemporary European, narrative film—an opposition to which I will return in the last chapter through the criticism of Jonas Mekas.

The essay concludes with an assessment that oddly predicts postmodernism: "cinema, on the verge of winning the battle for the recognition of its specificity . . . is now engaged in a reconsideration of its aims. The emergence of new 'intermedia' . . . the cross-fertilization of dance, theater, film . . . constitute a syndrome of that radicalism's crisis, both formal and social. . . . In a country whose dream of revolution has been sublimated in reformism and frustrated by an equivocal prosperity, cinematic radicalism is condemned to a politics and strategy of social and aesthetic subversion" (420–421). She gives the future over to eight-year-olds making films in their backyards—the noble dream of accessibility as a radical promise, one which resembles the video guerrillas and is akin to Mekas.

Form is the ground of the battle (the use of "radical" is culturally bound to the mid-1960s protest culture); her quotation of Eisenstein says it all: "to raise form once more to the level of ideological content." This position is rather similar to that of Lyotard, argued via psychoanalysis. The divide Michelson argues between the European and U.S. avant-garde was picked up and taken in the opposite direction by Peter Wollen in " 'Ontology' and Materialism in Film." Although Michelson wishes, during her talk, that she could show examples of the films, and while Jonas Mekas was sitting in the audience with a tape recorder, many contemporary debates have been waged over theories of film, perhaps more than the films themselves, which often serve as theories of film—which might be our greatest debt to the Soviets who taught and argued film theory perhaps as much as they shot or edited films. Michelson, with her aesthetics and politics grounded in French thought and Soviet art of the revolutionary period, has been a leading figure in the debates. That Soviet cinema had a great resurgence during the late 1960s, with student protesters applauding the ending of *Battleship Potemkin* and seeing the two parts of *Ivan the Terrible*, often for the first time, should not go unremarked. In many ways, Michelson was very au courant. The radicalism of aesthetics, or of form, can also be seen in the "look" and actions of the counterculture and protest movements—a series of tactics and strategies that could be shifted from issue to issue.

Around the same time, Michelson wrote of another significant event: "The film [Michael Snow's *Wavelength*] broke upon the world with the force, the power of conviction which defines a new level of enterprise, a threshold in the evolution of the medium." Others, too, invoked an evolutionary model of film history, imagining avant-garde as a powerful weapon in a cultural arsenal, a tactic resounding with the militant overtones of earlier avant-gardes, particularly in the Soviet Union in the revolutionary period, but including Italian futurism and surrealism. As Foucault reminds us, "The history which bears and determines us has the form of a war rather than of a language: relations of power, not relations of meaning."[4] In the midst of the Vietnam War protest and brutal civil rights struggles, which culminated in ending and losing a war, the slaughter of Kent State students, and the assassination of Martin Luther King, Jr., the U.S. avant-garde waged artistic struggle without much direct engagement with these political issues. Censorship battles were fought (there were confrontations and arrests). Journals (*Film Culture* and *Cinema News*) were created to spread the gospel and films. Accolades were garnered at international film festivals (with whispered rumors of aesthetic conspiracies). Coastal collectives (Canyon Cinema in San Francisco and Film-makers' Cooperative in New York) were organized. There were heroes (Jonas Mekas, Maya Deren, Bruce Baillie, Stan Brakhage, and Michael Snow). There were deaths (Ron Rice and Deren). There were champions of the cause (P. Adams Sitney and John Hanhardt).

Outside existing institutions (including, then, commercial cinema, art galleries, museums, and universities), artists banded together in guilds, forming collectives yet rarely collaborating, preferring the complete work by the total "artist." In alignment with countercultural politics and with a fervent nod to Soviet artists, including Malevich and Eisenstein, both strategies inverted the commercial model. Anyone could place films for distribution in the collectives, organized then and administered now by artists, and anyone supposedly had access to these embattled theaters for exhibition, thus reversing the Hollywood pattern of exhibition just as the conditions of avant-garde production rejected the studios' corporate canons of standardization and specialization. Films could be of any length or any quality, about any subject, with no subject; the makers were responsible for funding and maintaining their own prints, which belonged to them, as well as writing their own publicity copy. Without agents or galleries (although not uniformly so; some artists were represented by art dealers), filmmakers, to a degree, hawked their own works, tooted their own artistic horns, and relied on friendship for promotion, taking to the hustings like solo vaudeville acts. Like carnies, they found that eccentricity and brashness were assets. Catalogues listing and describing films available for rental from the co-ops were sources of publicity, along with word of mouth (the key source) and critical columns in, for example, the *Village Voice*. Art rather than commerce, the rough over the polished, and the group's cause over the fame of the individual were the radical rules of this game, which were, it should be noted, picked up and copied in, for example, England and Australia, co-op by co-op. Like the classical Hollywood cinema, U.S. avant-garde films and structures influenced other national avant-gardes, to a significant degree remaining artistically dominant.

Individuality versus collectivity (a contradiction built into this system in the gaps between production, distribution, and exhibition) has always been the catch-22 of the politics of U.S. avant-garde (and perhaps of the counterculture). The deeds were noble, the structure epic; yet individualism remained, as Foucault stated:

> And if from the early Middle Ages to the present day, the "adventure" is an account of individuality, the passage from the epic to the novel, from the noble deed to the secret singularity, from long exiles to the internal search for childhood, from combats to phantasies, it is also inscribed in the formation of a disciplinary society.[5]

If the intent of the artistic and political conflicts of the 1960s was to undermine the constraints of the "disciplinary society," it was compromised by "accounts" of individuality and avant-garde finally inscribed within a place of disciplines—universities. The young protagonists of this rebellion aged, crossing the generational divide and finally instantiating hierarchy.

Epic visual journeys charted the artistic progress of the youthful self as emblematic of the "collective consciousness." Cinema's conventions were challenged in an outpouring of poetic images, sometimes without sound tracks, stripped of accumulated constraints and conventions: Deren's fragmented, tortured "meshes"; Brakhage's mountains, stars, and riddles; Snow's central and regional encounters in lofts, gallery installations, and eventually the Canadian wilderness, his country; Hollis Frampton's Magellan voyage into the 1970s; Bruce Baillie's Parsifal; and Robert Nelson and William Wiley's Don Quixote, the comically heroic Blondino. Without the expected doses of the time and space of narrative and its historical conventions of continuity style, the spectator was playing an unfamiliar game, caught off guard. The frightening edge of looking (often a derailed or demonic voyeurism), as well as abstracted visual pleasures, came with the risk of misrecognition, of seeing and being seen, of not being able to identify the scene, of the realization of the split between the camera eye and our eye, of the physical disparity between sound and image. Outside the rules of intelligibility and pleasurable placement within memory created by story and repetition, we were shocked, ecstatic, confused, irritated, and bored by these films. By reminding us that our eyes must work, that we are desire's source and impossibility, that the text was not located on-screen but was a process *with* and not *for* us, these works engaged film's material apparatus, including the disruption of the comfortable place of the spectator at the movies and within culture.

The parallel with contemporary theory, particularly Barthes and Lacan, is uncanny, yet largely unremarked. It is likely that by the 1970s, by making the work of film apparent in more than a decade's outpouring of "experimental" films, by splitting the signifier from the signified, avant-garde had pushed film theory to explain this now uncomfortable, dispersed, bored, or blissful spectator. If that is the case, then avant-garde can be read historically, as and through theory. For the most part, however, academics clung to the safe familiarity and pleasure of narrative turf, and most artists disdained "theory."

As Barthes has suggested, "bliss may come only with the *absolutely new,* for only the new disturbs (weakens) consciousness (easy? not at all: nine times out of ten, the new is only the stereotype of the novelty)."[6] Unlike classical narrative's process of differentiation, invention within a set of constraints and conventions labeled "continuity style," avant-garde sought stylish difference, "the absolutely new." Of course Barthes's notion of the "absolutely new" bespeaks the problems of origin as well as the usual polarity between art and popular culture. (Still, the new as the stereotype of novelty is an intriguing third term which must be contended with, particularly in relation to postmodern art, theory, and fashion.) However, his distinction between texts of pleasure and texts of jouissance (the classical film versus the avant-garde film), invoking the readerly and the writerly, seems applicable to the historical effectivity and reception of avant-garde films. Many of the films were texts of bliss. "The text of bliss," Barthes wrote, "always rises out of it [history] like a scandal"; it is the "text that imposes a state of loss, the text that discomforts (perhaps to the point of a certain boredom), unsettles the reader's historical, cultural, psychological assumptions. . . ."[7] *Flaming Creatures* (Jack Smith, 1962) with its scenes of transvestite orgy, *Fireworks* (1947) with its homosexual reverie, and *Scorpio Rising* (Kenneth Anger, 1963) with its parody of Christ and celebration of the occult, drugs, sex, motorcycles, and popular culture (rock music—including 1960s black "girl groups" and Elvis Presley years before the 1980s nostalgic mania for both; movie stars—James Dean, Marlon Brando, and Elvis; and comic books and television) provoked outrage and were banned from the screens of art museums (after *Flaming Creatures,* the Milwaukee Art Museum stopped showing experimental films).

Additional films (Ken Jacobs's *Tom, Tom, the Piper's Son,* Paul Sharit's *T,O,U,C,H,I,N,G,* and Frampton's *Zorns Lemma*) illustrated that—to use Barthes's words—"difference is plural, sensual, and textual . . . difference is the very movement of dispersion."[8] Jacobs poetically remade film history. Sharits multilated the body. Frampton erotically dramatized the passage of light and deconstructed linguistics. Nelson and Wiley crazily careened their characters and fantasies through San Francisco. Brakhage showed us abstracted glimpses of light, refractions of swords, hints of naked bodies.

Brakhage had given the heraldic call in *Metaphors on Vision* (1963): the mythic eye of this heroic avant-garde (including the spectator) was to be "unruled by man-made laws of perspective, unprejudiced by compositional logic, which must know each object encountered in life."[9] Critics paid heed and analyzed the individual *experience* of these films as metaphors of consciousness, of light. Within Western representation's historical equation of sight with knowledge ("I see" meaning "I understand"), it appears "logical" (actually it must be historical—the phrase of the 1980s is "I hear you") that in cinema, vision has become both a sight of sensual pleasure and a site of struggle involving the place—*the experience* (impressions or feelings) versus the *construction* (history and context)—of the spectator.

A decade later in contemporary film theory, to which I will constantly return, funneled through the writings of Lacan, the "look" was delineated as a fundamental fault. Between appearance and the real is the look, a lack:

scopic castration in which the eye is separated from what it sees; this is modeled on the French photogenie debates in which the camera mediates the real, stylizing, altering and yet remaining true to the profilmic, as well as linguistics through which Lacan reread Freud. The eye and the "I" are versions of both the experience and construction of the spectator, depending on whether the subject is imagined as unified or split in language. Perhaps in historical coincidence with this conceptualization of the imaginary—of primary identification, narcissism, unity—eventually the camera of the avant-garde artist was thought of as anthropomorphic, as duplicating or extending the eye of the filmmaker. Ed Emschwiller claimed that his arm holding the camera, which swooped over bodies as physical terrain or landscape, was an extension of his eye. Brakhage had audiences make their own movies by pressing on their closed eyelids. While primarily applied to classical narrative films, the Lacanian model, with its linkages to surrealism, more aptly replicates the premises and practices of avant-garde.

However, in film theory, the divided subject of Lacan, descended from Freud, linguistics, and the surrealists, converged with Marx/Althusser and dissected the codes of narrative films, in the main sidestepping avant-garde until the late 1970s. This time lag should not remain unremarked: the premises and claims of avant-garde, including its international aspirations, were construed in the United States from the mid- to late 1940s, solidified in the 1960s, and were *radical* and unsettling in that political and intellectual context; contemporary film theory grew from the 1970s application in the United Kingdom of continental theory (from Brecht to Barthes, Freud, Marx, and, to a lesser degree, Foucault) to cinema, *after* an intense period of international, avant-garde activism and proselytizing. (The cross-cultural transmigration of film is fascinating and often unremarked—one condensed version might see it as the exportation of early U.S. mass film culture returning fifty years later as continental theory.) Rather than examining avant-garde texts within historical parameters and debates, many contemporary critics treat this variegated work as monolithic, timeless, eternal. Anger's citation of "Blue Velvet" in *Scorpio Rising* in the early 1960s is a very different story from *Blue Velvet* of the 1980s, which remembers and alludes to the earlier film. Reception itself—including temporality, repetition, legibility, shock, and scandal—was a focus of avant-garde's project and critique; what is forgotten in many accounts is that reception and spectators are historical rather than forever; context, including a politics of opposition and negation rather than incorporation and contradiction, must be taken into account. (I will return to reception and detail Lyotard's and Heath's respective but overlapping models of reception in a later chapter.)

Brakhage had banished sound from film art, reviving older debates, for example, Rudolph Arnheim, which circled around ontology; Andre Bazin's question "What *is* Cinema," film's very definition, was then, as it had been since at least 1915, along with deciphering the styles of film artists, a central question and debate, resembling arguments today around television, its very definition at stake. Strangely enough, while many films had sound tracks, although few had sync speech, perhaps due to cost, there was little theoretical talk about the intersection of sound/image, no matter how critical its function in particular films. That is also true of most contemporary film theory (with Noel Burch as a significant early exception and Mary Ann Doane and Rick Altman much later), which did not pick up Eisenstein's work on what he called "vertical" montage, demonstrated in avant-garde films, for example, Hollis Frampton's *Nostalgia* and *Critical Mass*. Vision, with its thorough grounding in the legitimacy of philosophy and art, has indeed dominated our thinking as well as our memories of films. This is even more ironic given that our theory is predicated on linguistics and semiotics and thus more snugly fits Framptom's visual and aural linguistics than it does Hitchcock or Berkeley.

For many filmmakers and critics, the subject was a transcendental one—neither split like Barthes's (through Lacan) nor heroically collective, but supremely individualized. The locus was the archetypal or apocryphal figure of the artist; it was often his (with a few hers) "creative consciousness" that was explored or excavated. Fragmented during the viewing, we were reassembled after the film by the presence of the filmmakers, who accompanied their sometimes silent films as speaking texts. As I continue to argue, this star system of personal appearances, in the Homeric tradition of oral history, combined with traveling circuits and repeated performances reminiscent of U.S. vaudeville to turn avant-garde into an *event,* an experience which exceeded or superseded the films.

Filmmakers regularly hand-delivered their "personal" films while telling tales of their arduous making, cost, and funding—stories structured on the Bildungsroman, stories of travail, eccentricity, meaning, and origin. One never missed spotting a visiting filmmaker at the airport—easily identifiable by the 16mm film case and the late 1960s leftist garb. (Morgan Fisher dressed more like an accountant, and Brakhage always looked too young to have made so many films; Land resembled a young, impertinent rabbi, his red-hair flowing when he strode; Conrad, a European 1920s intellectual or philosopher, was fashionably adorned in a single color; Woody Vasulka reminded me of Mel Brooks minus the abrasiveness, Sharits of a modern cowboy on the edge or under the volcano, Robert Nelson of the Marlboro Man, literally, and Jonas Mekas of a noble Lithuanian poet, which he was; Hollis Frampton would have been brilliant as God, Noah, or Abraham in a Cecil B. De Mille film—as he so comically said one night, "I was invited to the conference to play the wrath of God.") Like my experiential rap, the films were clearly framed by presence and anecdote (gossip granting personal familiarity). The unfamiliar was made familiar and often familial in the creation of a loyal band of disciples, students soon to be filmmakers or critics, for example, Diana Barrie in relation to Brakhage or Bruce Conner, Rob Danielson in relation to Owen Land. As Snow "writes" in *So Is This:* "Sometimes the author is present and poses questions. . . ." Or, it should be mentioned, answers them. Via cross-country repetition, avant-garde developed a history of heroic, mythic accounts, spiced with personal remembrance and gossip.

It is not insignificant that eventually the theaters were often university classrooms and museum corridors and meeting rooms—dispersed exhibitors with meager to bad facilities and without any systematic means of distribution except the energy of the single filmmaker, an occasional newsletter, and irregularly printed journals (sporadic publication was a mark of poverty, overwork, understaffing, and radical politics; journals of official culture are always on time). The Walker Art Center in Minneapolis, the Art Institute in Chicago, Pacific Film Archives and the Art Institute in San Francisco, along with the Museum of Modern Art, the Whitney, and the Collective in New York, SUNY in Buffalo and Binghamton were way stations in artists' cross-country treks, which were announced in newsletters. The University of Wisconsin in Milwaukee joined the list of welcoming exhibitors in 1974, documenting the visitors that year in a series of twelve one-hour video productions.[10] These places of hinterland exhibition corresponded with the passion of usually one sympathetic curator, faculty member, or filmmaker/teacher. Audiences (created by the local, resident aficionado's sheer enthusiasm) consisted of significantly more students than teachers; like the counterculture, this was a youthful, student-centered movement. Land taught at the Art Institute, where Brakhage also lectured. Tony Conrad, along with Gerald O'Grady, encouraged filmmakers in Buffalo, where Paul Sharits also taught, on a faculty that in the glory days included Woody and Steina Vasulka, James Blue, and Hollis Frampton. Peter Lehman and Guilio Scalenger invited filmmakers to the yearly film festival and symposium at Ohio University. Scott MacDonald invited and interviewed filmmakers at Utica College. Ken Jacobs, Larry Gottheim, and Maureen Turim kept the avant-garde fires burning at Binghamton. Milwaukee had Robert Nelson, Cecelia Condit, Valie Export, and Rob Danielson.

Like other manifestations of the artistic counterculture, the movement, which opposed institutions, was funded, recognized, and indeed made possible by institutions—universities via salaries and spotty purchases of basic equipment, and federal and state governments: the National Endowment for the Arts and some state arts councils, such as New York, funneled money to filmmakers (who still remain crucially dependent on various grant agencies). An NEA grant was both the financier and seal of artistic approval, a prestigious award which could be used to garner other funds, and an award which became self-perpetuating. Once an artist entered the grant pantheon, the chances for future awards were almost ensured; refinancing projects was a snowballing strategy of NEA grant panels. (In the early 1980s, a shift in public artistic policy occurred: from supporting media "experimentation" by unknowns to funding "established artists" with track records; given the emphasis on prior reputation, it became more difficult to enter the circuit of exhibition and financing.) Given the extreme cost of filmmaking, however, the amounts were relatively minuscule; this was a poor and struggling movement; innovative works were made for virtually nothing, brought off by the passionate energy of the maker, often made with novice student crews and edited on primitive equipment. (For example, George Kuchar, with an all-student cast and crew, has fashioned the most extraordinary super-8mm and video spectacles in class. His Bakhtinian extravaganzas of grotesque, zany bodies, often edited in camera, replete with special effects, rival De Mille in their sheer excess.) Audiences received the most for their investment—admission to most screenings around the country was either free or minimal. The movement was truly heroic, if not sacrificial, economically speaking. While fascinated by film's materiality, few artists were materialists in either the Marxist or the capitalist sense of the word. Although money was an obsessive topic, money was not the goal, merely an inconvenient necessity for film stock. Its lack became a social and artistic virtue, at least for a time. The economic history, including institutional connections, needs to be documented.

As crucial as the system of distribution of films and information was (and continues to be, although appearances are winding down as in-group events), it, like the financial linkages to officialdom, raised problems. Certainly word-of-mouth and hand-delivery distribution and exhibition were inefficient, particularly for filmmakers. Moreover, the personal appearance system, bound by its own decorum, risked placing "meaning" totally within the author; meanings *after* the film were then repeated as criticism *of* the film. The resulting interpretive translations were often nostalgic documentations, circumscribed by intention, remembrance, and anecdote. As Heath wrote in another context in one of the few theoretical essays on avant-garde films: "Generally avant-garde independent filmmaking has suffered from being provided with a history of its own."[11] Both systems—the circuit and criticism—hovered around the visibly centered artist. Both risked an individualism of "secret singularities," outside history, without politics, and thus without social critique, effects larger than the event, and audiences other than committed disciples. These problems have still not been resolved.

To return to the 1960 manifesto and a passage that predicted present debates: "We are concerned with Man. We are concerned with what is happening to Man. We are not an aesthetic school that constricts the filmmaker within a set of dead principles . . . we are not only for the New Cinema: we are also for the New Man."[12] New Men were championed and celebrated. The fragmented subject of Barthes was and still is construed in most theoretical writings and constructed by many avant-garde films as a male subject—albeit dispersed and now, perhaps, plural. As Yvonne Rainer wrote in the script for *Journeys from Berlin/1971*, "The therapist is still male."[13]

In the 1970s, feminist critiques of cinema not surprisingly circled avant-garde and grappled with the conventions of the look in narrative as the first site of debate. That this led to the present critique of the "theory of the subject" is also not surprising. In 1975 Laura Mulvey stunningly opened up the psychoanalytic terrain in "Visual Pleasure and Narrative Cinema," an

essay that caused a theoretical avalanche and to some degree buried historical, cultural specificity in its influential wake, including the fact that her
model was perched on an analysis of the films of Hitchcock and Von Sternberg. She wrote: "The first blow against the monolithic accumulation of traditional film conventions is to free the look of the camera into its materiality
of time and space and the look of the audience into dialectics, passionate
detachment."[14] Her strategy, marshaled first through and then against traditional narrative structures and within psychoanalysis and feminism, reversed
Brakhage's assault on the system of perspective in Western representation.
Avant-garde films might have "freed" the look, but where had it gone? Certainly not into Mulvey's dialectics and passionate detachment.

While it might be true that "woman" was not blatantly exchanged or grotesquely commodified by avant-garde films, neither was she centrally figured. "She" seemed to vanish with very few traces, except as allied partisan,
liberated lover, or filmed mother/muse—a "bearer rather than maker of
meaning" so literally enacted in Brakhage's films of the births of his children, starring his wife, Jane. "She" was no longer a problem, but "she" was
silenced only momentarily. Often "she" divorced "him," obtaining the rights
to his films as part of her settlement, as in the case of Freuda and Scott
Bartlett. Or in the case of Joyce Wieland and Michael Snow, her painting
and films were remembered in another film, by Kay Armitage in her artistic
biography of Wieland in 1987. From the mid–1970s on, the fervent outpouring of feminist writing and filmmaking etched a glaring historical absence
and affirmed a notable presence—as majority, as subject rather than object,
as challenge to networks of power. This work provoked avant-garde practices
to move in other directions—toward politics and an engagement with codes
of narrative.

As female film and video makers and feminism became increasingly prominent, the masculine avant-garde seemed lethargic; some bemoaned and
were bewildered by its decline, explaining it by economics and a conservative political climate. (New York was always an exception; recently, there
has been a resurgence of interest due to regular, ambitious, archival programming at two new venues in New York.) It was, however, the decline of only
a version of avant-garde, now out of step; instead of endings, perhaps beginnings could be argued; for women, the best, politically speaking, is yet to
come.

I don't mean to suggest that artists should have become male feminists,
speaking for or as women (although this did happen under the earlier aegis
of women's liberation); they, along with contemporary critics and theorists,
might have paid more attention to women—listening to them, reading their
writing, quoting their work, acknowledging their subjectivity, and overtly refusing to perpetuate subservience by assuming the dominant cultural role
reserved for male artists—turned to aware tongue-in-cheek in Martin Scor-
sese's Life Lessons (in New York Stories), but still true, parodied or not. Imagine a version starring Barbara Krueger in her studio—that is the future.

As I have repeated, the university was one site of the debates and one context of change itself. In 1965 students boycotted classes and occupied buildings. If only a few faculty members joined them, nonetheless a shift of pedagogical authority had occurred. Near the end of that turbulent decade, much teaching and telling converged around "theories of the text" as plural and heterogeneous. For many this was (and continues to be) and intellectual violence to humanist interpretations, a scandal of scholastic politics. As Barthes wrote of France in 1968, "power itself, as a discursive category, was dividing, spreading like a liquid leaking everywhere. . . ."[15] Universities became sites of activism (which was no longer the case in the 1980s, when power had stabilized, returned to conservative normalcy).

Today vestiges of old debates still swirl around theory as if it were an avant-garde practice. Just when I think this recurrent whine is history, I encounter yet another worried, famous, but out of style humanities professor, shaking his head forlornly and worrying about theory's language, its corrosive influence precipitating a Spenglerian decline of culture and values. It seems clear that discursive power was and is at stake; many of the former leading men of this opposition (like former stars of old TV series returning to *Murder, She Wrote* only to abruptly die) are still defending their territory without awareness that argumentative boundaries have dramatically shifted to include women. As Barthes archly wrote, "anti-intellectualism [which can also be anti-feminism] reveals itself as a protest of virility."[16] In the early 1970s, via theories of the text, women gained access to reading as a textual process of inclusion and/or revision; shortly after that breakthrough (for me, an extraordinary opening up and unraveling of hermetically sealed boundaries secured by "truth" or "empiricism"—a real *S/Z* rush), manifest in detailed textual analyses and sometimes called "deconstruction," theories of subjectivity enabled us to theorize and codify systems of representation and notice our inequality as spectators—there, as image; not there, as subject, a binarism which we later complicated. With these intellectual models as methods displacing "truth" garnered from informed but expert intuition, we could be critics and theorists—no small claim for knowledge.

Like the plural text as process, teaching was under siege in the late 1960s and the 1970s, no longer conceived as a consummable exchange of knowledge, smoothly flowing from the teacher/god to the student. Equally, knowledge was not to be valued as a commodity to be acquired as a truth, a single and comprehensive meaning, but as both production and process of reciprocal meanings amid historical and cultural intersections. Just as the concept of the perfect transmission from the author to the ideal reader was displaced amid the many debates on "authorship," so were relations between teacher and student. As Neil Hertz has written:

> Both figures—that of lineage and that of the closed circuit—depend for their intelligibility on a radical reduction of what is in fact plural . . . a reduction of those plurals to an imagined interplay of paired elements . . .

teacher and student. The power such figures exert over readers is in proportion to the reduction they promise to perform.[17]

In addition to "paired elements," these "reductions" take many forms, including "truth," knowledge, and answers. The power of the "reduction" can also be read as a seduction—the teacher promising truth or closure at the end, a truth which will be constantly desired and long delayed, as in the performance of narrative. Thus have both teaching and telling been narrativized.

Like narrative (as well as avant-garde), the name of the father is embedded in teaching, in pedagogy. For example, Shoshana Felman analyzes the pedagogical attributes of psychoanalytic practice, predicated as it is on dialogue, "the radical condition of learning and knowledge." With this as her paradigm of reciprocal teaching/learning, indeed their reversibility if not equation, Felman argues that

> the position of the teacher is itself the position of *the one who learns,* of the one who *teaches* nothing other than *the way he learns.* The subject of teaching is interminably—a student; the subject of teaching is interminably—a learning. This is the most radical, perhaps the most far-reaching insight psychoanalysis can give us into pedagogy.[18]

As enticing as this analogy is, the student—the one who learns and teaches—is still a "he." Fathers and sons teach and learn. Historically, an oedipal politics of pedagogy, whether real or symbolic, has been operative. In "Some Reflections on Schoolboy Psychology," Freud validates this assertion through his own experience: "These men became our *substitute* fathers. . . . We *transferred* to them *the respect and expectations attaching to the omniscient father of our childhood* . . . we struggled with them as we had been in the habit of struggling with our fathers. . . ."[19] Barthes reinforces the lineage of paternal intellectualism: "It is to a fantasy, spoken or unspoken, that the professor must annually return. . . . He thereby turns from the place where he is expected, the place of the Father, who is always dead, as we know."[20] This funeral dirge is only that of Lazarus. Barthes concludes: "For only the son has fantasies, only the son is alive."

One must ask about mothers and daughters, their fantasies. Where can they turn? The gender of the answer makes a substantial difference. We looked to male theorists in the 1970s; shortly after, feminist critics began to notice fault lines; from these oversights and blind spots, feminists worked out models of contradiction—and went from there to feminist theory. In film, women are still better served in criticism courses than in film production programs, although this is changing. Perhaps it is not only the metaphorical death of fathers and replicated sons which is desired but also the death of psychoanalysis' narrative reiteration of patriarchal hierarchies. But as Barthes argues, without Oedipus "our popular arts would be transformed entirely" because "what would be left for us to tell?"[21] Refraining from riddling, the Sphinx, in unison with women teachers, would have answered, "Plenty!" Thus, narrative is part and parcel of this double-binding dilemma. Some daughters are turning against this limited reading of Oedipus, remembering that he blinded himself at Thebes and that there was also Antigone.

Illicit in the 1940s, 1950s, and 1960s, hotly disputed in the 1970s, in the 1980s avant-garde cinema is legal tender, taught rather than fought. "Video" has been embraced in university production curricula by all but the most recalcitrant avant-garde film disciple—most of whom are working on independent feature films if not video. Like the history of Hollywood film, the short (or medium or long) experimental film has been replaced by features or video meditations, video experiments. If, as a discourse, avant-garde is not as "transparent" a "building" (Foucault) as commercial movies or broadcast television, patterns of power have emerged—in a period of decline, of fewer university jobs, and indeed real jobs anywhere. To a large extent, U.S. avant-garde cinema and counterculture video fulfilled their own prophecies: radical goals have, in certain practices, turned into conservative nooses. However scandalous, avant-garde work has been accommodated or incorporated *as* resistance. Perhaps now it is "art," safe as unusual if not overly profitable commerce, included and defused within the confines of the commodity art market and the university.

Yet unlike other commodities, the buyer's market for films and videos never substantially materialized. As 16mm market and distribution decline due to cost of materials, bulky and expensive shipping and projection compared with the easy portability and reproducibility of video, artists are trying to incorporate the half-inch video rental and sales market into their thought and distribution processes. I can rent *Scorpio Rising* and *Blue Velvet* at Video Visions for the same price. *Scorpio* costs slightly more than *Blue Velvet* to buy, although it is a shorter film. This two dollar a shot mass rental market or fifty dollar purchase price is paradoxical: is it the final blow to or realization of the museum's commodity market for film? Can avant-garde work imitate or use a commercial model, one which might provide substantial rental and purchase funds? Cecilia Condit says this is true in her case. Reproducibility has a dual edge: it mediates against collection as investment and preservation for scholarship, concealing for archivists the delicate nature of film and video, decomposing within our lifetime. At the same time, this marvelous fluidity and ease of distribution suggests an open market of exchange and sharing, as affordable as a television or a telephone. Historically, film or video rentals have not provided hefty if any incomes for most independent artists, who continue to be dependent on shrinking institutional grants (although Condit's and other artists' economic tale is different). Perhaps the weaknesses of the old system (with its linkages through opposition to the Hollywood studio model and the network broadcast spider web) will cause changes which will tap new audiences. Given reproducibility and immateriality, film and video were always less compatible with the museum than with mass culture practices. I wonder what would have happened if the stated opposition in the 1960s manifesto had been to art rather than to commerce. Oppositions are strategies, within contexts, and subject to change.

Today, independent avant-garde practices are moving sideways, outside the conservatism of academia into local galleries, performance spaces, community halls, politics, rock bars, and cable television (in certain venues, particularly the community access people, the dreams of free and easy public access embody the late 1960s countercultural values, dressed up a bit more, wearing shorter and less troubling hair); into other media and disciplines (music, theater, psychoanalysis); into forms of popular culture, including narrative and feature films. The disregard for the old hierarchies and divisions, plus constant examples of collaboration, suggest that avant-garde politics has altered. These heretical deviations from the 1960s canon are visible in the recent films and videotapes. There is indeed a new style, not predicated on purism, ontology, hierarchy—all exclusions. At the same time, the new style has been there all along; interpretations and pantheons obscured or blocked our vision.

Dick Hebdige, taking his cue from Genet and modeling his work on Foucault, argues that style is a "form of Refusal" which lodges objections and displays contradictions.[22] Social relations have been taken into avant-garde culture; practices have been mediated and inflected by history, infused by theory, feminism, and the work of artists from other countries. These are productive times of revision, of inclusion rather than exclusion. On the negative side, it is also a time of difficult distribution, exorbitant film printing costs, a shift to video distribution and video sales, without really a plan or organization (the Video Data Bank in Chicago and Electronic Arts Intermix in New York are terrific distributors); along with the cooperatives, a great deal of current distribution is primarily handled by individual artists from their apartments; exhibition is dwindling in the hinterlands, and scholarly criticism has been sparse. Feminism seems to be the only widespread political game of consequence. The radical but (seen in retrospect) paternal, antitheoretical ideology of the 1960s took a heavy toll on a once energized and pedagogic movement—now somewhat frantically trying to catch up with ideas, being caught with its political pants down one time too many. For many once active filmmakers it has been years between exhibitions. "Maybe I'll make a videotape," say the former "fathers." Ironically, along with Barthes's erotics and Foucault's "perversions," dispersion and fragmentation also have disadvantages. The things the 1960s embodied were not only ideas but structures and tactics for achieving them; protest practicum was debated and invented and put into action. We need a different activism for the 1990s. Almost anything would be better than the Spenglerian plaints and whines of Marxists about the decline and fall of postmodern culture in the 1980s.

CHAPTER
2
VISIONARY FILM AND SEXUAL DIFFERENCE

The avant-garde melee has been a contest of contrarieties: popular culture versus art, narrative or not, epistemology against phenomenology, or ontology contraposed to ontology.[1] Intriguingly, the demarcations have been adduced not from films but from criticism. To an uncanny degree, P. Adams Sitney's *Visionary Film*, published in 1974, has haunted subsequent renderings.[2] It is Sitney's sectarian disquisition, in lockstep with the films, diaries, and letters of Brakhage, that is repudiated or upheld. Equally efficacious for feminist theory has been Laura Mulvey's essay "Visual Pleasure and Narrative Cinema," published in *Screen* in England in 1975.[3] This essay paved a yellow brick road for sophisticated books on female subjectivity and cinema, such as *Alice Doesn't* and *The Desire to Desire*, and for the films of Sally Potter and Yvonne Rainer.

The mutual mise-en-scene of Sitney and Mulvey was the tail end of the counterculture and protest movements. Sexuality, work, liberation, negation, and opposition were key words which hooked up in popular slogans, art criticism, and continental theory. Freud's sexual fetish linked up with Marx's commodity fetish and reconnoitered in art and popular culture; this odd coupling overtly and covertly had a cultural field day. Both Mulvey and Sitney set their theorems in discord with institutions (including the economics and stylistic conventions of commercial/narrative cinema), endorsing alternative practices and sharing the "anti-establishment" conviction, so sovereign in the late 1960s and the 1970s, that aesthetics (the foregrounding of the cinematic apparatus) elided with "life-style" would precipitate political change, or at least signaled a radical break with the past. Both writers reflected (1) the decade's obsession with sexuality, and (2) the rhetorical tactic of binary opposition. However, the similitude ends here. The differences were glaring. Regarding their respective use of theory, particularly psychoanalysis, never would the twain meet. Mulvey begins from a place and with a question which "visionary film," aesthetic modernism, and the historical avant-garde cannot imagine: female subjectivity, pinpointing its exclusion.

Before I proceed with sexual difference, another skin-deep similarity between these two texts was a fervent belief in the radicality of form, the revolutionary aura of raw, revealed signifiers. It is important to note and remember the political depth of this conviction—that form, its disruption, alteration, and revelation, could change the world, or at least cinema. Along with Freud's sexual fetish, Althusser's rereading of Marx had instated imaginary relations, triggering analyses of the concealed "work" of films. The theoretical paragon advocated that deconstruction of techniques would uncover repressed social structures, including sexual difference. Or, from Brecht and later Godard, form as the intrusion and marker of ideology would disrupt and derail the text and spectator, casting illusionism aside for the new day to come. For Mulvey, unraveling the tight nexus of film's system of looks (of camera, of spectator, and of characters), freeing the camera into "materiality" and the "audience into dialectics" is "the first blow" against "traditional film conventions" by radical filmmakers.[4] "Continuity style" was under siege more than narrative per se. On the other side of this Maginot line, the visionary reading professed that this work, if already revealed, was the sign (signature) of the artist, equated with the ontology of cinema. For VF (my shorthand for Sitney's Visionary Film), figuration and form were the signifiers of art and the "secrets of a soul."

The acute differences between the aesthetics and the politics of form were concealed by critics on both sides of the humanism-theory divide calling up Soviet constructivism and Eisenstein as precursors. For example, Annette Michelson, in "Film and the Radical Aspiration," a key text of the period, proclaimed a "divergence of radicalisms."[5] Janet Bergstrom invoked Eisenstein as an exemplar of form pointing to political meanings.[6] To complicate these divergent overlaps, both positions ascribe to a comparable take on "modernism," one derived from Clement Greenberg in defense of abstract expressionist painting, against representation, and on the side of "materialist" ontology and art. (As a qualification: Michelson begins with Eisenstein and does cite Harold Rosenberg, Walter Benjamin, and Marxist thought. Her premises are not Sitney's.)

Another way to envision modernism is from the side of mass culture. This view is comparable to the "Americanism" endorsed by the Soviet avantgarde and the Prolecult in the 1920s, with a model of work and mass production derived from Detroit, Henry Ford, Taylorism, and the WPA, or to Walter Benjamin, who already had conjoined Freud and Marx, along with taking art into mass culture. If the latter sites (like Diego Rivera's murals in the Ford Museum) had become the intellectual objects beneath exegeses of modernism, the illusory division between mass culture and art might never have been instantiated as the tasteful, aesthetic standard for intellectuals which it is, in the United States.

As I stated, Mulvey and Sitney fixate on sexuality as both clue and answer to interpretation. While Mulvey stars Freud/Lacan, along with Hitchcock and Sternberg, elucidating her method, Sitney repudiates psychoanalysis. His denial, however, is merely a disavowal, the repressed as a structuring presence, or major premise. Sitney's model, on the side of art (abstract expressionism) and predicated on the tenets of romanticism, is inspired by Harold Bloom and his *Visionary Company*. For Bloom, psychoanalysis agonistically functions as wellspring and raison d'etre of art (poetry) and patriarchy. Mulvey's construct, on the side of popular culture and triggered by Lacan's rereading of Freud through linguistics, is inspired by feminism and is akin to Juliet Mitchell, who takes Freud as an analysis rather than a defense of patriarchy. Mulvey divided and gendered the subject in the unconscious, in language, in representation. For Sitney, as for Brakhage and Arnheim, cinema existed outside the symbolic of language and beyond, or in spite of, the real—to a degree conflating not only the unconscious with the conscious but also the symbolic with the imaginary. Under the analogous sway of the romantic poets, *VF* detailed artistic form as a mythical pursuit of cinematic and sexual identity, reconstituting the triumph of the male artistic ego in its insatiable, and hence impossible, pursuit of desire, predicated, for Lacan, on loss and absence.

The unnoted centrality of Bloom and psychoanalysis to *Visionary Film*, along with the similarities between Brakhage and Bloom, is acutely ironic. While avant-garde devotees bemoan and smirk at contemporary theory, equating psychoanalysis with feminism and then denigrating both as obstacles to innate creativity, they fail to notice that psychoanalysis is at the heart of their favored romantic exegesis. Critical theory has mapped the debate as phenomenology versus epistemology, rarely mentioning psychoanalysis, itself historical, as a common site of these divergent analyses. Both sides have muddied the waters. Whether epistemology or phenomenology, whether theories of the unconscious or "ego psychology," Freud provides a model of sexual difference which can only be denied with arduous difficulty.

For *VF,* sexuality was an internal, erotic, personal quest, a liberation into identity. For "VP" (again, my shorthand for Mulvey's "Visual Pleasure"), sexuality was constructed by difference embodied not in the artist but in the social, including representation and fiction. For *VF,* the answer lay deep inside the unique, eternal "self"; for "VP," the "subject" was a social construct. Or, as Teresa de Lauretis put it much later, it was "the problem of seeing, not as . . . a problem of 'art,' but as a questioning of identification and subject identity."[7] *VF* remained within traditional interpretations of Freud, beholden to the brave story of Oedipus; "VP" dissected its strategies, unraveled its system. While *VF* enshrines the world's oldest hero, the suffering, creative male artist, giving him an international film pedigree dating back to Melies, "VP" investigates the tactics of this figure in narrative and theory.

Because these mighty renditions have been so imperious, so peremptory, burying many films in the wake, I will relentlessly belabor this pivotal section. The dispute over romanticism has become an "of course" for theory dissenters, a dismissive one-liner, a free-floating axiom like "essentialism or idealism," killer points eliciting in-group assent in debates, but negative, one-word truisms rarely dissected. Thus, like *The Terminator* or Lazarus, romanticism returns to trouble theory. But this is the big city or *Blade Runner* version. Romanticism has been living a happy, suburban, authoritative life in English departments across the land. A 1980s version of what an early 1960s countercultural film might have been is *Dead Poets' Society*, a big box-office draw where the unknown, sensitive, and supportive students break the rules, meet in a cave, read the romantic poets, and become actors, incited to learning, generational dignity, and rebellion by the modest antiauthoritarian, Robin Williams. Predictably, the site is an upper-class boys' school in the 1950s, with young blonde things merely lustful objects. Fathers and school administrators are dogmatic to fascistic, old before their time, and the meek, downcast mothers are silent, pathetic. Like so many memories of the 1960s, the nostalgia for romanticism can also be heard as overtones in postmodernism, when men were boys and knew which side they were on. As Bloom's reading of Freud, particularly his model of anxiety, now wends its way out of literature, wandering into film theory, it might be propitious to artificially resuscitate an old corpse in order to properly bury it—like the blood-soaked body of Asa Buchanan's nephew on "One Life to Live," which returns to haunt only the woman he raped; everyone else believes he is dead, and no one will believe her; she is hysterical, seeing things. Thus, rather like Freud telling endless bad jokes in *Jokes and Their Relation to The Unconscious* or like watching parades on television, this chapter involves a dulling dose of tedious repetition—or, positively, like a loop film, or filming someone eating, or reprinting the same image, becoming more granular with each generation.

Against academic humanism and eliding high theory with low but popular culture, "VP"'s theoretical dissection *and* salvaging of Freud, in tandem with the Films of Hitchcock and Sternberg, uncovers a system of bipolarities, between spectacle and narrative, between looking and being looked at (reminiscent of John Berger in *Ways of Seeing* and Foucault in *Discipline and Punish*), between the active male (spectator and mover of the narrative) and the passive female as the object of his desirous gaze and story. Drawing on Freud's *Three Essays on Sexuality*, particularly "The Sexual Aberrations," his very short elucidation of fetishism, and Jacques Lacan's writing on the mirror phase and narcissism, Mulvey reiterates Freud's assessment of scopophilia: "In these perversions the sexual aim occurs in two forms, an *active* and a *passive* one." Mulvey's tag line, that woman was the "bearer not the maker of meaning," is an apt epigram for the place of women within what can only be called "the dominant ideology" of both classical art and avant-garde.

Casting the spectator as voyeur or fetishist within the mechanisms of scopophilia or narcissism, a spectator analogous to the child in Lacan's mirror stage, "woman" was simultaneously the ultimate pleasure and source of terror—for Freud, the contradictory sign of plenitude and castration. "Woman" was an obstacle that had to be overcome on the journey to the symbolic and identification with the father. Mulvey's investigation is of classical narrative and its pleasured spectator, with a call, in the end, for the overthrow of its traditional conventions, which, since its inception, had featured beautiful, youthful women as stars. The critique of masculinity, aka patriarchy, is, however, a prerequisite for her political agenda as filmmaker and feminist, the reclamation of female desire in films and theory alike.

(The use of bipolarity, of opposition and conflict, was derived from Marx and dialectical materialism as argued by artists during the revolutionary period, for example, Eisenstein's theory of art as conflict. Noel Burch's analysis of film's formal dialectics was loosely based on conflict.[8] The second term of Marxism, *materialism,* circulated imprecisely as the revelation of film's material grain, light, screen surface, and form. Mulvey has critiqued her own rhetorical use of binarisms: "The either/or binary pattern seemed to leave the argument trapped within its own conceptual frame, unable to advance politically . . . or suggest an alternative theory of spectatorship."[9] While I agree with the delimitation of difference to the sexual, binary logic signaled political and academic resistance amid a very real politics of protest. While dialectics might have been simplified and materialism evacuated by activists and theorists, rhetorical opposition was a strategy, not an error, and continues to serve a political purpose. In addition, the linguistic models on which this theory was predicated—the Russian formalists, Saussure, the Prague structuralists, and Benveniste—also incorporated binarisms, each term defined by, or containing, its opposite.)

While women such as Shirley Clarke, Marie Menken, Carolee Schneeman, Storm De Hirsch, Barbara Rubin, and Yoko Ono were making films, the majority of avant-garde films, unlike the Hollywood star system of worship and idealization, ignored women, figuring them (I repeat) as off-screen muse, mother, critic, or curator. When on screen, women were incidental, brief eruptions signaling male fantasy, whether "lyrical," "picaresque," or "mythopoetic." I think here of Bruce Baillie's *To Parsifal* and the brief appearance of the young naked woman in the forest as the phallic train snakes through and conquers the wilderness, restaging the nature-culture, female-male biological divide in this Wagnerian epic.

In Robert Nelson's *The Great Blondino,* the Quixote hero falls asleep and dreams his recurring orgy footage of naked, pendulum-breasted party girls superimposed over his sleeping body. Along the mock-hero's comic journey through the streets of San Francisco—a parody of Oedipus clinched by the last granular shot, which is of the Sphinx, with dreams of a horse's castration and an ever-growing but fake penis joke along the way—a strutting prostitute lures the fool off the path, to a restaging of the breast/buttocks transformation scene of naked, artistic lust from *Un Chien Andalou.* (For Blondino, the woman dissolves into an easel; art is the object of his desire, interchangeable with sex.) She is a joke, truly lacking, signified as only sex/biology. Whether caricatured parody or emblem of nature and beauty, the female body is the guarantee of male desire and, I suspect, the declaration of the maker's heterosexual preference and commitment to sexual liberation.

In either case, the female body is only a brief, usually pathetic, marker, rarely an identity, character, or even significant presence.

When women do make the rare star turn, as in Warhol's films, often men as drag queens or transvestites, the tale and the pleasure, or in the Warhol/ Morrissey films, displeasure, is homoerotic—from Cocteau, Smith, and Anger on, one dominant position for the male spectator of avant-garde, and one frequently linked to death. The representation of homosexuality rather than heterosexuality (with few films about "the couple"), replicated by the creation of a masculine band of cross-country disciples, is, on one hand, a confusion of roles and a scandalous challenge to conventions of representation, codes of censorship, and heterosexuality; on the other hand, the structuration is adolescent, involving youthful liberation and rebellion, centering, literally, on the phallus.

In *Scorpio Rising*, via James Dean, Marlon Brando, Elvis Presley, and Scorpio, the repressed of Hollywood cinema and the star system is addressed, in addition to representing the male body as the site of spectacle and sadomasochistic pleasure, including a plethora of crotch shots as climactic moments. Studded black leather jackets, unbuckled leather belts, waist-high camera tilts, and yellow road markers sensuously document the pleasure zone (and foreshadow high fashion of the 1980s). Drugs, scandal, celebrity, rock 'n' roll, violence, death, and, of course, sex are celebrated. Unlike the agitation of the female body as the site of spectacle and desire, the male body, perhaps what Barthes called a multiplicity of homosexualities and Foucault described as a multiplication of perversions, becomes the source of fascination. (Perhaps this partially explains the snug fit between *The Pleasure of the Text* and the reception of avant-garde films.) But whether liberation took a hetero or a homosexual form—like *Blondino, Scorpio Rising* also has an orgy scene with male bikers—the on-screen woman was worse off in Soho or San Francisco than in Hollywood: she was either an ordinary sex object, without glamor or high fashion, or there as a masquerade male; or she was just not there at all.

Avant-garde criticism also inscribed a masculine bias, reminiscent of the surrealists who worshiped "woman" as muse, the woman behind the man ploy. That the avant-garde was located amid the counterculture, which endorsed women's liberation and the women's movement along with "sexual liberation," suggests a slippery paradox, a containment comparable to postmodernism in the 1980s, which argues that feminism (like "woman" to modernism) has been crucial to postmodernism but is not able to locate many examples or quote any feminist writing. The historical trail in this regard is straight and consistent: the historical avant-garde was fascinated with "woman" as muse, the U.S. avant-garde with "women's lib" as sexual liberation, and postmodernism with feminism.

Women are caught in a logic of contradiction, being slapped in the face and kissed on the cheek at the same time. We are crucial, but absent. Critics and artists, like the film spectator, enact disavowal, pretending that women have not made films or written about these issues. Clinically speaking, dis-avowal protects against fear of castration; from a social perspective, it is a power move of exclusion, applicable to differences of sex, race, culture, and age. If one grew up in these equivocations, without theoretical models of feminism, it took time to notice women's absence or unimportance amid all the radical politics, complimentary flattery, and brazen acknowledgment.

The lack of interest in female subjectivity is also covered up by displacing the problem onto other issues, leading the argument astray, often under a banner of radical change. The first displacement was onto a critique of the institutions of art; the second, into a devaluation of the tangible art object and artist (the central canons of the historical avant-garde, according to Peter Burger). With the U.S. avant-garde, coincident with the film theory of, for example, Jean-Louis Comolli and Jean-Louis Baudry, the concern was the revelation of the film's work, uncovering the apparatus, in concert with psychoanalysis, Marxism, and structuralism, leading to typologies of "structural" film or, in England, "structuralist/materialist" films. Postmodernism focuses on the dissolving divide between mass culture and art, distinctions (actually standards of taste, education, class) which cannot hold for either film or video, defined by reproducibility, intangible objects until projected or transmitted, and, like *Scorpio Rising's* rock 'n' roll score, allied with mass cultural techniques of distribution, exhibition, and economic concerns.

Taken together, the now axiomatic arguments of *VF* and "VP," particularly their respective uses of psychoanalysis (one as story, the other as system), render the contradiction of difference as the political, historical, and theoretical problem it has been and continues to be for the art world, popular culture, and critical theory alike. Thus, I have schematically placed these two texts in dialogue, although quantitatively the odds are not equal: Sitney's work is a lengthy book, while Mulvey's is an essay (to which I return in later chapters). I emphasize that regarding *VF* I am arguing about a particular interpretation or image of avant-garde cinema, a model rooted in literary rather than film theory, and not the specific films, not alternative women's films, but a historical discourse taken up as the definitive or dominant reading (like Metz's psychoanalysis of the apparatus and spectator and Mulvey's feminist model). Examining the canonized concept of U.S. avant-garde cinema, its imaginary, which resonates with the biases of the historical avant-garde, is a preliminary step toward the emergence of another cultural model, which might enable us to see the films differently.

In tandem with the romantic premises of the U.S. counterculture (to which I will tenaciously return), supported by close readings of hundreds of films and often the corroboration of the filmmakers, Sitney's ambitious history of avant-garde cinema traces the evolution of styles, with style also connoting metaphysics: the chapter subjects progress from "trance to myth" and "the lyrical film" to the central "major mythopoeia," "recovered innocence," and "apocalypses and picaresques," concluding with "structural film." The mythical taxonomy is also determined by filmmaker; "The Magus" is devoted to Anger, "Major Mythopoeia" to Brakhage and, to a lesser degree, Baillie. The book traces an avant-garde lineage from the early 1940s to the early 1970s in the United States, analyzing technical variants, "Graphic Cinema," and "Absolute Animation" and including European antecedents. Few contemporary filmmakers from other countries, except Peter Kubelka, are mentioned. Read another way, as the epic titles suggest, VF traces a Promethean national quest and elucidates male subjectivity as an art of brave, sacrificial narcissism. For Sitney, as for many of the filmmakers, this was their duty as artists embodying the romantic tradition where the traumatic, sometimes treacherous quest for self *is* art.

As Sitney repeatedly writes of Brakhage, his Diogenes, the "process of making film and the search for consciousness" are one and the same thing, equivalent to the "identity of the erotic and aesthetic quests" (177). Regarding James Broughton: "although he is deeply committed to Jungian rather than Freudian psychoanalysis, the nostalgia for the origins of cinema is fused in his work with an ironic quest for the origin of his own psychic development" (82). The equation of aesthetics and identity, the origin of cinema and the origin of the self, in many ways replicates the pedagogical history of art. The interest of avant-garde also shifts, from Freud to Jung, evolving to embrace the notion of the collective unconscious (153). In her essay on Michael Snow, de Lauretis analyzes this central, agonistic conceit as modernist: the view that "the 'origin' of art is (in) the artist, *whose* desire is inscribed in the representation, *whose* . . . longing . . . is both mediated and effected by . . . the apparatus; and *to whom* . . . the film returns as to its only possible reference, its source of aesthetic unity and meaning."[10] "Visionary film" is film made by a single person and in turn revelatory of that person, if person is read as primarily "man."

Constance Penley, writing six years earlier, made a comparable argument about British "structuralist-materialist" films, predicated, unlike U.S. avant-garde, on continental theory: "it could be asked if they offer nothing but a *multiplication of effects,* all striving towards a new recentering of the subject, this time not centered in a transcendental elsewhere but in the body of the subject himself."[11] And a bit later: "The subject constituted by the early avant-gardists and the structural materialists is essentially the same even if one constructs its subject in the name of a romantic humanism and the other in the name of science and 'materialism.' Both play on an infantile wish to shape the real to the measure of the subject's own boundless desire."[12] Penley neglected to gender the "subject" as male, although the implications are there.

I again reiterate that the conditions of personal rather than corporate distribution and exhibition contributed to this centering on the individual. Appearances, so it would appear, occurred out of necessity, with altruistic, pedagogic, and economic motives—to celebrate the art of cinema, to reach new audiences, and to receive minuscule honoraria for the next film. The presence of the filmmaker was the film's lure and promise, turning a screening into an event, or, like commercial exhibition until the late 1940s and 1950s, "presentation cinema" (which included short films of various styles and live performance). Whether we understood the film or not, we would come away with something, usually for nothing, from the person in the form of anecdotes, impressions, an art experience, or a conversion "in the way we see." Whether answer or performance by the maker, the film's real and only star/author/producer/director who singly made the film, almost by hand, we came away with a story, a feeling of collectivity, and perhaps the belief that, given enough history, we might have chatted with a future Great Artist.

Thus was fostered the cult of the artist, in name or body interchangeable with the film: filmmakers wrote their own descriptive copy and, like the voice of truth and authority called upon to sanction art, interpreted their films after the screenings in question sessions for audiences, eliding criticism with the moment of reception, merging film with maker (which the label of "personal films" already equated), speaking of their work as themselves, thereby transforming what Monroe Beardsley called "the intentional fallacy" into the cornerstone of interpretation. (Coincidentally, *filmmaker* has, in the course of twenty or more years, become a single word. Unlike the specialist labels or credits of commercial cinema, this is a totalizing and craftlike term.) This narcissistic staging, on film and in person, of the artist/self in which the unique person is both the beginning and the end of art—the artist's vision the penultimate source of fascination to the maker (and sometimes the scholar), with the presence of devotees as guarantee that the makers' assumption of their intrinsic fascination is correct—is the very familiar tale of geniuses and humanism, sanctimoniously intoned in art history classrooms and museum galleries.

However comparable to the Kerouac-inspired adventure and freedom of being undomesticated, of being on the road and sexually liberated, making films was also an economic deprivation, a constant search for support. Many filmmakers—I think particularly of Woody Vasulka, Robert Nelson, and Owen Land—were uncomfortable with the pedagogical imperative as their primary means of funding. With the premises of romanticism as underpinning, however, the funding became drama for the story. That we were often hearing an old tale, of Oedipus's struggles with either the Sphinx or the Muse and ultimately the Father, was complicated and perhaps concealed by what Penley called "a multiplication of effects" and what I call an aesthetics of pluralism (as in Sheldon Renan's taxonomy of periods and styles), rather than a politics of differences.

As I rapped earlier, films could be of any length, about any subject, of any technical quality, with the human figure or not, with or without sound, shown on one projector or four, exhibited or projected, edited or not, with or without errors, painted or scratched or filmed, made by anyone, trained or not, blurred or focused, shot or collaged, often without discernible beginnings or endings. While the maker should be singular and the aspiration an artistic rather than a commercial one, the factor that counted most was uniqueness, often left up to the artist to decipher. The history of art sustains itself by so many differentiations and taxonomies by period or epoch, artist or school, style or movement, which necessitate expanding official buildings in which art can embrace variant media and history in a global grasp while repressing differences and economic exchange as mundane. This reversal of the value of material concerns is intriguing, taking materiality out of the social, where it is trivial, and into art, which is then "radical."

As *VF* sees it, art has little to do with the real world; art is a journey inward, to new depths of consciousness raising, fostered by drugs and liberated by sex. Sitney refers to a moment in *Scorpio Rising* when "Scorpio takes a sniff of cocaine. . . . We see in one or two seconds of cinema the re-creation of a high Romantic, or Byronic myth of the paradox of liberation," " 'an ace of light' " which he calls a liberation and a "limitation" because "it is exterior" (119). (That addiction was the debilitating underside of both drugs and sex, de-eroticized commodities of exchange without pleasure and darkly represented in Warhol's later films, is a postmodern reality; both random sex and drugs have lost their glamor as liberation has soured to self-destruction.) The celebratory contours of the late 1960s and 1970s counterculture, along with Sitney and Bloom, drew inspiration from the premises (and drug practices) of the romantic poets. Thus, *Visionary Film* paradoxically exemplifies (1) what were then imagined as radical, or anarchistic, social currents, including Bloom's "iconoclastic" criticism of the romantic poets (youthful artists railing against their fathers to claim their place in the sun), and (2) an evolutionary *and* apocalyptic (rather than materialist, dialectical) model of art history as a linear, albeit chaotic or pluralistic, series of greats and firsts, accidents and intentions.

VF also documents the not inconsiderable reality that most films available were, in fact, made by men and enthusiastically received by women who believed, as did I, in the radical potential of the inquisition of narrative conventions by the revelation of "the apparatus," including the spectator. But after continuity style had been peeled away in avant-garde films and narrative conventions analyzed by feminist film theory, another double absence—the erasure of representations of women and the inscription of female subjectivity—came into focus. While contemporary theory came to my rescue with new intellectual models, I spent a great deal of energy discovering that in theory as well I was lacking; how to make theory, like avant-garde, listen to and work for women became an important issue.

The oversights and blind spots of the 1970s were particularly ironic given the activity and publicity of the women's movement, with women's issues becoming nightly news, still a rare occurrence. However, attending women's groups and political organizing was one thing; digging through the archeology of art, creating models to deal with the inequities of that real world of texts and power, money and myth, was quite another, and it took time, particularly when art in the United States made a countercultural swerve in the name of equality and access, presumably in tandem with the women's movement, the civil rights movement, and the antiwar efforts. Separate but equal, applied in different ways to women and race, is still the critical contradiction, endorsed now by separatist feminists and black militants as deliberately separate because unequal.

An early rejoinder to the critical approach epitomized by *VF* came in a joint letter published in *Screen* by Penley and Bergstrom, who critiqued "the dominant ideology" contained in several books on U.S. avant-garde cinema. Penley argued against the phenomenological method, pointing to a tautological flaw: "Criticism's function will be to refine our seeing and affirm the modernist credo of knowledge through self-consciousness. The discourse about the object becomes (is the same thing as) the discourse of the object."[13] I would add to her critique that the object of discourse was a celebration of the subject or self as romantic hero. Penley further pointed out that "this phenomenological approach" eliminates "consideration of the spectator's unconscious relation to the film . . . an aspect that has received much attention in French and English film theory."[14]

While I agree, with qualifications, the irony is that rather than eliminating the "unconscious," the romanticism of Bloom taken up by *VF* stars the unconscious as the battle between eros and death, good and bad art; the artistic unconscious, a battle with one's precursors, is wellspring, quest and goal, source and discovery. It needs, in the great films, no other actants than the filmmakers, struggling against and in the name of art history. To a degree, this drama resembles Poggioli's assessment of the stages, particularly agonism, of the historical avant-garde.[15] As Sitney writes of Brakhage and "the erotic quest" in his early films, "Freud has never meant as much to any other film-maker. Brakhage even initiated an ambitious *Freudfilm*, but failed to bring it off" (175). I will leave this Freudianism alone and return later to the central figuration of psychoanalysis in Bloom's romanticism.

Bergstrom, in her response to the same texts, argued that "modern formalism" is "by definition opposed to the possibility of a political avant-garde, which is necessarily concerned with meanings."[16] Like Michelson on the other side, she invoked Eisenstein and pointed to *VF*'s lack of "any consideration of audience, social context, or the operations by which meaning is produced by and for the spectator."[17] Given an interpretation of psychoanalysis as eternal rather than historical, as a journey inward rather than an engagement with material practices, discourses, and referents, "meaning" as a social construction including the spectator had become irrelevant for many critics. Bergstrom offered a critical agenda: the analysis of "filmic enunciation" and "the notion that every film is crossed by a heterogeneity of discourses, [which bears] upon the representation of women." She called for a "shift of attention to the entire process of signification, rather than limiting it to the play of the signifiers."[18]

In both these lucid responses, the erasure of women and its flip side, the vaunting of male subjectivity as art, are noted, but from the cool distance of theoretical knowledge. The revelation of the apparatus in the theoretical criticism of Metz and Baudry (and Comolli) is held up as a better "approach," albeit in writings which neglect women, constructing an illusionary machine for men only. Bergstrom cautions us to look for meaning, for an outside, toward reception and the audience, including her analysis of Chantal Akerman's *Letters from Home* as an alternative. While enunciation was analyzed, we initially cared more about what Benveniste called shifters, the formal parameters rather than content or subjectivity. That the concept of enunciation within feminist theory has been amplified to include the questions to whom, by whom, and about what must be noted.

Oedipus is the unspoken myth woven through *VF*'s typology of myth as a link between artistic form and artist consciousness. The great films are linked to the poetry of Wordsworth, Blake, and Wallace Stevens, then in high intellectual and countercultural fashion; "the preoccupations of the American avant-garde film-makers coincide with those of our post-Romantic poets and Abstract Expressionist painters. Behind them lies a potent tradition of Romantic Poetics. . . . I have attempted to trace the heritage of Romanticism . . . more generative of a unified view of these films and film-makers than the Freudian hermeneutics and sexual analysis which have dominated . . . previous criticism" (ix). That Bloom's romanticism draws heavily on Freudian hermeneutics, particularly *Beyond the Pleasure Principle,* is not taken into account.[19]

As I have ceaselessly reiterated, Bloom is the critical model, although he is cited only in brief references, without elaboration of his premises. Thus, he exists as a guiding truism certified by quick allusions. In "The Lyrical Film": "Harold Bloom's observation about Wordsworth's achievement could be applied to Brakhage. . . . 'The dreadful paradox' of Wordsworth's greatness is that his uncanny originality . . . has been so influential that we have lost sight of its audacity and its arbitrariness" (176). The "dreadful paradox" of Brakhage's greatness drives Sitney's reading and, to an extraordinary degree, criticism *and* filmmaking during this entire period. Brakhage just might be the imaginary of the avant-garde; his name is synonymous with it. "As Harold Bloom observed of the twentieth century tradition in English poetry, 'every fresh attempt of Modernism to go beyond Romanticism ends in the gradual realization of the Romantic's continued priority' " (170). Rather than the modernism usually ascribed to abstract expressionism, *VF*'s other operative analogy for avant-garde cinema, Sitney, led by Bloom and Brakhage, rescues romanticism, a "continued priority." It is this "gradual realization" of romanticism artificially resuscitated as the history of art that needs interrogation.

To reclaim modernism from a formalism of the signifier, as Penley and de Lauretis imply, and link it to industrial conditions of labor, of work, to the experience of modernity as did, for one example, Benjamin, contextualizing it within mass culture, city streets, electrical technologies, arcades, and public transit—locating it in the crowds, streets, and factories of modernity, which included working women—might result in quite another reading of the films, as I stated earlier. At the same time, placing U.S. avant-garde cinema within the critical sway of romanticism—a revival of earlier communitarian thought and experiment—takes it out of the city and into the country, away from the ideas, techniques, and politics of modernity. This is an old-fashioned, radical aspiration which partakes of the counterculture ethos, a move back to communal farms, crafts, and do-it-yourself-sufficiency.

Via a constantly renewed commitment to Brakhage's work, *VF* resolutely holds to this romantic stance—viewed as "inwardness." "The eye which both Stevens and Brakhage enlist in the service of the imagination confirms . . . as Bloom's view would have it, the Romantic divorce of consciousness and nature" (187). The only important struggle is in the mind's eye, the soul, with one's artistic forebears, in a chain, albeit disruptive, of difficult (opposed to easy) art. Brakhage's writing in the 1963 *Metaphors on Vision* (a special and expensive issue of *Film Culture* dominated by a negatively and positively printed image of Brakhage's face, with a cut-out peephole for his central eye), and his use of blindness as an early metaphor (for example, *Reflections in Black* has a blind protagonist, and in an earlier film the character had gouged out his eyes, shades of Thebes) in turn confirms the snug fit of Bloom, exemplified by the anecdote of Brakhage throwing away his glasses when he began to make films—his unfettering of the human eye argued in his polemic against the standardization and hierarchization of codes of vision of Western representation.

Writing Bloom's history, Helen Elam enthuses over his 1973 book, *The Anxiety of Influence:* "This criticism transformed the conventional landscape of literary history into a battleground in which each poet . . . enters into . . . an Oedipal struggle with his precursors."[20] Without a qualm or qualification, Elam argues that Bloom simultaneously attacks Arnold's humanism, the New Criticism, *and* deconstruction; he "stresses the importance of imaginative vision, one of self-presence and self-origination which goes to the heart of mythmaking" (36). In the sexual identity model of psychoanalysis, the Oedipus myth is accepted for the untroubled centrality it is to Freud, who, in addition, mapped out contradictions and considered femininity a serious question; for feminist theory, Freud, like Oedipus, is dismantled but instructive.

De Lauretis goes right to "the heart of mythmaking" in her brilliant essay "Desire in Narrative": "In this mythical-textual mechanics, then, the hero must be male . . . because the obstacle . . . is morphologically female . . . simply the womb . . . if the work of the mythical structuration is to establish distinctions, the primary distinction on which all others depend is not, say, life and death, but rather sexual difference . . . the hero, the mythical subject, is constructed as human being and as male; he is the active principle of culture . . . the creator of differences. . . . Female is what is not susceptible to transformation . . . she (it) is an element of plot-space."[21] (I would add that "the primary distinction is [also] not, say," mass culture and art, narrative or not.) If she is right, "if the crime of Oedipus is the destruction of differences, the combined work of myth and narrative is the production of Oedipus,"[22] then rather than counterpoint Hollywood cinema's staging of Oedipus, VF merely displaces it, playing it out backstage as a drama of unrequited art and authorship (the male's search for what Elam calls "self-origination"). If "mythical positioning . . . works through the narrative form,"[23] then criticism predicated on myth is yet another fiction, ironically endorsing the ideological tenets of the classical narrative which Mulvey so lucidly dissected.

Regarding Bloom's 1961 *Visionary Company* (revised and enlarged in 1971), the companion volume to *Visionary Film* (itself revised in a 1979 second edition), Elam writes that "this company of poets, beginning with Blake and stretching in unbroken fashion to the twentieth century, forms a 'visionary company of love' " (36); the most visionary in this company, Blake, like Brakhage in *VF*, becomes "a model of imaginative strength against which the other poets are tested" (36). With Blake as exemplar, this leads to a "visionary freedom in which the mind directly creates time and space."[24] As Brakhage writes in *Metaphors on Vision*, "After the loss of innocence [the infant's learning to see, to classify] . . . there is a pursuit of knowledge foreign to language and founded on visual communication . . . the optical mind . . . perception in the original and deepest sense."[25] Like particularly the later Bloom staging the battle as a biblical epic, Brakhage elides "the Vision of the saint and the artist" as "an increased ability to see." "To search for human visual realities, man must . . . transcend the original physical restrictions and inherit worlds of eyes . . . contemporary moving visual reality is exhausted."[26]

The divorce of mind and nature, or nature and imagination, along with banishing language and visual reality, emerges here: "My eye, tuning toward the imaginary, will go to any wave-lengths for its sights. . . . How long has sight's center continued pupil to other men's imaginings? This sensitive instrument must respond to all the gods who deign to play upon it."[27] Thus, Brakhage turns on "2000 years of Western equine painting," unfettering his eye in his mythological quest for origins—"thwarting the trained response link between retina and brain . . . as in the beginning . . . my eye . . . outwards (without words) . . . transforming optic abstract impressions into nonrepresentational language, enchanting non-sights into non-words. . . ."[28]

For Sitney, Bloom, and Brakhage, "the great works baffle the intellect . . . these artists become the great martyrs of aesthetic discomfort."[29] For Brakhage, this is "the only private personal key I have for the coffin lid . . . to re-awaken the self, re-illusion the dreamer, and thus prevent the death of the spirit . . . the dogs will tear me to pieces if ever I'm caught."[30] This battle with death by a very young man involves a claim for eros *and* reproduction, what Elam celebrates without a misstep as "self-origination"—Brakhage filming the birth of all of his and Jane's children—making origin, reproduction (always a problem for film's status as art), a literal struggle toward self-sufficiency, involving another usurpation of women. Blake's Apocalypse describes Sitney's assessment of Brakhage, a poet who, "with increasing power, overcomes the external world, until word and vision are one."[31] Banished from the kingdom of film art are narrative, reality, and now language, along with sound.

VF unsystematically adopts Bloom's ahistorical use of psychoanalysis which, as Elam asserts, "insists on the priority of psychoanalysis over epistemology, voice over text, a psyche that resists deconstruction's idea of the self as an effect of language." Bloom combines Nietzsche's "will to power and Freud's theories about psychic defense—wherein poets lie to themselves, and to others. . . ." And regarding Bloom's 1971 *Ringers in the Tower*, "the antithetical relationship between nature and imagination attends the concept of central man" (37). For Bloom, original poets are difficult poets; strong poets react against tradition; weaker poets idealize what they inherit. "This is poetic history written from the point of view of poetry rather than a critical perspective that assumes its own detachment and secondariness" (38). Likewise, Sitney writes film history from the filmmakers' point of view. And, like weak and strong poets, there are weak and strong filmmakers and critics— the strong ones react against the past, not, as Walter Benjamin argues, for a "revolutionary chance" but in the "prospect that freedom and self-origination are within its grasp" (38). The significant place Bloom accords the critic, or himself, on a par with the poet, is compatible with Sitney's. The critic is a central player in the agon.

Bloom's valuation of figuration is read through Freud's *Beyond the Pleasure Principle* as a psychic force, with eros linked to lack and desire, set against what he calls the literal as cessation, death. Figuration is tension; eros is figural, but a doomed figuration; hence, all human sexuality is tropological, while we long for it, says Bloom, to be literal. "Hence the sorrows and the authentic anguish of all human erotic quest, hopelessly seeking to rediscover an object, which never was the true object anyway."[32] For *VF* and Bloom, figuration is a "psychic force," "linked with power," a defense against the literal, a "constant movement and tension as opposed to rest or a coming-to-meaning"; "power and Art is thus lodged, in line with Emerson, in figuration—power ceases in the instant of repose" (45). I can think of no better description of Brakhage's work.

Along with enshrining Brakhage as the inheritor of romanticism, of the subservience of materiality to personality, of reality (or nature) to imagination, of the literal to the figural, something else is at stake. The biggest problem with male identity and pleasure, along with linkages to power, is that they are secured at the expense of someone else. In this regard, male desire is not like female desire, which still has borders, propriety, humility.

Almost immediately after Sitney's first reference to Bloom, a dramatic opposition is introduced; it is overtly symptomatic, unexpected, the clincher to the dearth of women as artists, critics, curators, or spectators. In his chapter on Gregory Markopoulos, "From Trance to Myth," a dispute is staged: "The

Romantic posture did not rest well with Maya Deren. She struggled against it in her own films, and labeled them 'classicist.' She opposed Anger and later Brakhage when his work veered toward Romanticism. Her contact with Markopoulos, though, was minimal. When she was exercising some limited power through the Creative Film Foundation, he was in Greece . . . she died soon after he returned" (170). This scenario bears some scrutiny. Their contact was minimal, he was in Greece, and then she—of some limited power—died? This reads like classical mythology, with Deren, a powerful woman, figured as an obstacle that needed to be overcome or slain, along with being placed in a subservient position.

Although Sitney has a chapter on Deren's work, "Ritual and Nature," with the biological determinism as giveaway, his sniping at Deren is scholastically questionable. It is a tactic of curtailment of a competing "legend" of subjectivity (then being researched by a women's collective, which he notes in an apologia in the second edition) set against the myth of Brakhage. The story of classicism versus romanticism, or women versus men, of Deren versus Brakhage, of mother against father/son, of female subjectivity, influence, and power, which begins in Meshes of the Afternoon and continues each time I screen it, ends in the first two chapters of VF. Sitney imagines that Deren's death in 1961 silences her opposition, allowing romanticism, a male purview, to emerge as the unquestioned victor—the Perseus model of avant-garde with Medusa now dead.

Yet, it's not enough that Deren died, unexpectedly, in 1961. VF puts Deren (who is both his Minotaur and his Medusa—a real blind spot) in her place of subservience to Hammid, her husband, and later to Markopoulos (although he was in Greece—perhaps lost in a maze, for this chapter was excluded, at his request, from the 1979 edition). Like "Snow on the Oedipal Stage," so is VF; not surprisingly, Oedipus is the myth which cannot be mentioned amid the hundred citations of "myth." In his opening Deren gambit, Sitney conquers "women," moving away from mother, journeying into the symbolic (he was a precocious critic, attending avant-garde films and writing criticism at age fourteen) and identification with the Janus father of Brakhage (too young to be Dad) and Bloom. The price is high, however; Deren's reputation is undervalued and Meshes of the Afternoon is misinterpreted.

"The collaboration of Maya Deren and Alexander Hammid shortly after their marriage in 1942 recalls in its broad outline and its aspiration the earlier collaboration of Salvador Dali and Luis Bunuel" (3). Thus, the film's first weakness: this is a collaboration, a containment reinforced by a comparison to another film, derivation being another negative in the canon of avant-garde aesthetics, although equivocating pains are taken to avoid the overt claim that Deren and Hammid copied Un Chien Andalou intentionally. The comparison is linked by the Freud of The Interpretation of Dreams; both films use dream logic and symbols.

Then, Deren's critical flaw: "We should remember that he [Hammid] photographed the whole film. Maya Deren simply pushed the button on the camera for the two scenes in which he appeared." The film in which she "simply pushed the button" "is also Hammid's portrait of his young wife" (10). He notes a "difference which obtains between the early American avant-garde 'trance film' . . . and its surrealistic precursors. In *Meshes of the Afternoon*, the heroine undertakes an interior quest . . . revealing the erotic mystery of the self. The surrealistic cinema . . . imitate[s] the . . . irrationality of the unconscious. . . . Deren, with her hands lightly pressed against the window pane, embodies the reflective experience" (11). Thus, *Meshes*, "as psycho-drama, is the inward exploration of both Deren and Hammid . . . the quest for sexual identity; in their film, unlike those that follow in this book, it is two people, the makers of the film, who participate in this quest" (18). In what follows the next chapter on Deren, women are banished, with the exception of short references to the work of Shirley Clarke, Marie Menken, Carolee Schneemann, and Joyce Wieland (in name only).

Rather than sexual identity revealing "the erotic mystery of the self," Deren's (and Hammid's) is a model of difference, of a woman divided in and by sexual difference. The violence and rage directed against the female body, the contradiction and frustration beneath the heterosexual couple, are almost palpable. Rather than the parodic tone and structure of *Un Chien Andalou*, this is a deadly serious film. *VF's* analysis of *Meshes'* violent conclusion is troubling: the look at the end, of the man at the body of the woman, is different; it is an outward glance; she is dead, strangled by a condensation of the film's images and scenes—seaweed, the telephone cord, the broken mirror or glass. The man is standing, looking down, dominant. Sitney argues that this conventional look "changes the film's dimension by its affirmation of dream over actuality" (14), an argument which contains her narrative death as dream rather than real. I would assert the opposite: because the last shot is from the conventional male figure's point of view and hence is marked as stable, the shift argues that her suicide, or murder, is not a dream.

VF's reading of the violent bedroom scene of Deren stabbing the mirrored face of the man, Hammid, interchangeable with a hooded figure of death or a nun, displaces female terror and heterosexual violence into an art reference, which it is, but much more than that: "In the construction of the scene in which the stabbed face turns out to be a mirror, they pay homage, perhaps unknowingly, to a motif of the painter, Rene Magritte" (15). An attack on representation, on the institution of art, on surrealism, on systems in which woman is merely the reflection or signifier of male desire, without a room or desire of one's own, is a more apt analysis.

That *Meshes* is about female subjectivity divided against itself, held in the violent social and domestic contradictions of sexual difference (including giving men most of the credit), a scenario directed against the male for whom she is merely a reflection, an anger tragically turned back on the self as narcissistic rage, with differences played out between the overt and apparent clash of symbols, the knife, the poppy, the key, amid the claustrophobic, disorienting domestic space, is never considered. That the home to which she runs is a frightening space, that the proverbial room at the top of the stairs, the bedroom as the place of the primal scene, is also terrifying, says something about the heterosexual couple when the point of view is female.

Rather than Hammid's view of his "young wife," this is a view from the woman's corner of the room and a system clearly coded in the film. This film is about Deren's terror and the unconscious; as much as she pursues the elusive, robed figure, she can find neither pleasure nor identity there—only death. If female subjectivity is pursued in the couple or by running after men, there is nothing for women to find except an image of themselves. *Meshes* is an early version of de Lauretis's proposition that "the work of the film should be . . . how to position the spectator and the filmmaker not at the center but at the borders of the Oedipal stage."[33] And this terrain, even if she is standing outside, looking through the window pane, and knowledgeable about psychoanalysis (her father was a psychiatrist), involves risk, unsettling disorientation.

While Deren broke the mirror which held women to the imaginary (yet remained its victim), history remembers her as image, referred to as "the Botticelli." The female editors of *The Legend of Maya Deren* wonder why Deren chose for publicity posters the still from the film in which she is looking out the window: "There are so many images she could have chosen—the woman as warrior in *Meshes*, rising from the earth with a knife. . . ." "The legend of the painting supposes the Venus figure to be modelled after a beautiful Florentine woman who had died quite young and was eloquently mourned by all the poets. Grief for the loss of beautiful young women is a tradition in art that precedes the Primavera and that will extend beyond the still from *Meshes*. . . . Perhaps it was neither youth nor beauty she sought to keep but the transparency of the glass." Earlier, the co-editors write that "as the years passed, the discrepancy increased between her appearance and 'the Botticelli' on her posters."[34] Perhaps Deren knew about the gap between the real and the appearance, the performer and the filmmaker, women and woman, the contradictions to which women are held. (I note that she was only forty-four when she died, hardly an old woman.)

In a letter written after her death, Rudolf Arnheim pays tribute: "There is a photograph of Maya Deren, so striking and so well known that some of us think of it when we think of her. It . . . shows a girl looking out through a window . . . and yet the image is not really she," no more than Maya was her name—Eleonora was. Later in the short piece: "What was she after? She was one of the artists and thinkers who speak of the great paradox of our time . . . the world of tangible things . . . in Maya Deren's films, the familiar world captures us by its pervasive strangeness . . . the sequences of her images are logical. They are neither arbitrary nor absurd. They follow the letter of a law we never studied on paper."[35]

That her law was not that of male desire or Western patriarchy is also suggested by her trips to Haiti, along with her interest in ritual. That she must have been profoundly isolated as a woman filmmaker in the 1940s and 1950s is apparent. Her look is from outside, what de Lauretis, after Barthes, might call "elsewhere" and Adrienne Rich, "another planet." Perhaps the photograph of Deren behind the window pane, a reminder of the power of the female gaze, a knowing look from the margins, remarked the gap between women and their image—a discrepancy familiar to women held to a youthful ideal even by other admiring women.

(Sally Potter's *Thriller* begins where *Meshes* ends and investigates the cost to women of romanticism and Oedipus, unraveling the mystery of *La Bohème*. Su Friedrich's *Dammed If You Don't* restages the pursuit of the hooded figure—who is a nun. Like Potter, Friedrich interrogates narrative, the amazing *Black Narcissus* and raging nun lust amid Powell/Pressburger technicolor, exotic excess, somewhere in South America. At the end of her film, as at the end of Potter's, women unite; for Friedrich, in sex, for Potter, in a fond embrace. Both filmmakers have also explored the uncharted terrain of mother-daughter relationships—new territory for avant-garde.)

The film juxtaposed to *Meshes* in *VF, Un Chien Andalou* (1929), was released in 1968 "after almost forty years of clandestinity," finally "deemed suitable for adult audiences."[36] As Phillip Drummond reports in his detailed analysis, Raymond Rohauer, "key exploiter of the silent cinema," obtained the rights in 1960 and, under Bunuel's supervision, added the original gramophone musical score.[37]

Along with the Oedipus complex as a personal quest, another prevalent use of psychoanalysis in the 1960s and 1970s was deciphering symbols, "the only method of investigation of the symbols" of *Un Chien Andalou*. In relation to the dream logic and Dali's boastful proclamations of the film's total and purposeful meaninglessness, *VF* asserts that "this method of compiling a scenario was the liberation of their material from the demands of narrative continuity" (4). Drummond repeatedly cautions against a delimited, "primitive, crude psychoanalytic" reading, arguing that "nothing could be less relevant in the face of such detailed intrication . . . of signifiers that form and block the passage of Bunuel's and Dali's text."[38]

Forewarned by both scholars of the pitfalls of either narrative or psychoanalytic critique and in basic agreement with the film's disconnections and multiplicity, I would, on the contrary, argue that *Un Chien Andalou* can be analyzed as operating within the constraints of psychoanalysis and narrative, even functioning as (1) a reenactment of Freud's essay "The 'Uncanny' " and (2) a critique of classical continuity style, its counterpoints as much as *The Interpretation of Dreams* and abstract or figural art, which the film claims to depose—what Dali called the "maniacal lozenges of Monsieur Mondrian."[39]

That *Un Chien Andalou* was a "reaction against contemporary avant-garde cinema of Ruttmann, Cavalcanti, Man Ray, Dziga Vertov, Clair, Dulac and Ivens"[40] places it within a historical conjuncture similar to U.S. and British debates in the mid- to late 1970s around three comparable terms—avant-garde, narrative, and psychoanalysis. For Drummond, the film "is of interest precisely as a turning point between the alternatives of dominant and counter cinema," with Bunuel "challenging formalism."[41] Ironically, by positioning a critique of abstraction (along with a claim for representation) within the coincidence of psychoanalysis and Oedipus with narrative, *Un Chien Andalou* sketches a 1929 theoretical project remarkably similar to the general terrain of de Lauretis's 1980s call for feminism: "The most exciting work in cinema and in feminism today is not anti-narrative or anti-Oedipal; quite the opposite. It is narrative and Oedipal with a vengeance, for it seeks to stress the duplicity of that scenario and the specific contradiction of the female subject in it. . . ."[42] (Whether or not it is appropriate for Andalusian dogs, de Lauretis's description could be copy for Potter's *Thriller,* which directly addresses the contradictions for women of the classical texts of cinema, ballet, theater, and opera, specifically Puccini's *La Boheme* and Hitchcock's *Psycho;* I will return to *Thriller* later.)

Whether the woman whose vision is attacked by Bunuel's razor slicing her eye and whose glances and amazed reaction shots paradoxically dominate the film elucidates contradictions of the female subject will remain, for now, uncertain. Drummond argues that "the face of woman . . . redefines and refigures the male presence and activity within the film," an argument predicated on the twelve-shot prologue. She "displaces . . . his dream of space," along with the co-author (Bunuel) and the male actors; the film is a "desperate, castrated compliment to woman," a conclusion qualified in a footnote that this is not "to suggest that . . . 'the woman' is eventually any less fetishised. . . ." "In the narrative surrealism of *Un Chien Andalou,* the mutilation of the female protagonist is the paradoxical guarantee of her unharmed survival, the doom only of her surgeon, true victim of his reverie."[43] Whether parody or tragedy, the male seducer sacrificing himself to his own desperate desire is a very old and familiar story.

Like the classical film, *Un Chien Andalou* is a story of seduction and the couple, separated, quarreling, united, and then buried in the sand—happily ever after or dead (with the concluding shot an allusion to Dreyer), the two endings of Hollywood film. Along with a tormented, schizophrenic, sensitive man and a nagging, demanding, impatient woman, the film features death and sex. Along with narrative figuration of characters, the techniques are modeled on continuity style: a system of rhyming and repetition threads the film together, for example, the recurring stripes on the tie and the box and the watch on the man's arm at the beginning and end. In the classical text, as Heath has argued, repetition and rhymes, fashioned in a symmetrical manner with the end circling back to the beginning, devouring or using up all the elements in the process, create verisimilitude, locating the spectator in a position of intelligibility, of knowledge and power. The details accumulate meaning according to a logic which, like the narrative, is cause-effect and chronological. In *Un Chien Andalou,* literal and symbolic meaning, like the striped box, is tossed out the balcony window or dropped in the sand on the beach. We have all the clues and techniques but none of the answers or explanations.

Parody, which involves a coded relationship between texts, a referential strategy, more accurately describes the film. Continuity editing techniques of eyeline matches, point of view shots, and matching action create a system in which space appears to be continuous and stable; in *Un Chien Andalou,* these techniques undermine that stability. The editing is predicated on cutting to the woman's reaction to what she sees, usually with astonishment and irritation for being interrupted in her reading. The central apartment, the scene of the attempted seduction, is not the concrete locale it appears to be, with a recognizable 180-degree axis—the front door leads either to a city street or to a beach. Like the movie theater, the room has a balcony from which to view death on the streets below. By cutting through discontiguous spaces, encountering impossible objects of the look, with off-screen space capable of containing anything, including grand pianos with dead donkey carcasses and two priests (one is Dali) tied to them, space, like the body, is inconsistent. As the intertitles inform us, times are random. Along with the deconstruction of space and the unraveling of time (arbitrary conventions in the first place), techniques of continuity editing, including the incoherence granted by intertitles, are revealed in their arbitrary randomness, like language, letting us see what is there in narrative cinema—the formal elements—but what usually remains unnoticed in the hold of story, action, and star.

Along with parodying the sheer strength of continuity style and thwarting audiences' Pavlovian attempts to make meanings, the film relies, superficially, on the similarities between the dream work and the film work, the dreamer and the spectator (an old theory today which must have been hot stuff then), with the substantial difference that unlike the dreamer, the spectator, assaulted by the slicing of the eye in extreme closeup in the opening twelve shots, is not asleep but awake and anxious—anticipating a recurrence of the film's primal scene. (Hitchcock does return in *Psycho* in the shower or bathroom scene, but Marion Crane does not return to the story, as Simone Mareuil does in *Un Chien Andalou;* while that avant-garde moment in *Psycho,* constructed with a style distinct from the rest of the film, is an assault on spectatorial vision, it is contained, framed by the narrative; the shocking sequence *means* murder and thus becomes plot; form is narrativized, in Heath's term.) In addition, techniques of continuity editing are comparable to dream mechanisms of displacement and condensation, with latent and manifest content, for example, the transformation of breasts into buttocks, pubic hair into sea urchins, tennis rackets into books and then guns, one man into his double (an uncredited actor in the titles).

The violent attack on female vision and the spectator plays against our expectations of a cutaway or a fade, a sequence which has been analyzed via the structure of metaphor/metonymy by Linda Williams.[44] The shot of the razor/eye is followed by a cut to a cloud slicing the moon; unexpectedly, this does not follow metaphorical, censoring logic but returns and, without decorum, slashes the eye in extreme closeup—a more shocking sight. The scene of visual avowal instantiates disavowal as the subsequent spectatorial mechanism, which, as Freud (and film theory) never ceases to argue, is predicated on fear of castration.

In fact, the film can be read through, or as a parody of, or as the film version of, Freud's 1919 essay "The 'Uncanny,' " which doggedly and directly links castration to a loss of vision or other organs.[45] The film is a taxonomy of Freud's examples of images which trigger the uncanny experience of anxiety, "what arouses dread and horror," having to do with "silence, solitude and darkness" (246) and hence comparable to being at the movies. The experience of the uncanny, tested against and in defiance of the real, is akin to disavowal. The androgynous woman on the street, poking at the severed hand, and the double "become the uncanny harbinger of death," suggested by "dismembered limbs, a severed head, a hand cut off at the wrist" (244) with its "uncanniness springing from its proximity to the castration complex . . . including being buried alive by mistake [as] the most uncanny thing of all, but which is a transformation of another phantasy . . . qualified by a certain lasciviousness—the phantasy . . . of intra-uterine existence" (244). Thus, if read as an experience of the uncanny, the film's ending, rather than being meaningless and random, returns precisely and logically to the beginning of the film—loss of vision, castration, the woman's body, and the narrative logic of death.

"It often happens that neurotic men declare that they feel there is something uncanny about the female genital organs" (245). Female genitals, the unheimlich, or woman is the ultimate, and lascivious, fear. And Drummond is not completely correct—the woman does not survive the surgeon's scalpel, although she is the motivation, the bearer, of the film's meaning, perhaps resulting in Dali and Sitney proclaiming the film's meaninglessness by illogic, and Drummond its meaning infinitely more, by multiplicity. As Mulvey argues, "Woman [is] bound by a symbolic order in which man can live out his phantasies and obsessions . . . by imposing them on the silent image of woman still tied to her place as bearer of meaning, not maker of meaning."[46] After the opening twelve shots, the rest of the film "depends on the image of the castrated woman to give order and meaning to its world . . . the symbolic order . . . speaks castration and nothing else."[47] I question the value of castrated compliments.

Yet, in Freud's essay, which is an analysis of aesthetics rather than a clinical study, lies another issue. Beneath our civilized or adult veneer is an animistic proclivity, which he links, in his analysis of *Der Sandman*, with gothic romanticism. For Freud, "the unrestricted narcissism of that stage of development strove to fend off the manifest prohibitions of reality" (240), involving the "over accentuation of psychical reality in comparison with material reality—a feature closely allied to the belief in the omnipotence of thoughts" (244). It would appear that Bloom's reading of anxiety has taken

Freud literally, rather than as a critique, and banished material reality, declaring "the omnipotence of thoughts," as does Brakhage. This view has been taken up as a central canon of U.S. avant-garde cinema; yet it is only an interpretation. Freud, in passing, notes a crucial contradiction: the child in "unrestricted narcissism" desires rather than fears the uncanny. Freud's animism, linked with narcissism, resembles romantic mysticism, which the surrealists elided with Freud's discovery of the unconscious, believing, in accord with the parapsychology of F. W. H. Myer, that our bodies are inhabited by spirits who can speak through us automatically if we remove conscious, rational logic.

What is not noted regarding *Un Chien Andalou* is the parody of the romantic hero, the tormented man whose anguished desire is just barely tolerated by the bustling woman, irritated and impatient with all his transformations, suffering, and unrequited lust. The hero, divided against himself, appears in various guises which drive her nuts: the doppelganger of German romanticism, the fool on the bicycle, the Christ figure with stigmata in his hands and blood dripping from his mouth. Romanticism also circulates on the reissued sound track, which combines Wagner—the Liebestod from *Tristan and Isolde*—with two popular Argentinian tangos, dances of conquest and seduction.[48] Thus, the divide between art and mass culture is undermined, as is the serious equation between the erotic and the aesthetic quests, two illusions by which intellectuals, like artists, live their lives.

(This collage resembles Potter's intercutting of Puccini with Bernard Herrmann in *Thriller*. Abigail Child's 1988 *Mayhem* might be the postmodern, feminist remake of *Un Chien Andalou*, an eye-opening rather than a slasher revision which eliminates all narrative excess, rapidly intercutting highly stylized, gestural moments, allusive glances, poses, and snatches of sounds figuring the mystery of desire, a multiplicity of perversions rather than a bipolarity, with the film leading to (lesbian) sex rather than sex becoming story. *Mayhem* crosses and blurs the boundaries not only of gender and race but also of nation—its style is, indeed, international.)

The hero of high art and even higher thought is parodied also by his links with popular culture, as pointed out in Drummond's essay. Pierre Batcheff, "the French James Dean of the 1920s" who had previously appeared in "conventional romantic roles, in particular . . . *The Siren of the Tropics* . . . with Bunuel as assistant director and Duverger director of cinematography, as for *Un Chien Andalou*," resembles Buster Keaton.[49] Along with citing Bunuel's 1927 review of Keaton's *College*, Drummond suggests that the donkey carcasses/piano sequence is a reference to Keaton's brilliant *One Week*, in which the newlywed hauls a piano into his newly built, do-it-yourself house via elaborate pulleys, destroying the living room in the process. That this short film is a critique of domesticity, the couple, and the travails of marriage is of significance, at least to my argument. Keaton's rope apparatus for hauling the piano might also be linked to Dali's iconography. The principles and logic of mechanical physics so brilliantly employed by Keaton also comically turn against him. Thus, not only was *Un Chien Andalou* at "the turning point"[50] of dominant versus counter cinema, it also addressed the artificiality of the divide between art and mass culture.

Rather than liberation into the freedom *from* meaning—what Jean Baudrillard also celebrates when he claims that audiences, what he calls the masses, don't want meaning, preferring fascination, which resembles mesmerization—I prefer meanings as social, historical constructions tied to representation and determined by institutions and experience rather than psyches. The psychoanalysis of "liberation," posited on what Foucault calls "the repression hypothesis" (which avant-garde expanded to include the repressive constraints of narrative and commerce), smacks of romantic mysticism, so aptly described by Freud. Foucault's critique of Freud and "the repression hypothesis," published in France in 1976 amid debates centered on Lacan's rereading of Freud, can be seen as an intervention in that French context.[51]

The History of Sexuality can be taken as a response to the U.S. counterculture of the late 1960s and 1970s—predicated on liberation from the familial, educational, and religious monitoring and instantiation of proper sexuality and the work ethic. That the classical narrative reenacts the scenario of the couple coupling, becoming families, suggests one reason for the desire to be liberated from narrative. The generational rebellion, set against Family, School, Church, and State as the repressors of sexual freedom, argued that the new and creative life-styles of polygamous, casual, and frequent sex would lead to new social institutions and allow practitioners access to new, personal realities. "Free love" echoed the surrealists, who interchanged "love" with "liberty." The countercultural ethic, akin to romanticism, was a shift to collectivity, to crafts and do-it-yourself rather than precious art or mass production, away from the corporate world of work and fashions to creative life-styles of sleeping around, throwing pots, knotting macrame, baking bread, and wearing third-world, rural, or laborer clothing, along with removing makeup and growing hair; it was a critique of the "disciplinary society" and harkened back to earlier reformist eras.

That psychoanalysis is a deconstruction of the middle-class family in industrial capitalism that must be taken historically and culturally is true of subsequent interpretations, which are also historical and contextual. In the early 1970s, Lacan's rereading via linguistics and semiotics had not yet been taken up in the United States. And Lacan's snares and pitfalls had yet to be uncovered. Either biological determinism, the body as given or natural, or "psychologism," the mind as authentically experienced, or combinations of both were the dominant interpretations of Freud in the United States. This is one discursive context of *VF* and, from the diametrically opposite shore, feminism. U.S. feminists were leery if not dismissive of the theoretical potential of psychoanalysis to reveal anything of value to women, including an analysis of narrative and representation. That Freud could provide any insights into female subjectivity met with derision. For many feminists, Freud meant and equaled patriarchy. Psychoanalysis was seen as repressive for women, and women needed to be liberated from Freud. Hence the entire system rather than interpretations had to be dethroned—in a sense, throwing out the theoretical baby with the interpretive bathwater.

In a polemically impassioned response (a reprint from *Jump Cut*) to a summer 1975 issue of *Screen* which included a section from Metz's *The Imaginary Signifier*, Julia LeSage accused Heath and Colin McCabe's earlier editorial on psychoanalysis of being "overtly sexist": "I am referring to the *Screen* writers' accepting as an unquestioned given the Freudian concepts of penis envy . . . and fetishism."[52] The recent theorizing of psychoanalysis "is strange to me as an American, since the US gave Freud his greatest acceptance . . . in the Vulgar Freudianism that flowered in the 20s and 30s here. . . . In the 60s one of the first victories of the women's movement in the US was to liberate ourselves both academically and personally from the Freud trap . . . when I see intellectuals such as MacCabe and Heath . . . ground their ideas in an oppressive orthodox Freudianism that takes the male as the basis for defining the female, my first reaction is one of political and intellectual rage" (78). For women, the stakes were high. The raging disputes around the importation of theory (labeled unintelligible jargon), particularly psychoanalysis, into the United States were intense, including the boycotting of the Milwaukee conference in 1977 amid whispers of exclusion and elitism.

In her look back at the radical feminist movement in the United States, Ellen Willis assesses feminists' repudiation: "The movement's second major weakness was its failure to develop a coherent analysis of either male or female psychology . . . radical feminists as a group were dogmatically hostile to Freud and psychoanalysis . . . especially its concept of the unconscious and . . . the role of sexual desire . . . had almost no impact on radical feminist theory . . . an intellectual and political disaster."[53] Mulvey, in line with Juliet Mitchell, uses psychoanalysis to analyze systems of male subjectivity, including its operations within specific conventions of classical Hollywood cinema. For her, this was a prerequisite leading to an analysis of female desire and the overthrow of the conventions of the classical text. "Women . . . cannot view the decline of the traditional film form with anything much more than sentimental regret" is her last line (18).

In tandem with Heath theoretically, de Lauretis reclaimed narrative for feminism in her critique of Snow, and in 1983, in "Desire in Narrative," analyzed myth as narrative: "the movement of narrative discourse, which specifies and even produces the masculine position as that of mythical subject, and the feminine position as mythical obstacle or, simply, the space in which that movement occurs" (143). She goes further in this essay to assert that "one feels indebted to Freud more than any other male theorist for attempting to write the history of femininity, to understand female subjectivity, or simply to imagine woman as mythical and social subject" (131). In concert with Freud's continual modeling of contradictions, a both/and rather than an either/or logic, de Lauretis's method also posits contradictions: "the contradiction by which historical women must work with and against Oedipus" (157).

What LeSage rails against is an interpretation of Freud "where psychoanalysis promised the middle class solutions to their identity problems and angst, and where vulgarised Freudian concepts were part of daily life in the child-bearing advice of Spock and Gessell" (77–78). While de Lauretis inscribes the female spectator and theorist within the project, LeSage, concluding her critique, points to an early dilemma of film theory, in which gender did not figure as determinant. She also expands what remained a limitation for most feminists until very recently—the concept of difference as a bipolarity. "We not only have to recognize differences of class but entirely different social experiences based on the fact of the oppression of one sex" (83). Thus, in 1974–1975, she called for a model of difference that is not only sexual but also racial, cultural, and economic. Even the sagacious de Lauretis acknowledged the broad accuracy of LeSage's charge much later, adding that differences within and among women could be productive.

As I have reiterated, a central notion was that aesthetics (like drugs, clothing, sex, and new technologies such as video), would alter our lives and politics. The revelation of form and a critique of "work" beneath the commodity fetish, like the altered consciousness of drugs, were among the artistic tools of everyday life which would lead to liberation—one version of the personal is political, replete with paradoxes. These techniques of daily life would enable us to bypass social structures and alter economic, political conditions; the new aesthetics of revelation and confrontation would change "consciousness" and hence the world. As Andreas Huyssen writes: "The belief in consciousness raising by means of aesthetic experience was quite common in those days."[54] The confluence between revealing the work beneath the art, or separating the signifier from the signified, and the dismissal of the corporate, capitalist work ethic, or getting a nine to five job, must be noted.

This argument divided along at least two lines. For Godard, along with various U.S. cinema verite exponents, political filmmaking must reveal the seams of the apparatus, along with the presence and complicity of the filmmaker, reposing the Soviet avant-garde artist's question of the intellectual's relationship to the revolution and the working class. Theoretical writings by Baudry and Commoli, predicated on psychoanalysis, analyzed "the ideology of the cinematic apparatus." If the technique were revealed, the repressed uncovered, then another politics would emerge, including a repositioning of the now aware spectator. It could be argued that avant-garde's claimed evacuation of narrative, sometimes including characters and the human body, and its critique of representation dependent on the body, along with eliminating dialogue and sync sound (economic limitations must also be considered as explanations for various absences), precipitated this theoretical endeavor (with the caution that this is a very narrow description of avant-garde practices, although the most common in criticism; few filmmakers actually performed these reductions). However, whether the analysis was predicated upon ideology or aesthetics was critical, as Peter Wollen suggests in drawing the lines between two avant-gardes—the variant traditions in Europe, with a tie to narrative experimentation, and the United States.[55]

Issues of authorship (Foucault) coincidentally reentered film debates, linked to analyses of the apparatus. Within avant-garde, in line with the auteur policy, the sanctity of the author was upheld but pluralized: anyone could be an artist. The aesthetics of liberation read signifiers as marks of the maker; the emergence of a personal rather than professional style separated this work from the anonymity of commercial film, making even the humblest effort more interesting. Along with an inclusive shift in aesthetic standards, authorship was art. For the theoretical side, inscribing the presence of the filmmaker was a disruption, a declaration of enunciation, a political position.

Both approaches grew from the 1960s auteur policy, which attempted to discern authorship amid commercial conditions of corporate production. Issues of individual authorship and anonymous collaboration relate to the critique of private property, questions of standardization and specialization. To ensure personal authorship, avant-garde filmmakers would, indeed must, take on all aspects of filmmaking, particularly cinematography, repeating early film history and combining the amateur, do-it-yourself craft impetus of the counterculture with the fine arts tradition of individual artists. However, what must be remembered about the emergence of the auteur policy around *Cahiers du Cinema* in the 1950s, spreading to *Film Culture* in the 1960s with its historical pantheon which includes Welles, Von Stroheim, and Keaton, is that, like theories of the text and feminism, the auteur policy was a claim for access to the means of production. Films by untested directors, outside the rigid labor union and studio structure, made for small sums of money, became possible and fashionable.

If the corporate institution of filmmaking, with its divisions of labor which relied on years of training and apprenticeship, with expertise traded for money, with its system of production modeled on standardization and specialization, with the expenditure and potential profits of huge sums of money, could be overturned, then anyone with a particular vision could, for a minuscule amount of money, make a film, control its circulation, and own the work—gaining access to and then revealing for us the conditions of production. Hence, the contradictions in the United States: the values of a folk/craft culture hooked up with fine arts individualism. Handmade films were mechanically reproduced. Avant-garde rejected standardization and specialization with a vague critique of capitalism but with an eye on art and the purview of the museum.

Along with the rejection of the business suit in favor of blue jeans, of short hair in favor of long, a preference for the country over the city, the values of the craft movement and everyday life were ascribed to advanced technology—throwing pots, raising vegetables, hooking rugs, weaving shawls, building a house, shooting films, accessing information, and making video art were equivalent. Daily life was set against corporate and familial values of 1950s and 1960s upward mobility, a status secured by a job, salary, and home and visually declared by the possession of mass-produced consumer durables. Like competition, private property was critiqued (for example, in the de-emphasis on film titles) but paradoxically upheld: film collectives were organized so that individuals could produce their own personal films. Other values were inverted, for example, middle-class tourism of the 1950s: artist would travel, but not as tourists; they would travel in vans and camp out on cross-country treks, staying with friends rather than in motels. Work, or having a job, was displaced into life-style. Dropping out and turning on or being an artist took precedence. The concept of cinema as "work" and the deciphering of that process was culturally and strangely in tune with not working.

Paradoxically, what is taken today to be a conservative or old-fashioned politics of avant-garde was, like romanticism, not very long ago viewed as a radical practice. Context, like history, does make another kind of difference.

CHAPTER

3

VIDEO POLITICS

Video entered the U.S. cultural vocabulary in the mid-1960s as a technology *and* as a discourse. Like the post-World War II selling of the 16mm camera (the portable, trusty Bell and Howell was used by a single operator to record the war for movie screens), which coincided with the beginnings of the U.S. underground film movement in the late 1940s and 1950s, Japanese video technology was mass marketed during and after a televised war, Vietnam. Video zigzagged between the cultured art world and ragtag counterculture communes; the parallel politics, usually collapsed, did not necessarily intersect—one lodged with the art scene, the other with activist politics.

The founding video art story begins with Nam June Paik's purchase, with U.S. grant money, of a Sony portable video camera and recorder from Japan's first U.S. shipment to the Liberty Music Store in New York. As the tale is remembered, Paik's initial video recordings, taken in a cab on his way home, were of the pope's visit to the United States; they were previewed to an art audience that same night; "video art" was born. The art historical tale is, of course, more complex; also suspect is the inscription of a founding video father, no matter how anarchic or international his paternity. But while history has inscribed the man more than the machine, the star of video theory and practice was the Sony portapak. The irony today of Japanese consumer technology triggering an art movement funded by the National Endowment for the Arts and the Rockefeller Foundation is inescapable and logical. Video art allied itself with performance art and happenings, including Fluxus, pop, kinetic, and conceptual art, and coincided with the U.S. 1960s revival of the historical avant-garde, particularly surrealism, but the relationship between video and the museum was, and continues to be, hesitant and unstable.

Portable electronic technology coupled with a mystical/futurist metaphysics, linked up with communication theory, and nestled within the counterculture, particularly the student protest movement and the drug culture. The results, video art, guerrilla TV, or just plain video, were portrayed as personal, innovative, radical. It was fervently believed that simultaneity, feedback, delay, satellite/cable capacity, and electronic visions would foster, like drugs and random sex, new states of consciousness, community, and artistic and political structures. With its immateriality, erasability, easy operation, reproducibility, and affinity with mass culture, video was imagined as challenging institutions of commercial television *and* art, including the status of the precious art object and the central figuration of the individual artist, both of which were considered to be leftovers from "product" culture. No longer would the museum be the repository of culture in the form of rarefied commodities. If anyone could be an artist, and if art were no longer a product which could be sold or collected, then the structure of the art world would alter. Through cable TV, videocassettes, and amateur/home video, the television network monopoly would be dispersed, decentralized.

Dropping out, turning on, protesting, and experimenting with life-styles (like other key words, this collective concept in the 1960s has taken on opposite connotations in the 1980s: vapid celebrity and excess, as in "Lifestyles of the Rich and Famous"), were 1960s and 1970s counterculture responses and solutions to the increasing privatization and consumerism of daily life, which was filled with "consumer durables" and labeled "upward mobility." (*Consumerism* was then a Ralph Nader movement against corporate malpractices, but is now a negative practice, the first meaning in *Webster's* now subsumed by the second; and Nader is now a star reporter on *Inside Edition*.) Theodore Roszak was the guru and analyst of this making of a counterculture.[1] In opposition to technocracy and scientific discourses, including nuclear war and the military, Roszak prescribed a visionary culture of psychedelic drugs, Oriental mysticism, alienation (neither Marx nor Brecht), and communitarian experiences, an adversarial culture of romanticism whose heroes were Blake, Wordsworth, Emerson, Thoreau, and Tolstoy rather than Marx and Jung rather than Freud.[2] In the 1960s, when Peggy Sue did not necessarily get married, perhaps because she was wearing blue jeans rather than blue velvet, the global village of Marshall McLuhan, under the slogan (and theory) "the medium is the message," with elaborations of "hot" and "cool" media, was the electronic utopia, designed with the architecture of Buckminster Fuller, accompanied by the conceptual music of John Cage, and fostered by the drug experiments of Timothy Leary. In 1969, two art events addressed this confluence of cultural figures, technologies, and discourses: a thirty-minute videotape, "The Medium Is the Medium," produced by an educational station, and the Howard Wise Gallery exhibition "TV as a Creative Medium."[3] Inspired by acid and dope, the disciples of modernism's electronic triumvirate acclaimed Sony the new god of visionary liberation. The history of video includes citations of the purchase date of equipment, with editing decks available later; as Bill Viola says of much early video, "Life without editing is just not that interesting." (Unlike ships, cars, countries, and cinema, Sony, only a letter away from sonny, is not a goddess. However, the 1984 show in Paris, under the banner of "Electra: Electricity and Electronics in 20th-Century Art," gives pause to this remark.)

Along with the stoned, high, and radical romanticism of these Canadian and U.S. visionaries, another more political discourse was also influential: Hannah Arendt's introduction to the United States of Walter Benjamin's *Illuminations* in a 1968 essay in the *New Yorker* and the appearance of Benjamin's essays in translation in 1969.[4] That same year, the Museum of Modern art staged "The Machine as Seen at the End of the Mechanical Age," arguing in the catalogue that "electronic and chemical devices which imitate processes of the brain and nervous system"[5] were continuing the historical trajectory analyzed by Benjamin in his famous 1936 essay on art in the age of mechanical reproduction: that the passage of techniques of reproduction from manual to visual and now mathematical, the brain, replicated the passage from photography and cinema to television, electronics.

Indeed, Benjamin's essay suggested television as much as it pointed to cinema, as is seen, for example, in his quotation of Paul Valery: "Just as water, gas, and electricity are brought into our houses from far off to satisfy our needs in response to a minimal effort, so we shall be supplied with visual or auditory images, which will appear and disappear at a simple movement of the hand, hardly more than a sign" (219). Remote control and rapid channel switching are indeed "hardly more than a sign."

Benjamin's emphasis on exhibition versus cult value, his distinction between distraction and contemplation, describes both U.S. audiences of commercial television and video makers who took to the road in their vans. As Benjamin wrote, "the original meet[s] the beholder halfway . . . in new 'situations' and liquidates the traditional value of the cultural heritage" (220–221). Given that in the 1930s tinkerers and physicists alike were inventing uses for the electromagnetic spectrum, advertising do-it-yourself kits in trade periodicals, and promoting surveillance and ham TV, the compatibility of Benjamin's prescient theory (modeled on cinema) with television/video is neither far-fetched nor merely a handy analogy. (Benjamin was deeply influenced by Soviet filmmakers, one explanation for his translated revival in 1968, a critical year marking the resurgence of revolutionary commitments, including the question of the artist's or intellectual's relationship to the people. I think not only of Eisenstein's theory of shock and conflict but also of the agit-prop trains and steamers taking cinema and revolutionary thought to the rural peasants. Like Eisenstein, who embraced technology and mass cultural production, even wishing that he had made John Ford's *Young Mr. Lincoln*—a remark which may have triggered the *Cahiers du Cinema* textual analysis—and writing treatises on sound and color, Benjamin also situated himself within modernity in the 1930s.)

Besides Benjamin's differentiation between contemplation and distraction, a model drawn from comparing painting to film, he argues that another dimension of this shift is from art as ritual to art as political—a key distinction for the video guerrillas: "mechanical reproduction emancipates the work of art from its parasitical dependence on ritual . . . the instant the criterion of authenticity ceases to be applicable to artistic production, the total function of art is reversed. Instead of being based on ritual, it begins to be based on another practice—politics" (224). This is also a shift to reception, to exhibition, so important to Soviet film theory and practice. At the same time, avant-garde film and video, in some cases virtual theories of reception, have also operated within the premises of contemplation, within the contours of ritual. It has been assumed and desired by longtime proselytizers that U.S. avant-garde, its reception often structured as an event, was tied to ritual, with Benjamin's "criterion of authenticity" upheld in the name of the person and uniqueness. This reading is reinforced by various artists' interest in ritual, for example, Kenneth Anger's fascination with his guru of myth, Aleister Crowley. As I try to argue throughout, this presumption needs to be reassessed, as do the films.

Another of Benjamin's criteria for progressive art was the linkage between popular and critical reception: "The progressive reaction is characterized by the direct, intimate fusion of visual and emotional enjoyment with the orientation of the expert" (234). To close the "great divide" between popular reception and expert reception was one significant goal of video practitioners.

For video visionaries, the centrality of alternative systems of distribution and exhibition (Benjamin's "new situations") cannot be emphasized enough, especially since critics (including me), who fetishize the commodity by focusing only on production, largely ignoring distribution and exhibition, enact precisely what they critique. In an uncanny mimicry, the history of video, with its emphasis on access, systems, and distribution, parallels the development of commercial television, which directed its resources and energies toward distribution by the creation of national networks and exhibition by the manufacture and marketing of television sets. But there are critical distinctions: video advocated decentralization over network centralization and process over product. (By 1952, most programs were filmed, prerecorded rather than live, or filmed off the screen as kinescopes, so TV had tangible, visible objects which, like "I Love Lucy," could be sold and transported around the globe before videotape or satellite transmission was available.)

Like other manifestations of the counterculture, video theory was fashionable as well as useful. In big but zany books published by mainstream presses, video proselytizers like Michael Shamberg argued into existence a bricolage of renegade thinkers critical to the counterculture. The passionate premises of this eclectic melange of intellectuals were taken into video practice and daily life—a conflation of art and the everyday in a new coinage, "life-style" (which was not without precedent, however, among the surrealists). Because echoes or inversions of the late 1960s and early 1970s media visionaries can be heard in postmodern critiques for and against television (and mass culture), it might be pertinent to remember their specific claims, dated by a mere two decades.

Shamberg, a writer for *Newsweek* (and later the producer of *The Big Chill*), was a member of New York's Raindance, a video collective, and the author of the movement's bible, *Guerrilla TV,* a book commissioned in 1970 by a CBS subsidiary, Holt, Rinehart and Winston (with proceeds going to Raindance).[6] The first sentences declare a fundamental position: "The moon landing killed technology. The death of hardware is the ultimate transformation of America to Media-America. It embodies our total shift from a product- to a process-based culture" (3). *Radical Software,* the magazine distributed by Raindance, defined *video* (like drugs) as "software." In *Guerrilla TV,* key words—some now arcanely naive, others laden with inverse connotations—signal intellectual premises. "Media America is my own phrase. Other terms . . . are . . . words from videotape technology which seem to be analogous to thought processes. Still others, like 'junkie' and 'heavy' and 'hip' are taken from the dope/rock subculture. And finally, I have appropriated 'feedback' and 'software' and 'parameter' and other words from the vocabulary of cybernetics and systems theory" (6).

For Shamberg, Media-America was a positive concept linked to youth and the future. Video and other electronic systems comprised "an evolutionary stage in human development"; videotape was "a natural outcome of media evolution, giving us increased control over our psychological environment" (31a). This convoluted bio-logic (which paradoxically also argued a radical break with the past) was permeated by McLuhan and perched on Norbert Wiener's *Human Use of Human Beings: Cybernetics and Society.* In Shamberg's words, "What Weiner passed off as an elegant scientific breakthrough is also a major conceptual re-structuring" (5). For these "video freaks," information structures (which were "global," international rather than national) had to be "redesigned." Information (whose base was data) was energy, process, and power which had to be dispersed; "power to the people" meant access to information and video. Feedback was a central concept: "Only through a radical re-design of its information structures to incorporate two-way, de-centralized inputs can Media-America optimize the feedback it needs to come to its senses" (12). "Survival" and "ecology" pepper Shamberg's arguments. "The ultimate aim of Guerrilla Television is to embody ecological intention through the design of information structures" (9a). *Whole Earth Catalogue* is the paradigm—it had "use" (information) and "survival" value, as well as "feedback," telling the reader about the conditions of its production.

Print culture, the government, schools, and corporations, along with network television (what Shamberg called "beast television"), embodied product, centrality, and homogeneity rather than process, diversity, and heterogeneity (I think of Barthes, Deleuze and Guattari, and Paul Virilio). Beast television was regressive, tied to radio conventions, with spokesmen speaking above and for us, outside events. Shamberg: "Because radio men have been unable to model a visual language, only abnormal modes of behavior are considered news." "A lack of a true video grammar . . . also means that the actual experience of being at an event can't be communicated and therefore isn't considered news" (33). Along with "feedback,"

Shamberg advocated "action" against commercial television's tactics of "reaction." Government, he wrote, "is geared towards crisis management, not anticipatory response . . . the government doesn't know what to do unless there's a crisis or something stridently visible to manage" (14). Neither does network news, which wallows in crises.

Like crisis or catastrophe, media celebrity was another earmark of product culture, and Shamberg warned against the co-optation of the counterculture via celebrity: "Abbie Hoffman thinks he's getting his message across by going on the Dick Cavett show, but as somebody . . . once said: 'The revolution ended when Abbie Hoffman shut up for the first commercial' " (27). (That Hoffman was indeed a celebrity, even more nostalgically famous in the 1980s, was apparent in the front-page coverage of his death in 1989; his drug overdose was a deathly commentary on, a logical conclusion to, the false premises of the counterculture drug glorification.) Many of Shamberg's predictions have come true, as I realize when I read observations he made almost twenty years ago: "The Black Panthers . . . were created by TV. . . . But just as the media created the Panthers, they can destroy them, because the Panthers have no ultimate control over their own information. . . . No alternate cultural vision is going to succeed in Media-America unless it has its own alternate information structures, not just alternate content pumped across the existing ones. And that's what videotape, with cable-TV and videocassettes, is ultimately all about. Context is crucial to the amplification of an idea to prevent co-option" (27).

Shamberg's critique of commercial television was an acute prophecy of television's 1988 content: catastrophe, gossip, scandal. His assessment was very close to Baudrillard's on trivia, scandal, and publicity. "Movements and personalities burn themselves out very quickly when they're devoured by publicity" (28), wrote Shamberg in 1970, anticipating Baudrillard who, a few years later, also refers to Hoffman: "But transgression and subversion never get 'on the air' without being subtly negated as they are: transformed into models, neutralized into signs, they are eviscerated of their meaning."[7] Of course, this is simulation. While the two men's epistemologies are radically divergent, either could have written this: "The totality of the existing architecture of the media . . . always prevents response. . . . This is why the only revolution . . . indeed, the revolution everywhere . . . lies in restoring this possibility of response . . . presupposing an upheaval in the entire existing structure of the media. . . . No other theory or strategy is possible. All vague impulses to democratize content, subvert it, are hopeless."[8]

While Baudrillard claims a Marxist position (a perplexing conundrum for Marxist critics), the U.S. video counterculture uncritically embraced democratic pluralism and the politics of diversity. (These arguments are echoed but inverted in 1980s celebrations of the "subversive reception" of commercial television; however, this is the flip side of the video countercultural activists who wanted to open up production, providing alternative representations.) "Guerrilla television," asserted Shamberg, "is grassroots television.

It works with people, not from up above them . . ." (8a). The critical flaw was brushing over social systems in the belief that video was "a tool which promises a whole system that makes politics irrelevant, both right and left . . ." (9). Or, "The communications systems themselves, not philosophy, are what shape social structure" (9).

The confusing key to the entire superstructure (played out on a physical base or level; for example, an intellectual opposition to violence and war was carried out by bodily, passive resistance, equating thought and action, elevating body over mind), explaining why sex and drugs were so central (aside from pleasure and "liberation"), was that these "cybernetic strategies" were not envisioned as philosophical but biological, not ideological but technological, the dominant opposing dyads of countercultural thought. Herein lies the catch-22, the critical flaw: the choice of biology and technology over philosophy and ideology, with the latter terms taking precedence in 1970s theories which can be seen as countermands to the earlier beliefs. At the same time, the assault on classical philosophy's hierarchy of mind over body, reason over emotion, and men over women, reversing these poles of domination and subordination in favor of affect and the body— denigrated as the domain of the feminine—undermined the philosophical values of violence, torture, and rage, the privileged and masculine emotions in Western thought playing themselves out in the Vietnam War. The problem was the equation of sex with advanced technology, and viewing both as neutral or "natural"; the pleasures of both were masculine. As it has turned out, the medium is not the only message, although, as Baudrillard pointed out, McLuhan's assertion, "although not a critical proposition . . . does have analytic value in its paradoxical form" (172).

Technological determinism prevailed. Portable and affordable video equipment promoted artistry, populism, and utopianism. Like historical revolutionary movements, the political and artistic/social countercultures of the 1960s were marked by this instrumental conception of technology, which viewed the medium in terms of ontology or neutrality rather than as a system of social relations and discourses, including gender, race, and economics. With a fervent naivete and idealism in the face of massive commercial programming, the women's movement, the civil rights struggle, the Vietnam War, and cold war politics of containment, "video" would bring global salvation via access, circumventing institutions and going directly to individuals of conscience—"the people."

Conceived in opposition to commercial television, countercultural practices of video emerged in collectives on both coasts. People's Video Theater, Videofreex, Raindance, Global Village, and Video Freaks comprised a subcultural network and imagined liberation via the democratic pluralism of video: anyone could control the means of production, anyone could and should be an artist. In 1968, Ant Farm, a zany and ambitious group with outposts in San Francisco and Houston, founded by Chip Lord and Doug Michels and soon joined by Hudson Marquez, Curtis Schreier, and others, was created as "an army of termites in the subsoil of American officialdom."[9] Ant Farm has been described as a "family consisting of environmentalists, artists, designers, builders, actors, cooks, television children . . . university trained media freaks and hippies interested in balancing the environment by total transformation of existing social and economic systems."[10] This "underground lifestyle" was concerned with "education reform, communication, graphic design, life-theater, and high art." Aspects of the historical avant-garde reverberated in Ant Farm, including its mission to intervene in the everyday by using technology and its challenge of the sanctity of the art object and its author/artist who was imagined by Ant Farm as a worker, a builder, a constructivist, a member of a group of divergent interests and talents (an Ant/art colony). "Ant Farm accepts only worker ants, and by regulation, no queen ant or leader ant is admitted" was one of their tenets.

Along with the denial of hierarchy, Ant Farm's method of collective work included the systematic use of drugs to unleash "psychophysical information"; the use of grass, it was argued, brought the community closer and released creative energy; "free association" was encouraged by their "trips." Dope, like video, was defined as radical software in the magazine of that name distributed by Raindance. Or, in the words of Shamberg, "As with sophisticated uses of videotape and computers, it [dope] gives access to radically different ways of knowing" (18). Distinguishing between heroin (which was bad, linked to junkies and Vietnam) and marijuana (which was good), he asserted: "Americans will simply have to realize and sanction the notion that the widespread experimentation with drugs is not a symptom of decadence but, on the contrary, one of adaptation" (19). "For better or worse, it's perhaps the best psychological software we'll have until the electronic media are made more accessible" (17).[11]

Ant Farm sought commissions, toured universities, and won awards for architectural projects (for example, a polymorphous, organic, concrete house outside Houston and various inflatables, including a design for a convention center for the 1976 bicentennial).[12] The climactic moment of the group's video work is dated by the purchase in 1970 of a black and white Sony Portapak which, like so many 1970s video makers, was without an editing system. Their fascination with cars and critique of TV resulted in *Cadillac Ranch* in 1974 and *Media Burn* in 1975, both videotaped. The "customized dream car" in *Media Burn* and the car in *Eternal Frame* are central icons, as was "motorcade" a repeated signifier of the tragedy of Kennedy's assassination.

(This fascination with cars and culture has continued in the work of Chip Lord, culminating in a big book and a seventy-minute videotape, *The Motorist*. His 1989 tape of a cross-country trek to deliver a T-Bird, which the dealer/driver bought from his high school sweetheart at a class reunion, to its new Japanese owner in Los Angeles, demonstrates that the love between boys and cars continues well beyond adolescence, with struggles and identification with father along the road. This is the history of the family car as

Oedipus. Opening with the Diego Rivera murals in Detroit, intercutting advertisements and corporate films, and then traveling through fast-food America spreading over the desert landscape, the work is also a history of mass culture—not monolithic, not infinitely reproducible, as the Edsel demonstrates. The tape illustrates the passage from the mechanical age, concluding in the decade after World War II, to the electronic era of automotive production, the transition from a culture of difference and several choices— Ford, Buick, Cadillac—to an era of differentiation and hundreds to thousands of choices and fancy names. The car is history, memory; driving cross-country is a Bildungsroman, triggering adolescent flashbacks of the family and mass culture. John Ford meets Henry Ford, when men were men in Detroit or Monument Valley. In the last scene, the 1962 Thunderbird is loaded on a freighter/barge. The young Japanese man drives the car, the American icon, through the streets of Tokyo, as country western music wails on the sound track; the car has become a collector's item, now taken out of context; the divide between art and mass culture is no safer or more secure than our memories which can break in, altering the present.)

In the seventies, video vans spread the video gospel in a proselytizing/ pedagogic return of the agit-prop trains and steamers of the Soviet constructivist filmmakers, who would have loved the speed of video but would have been dismayed by the early problems of editing. Like the Soviets but without Marx, projects encouraged audiences to participate in productions, as well as preaching the new visions of society. For two months in 1971, Ant Farm went on the road with its Truckstop Project, a name which declared allegiance to working-class travel; yet it visited universities (a locus critical to the counterculture as well as video) in a "customized media van with antennae, silver dome, TV window, inflatable shower stall, kitchen, ice, inflatable shelter for five, solar water heater, portapak and video playback system."[13] The ecology movement combined with technology and mobile, unfettered domesticity as counterculture tourism. (Would any of this have been possible without the German Volkswagen bus/van?) Much has been said about video techniques; Ant Farm was insightful in addressing auto-technique.

Ant Farm collaborated with other groups, among them Video Freaks, T. R. Uthco (Doug Hall, Jody Procter, and Diane Hall) for *Eternal Frame*, and TVTV, Top Value Television—funny names of anonymity that identified shifting groups against the cult of the individual, the artist, the star. TVTV taped the last Apollo mission and interviewed the astronauts; Chip Lord of Ant Farm somewhere called NASA "a technodream state."[14] With funds from cable TV companies, the expandable group taped the Republican and Democratic conventions in Miami (they received a good review for the latter in the *New York Times*).[15] Unlike the networks, the group used Portapak equipment, producing "alternative" readings of the events from the convention floor, backstage at political parties and rallies, and from network booths (theirs is a fascinating and revelatory critique of network reporting which, for TVTV, is an integral part of the problem and spectacle). The result, *Four*

More Years, is an unsettling trailer for Reagan's presidency, completely un-fathomable and impossible then. In the 1980s, "Entertainment Tonight" has assumed this function, transformed into TV gossip, celebrity, and business.

Ant Farm's policy was to record real or imaginary events, disregarding distinctions between them, a structure of acceptable and necessary "paranoia" tied to drugs and TV. Like Lucy and Ricky and George and Gracie, Ant Farm did not need Baudrillard to tell it that TV confused the real with the imaginary, conflating reality and fiction as simulation. Although explicitly stated as a position of opposition to technocratic society and mass-mediated culture, its stance toward mass or popular culture, like its response to technology, was ambivalent or postmodern: Ant Farm used it while condemming it. By undermining the authority of print or book culture and posing audio-visual culture as a positive alternative, the poles of high versus low, or elite versus mass culture were slightly tipped.

Lest this all remain unfamiliar if not naive, I will detail one of Ant Farm's collaborative projects which resulted from all this video thought. For me, it is a complex critique of television, representation, audiences, history, art, and simulation.

Eternal Frame, a 1975 performance and videotape made by Ant Farm and T. R. Uthco, is a simulation of a catastrophe, a remake of the film of John Kennedy's assassination in Dallas. The recreation dissects representation, moving from the grainy film image imprinted in our memory as Greek tragedy, through the copy of the actors' preparations, rehearsal, and performance to a model—the videotape. Thus, it shifts from film to television, without a real except the Zapruder film which it takes on its own terms (it does not incorporate the point of view of the assassin, nor is it framed by the commentary and presence of network news reporters). The copy matches the original, which is only an image—an indelible one. That historical, silent image—along with the spectatorial mechanisms of disavowal or suspension of disbelief (reception)—is the mystery rather than who killed Kennedy and how, the usual concerns brought to bear on the Zapruder footage.

Unlike Baudrillard's theory of the simulacrum (which in large part was predicated on one of his trips to the United States, on his real experience of the many exported representations of the United States in films and television, an example of tourism producing theory), the videotape works through a series of contradictions, not the least of which is a definition of "art." It argues television as history, as a set of social relations *and* as a challenge to historiography and mastery which can provide a truth, a real. At the same time, the performance and tape grant answers and closure and reveal mastery through professionalism—the satisfactory perfection of their recreation and its effects. (The British television trial [broadcast on HBO] of Lee Harvey Oswald [which adjudged him guilty, to no one's amazement], the first in a series of planned restagings of history as courtroom drama, the "You Were There" approach, conducted by "real" lawyers interrogating experts, witnesses, and culprits and based on "real" evidence and documents, is a simpler investigatory simulation—looking for an imaginary real rather than interrogating its displaced representation.)

The resemblance of *Eternal Frame* to the work of Baudrillard is not coincidental, given the period and the common source in the thought of McLuhan. However, this work preceded by at least ten years the boom in the United States of Baudrillard's books, *Simulations* (imagine *Simulations* as the script for *The Last Judgment* co-starring Yves Montand as Charlton Heston, with Baudrillard in a cameo as a working-class God quoting Cecil B. De Mille) and *In the Shadow of the Silent Majorities*. While Baudrillard awaits the apocalypse (a process initiated by the postwar invasion of Europe by U.S. mass culture and thought, which heralded an end to mastery and classical education, so lucidly pointed to by Meaghan Morris[16]), a celebratory Ant Farm critiques catastrophe, collectively signaling the conclusion of 1960s rhetoric of youth and generational crisis. Fredric Jameson has suggested that "for many white American students—in particular for many of those later active in the new left—the assassination of President Kennedy played a significant role in delegitimizing the state itself," with Kennedy's "generation gap" setting off "political discontent" of American students.[17] This positioning of "Kennedy" within the U.S. left—glaringly emergent in the obsession of many of those on the left with uncovering the conspiracy of the assassination—is also undermined by the tape's irreverence, which paradoxically pays tribute as well. The tape also marks another ending—of a cultural politics of collaboration.

As the poster announcing the showing of the videotape to a San Francisco art audience cogently states, the piece is "An Authentic Remake of the Original J. F. K. Assassination." Early in the tape, the artist/president, Doug Hall, reprising his role in *Media Burn*, declares: "I am in reality nothing more than another image on your television set. . . . I am in reality nothing more than another face on your screen, I am in reality only another link in that chain of pictures which makes up the sum total of information accessible to us all as Americans. . . . Like my predecessors, the content of the image is no different from the image itself." Thus, *Eternal Frame* ("I am in reality an image") embraces the imaginary as dilemma rather than as tragedy, which is implicit in Baudrillard's view ("The space of simulation confuses the real with the model"[18]). This is, of course, the "hyperreal" in which all is statistic, memory bank, or miniature, abolishing representation. While Kennedy's death was, as the tape asserts, both a real and an image death, far from liquidating representation it enthroned the film image. *Eternal Frame* critiques that powerful hold of the image as history on our memory and emotions.

For Baudrillard, simulation is infinitely more dangerous than an actual crime, "since it always suggests . . . that law and order themselves might really be nothing more than simulations."[19] (This was the premise of the conspiracy theorists after Jack Ruby's shooting of Oswald on TV. It is an apt analysis of the Iran/Contra hearings, particularly Oliver North's testimony. If we take this in an opposite direction, nuclear war better be a simulation.) The crime and danger of art is boredom or bad taste, often disguised as an issue of realism by numerous platonic philosophers of false versus serious art. *Eternal Frame* includes responses to the videotape of the simulated assassination. Near the end of the tape, a middle-aged man, whose reactions were recorded outside the San Francisco theater after seeing the videotape, speaks for Baudrillard's insistence on denotative distinctions, on his desire for referents. "They didn't use anything original at all." They should have "either told what happened or made up their own story . . . they took a theme of a real man getting killed and they played little games with it. . . ."

As *Eternal Frame* suggests, not only the assassination of Kennedy but particularly the circulation and repeated viewing of the amateur/tourist movie footage, which has been endlessly rerun on television and scrutinized by real and amateur detectives for clues (the classic instance of close textual analysis of film, pre–Raymond Bellour), signaled the end of (imagined) mastery via brave individuality written in Arthurian narrative accounts of cause-effect logic and closure. (That this period of the Kennedy court was called Camelot is not without interest.) Because it had been recorded, the image, elided to reality and tragic drama, would yield an answer, a truth, if, like the riddle of the Sphinx, we could only get closer, could deconstruct it. But when deconstruction failed, recreation, or simulation, was the next logical step—a cultural shift analogous to the move from cinema to television as the dominant theoretical object or cultural metaphor.

It could also be argued that the assassination, linked as it was to film footage and given that it was not initially covered by the TV networks, was the first and last time for a united television audience: everyone compulsively remembered and minutely described, again and again, like reruns, where they were, in real life, and where they were in relation to television, representation. The assassination represented a cultural moment when television and our daily lives were still separate but merging. (We still remember that Dan Rather was physically there *and* on television.) While our emotional experience of the event came from television, our bodies remained distinct from television; meaning and affect occurred to us in specific places. Constant coverage of the event realized television's potential for collective identification and national cohesion—television's dream that by informing us and setting a good, calm, and rational example via the anchors, the populace will be united, soothed, and finally ennobled by repetition of and patient waiting for information.

Covering catastrophes is the ultimate test of the top anchorman's mettle. His stamina is measured by words, information, and calm demeanor. Television fancies that if we have enough news, if it stays on the air with us, a vigil like sitting up with a sick or dying friend, we will behave like adults. Baudrillard's prognoses of cultural (if not nuclear) catastrophe can be linked to television's instantaneous capacity to present live coverage of (death) events, both shocking and mollifying the audience, mediating and exacerbating the effects of the real which are rerun and transformed into representation. We can await live catastrophe on TV, signaled by ruptures in the flow of programs, a disruption of time, TV's constancy. Catastrophe argues for the importance, the urgent value, the *truth* of television. Its watching will be good for us, providing catharsis or, better, mastery via repetition of the same which is fascinating, if not mesmerizing. Castastrophe coverage thus functions beyond the pleasure principle as an essentially verbal rendering of the "fort/da!" hinged on a visual detail, in this case, Zapruder's footage. Perhaps masochistically, pleasure, aligned with death rather than life, comes from that game of repetition, with catastrophe as potent TV, coded as exception. It is a pleasure that doesn't come from TV techniques, which are usually of extremely poor quality—shaky, minimal, and indecipherable. Usually there are awkward editing glitches, missed cues and connections, filler speech and delimited language. There is endless repetition of the same facts and simplistic arguments which function like Muzak, overwhelming narrative, regular programming as we wait, with the anchor, either for further events and analysis or a conclusion before TV normalcy can return. The intrusion of the real is also the taking over of entertainment by the news division, the replacement of women by men. If the network merely breaks, momentarily, the crisis was not in the United States: our catastrophes demand twenty-four-hour coverage, nation over narrative. The assassination was "on the air" constantly. Continuous coverage later shocked us with a live rather than a filmed murder by Jack Ruby, an anonymous player soon to become notorious as he shot Lee Harvey Oswald on television, in jail, in footage which was then rerun and scrutinized.

After this riff of speculation, *Eternal Frame* revisited. After a rerun of the brief "original" (the Zapruder film is shorter than I remembered, a clip lengthened by history, slow motion, and stop-frame analysis), the reenactment of the assassination becomes, as the spectators of the rehearsals and real thing acknowledge, "more real" (there are progressively fewer errors or deviations from convention and expectations) until it is encapsulated as "art" and replayed for us as image, which it always was. After the Artist/ President Hall declares the tape's position in a Presidential Address, the first rehearsal of the assassination occurs in a car in front of rear-screen projection, flattening depth like a 1940s Hitchcock automobile ride. The studio is replaced by location shooting in Dallas (like the title, another bad pun), the scene of the real and artistic crime. Rehearsals of the event are intercut with backstage costuming and interviews with Jack (Hall) and Jackie (played by Doug Michaels), who comment on dress rehearsals, acting, and masquerade. Sexual difference is inscribed as a simulation: Jackie is played perfectly in a pink suit and hat, a performance of minimal film gestures. The hesitant actors, leery of, indeed fearing, reprisal, believing their act to be scandalous or sacrilegious (overstating the "radical" effects of art) emerge for the final performance, and restage the event for passersby, who appear to deeply enjoy it (as tourism, as "live" TV). The final color reenactment is then rerun as a rhapsody six times from various angles, becoming "authentic" and emotive in the process as patriotic music crescendoes on the sound track.

The clever interplay of documentary conventions of late 1960s verisimilitude (black and white versus color, wild sound, camera movement, address, and acting in, for example, the studio-staged speeches and the cinema verite style of the backstage and on the street interviews), document the arbitrariness of film conventions of realism. The interviews with the actors are critical moments of a presumed real; the actors' feelings as "simulated" rather than heartfelt is an unsettling suspicion. The level of the real intensifies when the tourist audiences react—at one moment with tears. This audience of casual passersby recreates that historical audience which lined the street (and Zapruder's film) for Kennedy's motorcade, later to become witnesses, critics, and stand-ins or extras for the nation-audience. Thus, the real players simulated an image, turning a film into a live performance which is measured by historical audiences against the famous footage as reality or later in the tape against standards of "art." That both memory and aesthetics, or history and art, are slippery calls emerges in the irony that the standard of the real is a bad "original" film, famous because of its singularity and hence "aura." Its existence is both the ultimate amateur filmmaker's fantasy and nightmare. "This is really bad taste," remarks Hall when watching the rear-screen footage on a television monitor in a hotel room.

The distance between *Eternal Frame* and Baudrillard can be measured by their conceptions of the audience. Baudrillard's mass audience is passive, fascinated, silent, outside; Ant Farm's series of inscribed audiences are vocal, actively involved in critique or, surprisingly, disavowal, yet producing, not merely consuming or escaping, meaning (like the end of representation, one wonders how this might be possible). One position is conservative, humorless, and without irony, predicated as it is on a model drawn from commerce; the other is refreshing. The spectators of the piece in Dallas compare the live performance to the real thing which is being recreated, they imagine, as a tourist attraction! rather than "art": "I saw it on television after it happened . . . it looks so real now . . . the characters look so real." Shots of these tourists photographing the recreation remind us of the anonymous maker of the original: Zapruder was just a person in the crowd filming Kennedy, and his film was introduced as evidence in the investigation, an unnerving way to become an artist. "He's re-enacting it. . . . I'm glad we were here. . . . It was so beautiful. . . ." After the performance, an incredulous Doug Hall comments: "I thought the most interesting thing was watching the people enjoy it so much. . . . How could they enjoy it so much?" This is the critical question of catastrophe coverage.

However unexpected this reponse of spectator enjoyment by the performers, who drastically misjudged reception and pleasure on many accounts, *Eternal Frame* incorporates response. Its various audiences exist in a dialogue with the recreation, acting as a corrective and participant/observer. (When the audacious performers, secure in the acceptance of their masquerade as tourism, enter the Kennedy Museum, a place of memory and souvenirs, they disrupt the sanctity of Kennedy as commerce and are kicked out.) The "live" event was edited into a videotape for a San Francisco art audience, which responded with the following remarks, later incorporated into the final piece: "bad taste but impressive," causing "bad dreams, disturbing but entertaining." Reception ("reciprocity," "feedback") alters interpretation. Chip Lord recently informed me that the screening of *Eternal Frame* in San Francisco (with a screening in New York the same day, November 22, 1975, the anniversary of Kennedy's death) was at the Unitarian Church, an event promoted by a local TV news station, another example of Ant Farm's galvanizing the media to cover art which critiques media; reporters are invariably baffled by work which crosses the boundaries between art and popular culture. Lord: "We traded them a copy of the Zapruder film for this plug on the air, but of course they described it as a 'who killed Kennedy?' presentation, so the audience included conspiracy buffs from the public at large as well as an invited art audience. I would imagine that the disappointed school teacher . . . was one of them. Our copy of the Zapruder film came from conspiracy theory sources and was originally bootlegged out of the *Life* magazine lab."

This sophisticated construction of and respect for audiences is a canny treatise on reception and context which resembles Gilles Deleuze's model of simulation. For Deleuze, the simulacrum circumvents mastery because it already includes the spectator, the angle of the observer. Thus the spectator/auditor is in tandem with the maker and can transform and deform the images. Deleuze argues that the simulacrum "subverts the world of representation" and is not a degraded copy but rather a positive one which denies privileged points of view and hierarchies.[20] Clearly another modeling of power is at stake—one which might unsettle "classical" scholars as well as patriarchy's parameters. Particularly intriguing in both the tape and Deleuze is the inclusion of the spectator's point of view in the very definition of the simulacrum—a position which is consonant with *Eternal Frame* (and the practice of Ant Farm, with their predilection for art works as events which critique and incorporate "the media" and audiences) and divergent from Baudrillard, who posits the "mass" outside as a skeptical force of negativity, for most critics the most troubling aspect of Baudrillard's position.

What fascinates me is the ping-pong dialogue of postmodernism with the counterculture. I suspect the game is determined by the age and memory, along with "class," of the writer, but leave my intuition of generational difference, including a personal history of television, untouched. But I am convinced that the passions of the counterculture sowed the seeds of their own reconstruction. For example, Shamberg praised "Media America's discontinuity with the past"; postmodern critics bemoan television's "eradication" of history. While postmodernism sighs with sad longings for the (realist or modernist) past of narrative, biography, art, and originals, video visionaries celebrated immateriality and the unraveling of print-product culture.

While video culture brazenly hawked communications as salvation, believing that political inequities would, like the domino theory of foreign policy, inevitably fall into line, postmodernism has disparaged "media ontology." On a more esoteric level, the "theoretical object" has shifted. If in the mid-1960s it swerved from cinema to video, this time it is shifting from film to commercial television. An unspoken image of U.S. television haunts postmodernism.

The counterculture's opposition to corporate, scientific, and technocratic structures is reiterated in Baudrillard's critique in 1972 of Marshall McLuhan, Hans Magnus Enzensberger, and Roman Jakobsen, who are linked through communication models (which are perhaps most dangerous in their boring and depleted language). Baudrillard: "The entire conceptual infrastructure of this theory is ideologically connected with dominant practice . . . still . . . that of classical political economy." For him, this "*scientific* construction is rooted in a *simulation* model of communication. It excludes, from its inception, the reciprocity and antagonism of interlocutors, and the ambivalence of their exchange."[21] While Baudrillard disputes thought cloaked in science as mystical, apolitical, and empirical, he shares the belief in "feedback" (what he calls reciprocity) and advances a critique of "media" which, as I stated earlier, is remarkably similar to Shamberg's (and, Nam June Paik's). For Baudrillard, by the 1980s, McLuhan's collective utopia of the 1960s, anticipating an electronic future, has soured into an obscene, private dystopia, marking the passage from pop art to postmodernism in the United States. (The shift has also been accompanied by a return to the Frankfurt School, endrunning French theory in many accounts, with *New German Critique* in a 1980s ascendancy over *Yale French Studies* of the 1970s. More of this later.)

Rather than going back to the future, I will fast forward to the past and back on my own analysis, and argue the bleak underside of visionary video politics and its "instrumental" view of technology: because the issue of consumer capitalism, like gender, was subsumed as an after-effect, the ultimate dream of TV populism—the home market or audience—is returning as a dystopia.

Because the enemy then (and now) was commercial television, it is ironic and logical that the networks, like academics in reverse, are rewriting the counterculture—containing the radicalism of the 1960s via parody and nostalgia for a lost, noble youth. For example, in "Family Ties," Steven and Elise Keaton are lovey-dovey parents, formerly Berkeley war protesters, seen in flashback wearing hippy, flower children clothes, looking very silly. What was an unimaginable nightmare then, a Reagan presidency, is the program's central joke (and reassurance) via the star of the show, Alex, the adorable, funny, conservative son and famous movie star, Michael J. Fox. A cliche of reversal twenty years ago has become a top-ten weekly situation comedy, a series with inventive "situations," elegantly clever scripts of one-liners and perfectly gauged, comic timing.

The ennui laden "thirtysomething" documents the hippy turned hand-some yuppy family, surrounded by remnants of a discarded, outmoded past, living the suburban, big old home life filled with work on personal relation-ships and the everyday, proclaiming the quintessential virtue of the nuclear, central couple relentlessly focusing on their pivotal fetish, the baby girl. Of course, the mother prefers staying home and looking at her child, and, need-less to say, the husband is "sensitive" and "involved" with the star of the series, domesticity. Sex is excellent. Their past drops by, embodied as the single, artistic long-hair and the single, neurotic female; for them, sex is not great. Unlike the upwardly mobile, central and married couple, these dissat-isfied friends/dinosaurs have failed to make the successful transition into the familial, corporate materialism of the 1980s. Like the loyal, secondary, but inferior characters they are, they visit and relive their shared protest past as the good old days; no matter how many forays these misfits make, they can-not break into the secure stronghold of the united couple now sealed off as "nuclear" family via many meaningful glances and long, bated pauses. The with-it message is clear; the past is childish, unproductive, unhappy. Grow up. Adapt. Get married and pregnant. Buy an old house. Get a real job. Cut your hair. What is startling is not the intricate conscription and defusing of the student protest movement via memory (the number of TV characters with countercultural pasts seen via flashbacks wearing hippie clothes is stag-gering), but the current recuperation of this blatant content. "Family Ties" is hailed because of the "liberal" producer Goldberg, who demanded a day-care facility on the set and stumped the Maine primary elections for child-care programs, including "maternity" leave for fathers; "thirtysomething" is praised by critics for its timely relevance, its innovative, "radical," hip-slick-'n'-cool style.

Baudrillard's "obscene" perfectly describes another contemporary mani-festation of portable, video, consumer culture, for women, very "rough trade." At the Merchandise Mart in Chicago in the summer of 1987, the now multiple video gods, JVC, Panasonic, Mitsubishi, devalued by competition, hawked their allures and wares at a collective ritual which travels to major cities in the United States each year, culminating in an orgiastic gathering in Las Vegas. When it comes to crude commerce, Baudrillard is right. The ritual was perversely fascinating and frightening. Dominated by the huge "seeing eye" of an enormous surveillance image/screen, the cavernous, echoing space was filled with suited business men eyeing and fondling the merchan-dise: old and familiar sexual technologies, the software of women and the hardware of video equipment. Burlesque collided with electronics.

The female carnies, garbed in flashy costume, used an old technique to sell a newer one, interlocking technologies and sexualities. That gender was technology and technology was gendered was literalized in each manufac-turer's miniature show: the male figure was robotic; the female was a real tease, a come-on; masculinity was the modern, high-tech machine, that place of invisibility and power, watching, taping while the low-tech women sang "Buy me"; video and the female body were available, multiple techniques for sale. (In defense of the original god, Sony, his display didn't discriminate and it was cute; both male and female were animated robots.) Consumer rape—(1) the powerful realization of the dream of accessibility and pluralism and (2) politics and art gone sour, taken into the home market—was metaphorically reenacted in a quiet scene on the lower level. A line of men with downcast eyes had very patiently formed. What awaited them, at the end? Pat Robertson and the new, electronic fundamentalism? The demeanor of devotion, including silence, provided clues. However, another object of desire was being worshiped: at the end of the line was a female porno star selling video cassettes of her films, provocatively autographing her image, flirting, available, with cascading, enormous breasts spilling everywhere—an image now real, a sight oddly prophesying the Jimmy (Bakker and Swaggart) sex scandals.

The private home as the modern theater of pornography might not have surprised the counterculture (who viewed home pornography as a positive "freedom of speech" cause, as well as a market for their work). In 1987, video, like TV, rather than meaning shared precepts, a common politics, means leisure, industry, domesticity—video bars, videodrome, video dating, the Video column of *Time,* rock video, video movie rental at "Video Visions" and other cassette supermarkets, and most importantly, amateur, home video equipment, and the circulation of video pornography, the latter a mass subculture, a real paradox.

At the risk of my own determinism and given that technology is not neutral, it could be argued that the way portable video equipment is currently being produced and marketed parallels the fetishistic history of the home stereo system; both have been taken into social/gender relations. Unlike machines marketed for women, machines addressed to men often have excess power, e.g., 160-mph sports cars, rifles, machine guns and hand-held missles, and the unearthly decibel levels of stereos. Washing machines or vacuum cleaners with excess power become either sit-com jokes, as in "Mr. Mom" or "Lucy," or a horror film nightmare. For women's machines, excess power is rarely a desirable, salable component. As well as being excessive, machines marketed for men are often infinitely extensible—there's always more to add, to buy, to build—linkages to do-it-yourself frontierism. Might one profanely suggest that these extensible machines evoke multiplicity and plurality, and are endless texts which demand endless mastery? In relation to stereo, the system—like certain theories of diffuse pleasures and sexualities which exist without referent or example—has become the dominant text; the content of the record is secondary, something which needs mastery by a system—like the actuality, the details of politics and events and personal experiences need mastering by a theory—which can jump over all those messy facts of oppression, cultural difference, and history?

It is not coincidental that the television set was introduced in the 1950s into the American home as a piece of furniture, a woman's dilemma and resistance handled by extensive campaigns in *Good Housekeeping* and other women's magazines; it was imagined as a potentially disruptive element which, however, could be smoothly managed by spatial redefinitions—the building of family rooms (TV as a baby needing a nursery, just as the home computer needs its own space) near the kitchen and accessible to and for Mom and food, or located in rec rooms away from the rest of the house. In this appeal to women to determine a predetermined space, Dad controlled the programs and, like Archie Bunker, lounged comfortably in the front-row center comfortable chair in numerous ads. Mom sat in straight-back chairs, darning, or she served Dad by turning the dial in this antediluvian era before remote control. Now that we are purchasing infinite "video systems" of component TV parts (including stereo systems) rather than single pieces of furniture, Dad has become the major buyer and assembler—not an uninteresting historical development. Rather than providing the mass, plural, utopian, alternative market for art (although forays and reconnoiters are still ventured), home video is a family plot, is video about the private home and the nuclear family—another replication in technology of ideology—of privatized spaces of unequal economics and labor.

Finally, without the intent to heroicize a spirit of an age or to portray a nineteenth-century drama of generations, but with the advances of the women's movement in mind, the countercultural stance against polarities, particularly the reassessment of private versus public spaces, art versus commerce or life, word over image, the book over cinema or TV, mind over body, as well as hierarchy among media, cultures, and nations are important, perhaps—in the dazedly conservative United States—more now than ever. However visionary, apolitical, and in the end at least quasi-patriarchal, the moment was a brief space in which, to quote Althusser, "the ideological state apparatus did not reproduce itself automatically."

CHAPTER
4

SURVEILLANCE AND SIMULATION

In *Discipline and Punish: The Birth of the Prison,* Michel Foucault tells us to look at the political and social margins rather than the center, at the ruled rather than the rulers, at the measured and disciplined body caught up in everyday techniques of power. The 1975 treatise can be interpreted as modeled on contemporary theories of vision and 1960s–1970s activist or drop-out politics (two mutually exclusive techniques which were derived from the same premises). Although Foucault does not speak directly to this period or these events, given the after-effects of 1968 in France, this is hardly a novel assertion.

In the United States, it was an era, beginning in the late 1940s with Mc-Carthyism, of governmental surveillance through wiretaps, infiltration, and photographic spying, all compiled in FBI dossiers. In the United States, women, blacks, and students organized and spoke up, taking local issues of daily life to the center of U.S. culture. They used the available and cheap techniques of bodily resistance in sit-ins, marches, and masquerade—hair length, blue jeans, and bralessness. Liberation from the disciplinary constraints of the family, corporations and work, school, the military, and the church, a nexus making up what Foucault calls "the disciplinary society," was the hue and cry (and plan of attack) of the counterculture and protest movements. This local, personal, and generational rebellion internally addressed the civil rights struggle, the end the war in Vietnam protest, the women's movement, endorsed personal life-styles of ecology, nonviolence, and peace, and sided with guerrilla and international struggles for political liberation. Silenced voices spoke with their bodies, bursting into the nightly TV news and newspaper headlines—places usually reserved for white men wearing suits.

The actions involved persecution, loss of jobs, and imprisonment; activism was documented by the number of arrests (which the Berrigan brothers are still compiling; Abbie Hoffman's obituary listed his forty-two arrests). That imprisonment, along with capital punishment, became newspaper headlines and nightly news, with footage of protestors being carted off to jail, might have something to do with Foucault's opening *Discipline and Punish* with a historical execution and the extraction of confession.

The key premise of both personal, everyday action and collective, global politics was repression, an hypothesis which included, perhaps privileged, the sexual; repression was taken out of the clinic and seen in every niche of everyday life. In *The History of Sexuality* (1976), Foucault's argument against Freud's "repression hypothesis" can be read as a response, or a corrective, to the counterculture and such visions of liberation extolled, for example, by Gene Youngblood in *Expanded Cinema*. Like his model of power as productive, with positive effects and pleasures along with negative constraints, Foucault complicates the interpretation of so many actions and so many pleasures based on lifting repression. To put his argument simply: rather than sexuality being repressed or kept in the dark, it has been an ongoing obsession of the family and state, imagined as a key to identity, a definitive secret about which we constantly speak.

Thus, when taken together, these two texts, published within two years, provide a model which epitomizes and critiques the 1960s and early 1970s. One book echoes the other. Regarding repression, Foucault posits that "if sex is repressed, that is, condemned to prohibition, nonexistence, and silence, then the mere fact that one is speaking about it has the appearance of a deliberate transgression."[1] Avant-garde or underground films from Anger's 1947 *Fireworks* on, in the United States, but including earlier films, for example, the censorship of *Un Chien Andalou*, are presented and defended as deliberate transgressions. As with Jack Smith's *Flaming Creatures*, legal court cases over censorship occurred after disruption of screenings, confiscation of equipment (the projector was perpetrator and evidence of a crime), and the arrest of viewers. If Smith or Anger had been caught seeing their own films, they could have been imprisoned. Going to underground films involved the threat of jail, the courage of one's convictions, the excitement of risk.

Foucault assesses, correctly for this period, that speaking of "sex in terms of repression . . . is . . . to speak out against the powers that be . . . to link together enlightenment, liberation, and manifold pleasures" (7). Protest movements and avant-garde film alike sought "enlightenment and liberation." What is not often noted is Foucault's third term, "manifold pleasures." The manifold pleasures of that period are all that is remembered in the innumerable 1980s revisions of the 1960s in criticism, films, and television. These often nostalgic references recall a time of youth when pleasure meant something—the linkage of personal pleasure to political commitment and concrete action, without risk of deadly disease. "The personal is political" was the politicizing of pleasure with one's real rather than metaphorical body by having sex, by taking drugs, by sitting in, by marching, by recycling, by conserving energy.

As I previously described, "thirtysomething" is sentimentally located in that history as personal memory of friendship, as irrevocable loss and free-

floating desire amid the familial ennui of present failures and daily medioc-
rities. Having been active in that period grants middle-aged scholars and
television characters political credentials. (Paradoxically, activists who are
still carrying on a 1960s politics appear as unsavvy, simpleminded, ineffec-
tual anachronisms; long hair for men has returned but as style not protest.)
Whether real or imagined, participants fondly remember occupying buildings and being gassed by local police wielding billy clubs and abusive language; the memory has lost specificity, along with fear, and become fuzzily,
sweetly collective and apolitical; forgotten is the real terror of police brutal-
ity and the paranoia of FBI surveillance, the loss of jobs and imprisonment,
the anguish of the struggle with family, the guilt of being polygamous after
years of inculcated monogamy and virginity.

Candace Bergen as "Murphy Brown" and the canceled Mary Tyler Moore
as "Annie MacGuire" were given sit-com pasts of being activists; on their
1988 series, they both attended the Democratic convention in Chicago in
1968 as lefties (we know, however, that Mary was on her way to Minnesota,
wearing lipstick and dyed-to-match rather than blue jeans). Murphy's former
lover, a Tom Hayden activist, returns to her present in an episode which
restages their instantaneous, hot lust, which is all they had then or now in
common, equating precisely the sexual and the political pleasures of the
protest movement; the sexual, the political all bound up in a libidinal flow
that is youth, turned to memory, is also transformed into scholarship and
theory.

On a 1988 episode of "Murder She Wrote," a grandson who has been
missing for twenty years is brought to life by a con artist in a look-like inher-
itance scam; however, aided by the ever-alert and all-seeing Angela Lans-
bury as Jessica Fletcher (Foucault's "speaking eye"), he recovers his memory,
discovering he is the real grandson. He was in an automobile accident after
protesting at the 1968 Chicago convention. Like many revisions of the
1960s, he had amnesia, remembers, and will now inherit millions, becoming
a richer albeit more sensitive yuppy than he already is, to say nothing of
reconstituting the family, bringing the protesting sons home, as it were.

The family structure attacked by the counterculture is the dream of the
1980s, emblematized by owning a single-family home, the other fetish of
"thirtysomething," which in the United States is becoming unaffordable for
the first-time buyer (one can only afford to buy a home if one already owns
one). In the 1980s, we recreate the 1950s and remember the 1960s, paradoxically keeping the radical goals and beliefs safe in the nostalgic past rather
than anticipating an activism for the future. (We filled the students' protest in
China with our own memories, forgetting political differences.) We have, to
a great degree, also forgotten that the ecology, women, and race were central issues, a clear and ongoing series of possible actions.

Because daily life and the sexual were founding terms, everyone could
take action and be involved; the local and the global were elided; the per-

sonal *was* political. Along with domestic ecology, pleasure was granted a political agenda and assumed a noble purpose. Pleasure was taken out of the sphere of individual gratification secured by consumption, linked to a common cause which provided a specific plan of action. Along with speech as transgressive, one wore politics on one's sleeve, adopting fashions of the third, Native American, working-class, or rural rather than corporate or high-fashion world. Friend and foe alike could see, immediately, which side one was on. Burning draft cards or bras took on equal significance; sexual repression and militaristic repression were part of the same package. The body—costumed, active, holding hands and linked collectively as nonviolently powerful—was the material and immediately visible landscape.

Critically, the movement had correctly assessed the proclivity of the media for events rather than discourse or argument; it was a theater of immediately visible and antagonistic actions, staging a visual theatrics of costume, slogans, song, and simple, repeated actions performed on, by, and with the body as much as language—a strategy which the antiabortion movement has adopted in the 1980s (in yet another of the crazy inversions between the 1960s and the 1980s with dizzying swings of political reversal). Video artists like Ant Farm staged performance events which used and critiqued TV.

In *Media Burn,* a customized dream car, driven by two art pros watching closed-circuit TV, crashed through a wall of flaming television sets at the San Francisco Cow Palace. This Fourth of July celebration included a speech by the Kennedy artist president, Doug Hall; local TV news coverage of the anti-TV event, which had the trimmings and hoopla of a sports spectacle, including play-by-play, programs, T-shirts, and junk food, was incorporated in the subsequent videotape. The sophisticated countercultural critique of media was employed to advantage—in art and political protest alike—and broadcast on local news, albeit with bemused, condescending confusion by the local reporters. Video art, like body art, performance art, and conceptual art, partook of a body politics with an eye to media coverage—a dilemma of documentation versus the ephemeral, preservation versus dissipation, product or book/print culture versus media culture.

The emergence in the 1980s of theories of the body is coincident with the revision of the 1960s where the body as much as speech and writing was the site of action, change, and politics. The body was a production, created outside of, and set against, consumption, endorsing an ecology which conserved, recycled, and sometimes "went back to nature" by living in communes. We can hear this emphasis on the body early on in Barthes, who "writes the body"; in Bakhtin's grotesque, carnivalesque body; and in Foucault's disciplined body.

To reiterate: Foucault links the discourse on sex to "the revelation of truth, the overturning of global laws, the proclamation of a new day to come" (7)—an apt description of the euphoric claims of that period. It was believed that avant-garde films and video would alter not only our consciousness but the international institutions of filmmaking and broadcasttele-vision, changing the very course of film and video history on an interna-tional (for film) and global (for video) scale.

Against the founding premise of repression, however, Foucault inverts the argument, insisting that instead of a censorship of sex, we have "installed rather an apparatus for producing an ever greater quantity of discourse about sex" (23). One apparatus producing discourse about sex was avant-garde film, which equated cinema with the erotic self. Avant-garde films were viewed by censors as pornographic. And, for the repressive hypothesis to work as a premise, sex must be viewed as outside of discourse; only the removal of an obstacle, the breaking of a secret, can clear the way leading to the secret of sex. Thus, many films were posed as riddles, "outside dis-course" or representation, including Brakhage's *The Riddle of Lumen*; Nel-son's *The Great Blondino* concludes with a last quick shot of the Sphinx. Deciphering hidden meanings was the critic's task, aided by the filmmaker telling us the truth, or secret, behind the film. The secret that is sex (with sex linked to male identity) can be read back over Bloom's reading of romanti-cism, including visionary films.

Perhaps no one was more euphoric about liberation than Gene Young-blood. His passion over "expanded cinema" is orgiastic, downright orgasmic.[2] The key to the hyped, speeding, massively pleasurable future is the equation of sex and technology. His *Expanded Cinema* is a whoopee book of cybernetic/computer speak, with mind-boggling terms like "simulta-neous synaesthetic synthesis." A brief example of one very male utopian fantasy of this futuristic technodreamer: in "Synaesthetic Cinema and Poly-morphous Eroticism" he asserts that "underground" movies are "synony-mous with sex." "If we place any credence at all in Freud, personal cinema is by definition sexual cinema" (112). Later, invoking his guru, Norman O. Brown, he states that "we hold the radical primacy of the passions to be self-evident." He rails against monogamy and "specialization of sexual ac-tivity." He champions group sex, recording sex on videotape; in a breathless burst of sources he quotes R. D. Laing, Marcuse, Dylan, Fuller, and Joyce, then analyzes the Esalen Institute in Big Sur along with films (*Fuses* by Car-olee Schneeman and Andy Warhol). He celebrates the fact that "within the last three years intermarital group sex has become an industry of corporate business, particularly in the Southern California area where a new world man is evolving . . . compiling guest lists for orgies at homes and private country clubs . . . many attend two orgies per week. . . . They discover the truth . . . that you must live outside the law to be honest" (115). Living out-side the law at the local country club, after returning home from a day of executive vice-presidency, is a strange version of radicalism. Women or video, then, could be interchangeable, like *Sex, Lies and Videotape*; women, in multiples, in any size or shape, made of any materials, would be the re-placeable fodder for these heterosexual, male ecstasies. Is that what happens when one moves to California? However outrageous the equation of avant-garde with the orgies of middle-class couples at Esalen appears today, Youngblood's credo was taken very seriously into the academy—forming one premise of the avant-garde, the risk of abandoning ideology.

The secret of sex is the obsession of the classical film as well, although it employs different techniques. As a counterpoint, I will digress to Hollywood film, reviving an older argument. Within the historical parameters of the classic text, cinema *is* an everyday machine of the ideology of the family. It is an institution which relays and constructs objects of desire, finally conscripted within heterosexuality and the family through film's endless creation of new, youthful couples. The representation of the erotic, promenaded female body—the figure of exploitation—then the denial and containment of that dangerous and unacceptable eroticism by death, marriage, or German expressionist lighting (of women living alone, i.e., without a man) in The End is both the paradox and obsession of classical film. These film discourses of (hetero)sexuality parallel Foucault's analysis of the stated historical, rhetorical terrain: "What is peculiar to modern societies, in fact, is not that they consigned sex to a shadow existence, but they dedicated themselves to speaking of it *ad infinitum* while exploiting it as *the* secret" (35).

In classical film, the secret is embedded in the fade to black, protected by the safety and closure of "The End." Foucault defines sexuality as "the name that can be given to a historical construct . . . one relay of which is the body that produces and consumes" (105–106). The on-screen female body is produced as a representation for male consumption (1) by the narrative and (2) through the eyes of the male protagonist, the male spectator. Foucault further describes this historical body, dating from the middle of the eighteenth century to the present and foreseeable future, as a class body: "One of [the bourgeoisie's] primary concerns was to provide itself with a body and a sexuality . . . the endogamy of sex *and* the body. . . . The bourgeoisie's blood was its sex" (124). (Which suggests why the protest movement, as it grew older, returned to the middle-class family, state legislatures, and corporate jobs, leaving others, such as blacks, who could not be so easily [re]assimilated, out in the cold.)

Thus, sexuality, conducted on the plane of the body, is a particular production, a historical construct, erected since the eighteenth century by the institution of the family. This version of the family is the locus of a critical conjuncture between what Foucault labels the "deployment of sexuality" and "the deployment of alliance" (106): the family, later supported by psychoanalysis, anchors sexuality *and* the circulation of wealth and reproduction, whereas before, these functions and discourses had been distinct. For example, the gloriously sexed and air-brushed body of Rita Hayworth, fashioned in gold lame for eroticism (the deployment of sexuality) in *Cover Girl* is, in the end, coupled to Gene Kelly's middle-class Brooklyn body (the deployment of alliance.)

Splitting this alliance by rebelling against the institutionalization of the heterosexual couple and the nuclear family can be seen, then, as historically radical, just as the 1980s reconstitution of the nuclear family on television and in daily life must be thought of as a conservative move; whether argued in 1988 as the American dream by Republican or Democrat, there is little difference.

This collapse of two formerly separate systems within the family occurs because, among other reasons, mechanisms of power and knowledge are now centered on sex. Foucault's analysis of power is of particular interest in relation to classic texts. He defines *power* as "a multiplicity of force relations, a process . . . a chain . . . with domination and subordination as its terminal form" (92). In his construct, "power is tolerable only on condition that it mask a substantial part of [its operations]. Its success is proportional to its ability to hide its mechanism" (86). This depiction of an apparatus of sexuality matches analyses of the technical and narrative mechanism of classical films, as well as the relations between on-screen male and female protagonists as poles of the domination/subordination split—another binarism which is too restrictive. To place eroticism within the family and consequently to put women in their place of subordination within that family is often The End of the classical film. It is not insignificant that in order to accomplish this task of power, the apparatus must be masked.

Yet, paradoxically, and consistent with Foucault's rhetoric of simultaneous inversion (or cultural dialectics), along with masking, a parallel tactic is accentuation or excess. Foucault locates one of power's four major strategies as the "hysterization" of women's bodies. This strategy constructs the female body as "thoroughly saturated with sexuality."

> Thus, in the process of hysterization of women, "sex" was defined in three ways: as that which belongs in common to men and women; as that which belongs, *par excellence* to men and hence is lacking in women; but at the same time, as that which by itself constitutes woman's body, ordering it wholly in terms of the functions of reproduction and keeping it in constant agitation. (153)

The history of classical cinema could be written as an agitation of women's bodies. In cinema, sexuality becomes image—framed, fragmented, then unified for consumption. The addition of spoken language, in its historical subservience to the image, like the couple, marrying the image, increases the fragmentation, unified into a singular coherence, in the end. It is significant that *spectator* is the term for an individualized audience, with voyeurism, a perversion, as the acceptable concept describing the spectator's process and position. There is no equivalent analysis of the ecouteur, of overhearing.

The main currency of exchange is the erotically coded image of the sexed female—highlighted, halo-haired, feathered, furred, air-brushed by Technicolor, costumed by Adrian, and made up by Max Factor. This gorgeous, tantalizing concoction (attractive to women as well as men) uncontrollably, often powerfully, circulates through eighty-nine minutes of the film, only to be contained/possessed in the privileged seconds of the end by usually a middle-class male/husband. The moment of metamorphosis from sexuality to alliance is an immaculate conception, keeping cinema's virginal code intact in the unseen and the unheard of the fade to black—the secret that is sex. Sex "by itself constitutes women's body," and yet is "lacking in women." This is film's paradox and women's historical double bind. Film's solution— fade/family—keeps the secret of sex in the dark of censorship or romance while imaging its manifestations in the "agitated" female body. The couple's passage through the film into the fade then into The End literalized Foucault's analysis:

> It is through sex—in fact an imaginary point determined by the deploy-ment of sexuality—that each individual has to pass in order to have access to his own intelligibility . . . to his body . . . to his identity. (155–156)

Without a word or a sound or an image, cinema places us within the family after a text of foreplay. As Barthes so aptly stated, "The dramatic narrative [was] a game with two players; the snare and the truth . . . nothing has been shown . . . what [was] shown [was] shown in one stroke, at the end; it [was] the end which [was] shown."[3]

Foucault's system, so perfectly applicable to cinema, can also be applied to avant-garde, but in another way: the secret that is sex as the drama of the individual maker, granting him access to his body, to his intelligibility, to his identity. The avant-garde text multiplied our options, creating what Foucault labels, after Barthes, "a multiple implantation of perversions; sexual heterogeneities" (37) operating outside like Don Juan: "There were two great systems conceived by the West for governing sex: the law of marriage and the order of desires—and the life of Don Juan overturned them both. We shall leave it to psychoanalysts to speculate whether he was homosexual, narcissistic, or impotent" (39–40). Warhol did indeed operate outside the law of marriage and the order of desire. While Don Juan might be an apt metaphor for avant-garde (and Warhol), I will follow Foucault's lead and leave it up to others to speculate whether homosexual and narcissistic are pertinent analyses.

For Foucault, instead of repression, the new persecution of peripheral sex-ualities entailed an incorporation of perversions and a new specification of individuals. As he paradoxically argues, power and pleasure had twin func-tions—one that "monitors, watches, spies, palpates, brings to light," and the pleasure that evades this power or travesties it; there is also "power assert-ing itself in the pleasure of showing off, scandalizing, resisting . . . attractions and evasions" (45). The argument of "spirals of power and pleasure" con-cludes with "we must therefore abandon the hypothesis that modern indus-trial societies ushered in an age of increased sexual repression" (49). Instead, Foucault asserts the opposite: "a proliferation of specific pleasures and the multiplication of disparate sexualities" (49).

It should be noted that all this recorded multiplication within avant-garde had little to do with women, their pleasures, except perhaps repression. Rather than the backhanded (for Drummond, castrated) compliment of figuring woman as excess, as does Hollywood cinema, avant-garde criticism and films took up Foucault's second strategy, defining sex as that which belongs, par excellence, to men, who then sacrifice themselves to their own desire, to art, which is legitimately sanctioned by and equated with male desire. Yet, this is also true of theory; neither Barthes nor Foucault paid much attention to women; their desire is not my desire. (That Warhol overturned this "law of desire" and art's precious object status, being revealed after his death as the consummate, total shopper, with what should have been an estate or rummage sale of dishes and cookie jars turning into a mass culture/art auction, is more than a small irony—like a cosmic joke that also perfectly assesses the state of postmodern culture, and not a negative take at that.)

I will repeat a story well known in video circles, a parable which I will rewrite later on. In *L'Invention de Morel*, Casares tells the tale of an escaped convict who found refuge on an island with only a single building, "the museum." One day the convict (soon to be a film theorist or postmodern art critic) saw people strolling and talking. After voyeuristically watching them, he noticed that these beautiful people repeating actions and conversations were complex projections, machine-made images and sounds. For this eternity as illusions in space and time, they paid with their lives. By falling in love with one of the imaginary women, the hapless convict again imprisoned himself; he renounced his life to become her lover, an image, gradually dying, day by day. Taken at face value, this tale is a metaphor for the great paradoxes of art and life: real versus fiction, illusion, representation, the imaginary, and simulation—dilemmas now pondered by film scholars as/and postmodern philosophers. Of course, crucial is the concept of life, not art, lived in a museum—the imaginary restaged as history in a perpetual present.

Casares's tale details an apparatus of power (both a surveillance machine and a simulation), driven by desire and predicated on vision—love at first sight ensnaring film theorists and filmmakers, like the hapless convict. Modern film theory is predicated on a critique of vision—an enshrined circuitry of looks capturing the spectator and demanding textual deconstruction. Sight as knowledge, "I see" equated with "I understand" in Western representation, declares an ideology. Paradoxically, film theory first put the finger on this slippage and then perpetuated it. The look—of camera, character, spectator—was analyzed as the dominant system of narrative, wielded and controlled by men and directed at women. Film theory incorporated models of the visible from Freud to Lacan (from his writings on the mirror phase and Poe's *Purloined Letter*) to Foucault to Baudrillard and dissected dominant cinema—what Peter Burger, from Marx, has differentiated as "system-immanent criticism" as opposed to "self-criticism."[4]

Granted avant-garde's oversight of female subjectivity, absenting rather than starring women, film theory has, in large part and for good reason, thrown the films out with their interpretation. Avant-garde films—their frequent disjunction of sound and image, their undermining of conventional representation, including, continuity editing, point-of-view structures, and emphasis on the human figure (to say nothing of video, which multiplies perspective and dimensions)—which presented alternatives to narrative conventions were overlooked. Narrative was the quintessential pleasure, and theory made narrative more interesting and academically respectable.

The history of cinema reveals that entrepreneurs early on recognized that narrative was a more profitable and predictable commodity than other forms, particularly documentary. The switch between 1907 and 1908 to narrative fiction is astonishing and thorough. By centralizing production (and eventually distribution and exhibition) in the major studios, narrative could partially be subjected to standardization and to efficient cost-accounting methods derived from the business practices of Taylorism and Fordism, detailed in what came to be known as the "continuity script" which broke down costs along with story and scene. Narrative had become a set of economic conventions that could be repeated and differentiated, remaining within its basic premises. Thus, from 1913 on (and ensconced by the 1950s as the dominant exhibition strategy), the feature film replaced "presentation cinema" which included a plethora of forms, styles, and lengths. Avant-garde film, on the other hand, involved not only a break with the classical style and narrative but also differences with other avant-garde films. Each single work was imagined without rules, as an invention rather than a reworking. Avant-garde is in many ways an alternative "mode of production" which remembers an earlier history.

As a series of textual collisions, abrupt displacements, avant-garde films shift the position of the spectator, the points of address and view through a vacillation between second and third person while acknowledging conspiratorial, intimate, and knowing collusion with the first person author/maker. As materialism rather than moral, the frequently comic, postmodern avant-garde is the practice where work is manifest. At the same time, the spectator/auditor has a marvelous freedom to skip over, be involved with, be absent from, or be unruled by texts which have only oblique and tangential relationships to real things, bodies and spaces. Avant-garde filmmakers have known about surveillance and simulation and unraveled both social metaphors in ironic, if unwitting, comic remakes of Foucault and Baudrillard. Working against mastery, against institutions of discipline, whether art or pedagogy, they play with rather than decry panopticons and simulacra, in an irreverence for their context—academia.

Along with illustrating Foucault on sexuality, many avant-garde works critiqued institutions of discipline—their own conditions of production. This is not the pleasure which comes from spying or from being in the center of the panopticon; this is the pleasure of evasion, of resistance, on a local level, to the family and the school. Perhaps it is a childish or adolescent more than adult pleasure. If this is so, then Freud, a relentless theory of childhood, would be perfectly applicable. (Snow's evasion in *So Is This* is on another level—resisting by parody and absence both the censorship and the criticism of previous films.)

I will analyze several films which address their context of education, their conditions of production and reception within academia/art. These works are pedagogic (or game show) simulations which critique a "disciplinary society," thereby biting the university context (unaware of the theory) that feeds them. Like all metaphors, this suggests a double bind: the Gordian knot of simultaneously being within and against an institution. Beneficent inclusion usually defuses. These works—*Da Fort* by Rob Danielson, films by Owen Land, *Bleu Shut* by Robert Nelson, and *So Is This* by Michael Snow (all avant-garde versions of Keaton's *College*)—are microcosms of disciplinary intrigue and simulacra of educated banality. They move among image, copy, and model, thereby querying representation—there is no pretense of a real—and art—their shaky status as "precious objects." They challenge originals, firsts, unique essences and perhaps "aura" while emphasizing reception and complicit audiences. Enunciation is compounded; reception is "theorized."

Da Fort (1982) by Rob Danielson—an unfamiliar work, an assemblage of clips selected from some fifteen educational films—repeats the interminable return, in various guises and gray rooms, of "educational" relationships, hierarchies of power: parent/child, teacher/student, doctor/patient, male/female. The premises of this twenty-minute film uncannily parallel the power/knowledge theses of Foucault, giving everyday credence to his historical assertions. (I should add that theory is not inscribed in these films by their makers; rather, I lay it over, a different story from the way theory functions in the films I analyze later by Rainer and Potter. Those films are reconnoiters with theory but here coincidence is the rule.) *Da Fort* ensnares us as both subject and object within a living history lesson of the subtle operations of disciplines. Constructed in seventeen segments separated by slow, measured fades to black, the tape runs the gamut of power's repetitive institutions—the school, the family, the military, the corporation. While preserving the integrity of each "scene,"[5] *Da Fort*'s rigid, unwavering, sometimes plodding segmentation both portrays *and* undermines Foucault's vision of a panoptic society of disciplinary space and disciplinary time—the very definition of things "educational," including films.

"Disciplinary space is divided, partitioned . . . breaking up groups, collectives. Each individual has his own place," wrote Foucault in *Discipline and Punish*. Thus, it is not surprising that educational films are rigorously partitioned and spatially confining. Every character has a narrow place, a claustrophobic space that curtails movement of body and camera. As Foucault explains, "the first of the great operations of discipline is, therefore, the constitution of 'tableaux vivants,' which transform the confused, useless or dangerous multitudes into ordered multiplicities. . . ."[6] (Lyotard takes the "tableau vivant" oppositely: as an immobile, static means of agitating rather than ordering the spectator.) *Da Fort* is a Hale's Tour of 'tableaux vivants,' living pictures of our educational histories which turn back and comment on each other as miniatures of everyday monotony; the tape walks a fine line between being monotonous and revealing monotony.

The deliberate, formal pacing, both within the artificially arranged scenes and in the metronomic timing of their duration, illustrates a punctilious temporality. "It is this disciplinary time that was gradually imposed on pedagogical practice . . . detaching it from the adult time, from the time of mastery; arranging different stages, separated from one another by graded examinations (159). *Da Fort* both amplifies and rebels against the imposed times of "pedagogical practice" by condensing the films' times and inserting wry comments on the tape's soundtrack. However, the performers, linked to the spectator, are locked into disciplinary time—outside "adult time," without power (like the adolescent counterculture and youthful avant-garde). They rarely see the agency of control; usually they (and we) only hear its imperious voice. We can almost *feel* power's presence and know it as the films' sponsoring agencies, as well as our parents and teachers.

By using off-screen, tonally constant, male voice-overs giving commands or guidance, the soundtrack reverberates Foucault's assessment that as power becomes more anonymous, those over whom it is exercised become more individuated: "In a system of discipline, the child is more individualized than the adult, the patient more than the healthy man . . . the madman and delinquent more than the normal" (193). (Think of the relative personal anonymity of powerful Hollywood moguls and the presidents of today's conglomerates which own film and television companies compared to our minute knowledge of avant-garde filmmakers.) Four off-frame, modern voices, taped at the film theory events in Milwaukee, are somewhat defensively added by Danielson as ironic echoes: Stephen Heath delivering a machine-gunned, brilliant summation of family romance and cinema, Vivianne Forrester breathlessly speaking of French "femininity" and silence, Jacqueline Rose forcefully explaining Lacan's mirror phase, and Jean-Louis Comolli arguing avant-garde and the apparatus (coincidentally with Peter Gidal, although neither auditor nor Danielson could know this).[7] These famous voices of French, Italian, and British film theory (vocal overtones found in miles of tape from six conferences) are exotically "foreign"; their difference collapses the Midwestern monotones into a single entity. Or perhaps, on the contrary, these "educated" voices of continental theory are terrorizing intellectual authority; at the same time, their meanings are undermined by the bland mise-en-scene into which their words are edited. We are reminded that theory, too, is institutionalized discourse.

Da Fort begins in a classroom with a tracking shot over wooden desk tops to the student teacher, Bill. A 1950s gray-suited, cropped-haired supervisor tells this bland soul: "I'll be at the back of the room. Pretend that I'm not there." Thus is inaugurated a sardonic and perverse network of "gazes that supervised," a system of film surveillance in which the performers are in a constant state of being seen (and dreadfully aware of that state—a difference from other movies, known as bad performances, bad actors) by the off-screen presence; their bodies are contained, measured, and scrutinized by "eyes that must see without being seen" (171). Controlled finally by voice, three gazes organize the videotape's surface and parlay our identifications: the student performers, the teachers, and the unblinking, static, and rather bored stare of the mid-placed camera.

The spectator is simultaneously the surveyor and the surveyed, always in a split and uneasy allegiance between the off-screen authority and the on-screen performers. Thus we are held in a double identification (perhaps a simulation) between sound and image, between domination and subordination, between seeing and being seen. Historical clues—1950s fashions, domestic norms, and technical indications of film's past, like television reruns—distance the segments from us. Yet like the performers, we still experience the recognition—or threat—of punishment and failure. Caught in the present of the tape's polarities, yet made safe by the marks of history and the lowly status of the educational film genre, we are reminded that we have already been normalized. We are literally historical subjects, or merely objects. At the same time, we are superior; that was then and this is now and aren't we smart—for me a serious problem of much TV history and compilation films in general (less so here, but including *The Life and Times of Rosie the Riveter*, ameliorated by incorporating present-day segments, and *The Atomic Cafe*).

The tape's enigma (and comic, hermeneutic question/answer)—the truth of language, of speech—is initiated in the second segment. An anonymous, off-screen male voice hypnotizes a man and a woman, who eventually fall asleep (suggesting delightful similarities between spectating, learning, and therapy—the danger of dozing off being endemic to all three endeavors). A later clip from this found film concludes the tape. Aided by a word from the therapist—"gum"—the couple resolve their confusion. The result is a satiating resolution for the couple, closure, and the end of the tape. Speech, a one-word answer (the conclusion of true/false tests), is both clue and cure which can be bestowed or withheld.

All of the segments suggest that testing is inseparable from teaching and therapy. In a scene set in a psychology laboratory, shocks are administered by an on-screen experimenter (a middle-aged and suited male) to an off-screen male subject whenever he fails to state the "correct word pairings." Again the importance of one-word, correct answers is emphasized. The on-screen experimenter is given instructions from a deep-throated, off-screen male voice: "Whether the learner likes it or not, we must go on until he learns all the word pairs. . . . You have no other choice, teacher." "Teacher" eventually refuses. He swivels in his chair and addresses the voice off, and us. We then learn that *he* is the subject and victim being tested. He is being surveyed. The off-screen subject was merely a plant. This layering and multiple occlusion of gazes does indeed resemble Foucault's panopticon as a continual spiral of observations emitted from a central point that knows all and sees everything but which cannot be seen in return.

A rhyming collage of micro-powers, *Da Fort* lays bare the strategies of educational films, their amateur yet insidious enactments staged in anonymous studio twilight zones. Gray living rooms with wobbly sets, minimal props, and delimited entrances and exits suggest that there is no exit from education. Discipline is as inevitable as death and taxes. The forced gestures of the performers, squirming with goodwill and awkwardly pantomimed professionalism, reinforce the disavowal of the opening line: "Pretend I'm not there." (This disavowal structures all film, suggesting that *Da Fort* inadvertently pokes fun at film theory and its deconstructions of family romance and the psychoanalytic place of the spectator.) The mechanical actors are sample humans encased in monotone simulations as slices of studied lives. These recreations are doses of visual documentation which turn "real lives into writing" (182), thereby making these seemingly innocent *tableaux vivants* a means of control.

Da Fort (again unwittingly) is a play on Freud's *fort-da!* scenario of a child mastering absence and loss by making the unpleasurable tolerable—if not pleasurable—through repetition. As Freud asked: "How then does his repetition of this distressing experience as a game fit in with the pleasure principle?" The same question could be asked of avant-garde film in general. Unpleasurable play, the "wish to be grown-up," the movement of the child from "the passivity of the experience to the activity of the game,"[8] all describe our process as spectators, or students in naive cahoots with the teacher. We are projected through simulation back into childtime, remembering that unpleasurable game in its many manifestations, including the present context of independent avant-garde film.

Since the late 1960s, the films of Owen Land (a.k.a. George Landow; he changed his name in the early 1980s, I believe) have punctured education's pretensions and avant-garde premises and styles. His work stands comically against disciplines—artistic and pedagogic. This wry humorist deflates current fashion—avant-garde film tenets, audiences, and student films in *Wide Angle Saxon;* psychoanalysis and structural film in *On the Marriage Broker Joke as Cited by Sigmund Freud in Wit and its Relation to the Unconscious, or Can the Avant-Garde Artist Be Wholed?* In many ways, all of his work, including performance and then video, are critiques of avant-garde practices, including references to and reworkings of his own films ("Remedial Reading Condescension" in *Wide Angle Saxon,* with its references to Frampton's *Nostalgia,* and the literal remake, from another subject position, of *Institutional Quality: New Improved Institutional Quality: In the Environment of Liquids and Nasals a Parasitic Vowel Sometimes Develops*).

Land uses the stuff of education, including the arbitrary pleasures of language's puns and sounds, to marshal his attack on the lunacy of disciplines (Land, formerly Landow, was a teacher at the Art Institute in Chicago and tried for years to go on permanent sabbatical, trying to escape, like his films, the confines of disciplinary spaces). While *Da Fort* recontextualizes educational scenes, Land restages or reenacts them, often as television commercials, derailing their pretensions. His films depict simulations of simulations of "real" life that become increasingly fantastic and elaborate productions (for example, the astonishingly costumed, performing pandas as "panderers" in *On the Marriage Broker Joke as Cited by Sigmund Freud in Wit and its Relation to the Unconscious, Or Can the Avant-Garde Artist be Wholed?*). Found objects are coalesced with recreations, sardonic updates which intricately negotiate a "real" while erasing history.

The pleasure and play of language—in the punning and ever-growing titles of his films, in the use of such palindromes as "A Man, A Plan, A Canal, Panama" (a funny example of found TV news footage, retakes and outtakes of a news announcer who flubs his lines, repetitively printed almost as a loop with only the slightest difference in *Wide Angle Saxon*)—shift us within enunciation. Sometimes we are the third person auditor of Freud's joking process. Or we are the second person object. In either case, we are part and parcel of the film's process. For Land, after meticulous artistry, the joke is everything. Like Deleuzes's simulacrum, it's not "on us" but with us. Land's work is a playful theory of comedy and a compendium of the sound-image-audience triangle. His films address art with forms of popular culture, recycling old formulas into critique—of commodity culture *and* art, without the ponderous baggage of moral condemnation.

Foucault writes: "the examination . . . is a normalizing gaze, a surveillance . . . in all the mechanisms of discipline, the examination is highly ritualized. . . . the superimposition of the power relations and knowledge relations . . ." (184–185). In process with Land's films, we are being tested or encouraged to rebel with the filmmaker against discipline. *Institutional Quality* (1969) shreds the power/knowledge stranglehold, parodying the "truth" of vision and the imperative voice. *IQ* (intelligence quotient) is a test in fourteen segments. As the female teacher informs us, "It is a test of how well you can follow directions." After three closeups of her face and the back of her head, we hear only her monotonous imperatives in droning voice-over. Since her commands request the performance of physical tasks— "turn on the lamp next to the couch," "dust the picture that is over the television set," "put the umbrella away," "have some fruit"—we fail as subjects. We are children arrested in the submotor state of Lacan's mirror stage, quite aware of our immobile, silent spectating status at the movies.

Furthermore, we are instructed to perform tasks with objects not visible in the picture. The last command in segment twelve—"see if your face is clean"—completes the mirror analogy (possibly denying the application of Lacan's "mirror phase" while paradoxically proclaiming the (im)possibility of Metz's primary identification with self as the ultimate and final source of the gaze). For this film, the audience is essential. We would be the object of a reverse shot or point of view shot. Also, we are subjects, taking and failing the film while most likely sitting in an uncomfortable desk in a bland university classroom—the usual place of avant-garde film exhibition/education.

Segment two is a rephotographed long shot of a living room. Because the television in the room is banding, and because of our stolid adherence to film conventions, we believe—in spite of the teacher's telling us it is a picture on our desks—that the screen image represents a real, normal-sized room, not a miniature, not a refilmed television screen. We repeatedly ignore aural instructions and depend on vision. But the movement of a pencil-wielding hand into the frame as if it were our own surprisingly distorts this false perception.

The instructor's words are intimidating, reminiscent of our tested pasts as if we were multiple-choice criminals locked into disciplinary time for sentences ranging from twelve to twenty years in schools whose architecture and design intentionally resemble prisons. (While critiquing power's domains, Land is also analyzing the conditions of exhibition/reception of avant-garde cinema. The clever ploy of turning the tables on education and audio-visual aid films, of turning education into art, then sending it back into an educational context, should not go unnoticed.) A sample of the teacher's commands brings back some hauntingly familiar memories:

> It is a picture of the house. Now listen carefully and do not look at the picture. This is how the test will go. I will tell you to mark something on the picture. Listen carefully and each time do exactly what I say. If you do not understand something I say, do not put any mark on the picture. Do *not* ask any questions. Just wait for the next thing I will tell you. Then try to do it. Remember, do not ask any questions. Just wait for the next thing I will tell you. Then try to do it. Remember, do *not* guess any answers. You will probably not be able to answer all the questions. Do not worry. Just do the best you can. Now listen.[9]

Was there not always something infuriatingly cloying and deceitful about the closing "Do not worry"? From our point of view, the hand enters the frame and writes a number 3 on picture, television, and movie screen, a tripled metaphor.

The claim by education for intelligibility is undermined by the film's structure. The filmmaker ignores his teaching antagonist, inserting images of projectors, film reels, and psychological tests—all with no relevance to her contradictory game of imperative learning. This lack of obedience deflects us as well, while creating counterpoints and analogies between word and image. We are the object of the teacher's gaze in the opening segment and the privileged viewer of the rest of the film.

We finally fail the film, a test which was impossible, just as turning on a television set which was already on was impossible. Yet, we have escaped surveillance, the teacher's spying eyes on the lookout for gum (for various disciplines, gum seems to be a sticky issue—clue, cure, and crime), passed notes, and other studious felonies. We cannot be seen but are present and knowing. Neither do we survey a surrogate victim. By embracing simulation, we escape the normalizing and hierarchies of education and remain delightfully undisciplined.

Yet another "educational" title is *Remedial Reading Comprehension* (1970), a film loosely organized around negatively and positively printed images of a female dreamer/viewer, the spectator of the dream (a film or classroom audience, and in Land's work there is little difference), and the runner, Land, the filmmaker and dream actant. The divisions between subject, dreamer/viewer (or spectator), and filmmaker are dissolved by two superimposed titles, "This is a film about you" (segment five), a phrase repeated by a voice-over announcer and concluded in segment twelve in print, "not about its maker." "This is a film about you" echoes "This is a test" of *IQ* and anticipates Snow's "This film will look just like this" in *So Is This.*

A male voice-over, an announcer/actor, says: "This is really a film about you. Let's suppose your name is Madge and you've just cooked some rice." We are exhorted to play yet another television game, a facsimile of education—a commercial. A closeup of a dark-haired woman, who looks directly at us, says: "This rice is delicious, Madge." A dissolve to a closeup of two grains of rice is accompanied by a lush score plus the announcer's words: "pure, whiter, cleaner, and rid of the coarse, hard to digest parts as seen in the unprocessed grain of rice on the left. . . ." A reverse shot would reveal us, the audience, already rhymed in the film as bored college students. We've been dreaming that we've been watching television, but now it's time for this film's test.

A printed essay on teaching begins its movement down and across the screen as a speed reading machine. The words in this illegible text are revealed only three at a time—first clearly, then blurred, then clearly—in a decentered and linear pattern. Comprehension of the whole is irrelevant to this inhuman apparatus, an editing machine of two-frame intercuts controlled by the frame and intensified by the white flicker and hovering words. The speed is electronic, yet suggestive of untapped potential for processes of viewing and reading. The problem of language, or words as image, a found text that answers the teacher's imperatives of *IQ,* is again a critical concern of Land, who cherishes words, puns, their invention. A sample of printed text is a definition of "Hokum":

> It is words without meaning, verbal filler, artificial apples of knowledge. 9/10 of all teaching is done with words. Words should point to things seen or unseen. But they can also be used to wrap up emptiness of heart and lack of thought. The student accepts some pompous, false, meaningless formula, and passes it back on demand to be rewarded with appropriately enough—a passing grade.

Clearly Land would agree, at least partially, with the contents of this definition. Never the pedant, however, Land accelerates the rate of this segment into incomprehension. This sequence mimics the passage of film through the projector, thereby commenting on the standardization of speed with no possibility of looking forward or back. A caesura—the "Lights out" command in the film for that audience—is rhymed by us and the actual lights on after this film is over. In Land's work, which depends on our presence but allows us to elude surveillance, there is always an exit. We can daydream, as do his protagonists, or we can leave, or we can play "simulation."

Land's films, moving through layered models of (1) photography, (2) film, and (3) television—media corresponding to the shifts from subject to subject's fiction to dissolution; from trace to drama to screen; from spots to phantoms to the whole—all funneled through a pedagogical imperative gone berserk, are simulacra, "not simply a false copy, but [calling] into question the very notion of the copy . . . and the model."[10] Thus, I will digress to the writing of Jean Baudrillard.

In opposition to the arguments of Foucault, the socialist utopias of collective access to the media—a redistribution of media/power advocated by Hans Enzensberger and the Frankfurt School (and invoking Walter Benjamin and Marshall McLuhan on the same page of "Requiem for the Media"), Baudrillard declared the end of the panoptic system in *Simulations.* Authorized and divinely blessed by Ecclesiastes ("Requiem" invokes God as well by dividing the essay into stages of the Catholic mass), he begins the book with: "The simulacrum is never that which conceals the truth—it is the truth which conceals that there is none. The simulacrum is true."[11] This riddle challenges the priority of systems of the gaze and representation. In his model of the contemporary world (based in part on a trip to the United States), there is no source of or for the gaze (neither the Renaissance convergent point for the spectator to occupy nor the infinite perspective in the image), neither seeing nor seen, only screen and surface. This loss of the real to screen and surface is ironically an apt description of the achievement of contemporary painting and avant-garde films and videotapes, including the work of Brakhage, Frampton, and Paik, to name only a few artists.

Just when film theory had begun to incorporate Foucault's discourse analysis, Baudrillard comes along and imperatively tells us to *Forget Foucault!* The panopticon of surveillance has been transformed into a system of deterrence where the "distinction between active and passive is abolished . . . where the real is confused with the model . . . since *you* are always already on the other side. No more subject, focal point, center or periphery . . . no more violence or surveillance, only 'information' . . . and simulacra of spaces."[12] If restated as a double bind, the contradiction of being in two places at the same time, "deterrence" is very familiar to women and artists. (It oddly resembles John Berger's argument in *Ways of Seeing,* that women watch themselves being watched.) The quotation almost reads like a working premise for the films of Land, Nelson, and Snow.

For Baudrillard—willy-nilly scattering scientific concepts such as nuclear, astronomic, entropic, and genetic as metaphors, in hypotheses apparently generated by an encompassing model of a televised, computerized world (or derived from cold war rhetoric of nuclear defense rather than offense in which the effects of radiation, which could not be seen but only measured, were minimized, if not denied, for many years) which has eliminated the "social": "The eye of TV is no longer the source of an absolute gaze, and the ideal of control is no longer that of transparency."[13] His by now axiomatic and famous claim is that "the space of simulation confuses the real with the model."[14] This is the imaginary as everything, Baudrillard's "hyperreal" (another style of art in the late 1960s and the 1970s) in which all is model, statistic, memory bank and, miniature which, predictably enough, abolishes representation.

When it comes to commercial television (and 1980s U.S. politics), Baudrillard makes limited sense. Our images mask nothing, and thus it is dangerous to unmask them. Scandals such as Watergate and Irangate are uncovered and condemned only to conceal the loss of the real of politics, truth, and honor; Disneyland—a crucial place within this theory—is a scheme concealing that the entire United States is Disneyland. We have moved from appearance, an age of truth and secrecy, to an age of simulacra, by strategies of deterrence rejuvenating a fiction of the real. Thus, we prove the real by the imaginary and the truth by scandal; we prove the law by transgression. Bank tapes identified Patty Hearst as a gun-toting robber/performance artist; TV protected us in this "simulation of revolution" (perhaps a performance) from capital gone momentarily delinquent with desire. Baudrillard argues that the simulation is more threatening than the "real"; it revealed, in this instance, the absence or demise of radical action. The Oliver North hearings revealed a more blundering demise—the lack of *any* law, never mind logic and politics.

Because power can only exert itself on the real, the rationality of means and ends, of causes and effects predicated on a referential order, power is breaking apart; its exercise, using discourses of crisis or desire, is a simulation. The panoptic model is a "machine of truth, rationality, of productivity which is capital . . . without reason—a violence.[15] The most disturbing assessment of culture is Baudrillard's analysis of the mass audience: the silent majority, stronger than any medium, overshadows historical systems of power; they want fascination and pleasure rather than meaning; "For it is not meaning or the increase of meaning which gives tremendous pleasure, but its neutralisation which fascinates. . . ."[16] This is a model which can partially explain the pleasure of the "David Letterman Show," but it supplies only the first step, and a literal one at that. In many ways, this vaguely echoes the Frankfurt critique of commodity culture, taken from its time and context.

Finally, for Baudrillard the cultural forecast is bleak, and simulation the cause. There is no longer a staging of scenes, no spectacle, no mirror, no image or representation, all "effaced in a sort of an obscenity." (I continue to wonder how.) The postmodern subject is not hysterical or paranoid, but schizophrenic, "no longer the player on a stage, no longer produced as mirror, but a pure screen. . . ."[17] (This traces the historical passage from theater [the suspension of disbelief] to film [fetishistic disavowal] to television [avowal of contradictions]. It is technical and spectatorial history of a negative shift from person to image, from the live to its representation, from the tangible to the intangible.) I will return to Baudrillard in relation to postmodernism. Suffice it to say that fear of the loss of mastery is palpable; in simulations, it is impossible to discern subject from object, thereby vanquishing the stability of power's poles of domination/subordination, potentially overturning the name and place of the father.

Unlike Baudrillard's reading, in which simulation involves a certain perverse deception of an "image without resemblance," Land's simulations, like Ant Farm's and Nelson's, are playful pretenses. As Gilles Deleuze interprets the simulacrum, it has a radical or at least an anarchistic function: it circumvents mastery because it already includes the spectator. Simulacra "are those constructions that include the angle of the observer, in order that the illusion be produced at the very point where the observer is located. . . ." Thus, the spectator, shifted between second and third persons, in tandem with the first person narrator, "a double scandal and stroke of the enonce," can transform and deform the images, which would be historical and contextual—produced "at the very point where the observer is located." Deleuze argues that the simulacrum "subverts the world of representation" and is not a degraded copy but a positive one which negates both original and copy, both model and reproduction.[18]

In one reading, this argument electronically updates Walter Benjamin, who distinguished between "aura" and "mechanical reproduction," with the latter enabling the work to be taken into new situations where new meanings would be produced. Deleuze refuses to be trapped in hierarchies or bipolarities, refuses to bemoan the rapidly altering status and circulation of commodities, whether commercial or artistic products. For him, either subject or object, standing alone or taken out of context, on the side of Art or Commerce, are theoretical reductions. Thus, the one-way street of most arguments regarding "colonialism" (or power or sender-receiver communications models or notions of culture being imposed from above or radically being invented subculturally) in which, for example, U.S. cultural exports overrun the world, resulting in a silencing in which the "subaltern cannot speak," is anarchistically upset: the simulacrum is produced, precisely, "at the very point where the observer is located."

The simulacrum must, by this definition, be historical, be contextual, be connected to experience; at the least, it is a two-way street. It might also be a local strategy as well as an object, a series of acted-upon events. The simulacrum is a notion which includes time, perhaps more than space or place; it emphasizes the effects of time inscribed in space. It is a model which, in centering mutual enunciation, a certain reciprocity (which Baudrillard views as an impossibility for electronic media which "prevent response"), incorporates the possibility of change, over time and within context. After all, objects, like subjects and theories, do change, in time or in place, irrespective of truth or reality. One can imagine our film theories, produced within temporal contexts and for specific reasons, as useful and tactical simulacra. Thus, it's not so much a question of whether de Laurentis, in 1984, or LeSage, in 1977, are right for all times and in all places about Freud, but rather from what vantage points and to what ends their diverent readings were produced.

The observer partakes of the process of producing cultural meanings, which are in turn transformed, contextually and experientially. Watching the "Today Show" in Sydney at 2:00 A.M., fifteen hours earlier than the United States, with reports of U.S. weather by a fat man wearing silly hats and crazy T-shirts, and news which has not yet happened in the United States, is an avant-garde event, as Meaghan Morris pointed out to me. Framed by Australian TV images, voices, formats, and audiences, "Today" (or "Yesterday" for Australia; "Tomorrow" for the United States) becomes a different program, more of a retroactive event (whereas in the United States it is predictive). Land's restagings and facsimilies, with their moments of trompe l'oeil, denials of privileged points of view, "set up a world of 'consecrated anarchy.'" His films illustrate Deleuze's argument that simulacra—affirming divergence and decentering in their destruction of models and copies—set up creative chaos, assuring a collapse of foundations which is a "positive, joyous event."

Deleuze's inclusion of the spectator's point of view in the simulacrum is a position radically different from that of Baudrillard, who posits the "mass" outside the simulation. Deleuze's model of creative reciprocity in a simultaneity requires work on the part of the observer, credited with knowledge, maturity, ability. Baudrillard conceptualizes the masses as a force of negativity, of silence. He writes of communication: "The myth exists but one must guard against thinking that people believe in it. That is the trap of critical thought which can only be exercised given the naivete and the stupidity of the masses as a presupposition. The mass media destroy the social with its pressure of information. . . . However, the masses refuse to participate in the recommended ideals . . . and silence is the ultimate weapon."[19] Silence, like the neutralization of meaning via fascination, has not, to my knowledge, ever proven itself to be an ultimate weapon, particularly for women and blacks. Whether the mass is being vilified or glorified is also up for grabs in this riddler's prose.

In Land's work, both spectator and filmmaker "refuse to participate in the recommended ideals" of pedagogy as surveillance, as mastery, with power poles of domination and subordination. To a degree, his work, like other avant-garde films, overthrows/critiques power by restaging it as a simulation—an impossible test, a confusion of levels of representation which challenges both the notion of the art object as autonomous and the institutions of art and academia—in the postmodern era, an amorphous duo.

> We can only make ourselves understood
> (well or poorly) if we maintain a
> certain speed of delivery. We are
> like a cyclist or a film obliged
> to keep on going so as to avoid
> falling or scratching.
>
> —Roland Barthes [20]

Robert Nelson, the filmmaker/cyclist, celebrates his audience and unties power's polarities by including them in the process of his films, in this instance, *Bleu Shut*—a funny simulation of a sublimely ridiculous test: a multiple-choice guessing game of naming "pleasure" boats. The film is an allusion to TV game shows and a microcosm of pedagogy; the testing moments are the Pavlovian real of school (replete with controlled buzzers, numbers, and clocks), and the cutaways are brief daydreams which simultaneously comment on narrative—its hermeneutic enigma/question prolonged by lies, detours, and delays of expectation and resolution; genres of cinema; the arbitrariness of language; and enunciation, address, and audiences.

As if ordained by Barthes's analogy between cycling and film, *Bleu Shut* opens with home movie footage of two historical cyclists joyously pedaling to a friendly gathering in the country. Later, another cyclist—twice distortedly shot teetering on a too small bike while enclosed in a crystal ball matte—falls off into a mud hole, like the old "Laugh In" on TV. Carrying the cycling/filmmaking metaphor from Barthes to this film's conclusion, the filmmaker begins to "tell us what this movie is about": after attempting a scholarly, pedantic interpretation of the "two planes of involvement," a treatise on film viewing addressed to a "you," a second person audience as a classroom of students, the sound equipment fails, an interruption and an error, like falling off a bicycle (or teaching film). With irritation, the filmmaker asks "What's wrong?" and walks toward the camera, blocking our vision with his body, rudely ignoring his students and inquisitioning the film's technicians, there, on the set.

In the end, "we" are turned into a historical, absent, third person audience, while the filmmaker is silenced by technical difficulties. "Either the speaker chooses in all good faith a role of Authority, in which case it suffices to 'speak well . . .' Or the speaker is bothered by all this law that the act of speaking is going to introduce into what he wants to say . . . correcting, adding, wavering . . . to render less disagreeable the role that makes every speaker a kind of policeman." (191–192) This ending, this film, and this filmmaker—currently a Milwaukee film teacher (formerly at the Art Institute in San Francisco) in constant pursuit of sabbatical (like Land) and "bothered by all this law of speaking" never mind theory—waver and correct, choosing the role of irreverent student rather than authoritative teacher.

Speech is interrupted (or "glotally" stopped) not only by faulty equipment or tails out endings but also by laughter and inserted shots. Language and film laws are unmade, just as is the truth of vision. Neither seeing nor hearing are serious believing. The film screen becomes pedagogy's blackboard, painting's surface or ground, and Freud's mystic writing pad capable of receiving new impressions; going to the movies is equivalent to going to school. After a shot of an aquarium with a cautionary moral printed over as intertitle, followed by fingers and mugging faces playing with the upper right-hand corner screen clock, the film literally runs out, goes amok. (Going amok: "Among Malayans, the condition of being amuck," according to *Webster's*.) Cyclists and filmmakers don't avoid the pratfalls of falling or scratching. ". . . The need is to work at patiently tracing out a pure form, that of a *floating* (the very form of the signifier); a floating which would not destroy anything but would be content simply to disorientate the law . . . everything is there, but *floating*" (215).

Just as Barthes concludes "Writers, Intellectuals, Teachers" with this tranquil metaphor of floating, Nelson concludes his film with a shot of fish floating or swimming in an aquarium. The world beneath the static boats of the film's test is a miniature ocean, a comic special effect's simulation of the sea/see, perhaps a reference to the conclusion of Bruce Conner's *A Movie*, an enigmatic, archeological, tranquil shot of a deep sea diver swimming into an underwater shipwreck, after catastrophe. On another level, the film's past of the opening, home movie, cyclist footage catches up to the present: the once upon a time of all fiction and of history is taken into the present of watching and listening to this film and this filmmaker; the film moves from nostalgia to process, from distanced, ignored third person watching and overhearing to second person listening, then to dismissed viewer.

The film is systematically ordered: the rigorous, relentless segments of the test are derailed by insert (or escape) shots—of a condensed rock band/ dance (too bad we can't stay at the party, but we've got to move along); of the filmmaker nakedly entrapped in a glass prism tower; of loops of a direct address dog asynchronously barking or not at the camera; of beans and a close-up hot dog loop—its repetitive circularity demarked by rising steam and its endlessness abruptly concluded by the synchronized finality of an aggressive, cutting fork; of musical performance clips from a B-minus Hawaiian musical; of a porno film; and a lengthy, overtly indulgent shot of rebellious brats in the crystal ball matte, maliciously and childishly misbehaving by sticking their knowing tongues out at the camera, the film, and us. All the segments are color keyed in a continuity palette of mainly sepia. The film is a "City Limits Film" musical comedy, "Presented" with defused fanfare and doses of narrative interrupted by presumedly pleasurable spectacle. Anything is better than school and discipline, even the worst (or best) movie.

The film's literal test, taken by the off-screen voices and the audience, of matching silly boat names to the on-screen still images of the boats, is administered by a gentle yet firmly insistent voice of a female teacher who times the two gleeful student buddies, Bob and Bill (Nelson and William Wiley, although it is difficult to tell one voice or attitude from the other). A clock in the frame/classroom untimes us, just as the film's subtitle lies to us about the thirty-minute length. The adult student buddies engage each question with dogged determination to master the illogical through logic and insight. "What fantastic boat names." It's "almost frustrating." "I'm gonna take a long shot." The filmmakers continually fail each question until Bill gets "Kant Budget" right—consoling Bob with "These are all very hard." Then, prior to the porno insert, Bill gets another one right. When he fails on the next question, "May Be So," he ironically replies: "I thought I was becoming an expert." "Guys II," yet another boat name and the real substance of this film celebration of friendship and collaboration, is failed, yet passed with dopey, "high" honors.

The film's test segments (like all tests) are miniature narratives: the question is the hermeneutic enigma, and the students' verbal musings are delays, snares before the closure of the end, the one word, correct answer of resolution and "truth" similar to "gum" of *Da Fort's* ending. After the right answer places them in a kindergarten of intelligibility, the hysterically laughing students roar on track with relief at the mystery's solution (putting the correct word with image), claiming, like novice Perry Masons, to have known or suspected (and what's the difference in tests?) the right answer all the time. In retrospect, test takers are always right. "As soon as one has finished speaking, there begins the dizzying turn of the image: one exalts or regrets what one has said . . ." (204). Language and education are childish but pleasurable and collective guessing games—replete with punning, mispelled arbitrariness. The impossibility of correspondence (in this film, perhaps as logical as resemblance ever is) between the object and its signifier (the *picture* of a boat and its image or name) is the very definition of a simulacrum. *Bleu Shut* was made in stoned fun; it is also a model of education and film as simulations—of space, of time, of the presence of an audience, of art. Disavowal—film theory's Freudian denial and guarantee of pleasure ("it's only a movie")—is a delightful actuality and thus a source of and for boyish play.

Pedagogy is an unabashed game, yet one which must be taken seriously: "Our intellectual debates are coded every bit as much as were the Scholastic disputations; we still have the stock roles . . . but where such roles would have been ceremonial and have displayed the artifice of their function, our intellectual intercourse always gives itself natural airs; it claims to exchange only signifieds, not signifiers" (202). (Contemporary film theory, which includes feminism, has an ironic blind spot: set against the biological or natural in favor of the historical, yet paradoxically arguing signifieds or absolutes when critiquing the avant-garde's signifiers as empty of meaning and bereft

of materialism—a critical tautology which also forgets history and context—
of the films and our theories.) As hard as Bob, Bill, and teacher try to pretend belief in the exchange of signifieds and the correspondence between
thing and image, they can only parody institutions, mocking the pedagogical
transmission of significant meanings. Bob and Bill will play by the rules as
long as the game is ludicrously ridiculous. And what could be more inane
than naming boats?

The answers, printed on the screen, are often held over the inserted clips;
thus "Bottoms Stup" renames the looped dog, and "Mick Stup Bunks" is
printed over the beans and hot dogs—both segments commenting on sound
and silence, loop and action. The direct correlation between sound and image, like word and object, is artifice, a game of learned conventions; learning, like art, is a random, lucky guess or simulation as much as it is a
surveillance. The spectator/auditor is held in a compromising position—
overhearing a test being administered and failed, after being brought into an
initial conspiratorial position by the whispering, off-stage teacher (reminiscent of TV's golf announcers), who informs us about the film in an excita-
tory, verbal trailer of feigned expectation.

Thus, unlike Land's work, we don't directly take the boat test (which might
be analyzed via Saussure's, Jakobsen's, and perhaps even Benveniste's linguistic models), although we do go along for the ride. The insert shots, recycled footage, are simultaneously our film test of genres, conventions, and
history, and teasing, tantalizing tidbits of what we won't see in entirety. For
example, during the porno insert, two intertitles, interrupting intercourse,
are intercut: "I love you, Irene. I will never love anyone but you." Sex continues in closeup. Then, "And I love you, Andre . . ." Printed on the screen,
presumably from this found footage, is "The end" followed by a logo, "An
Official Film." During *Bleu Shut*, we went to a condensed dance, saw brief
musical spectacles, and now a two minute porno film—summaries of all
movies. Thus, we neither take, pass, nor fail *Bleu Shut*, just as the maker and
cohort/alter ego could not logically name (or not) the boats. We don't even
get the filmmaker's lecture at the end as an explanation or solution. We enjoy the elliptical experience but are constantly reminded that "we" are always outside pedagogy and cinema as spectators, overhearing private and
personal sessions: ". . . the teaching relationship is nothing more than the
transference it institutes: 'science,' 'method,' 'knowledge,' 'idea' come indirectly . . . they are *left-overs*" (196). Transference could be a sweet concept
to explain the triadic relationship of avant-garde film-maker-spectator, a process which would take the screening event into account.

This film has many "leftovers"—not the least of which is (the hot dog)
laughter at our pasts and our present conditions of viewing. In complex
ways, the spectatorial mechanism of *Bleu Shut* and of pedagogical simulacra
might not be identification and disavowal (which the simulacrum already
embodies) but transference. "How can the teacher be assimilated to the psychoanalyst? It is exactly the contrary which is the case: the teacher is the

person analyzed . . . it is not knowledge which is exposed, it is the subject (who exposes himself to all sorts of painful adventures). The mirror is empty, reflecting back to me no more than the falling away of my language . . ." (194). Nelson the filmmaker—bare ass exposed and trapped in the cold, colored, and beautiful tower (a monument to Art? a womb and disorienting ledge of glaring exposure) of glass prisms (narcissism berserkly refracted into infinity)—humorously risks the "falling away" of language and image. His mock-epic film journeys are fraught with comic peril, last laughs before "falling off" life. We are reminded that the search for identity in art, no matter what the sexual difference or preference, also involves the risk of revealing the self, in public; or more frightening, of not being able to make art. Theorists might also take a cue from Barthes by displaying our artifices along with pointing to those of others.

So Is This by Michael Snow (1982) refers only to itself, to the sport of spectating, to the presence and subjectivity of "this" rather than the distance and objectivity of "that." By referring to itself, this film paradoxically marks itself as theory, a Deleuzian simulacrum. As both history and theory through reversal, it not only recontextualizes reading, writing, and spectating but is also a comic turn on film language—starring writing, like intertitles in early cinema, the spaces between the image signs.

Writing has always been essential to cinema—in intertitles, subtitles, titles, and credits, all for the sake of ownership, narrative, and the location and intelligibility of the spectator. In silent cinema in particular (which this film is and commercial film never was), writing was an integral process with image (in many Douglas Fairbanks films, for example, almost half the time is spent reading lengthy intertitles). Writing in the intertitles was systematically part of the "continuity style," but also potentially a break with it. But perhaps the most direct historical connection with Snow's film is that intertitles frequently declared an enuciator with a position, a narrator (often the director) in collusion with the audience.

In *So Is This* writing is the only image, just as the only image is an iconography of language. Luminous, white-printed words are "flashed" for measured intervals. The size and duration of the words vary. The words repeat, reverse their order, speed up and slow down. The "look" as well as the sense of language is at stake. These imaged words, replete with potential stories, have their shadows, rhythms, and imaginary sounds—inflections, volumes, and accents. Signifieds slide into signifiers, sign into object. Letters become building blocks of pure light. The monologue which we read is transformed into silent dialogue.

Inner speech, that elusive psychoanalytic thing, becomes quietly heard, spoken in the imaginary of the film viewing. Are we thinking or reading? The split subject is caught somewhere between thing presentations and word presentations, between speech and silence. The split is also sealed by laughter, the momentary slip into the unconscious where all disruptive thoughts are stored for societal safekeeping. We are spoken and read to. Equally we are spoken *of* while we read in the dark privacy of a public ritual. Finally, we cannot talk back. However, we can block out language by closing our eyes. It's only a movie, after all. This tour de force of filmed words plays with the silent look of language. Yet ironically, this silent reading is disconcertingly loud, suggesting that between speech and image is always language.

Snow's direct "presence" (a postmodern version of avant-garde's traveling circuit) is in the first person "I." It's as if Snow wanted to declare the life rather than the death of the author. Yet his voice is not *over* the film but rather *in* and *on* the screen, existing as printed words rather than synched with moving lips. This "I" is a presence, yet in its silence, absent. During the film, the point of address doubles: the enunciator "I" maps out a schizo narrative for an embattled protagonist "author" who has specific intentions, who will, for example, be "very confessional about his personal life." Of course the system of the film is *exactly* that but not *about* that; it is always about this.

The horizontal string of words along the vertically moving film enacts a hermeneutic treatise: a stripped bare, meditative narrative play with and for the spectator who is suspended in the present while awaiting the promise of future pleasures, the satiation of closure, yet another variety of *fort da!* Thus, although *So Is This* does not use the content or "look" of things educational, the film, in its play with us, places us in a pedagogical position, in front of a blackboard, with all of our expectations of narrative pleasure intact. Snow's narrative is solely process and expectation—not expectations created by narrative but rather by the promise of traditional narrative which ironically we are already in, now. The film tells us: "The rest of this film will look like this. This film will consist of single words presented one after another to construct sentences and hopefully (this is where you come in) to convey meanings." After mapping out both the film and our options, the text then lies by reporting its length as "about two hours long." Later we read: "How do you know this isn't lying?" The viewer, constantly anticipating but surprised and amused by this question, is in a position comparable to that of the home audience for a television quiz show, *excluded* although illusorily coded in as present. This treatise on going to the movies is thus also about reception and the construction of the spectator as Snow's ideal and real audiences.

This film denies its originality and perhaps the notion of ideas as property. Words on the screen honestly declare that "this is not the first time this has been used. This belongs to everybody." However, just exactly what "this" is remains a question. Obviously, it is technique and cinema. "This" is a multiplicity, the arbitrariness of language, a beguiling present rather than an anxiously awaited and constantly delayed future. Retroactively we realize the political dimensions of "this." In our present world of constant sound, talk, and speeded up imaging, the very preciousness of silence, in the gaps and quiet spaces between words, is endangered. This, the moment, the present, the here and now, belongs to us. The future is only a promise built on expectations: it is an illusion, perhaps a deceit; to believe we can control it is a conceit.

At the same time, one can almost feel Snow's superior pleasure in evading representation and the audience, outrunning criticism by anticipating and thereby controlling our response, dominating the spectator precisely by his knowing absence; in many ways, this is a monologue, cloaked as a dialogic process, precluding any reciprocity. We laugh at ourselves rather than with the filmmaker, who might be laughing at us. On second thought, the joke might be on us.

> ... there may be a third textual entity;
> alongside the readerly and the writerly,
> there would be something like the *receivable*.
> The *receivable* would be the unreaderly text
> which catches hold, the red-hot text. . . . I can
> neither read nor write what you produce, but
> I *receive* it, like a fire, a drug, an
> enigmatic disorganization.
>
> —Roland Barthes[21]

Although not "red-hot," *So Is This*, like Land's and Nelson's films is "receivable," in fact, structured around reception. This film ensnares the spectator in a paradox when watching and referring to "it," the film. A silent playwriting which we read amid laughter and bursts of recognition, it literalizes and unmakes Barthes's dichotomous delineation between the readerly (simplified to the classical text) and the writerly (the modern or avant-garde text). It might have delighted Barthes, who had already undone his own polarity by introducing the intriguing third entity—the receivable, a concept particularly pertinent for a postmodern theory of contemporary avant-garde.

Certain "red-hot" films reek of a popularity, albeit a scandalous one. Like Manuel DeLanda's *Harmful or Fatal If Swallowed* and *Raw Nerves: A Lacanian Thriller*, reminiscent of the reception of earlier films by Anger and Smith, and the feature film by Lizzie Borden, *Born in Flames*, these films catch hold. Perhaps the *receivable* operates both at the intersection of art and popular culture and at the margins, within subcultures with distinct styles, fashions, audiences, and politics. The history of U.S. avant-garde practice is a treasure trove for postmodernism, including questions of reception as historical. That we can ask the question suggests a change in our cultural conditions.

CHAPTER
5
THEORETICAL OBJECTS

In "Acinema," Jean-Francois Lyotard's model of reception is analogous to pyrotechnics. Referring to Adorno, who fancied fireworks as the "only truly great art," Lyotard provides a metaphor for avant-garde films—the clarifying example of a match which "once struck is consumed. If you use the match to light the gas that heats the water for the coffee . . . it is a movement belonging to the circuit of capital. . . . But when a child strikes the match head to *see* what happens, just for the fun of it, he enjoys the movement . . . stated losses . . . dissipation of energy . . . intense enjoyment . . . *la jouissance.*"[1] Comparable to Barthes and predicted on psychoanalysis, Lyotard argues that "it is essential that the entire erotic force invested in the simulacrum [be] . . . displayed and burned in vain." Acinema will produce "vain simulacrums, blissful intensities instead of productive/consumable objects" (54). I think here of Ernie Gehr's *Serene Velocity* or Barry Gerson's *Luminous Zone*—where energy is intensely concentrated within the almost obsessive formal structure itself and perhaps dissipated during viewing.

The "pyrotechnical imperative" has two options or poles: immobility and excessive movement. These spectator positions of either paralysis or movement are inversely matched to what Lyotard calls "the tableau vivant," a staging of immobility, and its converse, lyric abstraction, "where agitation appears" (57). Brakhage's *Anticipation of the Night* is an example of lyric abstraction which, comparable to abstract expressionist painting, would immobilize the spectator, a "fascinating paralysis." Snow's *Wavelength,* on the other hand, is closer to the *tableau vivant* and would agitate the spectator. In both realizations (not Lyotard's examples), Lyotard's analysis suggests that "the represented ceases to be the libidinal object while the screen itself, in all its most formal aspects, takes its place," restricting "libidinal discharge" to very small, partial regions of the body, the eye-cortex (59).

Lyotard's double use of "vain"—dictionarily meaning empty, worthless, hollow, having no importance, without result, fruitless—which, for him, is a positive virtue resembles Bergstrom's negative critique regarding empty signifiers, bereft of meaning and materialism. Lyotard's invocation of the child as pure subject, logical given that psychoanalysis is resolutely a theory of childhood, takes Penley's negative critique of "infantile" also to positive ends. In all three instances, this "a" or not cinema is presumed to consist of effects and affects, elicited by formal work on pure signifiers without referents in the material world. At the same time, for Lyotard the "screen itself" is transformed into a libidinal object; for him, this is a good thing; for Baudrillard, screen objects are bad, simulations. This modernist presumption *about* the films recapitulates theory's emphasis on separating signifiers from signifieds and becomes a virtual premise (and a sine qua non) of criticism, including Lyotard's model of reception which appears to partake of Deleuze's version of the simulacrum.

However, theory is rhetorical, disputatious; it is also historical, strategic. As Barthes reminded us, theory gives itself "natural airs," an exchange of signifiers traded as signifieds: both Penley and Bergstrom critique a particular interpretation of avant-garde cinema, challenging criticism more than films, paradoxically repeating the fallacy they discover in avant-garde cinema whch they argue is without materialism, subjects without objects. To an intriguing degree, this is what Lyotard calls for in his "version of the sublime as a history of events, a tradition of happenings . . . of moves and rules" which "imply that actual artworks might be but the residues of such events." Postmodernism thus becomes an "injunction of formal eventfulness," the invention of new rules, unexpected moves, what Morris calls the *"traditional* imperative to break with tradition."[2]

She goes on to argue that Lyotard's sublime, which appropriates for postmodernism the "gestures of the historical avant-garde," has "the enormous advantage of undermining the persistent opposition made between *modernism* as . . . self-reference, purism, ontological preoccupation . . . and *postmodernism* (avantgardism) as an insistence on problems of reference." What the notion of the sublime dissolves, says Morris, is the proverbial opposition, "art/world," in which "some art talks about art while other art talks about the world." This dichotomy imagines that "loquacity is in either case intrinsic to the artwork . . . regardless of how, when, and by whom it is read." This ahistorical presumption, along with the binarism "self-referring/other-referring," has, to a remarkable degree, been the syllogistic premise of avant-garde film criticism, whether pro or con, even by feminists so opposed to arguments of inherent nature. Morris concludes that the opposition can only be understood as a "stake linked to conflicts in the discourse-genre of art criticism" (64).

One theoretical object for avant-garde cinema is film history. Sitney's analogy of film with poetry recapitulates one history of film criticism which justifies cinema's status as art by linking it with legitimate forms like music or painting, or like the history of Hollywood which aspired to the status of middle-class theater exemplified, for example, in Adolph Zukor's Famous Players in Famous Plays, later merging with the Jesse Lasky company to form Paramount Studios. The formal experiments of avant-garde cinema recreate and allude to film history in other ways, including artists' declaration of ancestry and lineage with, for example, Welles, Von Stroheim, Melies, Eisenstein, and Vertov.

One reading of early film history, which also reconstructs and amplifies the work of a 1905 film, deconstructing the cinematic apparatus, is portrayed in Ken Jacobs's *Tom, Tom, the Piper's Son*. This ninety-minute film investigates its one-reel antecedent by reprinting and repetition, focusing on details of the tableau staging, transforming the short or "primitive" film into an abstract feature by elaboration and elongation, revealing the early film as the complex narrative spectacle it was. "Primitive" cinema becomes modernist cinema, the old is made new, and mass culture shifts into the realm of art.

Jacobs repositions us as modern (and historical) spectators, taking us on a visual tour from the view to the detail, from theatrical proscenium staging to film editing and camera placement, from the human figure in action to peripheral, granular incidentals, from Renaissance perspective, resolutely centered, off to the margins and up against the flatness of the two-dimensional screen and a loss of focus, from the long shot to the extreme closeup, from legibility to abstraction, from the literal to the figural, or from the figure to the ground of the movie screen, thereby renegotiating that early contact of and for story. Thus, narrative becomes the materiality of the apparatus, the basis for a disquisition on temporality. Another mystery—of the time of the spectator and story—along with the theft of the pig unfolds; time is reversed, delayed, stopped, elaborated.

While film theory predicated on classical cinema analyzed film's spatial conventions, avant-garde films unsettled spatial configurations, addressing issues of time—its chronological, Newtonian, standardized, public times exchanged for money. In many ways, this complex modeling of time might have more to do with the unconscious—simultaneous, capricious, private times, with the past capable of erupting into the present, at the same time— or with thought and its disjunctive temporalities. Jacobs's film reminds me of the distinction, quoted by Benjamin, between memory, which is destructive, and remembrance, which is conservative or nostalgic. *Tom, Tom* is destructive memory through a radical conservation. That film's temporality was a concern of early film theory, a property of cinema which quite thoroughly inflected the thinking of modern artists and critics from the turn of the century on, running the political gamut from Eisenstein to Picasso, perhaps even determining definitions of modernism, has recently gone unremarked along with modernists' constantly stated fascination with cinema as an electric technology which could artificially rearrange space.

The film is also a critique of representation, remakes, and sequels—along with notions of originals and aura. The mise-en-scene or staging of the 1905 film was taken from a Hogarth painting, pointed out by Sitney; the scene is of a county fair, including a wire walker. Fine art and folk art converge, traverse, mutually informed by each other, making distinctions always historical and contextual. Film's economic basis in (1) popular or folk culture with immigrant or working-class audiences, and (2) mass, reproducible, technological culture is invoked. Film was a high-tech art of everyday culture. Jacobs restages cultural history by reminding us of the conditions of film exhibition in music halls, fairs, and circuses; the electric machine of movement, appearance and disappearance was a wondrous gimmick, like magic, a novelty act of (dis)embodiment, speeded up and and stop-framed times which magicians like Melies incorporated into their performances. These traveling sideshows of the spectacular, including the fascination of seeing the projector (the "concealed" or "repressed" or "seamless" "work" of the apparatus scrutinized by audiences then like textual analysts today), were frequently one-man operations, with the maker as the quintessential auteur, like Melies, doing everything from camera work, directing, editing, and processing to costumes, publicity, and projection. The similarities between "primitive" and avant-garde films' conditions of production, distribution, and exhibition become apparent. However, there is a significant difference: the maker of the 1905 film remains anonymous, suggesting that the place of the author is central to distinctions between art and popular culture. (I remember Malcolm LeGrice spending a day coordinating a multiple-projection film with meager equipment and then having to perform as artist, after his arduous technical day, in front of a ragtag band of UWM film students and faculty.)

Narrative film moved, some say evolved or developed, rapidly, to a system of standardization and specialization (and collaboration). Other shifts in history occurred—from films of short duration and variable recording and projection times to standard feature length and uniform speed, determined by sound; from "silent cinema" (always with music and effects) to films with synch speech and sound; from dispersed exhibitors at county fairs, vaudeville houses, and nickelodeons to legitimate theaters and centralization; from mixtures of the live (and bawdy) and the filmed to, by the late 1950s, only the filmed, with, today, only one film, the feature, rather than a mixture of comedy, news, and animation; from an era of flamboyant entrepreneurs to multinational corporations; from a system of local and regional to national distribution and exhibition; from sale by the foot to rental and now, via video-cassettes, back to sales again; from the national to the international, interspersed with periods of isolationism, trade protectionism.

As a not insignificant aside: avant-garde cinema, like the video visionaries and liberation movements, imagined an international structure, operating across and against national political and cultural barriers, connected by stalwart individuals, travel, films, festivals, and venues of alternative exhibition. This internationalism recapitulated two eras—the twenties (and earlier), when film was argued as a universal language which would unite countries (with intertitles in various languages in release prints), and the late fifties' opening up of the feature-length art cinema market for sound films with subtitles, accompanied by the growth of film societies, particularly around universities, which began to offer film courses. Since the recent cessation of the Cold War, along with the death of the belief in "the revolution," the international has recently become a free zone of rapid deregulation, a vast, open market for the circulation of commercial products and services, unfettered by differences in laws of exchange. McDonald's not Brakhage is what Moscow is waiting for.

Tom, Tom is also film history which concerns the writer's particular viewpoint, based on lost or disintegrating paper or nitrate prints, a history often without a real except an older representation—be it painting or nursery rhyme or film—whose cultural conditions of production and reception have been forgotten and whose historical meanings as political allegories have been lost. History, here, is a modern re-vision and invention; there is no real except another image and hence no need for a camera, only an optical printer, a doubled machine which combines a camera and a projector and whose relay function in creating special effects like dissolves, fades, superimpositions or correcting errors, along with making additional prints, is usually overlooked.

The optical printer makes, shoots, or records one film from another; hence, there is no real except the film image, no outside, no tangible referent, only mechanical reproduction. (There is a certain irony in critics unknowingly repeating films' material conditions of production as negative critiques derived from theory.) This reversed, closed circuit of projection-recording can correct (for television broadcast of cinemascope films which is really a reshooting), reproduce, or radically alter the film. In all three instances, the generation of the film alters, moving away from the "original," which was only a negative in the first place, decaying in some vault if still available. For many filmmakers, it became a critical machine (as it was in Hollywood in the early 1930s, hence all the wipes, calendar pages falling off walls and newspaper headlines' montage), eventually available in university film departments, often built by filmmakers. In *Tom, Tom,* we see as formal parameters what could be errors of printing or disasters of projection, for example, the film slipping through the projector gate, refusing to hold on its spockets, revealing the metric lines between the now twenty-four frames per second. Intermittent motion which yanks the film at regular intervals through the machine, stopping and starting, is discontinuity which only appears to be continuous. Thus, *Tom, Tom* also documents a series of significant, now taken for granted, mechanical inventions by anonymous tinkerers (recently being discovered, named, and credited in the new and empirical film history) which were ingeniously combined to make up the projector and the camera.

Or the film *is* what Comolli argues is repressed, the unseen of printing and processing, and enacts Baudry's analysis of the projector and camera mirroring each other, combined in the optical printer. This film is literally and figuratively what their theories urge us to arduously uncover in our analyses of classical narrative films. I would argue that this film, like many avant-garde films, is theory, informed by history—of technique, of style, of story. If Metz and other writers on the cinematic apparatus had studied avant-garde cinema earlier (or, for example, Buster Keaton's films, although *Sherlock Junior* would have been more than enough for an analysis of film work and dream work, or the conventions of revelation and concealment of the apparatus), the task of theory might have been simpler.

Avant-garde films critiqued the middle-class and economic determinations of commercial cinema (and our theories and their pleasures)—enacting the arguments of Noel Burch regarding the different rather than "primitive" conventions of early cinema, including their address at least for a short time to immigrant and working-class audiences. In one way, the histories of Hollywood and the avant-garde overlap: their mutual desire for respectibility, the sacrosanct imprimatur of the label Art—whether genteel good taste for Hollywood, or radical revelation for avant-garde, secured by authorship. Yet, as *Tom, Tom, the Piper's Son* so perfectly demonstrates, popular culture cannot be so easily separated from art; rather, the division is historical, including an economics of reception. Neither "original"—with Jacobs's disquisitions on origins and their impossibility in film with its layers of generations, reprintings leading *to* a granular materiality and decay of both legibility and image quality—would pack 'em in at the shopping mall multiplex in 1988.

Hollis Framptom's *Critical Mass* stages the domestic violence implicit in language, a dissection of the heterosexual, liberated, countercultural couple, trapped in the everyday of speech and relationships in a "scene" which can never conclude but only ends, arbitrarily.[3] In this implosive film, sound is really off, the amplifier/speaker split from the projection; we realize the physical differences between light waves and sound waves, the incommensurability of acoustic space and visual space. The frame often consists of black leader, but it is not an empty frame. The enigma "where were you," the verbal narrative sought by the woman interrogator, is answered by her partner's refusal to explain: "I can't tell." She tries to extract a story from him, a confession; he asserts privacy; she counters with commitment and intimacy; finally we don't know.

We are held in the position of ecouteurs, overhearing, like listening through the walls of an apartment to domestic quarrels. The sometimes vacant frame plays on our voyeurism as well, but deflects our desire to see as well as to know. Speech is a stammer, a stutter with the body, edited and stylized into a series of gestures, for example, her pointing, accusatory fingers. The squabbling couple, locked in language, is shot against the white backdrop, another version of the screen, only here, with real people in front of it, who are projections for us. Speech consists of circularity, refusal, cliches which cannot halt, words which cannot be retracted, accusations which cannot go anywhere. As Barthes says, this speech of domestic dispute can never conclude, it can only stop. Speech is aggressive—filled with consonants, aspirants, shit, fuck. We can hear the violence Barthes ascribed to speech and domesticity; the words, the repetition, move from banality to aggression. The subjects are literally divided in and by language *as* an irrevocable difference and a power play which includes not speaking, not answering.

As if the image cannot hold up against the assault of the words, it flickers out, then returns, with a series of differences. The film loses sync, body and voice separate—techniques which are catastrophes or errors of projection for the classical film. Finally, the image is taken out, and we hear the entire debate, now in complete sentences. The film ends with the last word, or getting the last word as both a power play and an impossibility.

In Frampton's *Nostalgia*, the dissipation of energy celebrated by Lyotard is enacted literally rather than figuratively by burning a series of photographs, destroying "the represented" as the "libidinal object" and paradoxically re-investing it; each new photograph of a famous artist and friend repeats this process of destruction/investment. The film's structure can be tongue-in-cheekily called dialectically materialist in that a series of conflicts, not merely formal oppositions, precipitate a third entity, a complex, overtonal montage which occurred for Eisenstein during projection: the asynchronous and difficult lag between image (a representation of a representation, a moving, still image) and voice-over (of Michael Snow but presumably of the film's maker), a vertical montage between the represented and the story, between the body and biography, between the past and the present, between expectation and recall or memory.

And, I would argue, the process is neither in vain nor does the film enter the circuit of capital, although these are the film's material concerns. It is also not merely work on the signifier, although it is that, literally; it is not merely the oedipal story of the artist and his work, although it is also that. It is all of these three critiques, which form its substance, taken to parody—and more. *Nostalgia* concerns language, its arbitrariness, the division of the subject, the rift between signifier and signified. It focuses on the sign, on the indexical, iconic, and symbolic aspects of photographic reproduction and its arbitrariness (image legibility is taken by many theorists as a value, a measure of the real as signified, or materialism). *Nostalgia* is a theory of cinema set against both the theory of the signifier and ontology/phenomenology, with ontology and the status of the imaginary signifier paradoxically serving as its ground.

The film's work parallels Barthes's 1971 call for a shift within critical theory. "The problem is not to reveal the (latent) meaning of an utterance . . . of a narrative, but to fissure the very representation of meaning, is not to change or purify the symbols but to challenge the symbolic itself." *Nostalgia* enacts the move away from "the destruction of the (ideological) signified" and performs "the destruction of the sign: 'mythoclasm' is succeeded by a 'semioclasm' which is much more far reaching."[4] Although cataclysmic, *Nostalgia* is a man's world, with women as incidental afterthoughts, desirable aftereffects. Making art is a man's tale, no matter how ruptured or parodic.

An overhead camera records in closeup the gradual burning of a series of photographs placed on a hot plate (like the Socratic dialogue about cooking and art and a challenge to point of view: like writing in *Poetic Justice,* and cooking, we look down at the screen), still images which begin to move and transform, taking on life as they are decomposing or being destroyed by the film's pyrotechnical imperative which shifts us from pleasure to pain (of dissipation along with remembering what that hot burner felt like as a child). The photographs and the voice over by Snow as Frampton the artist recreate a personal history through memory; *Nostalgia* tells a story of art and friendship and fame; at the same time, it is a critique of art criticism, a parody of the arbitrariness of interpretation. Is a picture worth a thousand words? Can words undermine, clarify, redefine the photograph, granting it a context and a politics, as Susan Sontag suggested? The status of description and the veracity of interpretation are up for grabs as the voice over tells personal stories about the photos or far-fetched tales of their subsequent analysis.

In any event, pictures, or representations, with words as their ally, inevitably and randomly lead to narrative, to suspense and mystery, *Nostalgia*'s ending: the voice over encounters an accidental reflection which "inspired such fear and loathing that I will never photograph again. . . . Do you see what I see?" (Owen Land and, later, James Benning allude to this film and scene.) While the still images, like the past, decompose, paradoxically transformed into moving images, there is no presence track, no sound of burning. The voice over, separate, like *Critical Mass,* creates expectations, often colliding with art history, the great names of modern U.S. art, for example, Frank Stella, James Rosenquist, Larry Poons, and Michael Snow; history is equated with story and person but unraveled into postmodernity. The obsession of commercial film, including its clapstick method of recording and complex dubbing and editing in post-production, is maintaining sync by keeping the sound with the image—at all costs. This film splits that imaginary unity, divorces that marriage.

The precious object status of reproducible media and the material fact that film, like photography and video, rapidly decays unless properly preserved, hang in the balance. From Cocteau on, the passage of film through the projector has been seen as a death, the destruction and loss implied by endings, the inability to jump back for a second glance akin to the relentless passage of time. The projector lamp burning a hole in the film (which Land prints in *Wide Angle Saxon*) is a clear danger of film, particularly when film stock was nitrate and when the artist is responsible for replacing damaged and costly prints; if the image doesn't move, it will be destroyed. (Like stop frame analyzers, video has granted us the ability to stop and reverse the image, although we cannot reverse or freeze the sound track; while video can be erased, it does not run the risk of burning.) We reassure ourselves that the prints are burning, not the negatives from which they were made. But where is the original? Whose story of art is this? The spectator is untimed by sound; the passage of the film through the projector and us is asynchronous, a collision of the present with the past on its way to a future which is uncertain.

In "On Some Motifs in Baudelaire," Walter Benjamin quotes Reik: " 'The function of remembrance . . . is the protection of impressions; memory aims at their disintegration. Remembrance is essentially conservative, memory is destructive.' "[5] While the image track records willful destruction of memory, the sound track tries to conserve the past, arranging it in chronological order determined by person or drama, interpreting it, mastering it according to an art historical logic all leading up to a dramatic moment, a finish which serves as an explanation, a cause-effect logic. If, as Benjamin, quoting Proust, writes that "the past is 'somewhere beyond the reach of the intellect, and unmistakably present in some material object' " (158), *Nostalgia* documents a struggle to relinquish *and* preserve the past, the materiality of the photographs, by the intellect, the voice-over which can neither capture nor catch up with history, a loss.

In "Repetition Time," Stephen Heath's "Notes around 'Structuralist/Materialist Films' " hinge on the process of reception, drawing on the writings of Barthes, Lacan, and Metz: "the disunity, the disjunction . . . is exactly, the spectator . . . what the practice addresses is not a spectator as unified subject, timed by a narrative action, making the relations the film makes to be made, coming in the pleasure of the mastery of those relations . . . but . . . a spectating activity, at the limit of any fixed subjectivity . . . dispersed in process, beyond the accommodation of reality and pleasure principles."[6] This experience of disjunction is akin to Lacan's model of being divided in language and Barthes's famous quote about boredom: "jouissance seen from the shores of pleasure." It is difficult to define *Nostalgia*'s process, its passage, its reception, after the fact. Avant-garde might be an affect, an experience of disunity, one which is literally dramatized in Frampton's radical separation of the time of the telling from the content being burned. We watch while history is being parodically eradicated by a match and revised by being incorporated into narrative or wild criticism. However, it is not dissipated: we can watch the film again. (*Tom, Tom, the Piper's Son* works another way—as a radical conservation which might be too long to watch a second time.)

Like Lyotard, Heath invokes *Beyond the Pleasure Principle* (as does Bloom) as a theoretical explication of both the film's formal strategy of duration and repetition *and* the spectator's response, "the production of a certain freedom or randomness of energy, of no one memory," what Heath calls, after Lacan, "the *radical* new" (7). Bloom's deployment of *Beyond the Pleasure Principle*, with death as the literal, set against movement, the figural, is replicated by Lyotard and, to a degree, Heath. Patterns of identification are broken with "no place for the look, ceaselessly displaced . . . anti-voyeuristic" (8). Because voyeurism depends on being safe because distant, without risk of being seen, I partially agree with his assessment; at the same time, the spectatorial look is granted such power, is often so resolutely focused and addressed as to make it almost hypervoyeuristic. For example, in Brakhage's *The Act of Seeing with One's Own Eyes*, the aggressivity of the camera's intrusive action, swooping into crevasses of corpses, darting into skulls while skin is being folded back, almost forces us to see what we don't want to watch. The editing of the film, like the probing camera, repeats the cutting up of the inert bodies in the autopsy room.

Heath elaborates three phases of "the spectator as subject": "preconstruction, construction, and passage." For avant-garde film, he argues that passage is the key: "Passage is the performance of the film, the movement of the spectator making the film, taken up as subject in its process" (9). The work of the film is "the presentation of the process of a film." If passage is central, and if this process does not enter a chain of consumption, is dissipated rather than preserved or consumed, then avant-garde film, like Frampton's burning of the photographs, must always be historical, caught up in the moment and its loss, over time becoming out of sync with the present—*Nostalgia*. (However appropriate this analysis, I would argue that preconstruction, the context of the films, their dialogic engagement with other films, media, theory, and social issues, cannot be fruitfully ignored.) Avant-garde then can only be destructive memory, can only occur in *contextual* moments of struggle and resistance, which the critic or theorist tries to conserve and order, transforming memory into history, remembrance—*Nostalgia*.

For Benjamin, however, history does not need to be dead or over: a dialectical or materialistic analysis might "blast a specific era out of the homogeneous course of history—blasting a specific life out of the era or a specific work out of the lifework [which] is preserved . . . and at the same time cancelled."[7] *Nostalgia* is both a process of preservation and a cancellation. Benjamin's "conception of the present as the 'time of the now' which is shot through with chips of Messianic time" (263), too grand for a short film titled *Nostalgia* rather than *History*, has some relation to Adrienne Rich's call for revision. For her, "entering an old text from a new critical direction" is, for women, "more than a chapter in cultural history."[8] Re-vision can, as Barthes also argued, "change the object itself." Rereading avant-garde films in spite of the Great Art by Great Men hypothesis can produce new readings along with deconstructing mythical tales of Art.

Thus, while the myth of the questing male artist relentlessly circles through avant-garde criticism and certain films, as de Lauretis, I, and countless other critics have argued; and while the films do perform work on the formal attributes of the signifier, as Penley and Bergstrom state; and while avant-garde does enunciate reception as a process, the films themselves, like the theoretical presuppositions, also exist within and engage with the social and the historical. The postmodern avant-garde is art not merely of signifiers but of signifieds, meanings, signs, including the history of cinema as mass culture.

However, not only can history be homogeneous, as Benjamin argues, but criticism as well. Contemporary film theory has gone through a modernist period—with semiotics, for example, as a supertext over and above the referent and context—placing film, a "science of the signifier," on the side of the imaginary, par excellence. We set one theory against another, relegating our cultural objects to incidental or symptomatic status—illustrative or decorative racks on which to hang our theories, which also warred with history. Not surprisingly, this dispute between theoretical signifiers is similar to one interpretation of the vacuity of avant-garde, argued as operating outside the social, meanings which were there but we spoke of other things; our eyes were on the signifier and the apparatus, and we saw manifestations everywhere.

On one hand, this explanation is historical: theory opened up the field of film studies (both marginal enterprises within universities) to particularly literary critics not trained in the discipline. Film History was not a prerequisite. Thus, theories of film could be generated by seeing only a few films cold, as it were. Avant-garde was as openly invitational—history and training were not required and might be hindrances for filmmakers. Anyone could teach cinema. After all, it's only a movie.

In superstructural theory, we either went beneath the object with microscopic scrutiny to reveal deep structures, or we springboarded above it to find subjectivity. In neither instance were our critical objects central. The real scrimmage was over theory. In many ways, postmodern theory focuses on objects, sometimes humble artifacts taken from everyday life, popular culture. After ignoring artifacts for at least a decade, critics are now amazed how cultural objects have changed. Meanwhile, theory has wandered out of the academy and is having fun on television and in journalism. Rather than the earlier scandal of taking mass culture into art, postmodernism sends art and theory into popular culture, a devaluation for intellectuals. Or, perhaps, the focus is on art as popular culture, with the difference being history, genteel good taste, and money.

Perhaps it is not so much the theoretical object which has diversified, multiplied, crossed over borders once imagined as solid and sacrosanct but our theoretical models, no longer locked into oppositions or warring camps. Perhaps it is not so much the art world that has qualitatively altered, or even popular culture, but our theoretical presuppositions. Engel's "law" of the transformation of quantity into qualitative change might be occurring on both fronts; his second formulation that systems contain their opposite is certainly proving itself true, as the radical 1960s became the conservative 1980s, rewriting Marxism in theory and in the world. The postmodern return to cultural objects within contextual sites, including economics and other empiricisms, rather than their received interpretations, can change the object, producing new critical models beyond the stagnation Barthes already calls in 1971 "catechistic declaration." This rhetorical practice hit the United States around ten or more years later and safely lodged in graduate schools, where "a mythological doxa has been created: denunciation, de-mystification (or demythification) has itself become discourse, stock of phrases."[9]

If Barthes is right, and I think he is right on, that the doxa now unmasks myth (and television, for example, David Letterman's funny ripping of General Electric and NBC is a good example of that), routinely unhinging signifier from signified, then it is the sign itself which must be shaken. But in order to shake the sign, we must first see it or hear it. As Barthes cautions us, it is no longer so easy to separate the signifier from the signified, the ideological from the phraseological, because the distinction itself has become mythical: "any student can and does denounce the bourgeois" (166).

Barthes's very short sketch (in my translation, only five pages), "Change the Object Itself," to which I am referring, a revision or addendum to his influential essay on myth, is an uncannily accurate sketch of, or blueprint for, U.S. postmodernism as well as British cultural studies—an interesting cultural divide with postmodernism's writers focusing on art and representation and cultural studies writers starting with popular culture and the audience. If this perception is accurate, the focus on either audience or representation is thus imagined as a political choice and a binary opposition. While theory migrates unmoored from context, in this instance a class-based and differentiated society, Britain, versus U.S. society in which "class" has not been determinant in the same way, we are discovering that intellectual premises and hence enunciation are determined by culture as well as history, that cultural difference indeed matters no matter how many international conferences we attend. (I realize the incongruence of sealing the difference via French theory which I did earlier with Foucault.)

Barthes posits that the future of criticism will involve what he calls idiolectology (fortunately, not an adopted term, reeking of jargon and suggestive of idiocy and a rectal exam), a term somewhat comparable to Bakhtin's dialogic: "rather than myths, it is sociolects which must be today distinguished . . . whose operational concepts would no longer be sign, signifier, signified, and connotation but citation, reference, stereotype" (168). The latter—"citation, reference, stereotype"—reads like a checklist of recently discovered postmodern attributes. "If the alienation of society still demands the demystification of languages (and notably the language of myths) the direction this combat must take is not, is no longer, that of critical decipherment but that of *evaluation*" (168). Was Barthes asking for a return to aesthetics? In 1971? (I must note that feminist theory [not its catechistic derivations as jingles] has always been concerned with evaluation, along with practices of resistance.) In this seismic, 1971 shift of the terrain of theory, in fact not that surprising, Barthes includes "conversation, newspaper articles, advertising images" (169) among our theoretical objects. The problem then and today must be to ask "what are the articulations, the displacements, which make up the mythological tissue of a mass consumer society" (167). The point for Barthes was, however, to change the object itself, to produce a new object, one lodged in the premises of "the mature Marx" (169), the socialist goal of cultural studies in England. In 1989, this hardly seems possible.

I want to jump back even further in time, to 1958, and another context, and look at a film of displaced articulations, appropriately called *A Movie*. As I argued earlier, *Bleu Shut* consists partially of leftovers, recycled, re-edited, reprinted film footage taken from other contexts—one postmodern technique of archival pirating used by avant-garde filmmakers, for example, Land and Anger. *A Movie*, like *Report* (1965), by Bruce Conner, consists entirely of film leader, bootlegged, recycled footage and found sound, materials which Conner reuses in later films. He refers to his scavenged artifacts, what Barthes calls "citations, references, stereotypes," as "lost" objects rather than the "found" objects of the surrealists. *Crossroads* is an elaboration of a short scene in *A Movie*—the Bikini Atoll, nuclear test footage; one spectacular and famous minute is expanded into an entire film through repetition and reprinting. These ordinary or shocking discarded objects, from the banal, like tails out and black leader, to the horrific scenes of recorded catastrophe, like the nuclear test footage, rather than being thrown away or incidental, become the very sustance of his assemblage.

In *A Movie*, Conner brilliantly edits movie chase scenes, sports racing scenes, and disaster footage, including the explosion of the Hindenburg, the collapse of a suspension bridge, and the Bikini Atoll explosion, with shots taken from National Geographic films of bare-breasted "primitives" and African animals shown in so many elementary schools in the 1950s which indoctrinated us with our cultural superiority, necessitating U.S. civilized imperialism. We could see the nakedness of black women as natural because inferior; naked white women, like the intercut shots of Marilyn Monroe, were illicit, sexual, pornographic—one difference between ethnography and pornography being racism. The footage escalates from silly bicycle races to violent and deadly collisions of race cars. Our laughter turns to silence as the film progresses, accumulating meaning and a history of imperialism over race, sex, animals.

A Movie is a history of cinema and technology as catastrophe, including the interruption of narrative pleasure within the film by intercutting titles (critiquing film's history of ownership and art's equation of the artist's name with his work, here a repetitive obsession), black and white leader, and Academy leader—the numbered footage for sync resembling the nuclear countdown. The history of cinema becomes the history of Western culture or the United States—a history of colonial conquest by technology, resolutely linking sex, death, and cinema—questioning our very desire for cinema (a fetishistic, deathly pleasure within the safe, perverted distance of voyeurism, economic superiority, and national boundaries). Cinema and our perverse pleasures are technologies which accompany, document, and restage imperialism as narrative and visual spectacle in, for example, the Western and the U.S. government's nuclear experiments, which were rehearsed, performed, and released as educational/promotional films in the late 1940s and early 1950s. These military films made for the public reassured us that radiation would not harm us if we would take minimal precautions. Film was an instrument of nuclear policy, turning the destruction of the Bikini Atoll, along with the displacement of its "natives," into an aesthetic spectacle, eradicating the islanders just as narrative conventions erase film's conditions of production in the name of illusion or the commodity fetish. An early shot of a submarine periscope rising, its operator catching an illicit glimpse of old footage of a nude Marilyn Monroe, followed by the expulsion of a torpedo, is funny, but sexist. By returning to the submarine later, this time followed by the nuclear explosion, the earlier reading is revised. The fetish is politicized, turned into governmental policy, which is destructive.

The date of this film, 1958, must be remarked; in many ways, it is a landmark of postmodernism, anticipating and exceeding current left debates about mass culture by thirty years. Critically, it raises issues of imperialism, colonialism, and the eradication of cultural difference. *A Movie* partakes of situationist strategies and politics, devastatingly demonstrating DeBord's "society of the spectacle"—the Bikini Atoll explosion turns into beautiful art, a sublime image, eradicating the blowing up of the islander's culture; it links models of simulation with nuclear policy and other theories of catastrophe. In fact, Conner's films, like Warhol's disaster art later, are arts of catastrophe: *Report* is about the coverage of Kennedy's assassination, including the fact that very little was recorded, a catastrophe of vision; *Crossroads* walks a fine line between critique and aesthetizing the Bikini Atoll explosion. The context of *A Movie* is post–World War II, within the terror and disavowal of the cold war and U.S. expansionism argued as defensive containment, which included the development of vast consumer markets; consumption and shopping would assuage our fears of nuclear decimation.

The historical spectator, not so familiar with these emblems of catastrophe which are still fascinating in 1988, and living amid the denial of radiation's effects, the Korean War, the fear of Soviet bomb attacks and the paranoia of McCarthyism and communist conspiracy, must have received this film very differently from the spectator of 1988—the end of the cold war. Conner's use of Monroe anticipates Warhol by several years, as well as her obsessive, worshiped resuscitation in U.S. culture throughout the 1980s as a necrophiliac fetish. Anger anticipated, around the same time, the other cultural leftover from the fifties, now regularly sighted in consumer warehouses—Elvis—as did Warhol, keenly attracted to celebrities of death and drugs. Indeed, fetish objects (including Anger's Rudolph Valentino memorabilia and the sex/death/drugs sensationalism of *Hollywood Babylon*), which Conner's sculptures unsettlingly equated with the ovens of the Holocaust, linking dead, burned babies with nylons and pubic hair, politicize the sexual and link it to power (not the least example is the phallic, mushroom cloud), arguing a history of politics as perversion which is violent and destructive and quite unlike the arguments film theory gives to the various perversions ascribed to the film spectator. This is history clearly marked and critiqued as male, not safe in either the dark of the movie theater or the past tense but always present, immanent, and dangerous.

Amid the beginnings of throwaway culture and legitimate fetishes, Conner recycled old, dead, and illicit objects from mass culture and psychoanalysis, like fur, feathers, lace, and dime-store jewelry. Conner's work is a virtual catalogue of postmodern attributes, including a dystopian prognosis of technology, with cinema as his theoretical and material object. He uses banal objects to reveal the fatality of technology. "The death symbol in Conner's work is always the dead object, and the dead object is always present. . . . Conner's concern would appear to be less with death itself than with the hideous forms death has taken in our times."[10] This is not an internal quest for male identity as the sexual but is work firmly within the social, the political, the historical which includes sexual and racial difference. For Conner, the effects of masculine power are catastrophic.

I want to take this 1950s fetish and culturally exaggerate it. If, as Freud argues, the fetish refers to the moment just before the frightening revelation of sexual difference, is an object invoked to ward off the fear of castration, instantiating denial or disavowal, a specifically male defense, perhaps it can also be invoked historically and collectively; Marilyn and Elvis are the twin emblems. The moment before, the time of difference, might be post–World War II, with the coincident expansion of mass culture and a foreign policy of containment secured by nuclear power, dependent on denial of its dangers and its use in the future—an argument of dissipation rather than conservation. We would develop the bomb and test it but never use it militarily—a policy of squandering which, as a recent television film suggested, Oppenheimer and the military could not stand; thus the atom bomb was dropped on Japan. Nuclear denial—a logic of inversion where offense became defense—and product differentiation and commercial proliferation (a term applied to nuclear proliferation, that U.S. fear)—sameness sold as incremental difference—replaced acknowledgment and difference as argument and logic. We were held, thus, within the beginnings of simulation as positive.

Mass culture is not so much defined in the 1980s as the commodity fetish, although it is that; rather, it is packaging, a series of differentiations, a proliferation of products as choices which, as John Berger argued in the early 1970s in *Ways of Seeing* (along with the polarity of sexual difference, his second argument picked up by Mulvey), conceals the fact that we have few political choices left. A seemingly innocent and funny moment occurs in the compilation film, *Atomic Cafe*: after footage of nuclear tests and politicians defending the bomb, a shopping center magnate urges us to forget our fears by shopping in the newly designed centers (which, as I mentioned earlier, Warhol apparently did with a vengeance, accumulating massive consumer items which were sold, after his death, in an art auction). A politics of difference—including cultural, racial, sexual, political—gives way to a packaging of differentiation, a culture of incremental sameness argued as difference and predicated on disavowal or denial.

Peter Wollen has proposed a model of postmodernism, drawing on film and popular culture in general (albeit remaining within a model of pop art), around the triumvirate of Godard, William Burroughs, and Warhol, and set in the late 1950s.[11] The similar concerns among the three artists are traits or techniques of postmodernism: an emphasis on the vernacular and situationism, including forms of popular culture (rock 'n' roll, B-movies, journalism, news photography) and street and drug subcultures; the use of various media of reproduction, crucially, without qualms, for example, the tape recorder, Polaroid, video/TV, thereby dissolving ontologies and borders, recycling, quoting, and bootlegging from various sources; and their comparable social metaphors of prostitution and/or addiction. Although it is unfortunate that the early critical edifice of postmodernism, no matter who the constructivist or what the viewpoint (from literature and painting, for Huyssen; from film for Wollen with, however, both arguments, including a comparable Marxist emphasis, located within pop art of the early 1960s), was constructed without women, I would add to this archeology at least the work of Conner and Anger.

CHAPTER
6
POSTMODERN TV

Within the great debate over the status of art and philosophy, or beauty and truth, Plato ranked representations—from image, through copy, to simulation, with resemblance as the test of validity. Although Plato's polarity, art and philosophy, has either been eroded or collapsed in contemporary theory, a comparable hierarchy of authenticity can be charted with modern media—from painting, to photography, cinema, and the contemporary illegal alien, the medium without an artistic passport, or better, without demarked material borders, television. In an era of electronic metamorphosis—pointillist image masses of continuous, particle movement, without visible support until televised or material base until taped or printed out—tangible objects are being replaced by labyrinthian circuitry; equally, like physics' unexpected, proliferating particles named leptons, bosons, muons, and neutrinos, the "subject" is multiple and heterogeneous. Thus, mastery—through vision—over tangible objects and manageable subjects is lessening, as are originals, origins, a real, and singular truths—including (in the United States) the hold of unitary, classical, European systems of thought. For many art and literary critics, the anti-Christ has reached Bethlehem.

For intellectuals, illusory pleasure machines—in the twentieth century including vaudeville, cinema, and television—demand reparation, or at least a certain amount of guilt and condemnation, until replaced by another desiring, public machine as the new object of contempt. Preachers harangued vaudeville as a place of moral corruptness until the growth of the nickelodeons, and expressed religious outrage at photoplays. Video game parlors were prophesied as imminent doom, until most folded. At the same time, the contemptible medium provides, without direct acknowledgment, the very definitions of the theory, e.g., certain writings of Foucault in relation to cinema and other profitable machines of the visible; Baudrillard's thesis as predicated on television and other electronic systems; and Freud's, as well as Foucault's, use of terms taken from opics—diffusion, diffraction. More generally, media, with specific modes of production, are turned into metaphor by theories and applied as historical symptom. These arguments follow a rhetorical pattern: a collective (un)conscious is often pessimistically if not catastrophically analyzed as altered by the "new technology" (better defined as a mesh of discursive techniques).

Fashionable and popular critiques of postmodernism can be interpreted as predicated on the reality and features of popular culture, particularly television and other electronic systems. Indeed, "video" (for museums) and television (for intellectuals) portray a virtual catalogue of traits of postmodernism, suggesting that TV serves as premise without acknowledgment. A compilation of postmodern features is in order: stated negatively, historical eclecticism, replication, and simulation; plagiarism and pastiche (rather than parody); bootlegging, recycling, plundering, and raiding the art of the past; nostalgia, ahistoricism, and apoliticism; or, more positively argued, bricolage and assemblage; the denial of dichotomies, bipolarities, and the ontology of media boundaries, including the breakdown of genres and the distinctions between art movements such as pop, op, and kinetic; the blurring of the borders and status, the distinction between art and popular culture, and overturning the rigid divide that separated modernism from mass culture; the vanishing of the utopian belief in the project of modernization, along with the fervid faith in technology. Eptitomizing every blemish or glow, television is the quintessential embodiment (or emblem of decline) of postmodernism's central traits.

As television is the dominant object that is either repressed or disparaged with noble condescension, so too are women, the majority subjects, acknowledged only with great difficulty; in postmodern treatises, feminist critiques, when acknowledged, are at best marginal or Other; in most exegeses or condemnations of postmodernism, they exist beneath the surface, incorporated as argument with neither foot nor love note.

Some critics have been more gallant than others—debonairly inviting feminist theorists and artists, along with other "minority cultures," to join their debates. Andreas Huyssen, an influential explicator of the historical relationship between the avant-garde and postmodernism through the intellectual venue of German philosophy and U.S. art since the 1960s, has critically influenced the current debates through, for example, a special 1981 issue of *New German Critique* on modernism, as well as through his own essays.[1] In "Mapping the Postmodern," which contextualizes German, French, and U.S. arguments, lucidly explicating major premises and posing questions, he writes: "It was especially the art, writing, filmmaking and criticism of women and minority artists . . . which added a whole new dimension to the critique of high modernism and to the emergence of alternative forms of culture."[2] Like Craig Owens in his widely read essay, "The Discourse of Others: Feminists and Postmodernism,"[3] Huyssen agrees "that women's art, literature and criticism are an important part of the postmodern culture of the 1970s and 1980s."[4] These comments acknowledge women's avant-garde and postmodern practices, while attributing effect to feminist critiques of modernism—the quest for ontology, the centrality of the author/genius, the uniqueness of the precious object of art, and the sacred distinction between art and popular culture. The essay does not, however, mention feminist work on representation of women in forms of popular culture—not a slight oversight. As forthright and flattering as Huyssen's statements are, feminism remains peripheral, outside, although holding an engraved invitation.[5] However, it is apparent that Huyssen is politically committed to crediting feminist practices with significantly altering our culture; he wants answers from feminist discourses and writes: "In light of these developments it is somewhat baffling that feminist criticism has so far largely stayed away from the postmodernism debate which is considered not to be pertinent to feminist concerns. . . ."[6] Given postmodern criticism's appropriation/avoidance of feminism and its doomsday terror of mass media—resulting in some form of disparagement of postmodern art—feminists are equally baffled; the territory of postmodernism is so familiar and alien, at the same time. Feminism has already been spoken for without an official announcement of the betrothal. Thus, accepting an invitation to this fraternity dance is intellectually difficult. However, because Huyssen's sagacious, comprehensive essay has significantly influenced me, I will try to articulate our mutual—and different—bewilderment.

One text manifesting symptoms of male "mass" hysteria is the influential *The Anti-Aesthetic: Essays on Postmodern Culture*.[7] While the fascinating collection of essays importantly illuminates many contemporary positions across wide-ranging and difficult terrain, the blatant absence of feminist issues and writing, with the exception of Craig Owens's essay, proclaims an exclusive politics—as well as inscribing a blind, male figure of postmodernism (the Colonus stage of Oedipus's tragedy). Hal Foster's introduction, which lucidly clarifies and defines the contemporary debate while perhaps excluding feminism, evokes a substantial reservation. Foster's two politics of postmodernism—one of resistance, "which seeks to deconstruct modernism and resist the status quo and a postmodernism which repudiates the former to celebrate the latter,"[8] one of reaction—which are so clear on first glance, are disconcerting on second thought. Without celebrating the status quo, feminist discourses contradict, lodge "in between," these two politics by deconstructing *and* repudiating "modernism," which, after all, had reserved few places for women other than nurturing mother or muse.

While acknowledging feminist critiques of modernism and mass culture, the major dilemma of Craig Owens's essay stems from using Lacanian psychoanalysis—a system which denies women's desire, among other things—as a logical or even radical basis *for* a feminist argument rather than as part or symptom of women's historical situation. This might explain why and how Owens, like Lacan, can ignore the issue of women's desire by locating it simply within (negatively, to be sure) a masculine imposture. In forgetting, like Lacan, that women are not merely male surrogates or masquerades but historical subjects with real experiences, knowledges, and histories, Owens is able to use feminism as an object of investigation existing in relation to male rather than female subjectivity, as the estranged Other of his title. At the same time, Owens places feminism centrally within postmodernism, quotes feminist theory, endorses feminist work, and analyzes feminist writing and art as intersecting practices of theory and politics. He finds in French theory what has attracted feminists (and what repels postmodern theory predicated on German philosophy, including Huyssen, which mourns the loss of narrative and history, including personal stories of authors, thereby asking for a return to modernism, if not realism). As Alice Jardine said during a Milwaukee presentation: "What most critics of 'French Theory' do not or will not deal with are the connections made possible by radical psychoanalytic theory among the libidinal, political, and capital economies. Possibly because these connections make gender and sexual difference intrinsic to all of these systems and all of their discourses, especially those of capitalism. . . ."[9] I am not sure whether things French are quite so sweepingly rosy; yet Owens grasps this affinity and refuses the current, postmodern assault on, for example, the work of Barthes and Foucault.[10]

Equally, it is difficult to imagine the subtitled "postmodern culture" as a culture which excludes mass culture, particularly television or video, except by inference or negative example. In his essay in *The Anti-Aesthetic,* Edward Said refers, in the name of John Berger, to "television, news photography, and commercial film" as visual aids "all of them fundamentally immediate, 'objective,' and ahistorical."[11] While television is marginal in Said's impassioned polemic against academia which calls for interference, "crossing of borders and obstacles,"[12] and stands against elitist, academic specialization (and presumably the polarity art and popular culture), women are resolutely absent, not mentioned even if feminism seems to be a glaringly obvious argument. For example, Said states that one negative function of the humanities is "to conceal the hierarchy of powers that occupy the center, define the social terrain. . . ."[13] Clearly, the revelation of hierarchies of power has been a goal of virtually every feminist discourse.

For two other critics, Baudrillard and Fredric Jameson, television and feminism (in a double popular culture whammy) are the barbarians, imagined to be securely outside the artistic and academic gates, yet threatening or known to be trashing from within, signaling yet another decline of contemporary society. Ensnared in pessimism, these writers are anxiously worried. For Baudrillard, whose writings are teasingly attractive, on first glance, to theorists of mass media, the cultural forecast is catastrophically bleak. While his metaphors are nuclear, astronomic, and electronic, finally his position is politically implosive. Beneath the surface, his work suggests a close allegiance with the Frankfurt School's premises of decline through the mass culture industry (without, however, their careful, illuminating, textual analyses). In his assessment, there is no longer a staging of scenes, no spectacle, no mirror, no image or representation, all "effaced in a sort of an obscenity. . . . The obscene puts an end to every representation."[14] (I wonder how?) The contemporary subject in his unrelieved meaninglessness is not hysterical, paranoid, but schizophrenic. Among other things, Baudrillard's "obscene" is the present, which in history becomes scene/seen; yet his longed-for past is a nostalgic one of (pre)realism and denotative correspondence. Meaghan Morris's playful analysis in the Australian collection *Seduced and Abandoned* is ironic and acute: "This is not, after all, a modernist credo for a purely self-reflexive and 'non-referential' theory, and still less a post-modern conceit of scavenging; it is a claim that a discourse might be adequate to its world—it is . . . a realist claim. . . ."[15] Operating outside history, Baudrillard's interpretation leads to a numbing powerlessness; in the name of inclusion, his system, like Lacan's banishment of history and the denigration of the Imaginary, excludes us. As Morris suggests in a clever linkage: "Yet we may . . . wonder whether the fascination of television enthusiasts for Baudrillard is not like that of feminists for Lacan. The great seducer, says Baudrillard, is the one who knows how to capture and to immolate the desire of the other."[16]

Beneath the seductive, benevolent, yet acute pessimism is the terror of profane, popular culture, outside the preserves and premises of the Sacred Museum of Art. The mundane museum of dead styles is historical—earlier, a movie theater, currently, television, both brothels of disembodied images, both transient, nomadic, illusory objects without proper and tangible artistic passports. Behind the scenes, film theory has always suspected this. Forlornly, in the same collection, Jameson intones cultural stagnation: "all that is left is to imitate dead styles, to speak through the masks and with the voices of the styles in the imaginary museum."[17] Of course, crucial is the concept of life, not art, lived in a museum—the imaginary restaged as false history in a perpetual present. In this cultural mausoleum of dead styles, while Baudrillard gives the last rites to realism, Jameson eulogizes modernism. As divergent as their political positions might be, both long for Art or originals—for truth and mastery, when men were men and art was art—reminiscent of Walter Benjamin's "aura" and grandmother's gift-giving in *Remembrance of Things Past:* "She would have liked me to have in my room photographs of ancient buildings. . . . But at the moment of buying them . . . she would find that vulgarity and utility had too prominent a part in them, through the mechanical nature of their reproduction by photography. She attempted by a subterfuge, if not to eliminate altogether this commercial banality, at least to minimise it, to supplant it to a certain extent with what was art still, to introduce, as it were, several 'thicknesses' of art. . . ."[18] Perhaps one postmodern subterfuge, at least Baudrillard's, is to "introduce, as it were, several 'thicknesses' " of theory. The passing of a culture of precious, unique, tangible, man-made objects and the autonomy of the sanctioned institution of Art are mourned with the remembrance of things past.

One way of representing the decline into vapid popular culture is to feminize it, as Tania Modleski has argued;[19] another is to decry popular culture's absent (in postmodernism through acceleration and simulation) discourses of history, just as women have been denied history and consequently are represented as ahistorical, as eternal mother/muse, virgin/whore. In "Postmodernism and Consumer Society," Jameson does both, after delineating two features of postmodernism—pastiche and schizophrenia, "the transformation of reality into images, the fragmentation of time into a series of perpetual presents."[20] Both traits could describe either commercial television or strategies applied to women—the representational conventions of fragmenting the female body and transforming woman into image, the perfect, fetishized whole, have been extensively deconstructed by feminist critiques. Surely Jameson must suspect the source of both his analysis and his depression—mass media, particularly television, and feminism. Following in the footsteps of Foucault, who equated women with patients and children, and Freud's investigation of female hysteria, the grand, scholastic finale is to perform a psychoanalytic diagnosis and assign a label—in this postmodern case, like Baudrillard, *schizophrenia*. Unlike Freud, however, Jameson avoids naming his real problem, indeed refuses, except indirectly, the word: *woman*—the stumbling block of language for so many modern male theorists. As modernism was so fascinated by woman, so does feminism intrigue postmodernism.

Thus it is not surprising (although encountering *any* reference to women as subjects, let alone female subjectivity, by men is *always* startling) that after invoking a historical male cast of modern/heroic writers and filmmakers, and neutral, plural pronouns, suddenly a slash appears in Jameson's discussion of the postmodern subject as a schizophrenic, a pronoun divided, in drag, a transvestite "he or she." Although "he" is munificently included, a close reading suggests that the actual postmodern schizophrenic is either female or masquerading as a woman. Because I recognize myself in this postmodern subject, I will, as women are wont to do, interrupt Jameson's treatise: "But since the schizophrenic does not know language articulation in that way, [Lacan's positioning women as other, outside language, the symbolic, the law of the father; 'that way' as the language of proper discursive power which excludes and hierarchizes] he or she does not have our [a neutral pronoun which presumes but does not include me] experience of temporal continuity either, but is condemned to live a perpetual present [the effects of eradicating women from official histories and places of power] with which the various moments of his or her past have little connection [linear, cause-effect chronological history, as Hayden White suggests, is yet another way narrativity overpowers and hierarchizes us] and for which there is no conceivable future on the horizon. In other words, schizophrenic experience is an experience of isolated, disconnected, discontinuous material signifiers which fail to link up into a coherent sequence [as good a description for strategies of representation of women within Western art as I've encountered; equally an apt description of women's consigned, fragmented, discontinuous domestic existences]. The schizophrenic thus does not know personal identity in our sense [that of the unified, male, individual, genius ego], since our [whose?] feeling of identity depends on our [yours!] sense of the persistence of the 'I' and the 'me' over time."[21] Women have been speaking in the first person, rarely and recently, usually with awkwardness.

While Jameson's *our* tries to include me, finally it excludes me; paradoxically, he has written an apt summary of feminist critiques of representation of women and perhaps even described women's daily domestic lives. His analysis is then applied to television which, like the bisexual postmodern subject, is historically, intellectually, or metaphorically ill. "The media" involve "the disappearance of a sense of history, the way in which our entire contemporary social system has little by little begun to lose its capacity to retain its own past, has begun to live in a perpetual present and in a perpetual change that obliterates traditions. . . . Think only of the media exhaustion of news . . . to relegate such recent historical experiences as rapidly as possible into the past."[22] (Women have been the objects of historical, aesthetic amnesia for centuries; now, in this bleak prognosis, as schizophrenics, outside history, like television or mass culture, they will be postmodern subjects—yet another double bind.) As tantalizing as his pessimistic analysis is (particularly significant as a Marxist reading *for* history, marked within periods of capitalism), it is a peculiarly deaf assessment of contemporary feminist debates argued from vantage points other than white male narratives.[23]

While much postmodern theory is constructing its object by trashing commercial television, ignoring video with nary a glance, and defining its subject as singularly male (both strategies involving a reclamation of mastery), many video artists are mapping out their own postmodernism, including a critique of contemporary media culture as/and politics significantly at variance with, or in advance of, the literary version which ignores them. At issue is the relationship of institutions of art, mass media, and academia; at stake are theories of subjectivity (including sexual difference) and reception, strategies of narrative and representation (the very status of the image, its relationship to sound), delineations of history, and questions of address and audience. Whether inadvertently or not, certain video works exist simultaneously as theory and criticism of literary theory (with which, in an ironic reversal of the way the scholar examines art tradition, many artists are familiar).

For example, while the delineation of the simulacrum in the writings of Baudrillard masquerades as a celebration of the "masses," it decries illusion, the preoedipal hold of the Imaginary. Certain TV or video artists—including the extensive range of work by feminist artists on female subjectivity, but including work that does not directly address feminism, e.g., William Wegman and Michael Smith—star the paradox, trying to outmaneuver mastery via the imaginary, thereby positing different versions of the masculine "theory of the subject." This frequently parodic work critiques power/surveillance by restaging it as simulation—a confusion of the levels of representation which challenges both the notion of the art object as autonomous and the sacredly entrenched institutions of art and academia.[24]

William Wegman's one-shot scenes, produced between 1970 and 1977, have a complex concern: the dissembling of mastery (including the hold of sound/image synchronization over the spectator/auditor) through performed

schizophrenia—funneled through elegantly witty parodies of the doubled institutions of academia and art. These vaudeville simulations of pedagogy, art
historical or psychoanalytic burlesque, undermine institutions of authority.
Wegman is the schizophrenic as stand-up comedian; he is, as in Freud's
joke, "a double-dealing rascal . . . (the Janus-like, two-way-facing character
of jokes). . . ."[25] Wegman is his own straight man, in conversations with
himself or with his dog, Man Ray, as performer/viewer/student in elisions of
pedadogy, commercials, and "art." Our position as spectator/auditor is unstable yet essential, resembling another interpretation of the simulacrum,
one which is not pessimistic, and one which will be familiar to artists and
feminists, suggesting its derivation—of course, without ackowledgment.

As I argued earlier regarding Owen Land's films and *Eternal Frame*, in
"Plato and the Simulacrum," Deleuze's refreshingly postmodern reading,
the simulacrum has an anarchistic function well suited to this comedian: it
bypasses mastery because it already includes the angle of the observer. (In
this regard, the simulacrum resembles the joke which necessitates a third
person listener.) In his minimal, quiet studio—almost a vacuum without the
ever-noisier presence track of television—Wegman usually performs alone,
with only a man's best friend—his art historical dog, Man Ray. Briefly the
set-up: a stationary, unmanned camera, a closed-circuit monitor, usually
one shot takes, and no editing. Wegman's gaze and address are not direct,
but at a mediating, off-frame monitor—his unblinking audience, cohort and
mirror—enabling him to manipulate the image by, for example, syncing
his voice with his body, altering the sound sources of his body, and by
entering and leaving its field of vision. The audience is not imperatively
addressed; enunciation, including its humorous collisions with the
enounced, is deflected away from authoritative commands into a lesser
form, description (according to classical rhetoric's hierarchy) or anecdotal
conversation. Because we complete the circuit of the joking process by traversing his leaps of metaphor, we slip into the unconscious with Wegman
who might be parodying the conceits of body art as his stomach sings a duo;
or performing a TV commercial via a Bauhaus/art school discourse with an
exercise/vibrating chair—transforming objects by layering the discourses in
the intricate process. As Barthes so elegantly suggests: "and if these emblems are perfect, it is ultimately because they are comic, laughter being
what, by a last reversal, releases demonstration from its demonstrative at-
tribute. What liberates metaphor, symbol, emblem from poetic mania, what
manifests its power of subversion, is the preposterous. . . . The logial future
of metaphor would therefore be the gag."[26] Wegman's work is a logical future (Barthes was speaking about the Marx Brothers films); the art history/
academia gag is a critique and a resistance to the outlandish promises of
commerce through art.

The enunciation, the point of address of other scenes, the "Hey, you, I
want you to hear something," leads to a conversation, a dialogue with self,
with body. "The pleasure of the text is that moment when my body pursues

its own ideas—for my body does not have the same ideas I do."[27] Just as the gaze is deflected through the monitor, or by eliminating eyes and altering the lips as source, or by using objects to replace the human figure, so is the source of the voice derailed, as we become both analyst and analysand. In *Rage and Depression*, Wegman, sitting on a chair, legs crossed, manically smiling, recites to the off-frame monitor/confessor/auditor/analyst: "So what am I gonna do. I had these terrible fits of rage and depression all the time . . . finally my parents had me committed. . . . They tried all kinds of therapy. Finally they settled on shock, and the doctors brought me into this room in a straight-jacket. I still had this terrible, terrible temper. I was just the meanest cuss. And then, when they put this cold, metal electrode to my chest, I started to giggle. And then when they shocked me, it froze my face into this smile, and even though I'm incredibly depressed, everybody thinks I'm happy. I don't know what I'm going to do." Wegman then stands and exits while the tape ends as abruptly as it began. In a later, color tape, this schizophrenic returns; in an extreme close-up, only the grinning mouth remains: "Hi! Do you remember me, from a long time ago?" By changing the shape of his mouth and without a cut, Wegman answers his own salutation: "You look familiar." Then the two yous—what about us?—discuss the pleasure of going to bad movies. Unabashedly, Wegman talks to himself. In another tape, a close-up of his face wearing Ernie Kovacs as Percy Dovetonsils cross-eyed glasses engages in another cock-eyed dialogue regarding the respective merits of playing horseshoes or baseball.

At the same time that the body and voice are divided or fragmented, so is image split from sound or meaning. For example, the image of Wegman on the hard, industrial relaxing chair denies the pleasurable promises of his sales pitch of sinuous, relaxing vibrations created by rhythmically striking the chair with a lead pipe. In *Man Ray, May Ray* (1981), with additional performers and longer than his earlier works, Russell O'Connor's cause-effect narrative of the life of Man Ray, "human artist," is intertwined with images of Man Ray, dog artist, or artist's model. The seriousness of visual documents as support for scholarship's precious discourse is undercut by the "truth" of the image as the tape intercuts old yearbook pictures, irrelevant newspaper photographs, and scenes of the romping dog. In other pieces, the conventions of sync are the source of comedy as we see Wegmen playing Man Ray's nose or, in another tape while watching the bystanding monitor and grimacing, Wegman syncs up his facial expressions with Man Ray's growling beneath the frame. When he (or man and beast) gets in sync, the tape ends. Source, enunciation, address, the status of being a human or an object, and our positioning within the sound-image complex—usually an authoritative place of synchronized, transparent legibility—are Wegman's seriously comic concerns.

Wegman's work dissects art history genres, movements, and discourses, mixing languages of commerce with art, leveling dichotomies including sound and image, human and nonhuman, and exposing the artificiality *and* seriousness of artistic gestures, as well as displacing the centrality of the revered notion of artist. Jean Francois Lyotard described experimentation: "With satire, however, you have free rein . . . you can turn pedagogical, dissertational, narrative, conversational, lyrical, epic. . . . In satire, genres are mixed because the persons speaking are varied. . . ." Lyotard argues for and celebrates the reversibility of satire, "of what is visible with what sees, of what can be said with what speaks."[28] (This assessment resembles Deleuze's model of the simulacrum, incorporating the angle of the observer within it.) Paradoxically, by being both subject and object of his work, Wegman reveals, simultaneously, originality and the stereotypical gestures involved in "being an artist," a "dog/star/man's" life. With or without knowledge of body, conceptual, minimal, or performance art, we can "get" Wegman's accessible art on several levels. Man Ray can be "read" as dog or human stand-in, as art performance or vaudeville dog act. Like Wegman, Man Ray is both subject and object, both artist and performer, both deflected source of the gaze (in the spelling lesson when, by admonition, he had mispelled *beach* as *beech*) and object of Wegman's gaze in, particularly, the Polaroid photographs. Miniature dog narratives are predicated on "looking," parodying the "truth of vision" and the status of the real and important. (Deleuze and Guattari's concept of "becoming animal" is literally embodied in Wegman's photographs and videotapes, particularly his parody of portraiture and conceptual art, with Man Ray a historical still subject or performance artist. Man Ray is both the "libidinal object" and the maker's alter ego—truly an artist's best friend.)

The structure of jokes as miniature narratives, through time, with a reciprocal relation between image and enunciation and its effect upon the spectator resembles the structure and process of Wegman's work. Freud locates the joke's work and its sources of pleasure in relation to (1) the technique (an envelope, a container—in Wegman, TV conventions and Art History discourses); (2) the play of words and sounds; and (3) the lifting of inhibitions— in a join, or a brief, mutual, disparately timed slippage into the unconscious, between the first person maker and the third person listener. Jokes work by "consciously giving free play to unconscious modes of thought" which have, through acculturation, been rejected as faulty. The joke is a *process* and is temporal in its passage, finally dependent on intelligibility. Jokes have both a retroactive and an anticipatory narrative movement in time. Thus, the process depends on telling. "The psychical process of constructing a joke seems not to be completed when the joke occurs." The need to tell is connected with the laughter produced; and thus, the critical function of laughter from the third person, absent from the event, is performed by the spectator/auditor who "laughs his quota off." Pleasure paid for with laughter signals the joke's completion.[29] Thus, unlike (or in spite of) both the structures of narcissism usually connected with the solo video performer interacting with self-image and commercial television's declaration of "live" audiences and use of laugh tracks to signal completion, Wegman's work is open ended, inclusive of the audience. We complete the tapes at other times, in other places, posing a central concern of contemporary theories of subjectivity: reception, within historical moments and local contexts, within mixed discourses of "art" and "mass culture."

These gentle, comic performances of theory enact Barthes's dictum: the work produces "in me, the best pleasure if it manages to make itself heard indirectly."[30] Wegman's wit has a marvelous indirectness, a brief, clever circumlocution of reversal, with a sharp aim and target, illustrating that pleasure and knowledge need not involve mastery: "The pleasure of the text is not necessarily of a triumphant, heroic, muscular type. No need to throw out one's chest."[31] And, in another pasage: "Far too much heroism in our languages . . . muscular, phallic. . . . The pleasure of the text . . . is on the contrary like a sudden obliteration of the warrior *value*."[32]

The context of Wegman's work can be traced from U.S. art history discourses of the late 1960s—pop, op, minimalism, body, and conceptual art—a time when labeling according to stylistic difference was almost obsessive, as if to postpone the inevitable dissolution of genres and hierarchies, including the polarity between Art and Popular Culture. Equally challenged was the determining centrality of the singular, serious, heroic "artist" as both enigma and answer. Michael Smith's 1980s performance/installation work (taken into video) is emblemmatic of the critical changes between the 1960s and 1970s. Performance (which is historical, e.g., happenings, Italian futurism, etc.) is an amalgam which disrespects ontologies, divisions, borders, and precious objects whether in media, academic disciplines, or traditional notions of "professionalism" and career; unlike theater, the artist is both inside and outside the work.

While Wegman also draws on a tradition of performance, the critical difference between the work of Smith and Wegman emerges in the use of, or generational relationship to, commercial television genres. In his 1970s tapes, Wegman operates within the sixty-second partitioning of commercial timing—a narrative/structural, one-liner span used in the black-outs and sound/image play of Ernie Kovacs, involving the mixture of genres comparable to 1950s "vaudeo." A decade later, with direct quotation/critique of 1950s and 1960s television programs, Smith's tapes resemble the more sustained, repetitive, continuing character format of sketch or situation comedy. "I have such a hard time putting a story together that I thought a good solution would be to use the same story over and over and do different things within it."[33] Like situation comedy and sketches, Smith's work is edited to include reaction shots, scene changes, and intertitles, with elaborate props which are condensed and displaced in his dream logic, TV nightmares, confusing or conflating the real with the imaginary, turning television into a friendly or frightening companion/simulation. Smith's segmented, chronological, cause-effect narratives of the unpopular, uncool bachelor Mike are serious critiques of, among other things, television reception and commercials' fantasy scenarios.

In *Secret Horror*, a 1980 performance tape, narrated in the beginning by a voice-over, the sleeping Mike is awakened by a scream/a dream of a falling (art historical) grid ceiling. Obsessed by laundry, the high drama of ironing (replete with all the dream mechanisms) and other domestic travails, and edited with a Hitchcock parody of ringing telephones and knocks on the door, the protagonist is caught by popular culture—trapped in the nightmare of a hyped quiz show, taken with troubling anxiety in his underwear to a ghostly come-as-you-are party—in a life scored by irritating, cheery, constant muzak. This drama of the home TV viewer in his boxer shorts and T-shirt depicts the postmodern male subject: fraught with anxiety, obsessed with bridge mix and other small pleasures, imperiled by a lack of social skills, he is a comic clown of inept loneliness. The Ghosts, a condensation/displacement of his laundry and the ghostly presence of TV, pursue and torment him until the end when, dressed in his 1960s "fashionable" blue jean outfit (designed by Kenneth, as the end credits inform us) and large "Mike" belt buckle, Mike dances alone to a popular song, "Forever in Blue Jeans." Mike is in tune with television but out of step with sociability. He is always an imitative chorus, pantomiming mass culture's scream for popularity through sex and fashion. Via his direct looks at the camera, bewildered, eyebrow-raising reactions to the off-frame intrusion of dictates, his plight is comic and sad. Alone, Mike imitates fashion and waits for life—the version of controlled and cool masculinity promised and proclaimed by television.

Down in the Rec Room (1981) is another performance of anxiety-laden male adult adolescence and its terrors. In this tape, Mike is the party-giver; no one attends. After preparation and performance—including a perfectly synced pantomine of Donny dancing with Marie in which Mike, at one point, leans on his partner, the television set as another dancer—and inspired by the voice-over exhortation of a children's song, "Make Believe" (an earlier, childish version of disavowal but no less accurate an assessment of subject mechanisms), the concept of TV as a collective ritual and as a friendly companion is poignantly challenged. The tape has two voices, a voice/over and a voice/on: his inner monologue, to which he reacts with amazed, double-take looks at us; and the confident voice of knowledge, the paternal assurance that "make believe" will make everything OK. Mike responds with first eagerly compliant then disbelieving reaction shots to this voice. However, just when he is about to quit, to stop pretending, the record cuts in: "But there's one thing you must do. . . . You must be sure that you believe or nothing will come true." After this warning, Mike continues to play the game of simulation with incredulity but resigned determination. This Mr. Rogers version of belief in imaginary friends is evangelistic if not propagandistic. TV as the imaginary arbiter and teacher of socialization is severely questioned; the tape concludes with "I didn't invite *them*" as a record invokes storybook figures, including Santa Claus. Thus, popular culture becomes estranged as imaginary Other. We are defamiliarized as the everyday is made strange and vaguely threatening. "Make believe" is as risky, isolating, and bewildering as the psychoanalytic mechanism of disavowal and theater's suspension of disbelief.

Mike's voice is separated from his body in a version of inner speech or a dialogue between the inadequate, lonely ego and the superego—a private conversation to which we are invited ecouteurs. Smith's work makes us aware of the profound isolation of the contemporary individual and the television viewer, caught in the imaginary of communication. Conversely, television might not be merely a culprit, a false and trivial ego ideal of glitter in Donny and Marie, but the only friend, with "let's pretend" the only solace and escape. Mike has no one to talk with except television and us, watching him on television. Like all clowns, the character is caricature, knowable and lovable (sometimes adorable) in the tradition of Chaplin's tramp rather than Keaton's acrobatic lover/bumbler. Like most of us, Mike is an amateur, trying to disguise his acute "self-consciousness" with the latest fashion—in this case the styles of 1960s television—in reruns and thus out of history and out of style. This notion of media as obliterating history, causing us to experience an accelerating present tense, describes nostalgia and Jameson's schizophrenic subject. Yet, Mike—a postmodern male inscribed in the imaginary, outside power's domains—is also a challenge to traditional systems of dominance and power, including those master narratives and reassuring male voices of childhood.

Smith's work resembles Freud's definition of the comic, a two-person operation dependent on the memory of childhood dilemmas, involving a process with the audience different from Wegman's three-way "joke." Smith's work denies commercial TV's declaration of participation and inclusion while simultaneously promoting our identification with Mike; Wegman's videotapes demonstrate reciprocity while defraying identification which is only possible with a dog or a schizophrenic. Yet, in uncanny ways, the similarities are more intriguing than the differences: the creation of below average, lonely, sometimes weird guys, out of sync with fashion, popularity, barely able to manage daily life, with TV as their collaborator; the use of self-dialogue and the separation (or doubling) of voice from body; but most importantly, the gentle, resistant comedy as critique of mastery, constructed on the premises of postmodernism—simulation, the schizophrenic subject, and dissolving the divide between art and popular culture. Both artists refer back to the history of commercial television—which has had scant respect for sustained great narratives and complex character psychology, preferring instead comedy and "variety," the performative codes—and art. Like power and mastery, both commercial television and modern art are scrutinized. "When I learned how to juggle, I looked at the end of the book and saw a picture of this guy juggling a tennis racket, a garbage can, and a chain. I wanted to be able to do that, but I realized it would take a really long time."[34]

Recuperation is, however, the risk of parodying television—historically a medium of parody, particularly of itself, from "I Love Lucy," to Jay Leno's critiques of popular culture, particularly television commercials. For forty years, television has been the domain of situation comedy, with its own quite brilliant classical set of conventions which privilege performance over narrative, a form which incorporates audiences within the enunciation. I don't think performance art is equivalent to playing a second banana on a situation comedy. Yet, if that were the case, then the "Bob Newhart Show," with its parody of Michael, an hysterical male yuppie with his blonde bimbo mate, Steffie, to say nothing of its parody of local television talk shows, would rank as the best art. For a generation raised on television, coming to terms with television is not the same thing as taking television on its own terms, which appears to be the postmodern case. I hope this is not the future of the character, "Mike."

I want to conclude with a rigged comparison between what is called video art and feminist video, or Martha Rosler versus Nam June Paik. This setup illustrates the countercultural preference for biology/technology, distinguished in their thought from philosophy/ideology. Paik and Rosler sit on opposite sides of this intellectual rift. The work of Paik, linked to/derived from the historical avant-garde, conceptual art, and the Fluxus movement, presages both Baudrillard's writing on simulation and 1980s exegeses of postmodernism, although paradoxically his collaborators are known as modernists. The dance of Merce Cunningham, the cello performance pieces of Charlotte Mormon, and the music of John Cage, along with Japanese television commercials and various New York scenes, are starred and recycled in his early tapes. The pastiche combines performance art like the smashing of pianos, or Cage's performance in Harvard Square, with journalism, on the street interviews with passersby.

The Selling of New York (1972) consists of tapes broadcast on late-night TV in New York, with sections recycled in 1975 and revised in 1977. An art critic, Russell O'Conner, imperiously, monotonously intones ponderous sociologies, among them the statistical efficiency of the New York City police force compared with that of the force in Missoula, Montana. A woman in a beauty parlor chair angrily talks back to this authoritarian, boring voice, now on television. In one context O'Conner is an art critic; in another the voice of any authority, whether selling art, scholarship, or detergent. He is not a voice-off except metaphorically, but on, Foucault's "speaking eye," a truncated body of incessant, insistent speaking lips.

Paik undoes Barthes's insistence that power operates through language: "The object in which power is inscribed for all of human eternity is language . . . language is legislation, speech is its code . . . to speak . . . is not, as is too often repeated, to communicate; it is to subjugate."[35] Paik unmakes the decorum and pretense of language's ruling discourses. The infuriating talking head appears on a peepshow screen at a porno parlor. A woman taking a bath shouts at the unavoidable, irritating set. Finally a masked cat burglar enters a bedroom, unplugs the oblivious but noisy TV set and steals it. Blessed silence occurs through theft, a simulation of a crime which is pleasurable rather than dangerous.

The imperative male voice-over of information and statistics is undercut by a cynical audience, which ignores it or turns it off. TV is a constant selling but one which perhaps audiences don't buy. TV is depicted as an ensemble of scenes and a conflation of genres and media, rapidly edited. Paik's depiction of the "masses'" resistance and refusal might be comparable to Baudrillard's; yet Paik's conception of audiences is joyous and dynamic—they take action, they talk back, they are not fooled by simulation or information.

Paik's sculptures or video installations, with their metaphorical titles, provide another treatise on watching TV, illustrating a paradox: the video sculptures are displayed in galleries and museums as public, discrete events of individual viewing. These works dramatize that TV, rather than being a monolith or a singular machine, can be anything, given context. The titles redefine the function of television—a variety of interpretations: *TV Chair, TV Bed, TV Cello, Video Fish,* and *Moon Is the Oldest TV.*

Video Fish (1975), a many-monitor installation, conflates the real with the simulation. Aquaria filled with fish are placed in front of TV sets with images of fish in aquaria: TV is an illuminated fish bowl, a fish bowl is TV, TV can be an image of a fish bowl, or an appearance of fish. It suggests the sense of random movement, slithery traces; the public aquaria where we go to watch fish swim; the use of water rather than air as the medium for the image; Jacques Cousteau and Lloyd Bridges.

TV Garden consists of color monitors on their back, screens up, amid green plants. Given the context and title, the colors and images on the monitors become representations of light or flora. The sets appear to waver as the images reverse direction like flowers in the missing breeze. The status of the monitor (an officious word of discipline and surveillance) as an object is transitory; it can be altered; it is not merely a piece of furniture but can be transformed into a cross, a cello, a penis, brassiere cups, or a fish bowl. Nothing is precious; things exist to be redefined, deformed, recycled. As Baudrillard writes, "Reciprocity comes into being through the destruction of mediums. . . ."[36] TV as a machine of bland banalities and consumption can be transformed into a medium of reciprocity—Paik's dream of video as participatory TV, with an international, live satellite broadcast in the 1980s. Paik's image-making machines unmake and reconstitute TV, which he knows is profoundly reliant on and defined by sound as much as image.

TV Chair, TV Buddha, and *Moon Is the Oldest TV* also address the watching of TV. (We rarely watch—another term for surveillance—TV contemplatively at home; ironically, this is what we do in galleries and museums.) In *TV Chair,* the spectator can look through the open "chair" at the monitor and see the TV screen as object or self-image from the camera; or the monitor/camera looks up and imprints faces looking down or buttocks sitting in the "chair." On another level, the chair resembles a toilet—a condensation of Archie Bunker's chair with the sound of an upstairs toilet flushing. That chair, now in the Smithsonian, was a command post of patriarchy which this chair mocks.

TV Buddha, a statue, contemplates a monitor which returns an image of the statue. The mysterious, static Buddha is a spectator in stoic contemplation and an object of worship. Both TV and Buddha are icons of worship, one sublime, the other ridiculous. Their juxtaposition represents the collisions of history and cultures. Using cameras and monitors, *TV Buddha* looks and takes in the spectator's look and image, at the same time. The look (and the joke) is simultaneously absorbed, refracted, and reenacted. Instead of a hyperreal, a simulation in the face of the absence of the real as Baudrillard argues, Paik's work is a real simulation, posing riddles of another kind.

The Moon Is the Oldest TV, an installation of twelve monitors suggesting the phases of the moon, has an ironic edge. The global notion of the world all watching one TV set, the moon as fount of romantic poetry, the moon as a heavenly network of satellite hookups and downlinks, historical time versus TV time, all lead to the ultimate simulation: the 1969 U.S. moon landing. It was impossible initially to identify the network's replay of simulated landings until "simulation" was finally printed over the image. The word declared whether real or not. After the moon landing (maybe it never happened), we could distinguish: the real footage was not of comparable image clarity and resolution. Bad technique was a mark of truth. Error or flaw meant real; but the live and real, the noble dream and promise of TV, can also be simulated, as imperfect.

Paik is known as the inventor of machines. From electro-magnets to synthesizers/computers and now lasers, his machines derail continuity, deforming image, unhinging power. His videotapes "baffle and loosen" the hold of the gaze and the formidable power of language. This comedy (a comedy of errors?) dissolves divisions and structures of difference—art and popular culture, East and West, active and passive, seeing and being seen—with always an eye and ear directed toward irony. The work is collaborative, participatory; sometimes the tone is raucous, sometimes darkly disquieting, as in *Guadalcanal Requiem,* 1977. Charlotte Mormon, his performance companion, and her cello on that historical beach of ravishment, is an image recalling their past censorship battles as well as military battles between cultures. I value his collaborative, international spirit. Given Paik's connections to Fluxus and happenings, he is a direct descendant of the historical avant-garde, with the addition of cultural dissonance or difference: U.S. popular culture and art is seen from Korea (and Germany). Andreas Huyssen's early call for avant-garde is apt:

> The point is rather to take up the historical avant-garde's insistence on the cultural transformation of everyday life and from there to develop strategies for today's cultural and political context.[37]

Mormon's presence also raises the very sticky issue of the representation of woman within avant-garde. Her status within his work is, for me, a real problem, the equation of biology and technology, a mental set vehemently refuted by feminism in the late 1970s, but returning in the 1980s, revised, in theories of the body. I also question the historical accuracy and political value of enshrining Paik as the father of video art, the twin of Brakhage; we don't need any more fathers. Martha Rosler's *Vital Statistics* is a feminist critique of both dilemmas.

Foucault's emphasis on vision, a "pure Gaze" with "pure Language" as a set of effects which can be seen—a "speaking eye"—is a metaphor made literal in his use of Jeremy Bentham's penitentiary design (and realization) of the Panopticon as a model for the carceral society of surveillance. The prisoners are unable to see each other or the authority in the central tower who watches them—never sure whether they are being looked at, constant, potential victims of the Gaze.

> Visibility is a trap. . . . He is seen, but he does not see; he is the object of information, never a subject in communication. . . . The Panopticon is a machine for dissociating the see/being seen dyad. . . .[38]

The dissociation of the see/being seen dyad as the sense of permanent visibility reenacts Casares's fable of the imaginary museum, the convict, and the beautiful woman. Foucault's scenario describes the inmate in Bentham's prison and women, a theoretical model embodied in this 1974 videotape. Rosler, a performer like Mormon, interrogates the unquestioned use of the female body, the passive object of the "speaking eye," staging Foucault along the way. For, "defined in terms of visibility's conventions, she carries her own Panopticon with her wherever she goes, her self-image a function of her being for another."[39] Foucault's divide resembles Berger's assessment of women seeing themselves being seen, as well as Mulvey's split between seeing and being seen, between male and female. Like some feminist critics later, Berger posits the surveyor inside women as male, which resembles Sally Potter's concept of internal, colonized space. However illuminating and groundbreaking these models, I now take issue with these analyses which, like Lacan's lack and desire, depend on the centrality of the phallic signifier. This is not the way we are; rather, these divides and internalizations, which exist within the unconscious as well, are the social and historical constructions by which we live, at least for now. *Vital Statistics* employs and dissects the cruelty and power of surveillance while simulating the scrutiny of women by medical or scientific institutions. The unblinking gaze is a passionless stare at a woman's body, Rosler's body, stripped bare then garbed as masquerades of the divided woman—the bride in frilly white or the sexy woman wearing a basic-black evening dress.

The claim of the voice-over in its litany of crimes in the name of science, of statistics, against women and humanity, intersects and challenges the scene of Rosler undressing, being measured by the doctor/scientists wearing white coats. Her nakedness, shot from a careful and steady distance to avoid voyeurism is, for me, a dilemma of representation as victimization. The doctor's anatomical sketch of her measured body is a commentary on woman as model in several senses of the word, yet stripped of erotic, fantasy overlay; a statistical pinup of literal measurements has replaced and negated woman. For me, the routine, flattened, and ritual pattern of the mise-en-scene, performances, and editing suggest the domestic regime of suffocating repetition, of women's nonexistence except for others.

Vital Statistics's insistent, didactic voice-over undermines with data, or competes with, the authoritative, dominant status of vision, intersecting the sterile, *tableau vivant* of the victim/model ensnared in, immobilized by, the gaze of the camera. The assertion of the voice, reading a historical roll call of crimes against women, a list of catastrophe, a history of abuse, countermands the passivity and muted silence of the image. This voice is not like the mellowed, trained truths of newscasters, the TV male voice defining bodies and soothing audiences, drifting from room to room, our constant companion—male authority. These voices are grating, droning on about inhumanities we would rather not hear. For women, power and surveillance might not be so funny, so easy to evade, so pleasurable to resist. The underside of Foucault's pleasures of perversions and Deleuze's playful simulacra are real atrocities against cultures, races, and women. Whether pleasure or pain depends on the vital statistics of what side of domination/subordination one is on.

International video artists also know about surveillance: Michael Klier's *Der Reise* is a science fiction surveillance tape, edited from cameras placed round a modern city—a tale of barren modernity and nonaction. Elsa Cayo's marvelously clever *Qui vole un oeuf vole un oeuf* (France) is a simulation of shoplifting in a supermarket seen from the point of view of surveillance cameras, their silence narrated by an off-frame, conspiratorial voice; and in *Great Mother Sachiko* (Japan), the agonizing soap opera of daily life is doubled on a domestic television set. In many ways, these and other U.S. video works, like Cecelia Condit's *Beneath the Skin* and *Possibly in Michigan*, overthrow systems of panoptic power, mastery, and the gaze by simulations—which include us in the game as player rather than object.

CHAPTER
7

UNCANNY FEMINISM

The traces of the storyteller cling to the story
the way the handprints of the potter cling to
the clay vessel.

—Walter Benjamin[1]

The princess may very well have had an uncanny feeling, indeed she very probably fell
into a swoon; but we have no such sensa-
tions, for we put ourselves in the thief's
place, not in hers.

—Sigmund Freud[2]

Before analyzing Cecilia Condit's videotapes *Beneath the Skin* (1981) and
Possibly in Michigan (1983), marvelous tales told from the princess' point of
view, I will wander through the metaphorical, treacherous forests of other
stories, discovering "invisible adversaries" along the path. The first is a
handsome prince in a cautionary fable, "The Twelve Dancing Princesses":[3]
"Once upon a time there was a king who had twelve daughters, each more
beautiful than the other. They slept together in a hall where their beds stood
close to one another. At night when they had gone to bed, the king locked
the door and bolted it. But when he unlocked it in the morning, he noticed
that their shoes had been danced to pieces, and nobody could explain how
it happened." Although imprisoned by patriarchy, these dancing daughters
gleefully and confidently escaped the king's gaze of surveillance and power;
together "they danced, every night, on the opposite shore, in a splendid
light, till three in the morning, when their shoes were danced into holes and
they were obliged to stop."

In this celebration of female adolescence and adventure, however—as in
most of the "once upon a time" of fiction—something is wrong, and the
youngest sister is suspicious: "I don't know what it is. You may rejoice, but I
feel so strange. A misfortune is certainly hanging over us." For women, on a
par with being scrutinized and contained by vision, the end is the dire,

dreaded misfortune—in this fairy tale, marriage to a prince, a quick and unhappy conclusion which separates the sisters and censures their nightly escapades. Anne Sexton's rewriting: "Now the runaways would run no more and never / again would their hair be tangled into diamonds, / never again their shoes worn down to a laugh, / He had won."[4] A fellow had been given a cloak of invisibility by an old woman and had secretly spied on their nightly pleasures and reported to the king. For his voyeurism (and successful surveillance), he was given the kingdom and a princess of his choice. The peril of being the visible, private object of desire and the safe power of being the invisible, desiring, public subject are two morals of this and contemporary theory's story. The undisciplined sisters had transgressed the patrolled frontier between private and public—that demarkation line of power—and their passionate, dancing bodies were duly arrested.

Although the prince inadvertently revealed his presence through touch and sound, eleven of the princesses paid no attention: "And, as he broke off a twig, a sharp crack came from the tree. The youngest cried out, 'All is not well! Did you hear that sound?' " No one else listened to these sounds, which made "the youngest princess start with terror." While many feminists are proudly standing on opposite shores, watching the "splendid light" of independent films and videotapes and being invited to the intellectual dance of postmodernism by scholars and the art world,[5] we might heed the alarm of the youngest sister, for there are warnings in the academic air of godly wrath and signs of virulent condescension, brazenly heralding a resurgence of reactionary, antifeminist positions—signaled by arguments for women's return to private space, the home. "New traditionalists," we are told in magazine ads, are women garbed in tailored, professional fashion; rather than being in the office, they are photographed with children, in domesticity, preferring to remain at home.

Lawrence Stone, Dodge professor of history at Princeton, another prince of a fellow and the second adversary of this essay, caused me to "start with terror" and conclude with furor at his patronizing, biblical admonishments in the *New York Review of Books*—at best a naked emperor when the topic rarely turns to feminism; at worst, which is usually the case, a wolf without the guise of sheep's clothing. In the first paragraph of "Only Women," a foreboding title, King Stone speaks to the princesses: "I must first set out the ten commandments which should, in my opinion, govern the writing of women's history at any time and in any place"—certainly a specious claim when discussing the writing of history. (Ruminous sounds, awkwardly famous movie stars, and unearthly special effects restage this spectacle in the film version of *Only Women*, co-directed by Lizzie Borden and Cecil B. De Mille, in which Stone plays himself and is duly disemboweled in the film/theory remake of the beginning of Michael Foucault's *Discipline and Punish*.) Having claimed truth and the world for all times and all places, the Stone tablets are thus writ by this Moses impersonator: "1. Thou shalt not write about women except in relation to men and children. [The wife/mother plea suppresses the very reality of women's lives, forgetting both women's relationships with other women and the exhausting fact that most women always have at least two full-time jobs—taking care of children and men.] Women are not a distinct caste, and their history is a story of complex interactions; 2. Thou shalt strive not to distort the evidence and the conclusions to support modern feminist ideology. . . . 4. Thou shalt not confuse prescriptive norms with social reality. . . . 9. Thou shalt be clear about what constitutes real change in the experience and treatment of women."[6] Because Stone is male and thus omnipotent, he, like his godly predecessors, knows "what constitutes real change" in the experience of women or "thou."

This catalogue of imperative "shalts" is an intellectual aberration—a paranoid delusion of divine intervention into feminist scholarship and history. I "start with terror" when I imagine the collective, knowing laughter of educated readers at his chastisement of women writers and feminism. For Prince Stone, women (not just feminists) have broken the bonds of propriety and chastity by entering priestly male domains of "history"; he marshals his defensive attack on women under the disguise or banner of research. Like the prince's cloak, scholarship and prestigious chairs (a veritable star system of academia reminiscent of the Hollywood studio era, replete with gossip and credits, is operative in this magazine) provide various screens, briefly concealing, like the prince's invisible presence, the argument.

American Film joins the *New York Review of Books* in mockery through the terrain of "with-it" popular culture in a breezy piece by Raymond Durgnat on Grace Jones—an essay and a female subject made strangely respectable (as if Jones were not) by dropping sundry names, e.g., Visconti, Renoir, and Vertov, in a swaggering display of his superior knowledge of and desire for her "phallic-narcissistic swagger and strut." (This lurid psychoanalysis suggests Lee Marvin's black-leathered Liberty Valence in John Ford's film and describes Durgnat's argument and style.) After glorifying Jones and her traversals of boundaries, Durgnat suddenly turns on feminism, on women as the objects of his contempt, the real reason for his essay. He smugly writes with scorn: "Jones disturbs the Brand X forms of feminism. She's too frivolous for its schoolmarms, too sexual for its puritans, too strong for its sensitive plants, too competitive for its pacifists, too capitalist for its radicals, too effective for its neurotics, too hetero for its separatists, too responsibly independent to put the blame on pop for everything (war, the weather, old age)."[7]

Durgnat's dismissive compendium, modeled on Linnaeus rather than the Bible, reiterates the nauseating typologies used to assault feminism and employs biological arguments used to contain women, e.g., frivolous, sensitive, pacifists, puritans, schoolmarms, and, of course, neurotic and dependent. It is not insignificant that *American Film* would publish, without notation, words of undisguised racism and sexism, setting women in opposition under the cover of praising a black woman—the imperialist tactic of divide and conquer, the king's move against the sisters, a gambit of subjection rather than subjectivity.

These all-knowing enunciators protest too much, however; perhaps they are afraid of something, including the assertive, stylish representations of Grace Jones. Perhaps women, white and of color, are upping the ante, redirecting the terms of vision and spectacle in stories and theories which dance on opposite shores without the fatal end of patriarchy. In vastly different ways, Condit and other feminist artists "play with our curiosity and finally refuse to submit to our gaze. *They turn being looked at into an aggressive act* [my emphasis] . . . they are playing with the only power at their disposal— the power to discomfit, the power, that is, to pose . . . to pose a threat. . . . They must exceed definitions of the proper and the permissible. . . . And there is pleasure in transgression."[8] (As a qualification or addition to this acute remark by Dick Hebdige, women also have language "at their disposal"—for some, a troubling incursion into grammars of power as women interrupt the masculine ecology of speech *and* dispose of, or trash, kingly discourses—which Condit does in the garbage sequence which concludes *Possibly in Michigan*.) Along lines similar to Hebdige, Mary Russo writes about masquerade: "To put on femininity with a vengeance suggests the power of taking it off."[9] Condit does "pose a threat" by putting on femininity with a visual and narrative vengeance; her disconcerting irony and sweetly gruesome stories also put on and undo societal prescriptions and taboos regarding women's options to subjugation by violence or the gaze, letting us see and hear what often remains hidden, behaving with impropriety. Feminist films and video are telling stories differently *and* looking at difference differently—the latter, a key to feminist influences on current debates on postmodernism, particularly the issues focused on notions of the Other. As I argued in the preceding chapter, women are posited as the schizophrenic subject of postmodern culture, just as television is its latent object—the embodiment of every emblematic feature. Yet rarely are either subject or object acknowledged other than for feminism as Other—as a "great divide"[10] or bipolarity (containing, in order of historical fashion, vestiges of Lacan's endless division of the subject in language, the split between "I" of enunciation and "I" of enounced, the separation of the inner world of the "self" from the outside "world" of reality and facticity which can be mastered and owned, the division of subject from object, men from women, women from women, word from image, and soul from body.[11])

I want briefly to elaborate on this strange situation of feminism's acclaimed marginality and unstated centrality through a selective reading of an *October* essay, "The 'Primitive' Unconscious of Modern Art," by a leading figure in the debate, Hal Foster. Among complex, political issues, he explicates *bricolage*: "Myth is a one-way appropriation, an act of power; *bricolage* is a process of textual play, of loss and gain: whereas myth abstracts and pretends to the natural, bricolage cuts up, makes concrete, delights in the artificial." (Condit's work literally "cuts up" and "delights in the artificial.")

Up to this point, drawing on Levi-Strauss and Barthes, Foster's definition of the "primitive style" is uncannily similar to feminist art and argument— against biology, which for women emerges as the "eternal," the goddess/ whore myth. Foster provocatively asserts that "the rupture of the primitive, managed by the moderns, becomes our postmodern event"; he concludes by invoking feminists for whom "there are other ways to narrate this history."[12] Thus, by extension and in/direct elision, feminism becomes the repressed, managed rupture of postmodernism—posited, like "primitivism" earlier, *outside* the debate as the estranged, unknowable other, along with other races and cultures. I repeat: in postmodern discourses, "woman" is not fascinating as she was to modernism; "feminism" is.

If feminism is going to be invoked as a desirable dialogue or a discourse of salvation, it is time to realize that at least white, intellectual, middle-class feminism is not Other in the sense of being outside a shared history and politics of class and race; white women are Other for psychoanalysis' male subjects and analysts for whom "woman" *is* the problem; "she" is a para-doxical dilemma which grants male identity and exists as an inscrutable mystery, in both myths serving as the object of male desire/fear rather than as a subject. Indeed, an exceedingly primitive unconscious is posited by the modernists Freud and Lacan. Within this European, historical account of male sexuality/subjectivity, yes, "woman" is other and lacking, truly a prob-lem—with an essay by Freud "On Femininity" but no comparable piece on masculinity. But for political and fashionable U.S. writers on postmodernism? The blind yet concerned visage of Oedipus, now miserable at Colonus, again misreads women or feminism which is alluded to rather than translated and which servilely works, without recognition, as source of the argument and/or the condemnation of postmodern culture.

The task for feminists involved "re-vising the old apprehension of sexual difference and making it possible to multiply differences, to move away from homogeneity,"[13] a notion picked up, then amplified by de Lauretis to include "differences among women" and "differences within women": "differences which are not purely sexual or merely racial, economic, or (sub)cultural, but all of these together and often enough in conflict with one another."[14] These delineations of hetereogenity, together *and* in conflict, of historical women are resolutely against the notions of "purely" and "merely" usually applied to eternal "woman" and veer from princely mastery through colo-nization, bipolarity, hierarchy and otherness. These gambits which divide and conquer rely on a central, defining term or superior reality (usually white and/or male) rather than a series of equivalent or nonhierarchical options.

Several strategies of "hetereogeneity" are apparent in recent feminist cin-ema and video: (1) the emphasis on enunciation and address to women *as subjects* (including multiple voices in personal dialogues and the use of pri-vate speech), a reciprocity between author, text, and audience involving col-lective/contradictory identifications and shared "situations"; (2) the telling of "stories" rather than "novels" or grand master narratives as Walter Benjamin distinguished these two forms; (3) the inextricable bricolage of personal and theoretical knowledge; (4) the performance of parody or the telling of jokes, with irony and wit as women's allies rather than enemies; no wonder women in the audience laugh with such bursts of mutual delight; neither tale nor laughter are at their expense; (5) an implicit or explicit critique and refashioning of theories of subjectivity constructed by vision; and (6) a transgression of the boundaries between private and public spaces and experiences, entering with intimacy the "public sphere" and unsettling these metaphorical and real spaces of power through confinement by looking and talking back. I will scatter these intersecting issues throughout the discussion of Condit's sassy video work.

Beneath the Skin (1981) and *Possibly in Michigan* (1983) are unnerving and funny retellings of Oedipus as tabloid sensationalism. Imagine Freud's essay on the uncanny as either a feminist fairy tale or a murderous scandal, excerpted in the *National Inquirer* and *Art Forum*, illustrated by photographs of masquerade women or mutilated corpses, and accompanied by bold headlines of first person quotations. This lucid critique/lurid exposé would return—collapsing criticism's bipolarity of art versus popular culture, fiction opposed to fact, simulation against the real, canny against the uncanny—as a performance staged by Cindy Sherman with voices by Lily Tomlin. Scholarly explications via "theoretical" postmodernism would be published in *October* while personal stories of the artists would appear in *People;* clips from the piece would be shown on CBS on Sunday morning in the sacred art slot near the end of the program. Condit, Sherman, Tomlin, and Annette Michelson would intimately/polemically chat/assert on "The Phil Donahue Show" before a female audience of nonfeminists. Or as real life would have it, Condit's work would be broadcast on "The 700 Club"—without its sound track—and dubbed over with a poet reading his work about homosexuality. We would be held in a disconcerting uncertainty concerning origins, originals, mastery, truth, art, popular culture and "the real" (all of which are complex processes, dispersed discourses which, like mass culture, most criticism posits as monoliths or "things" which are locatable, almost tangible)— currently labeled "pastiche" and "schizophrenia" as the emblematic condition of the postmodern object and its confused subject.[15] Or, as Barthes argued earlier, "Taken aslant by language, the world is written through and through; signs, endlessly deferring their foundations . . . infinitely citing one another, nowhere come to a halt. . . ."[16]

Or, in another interpretation of this crazy return, we would be as ambivalently delighted and unwarily off-centered as we are by watching Condit's videotapes. Their status as hyperreal—the mesmerizing, fibrillating images of masquerade and the grotesque—is undercut by the irony of the smiling voice speaking of violence and death with the amazed, homey incredulity of backyard gossip or doubly displaced by innocent, sing-song exchanges and girlish operettas. Grizzly scandal collides with female adolescence, just as sound intercepts image, derailing spectators and interpretation alike; the real violence in women's lives coincides with fairy tales and princesses. Teresa de Lauretis concluded *Alice Doesn't* with a marvelous, riddling question: "it is the signifier who plays and wins before Alice does, even when she's aware of it. But to what end, if Alice doesn't?"[17] Cecilia doesn't and Condit's work unravels the sentence's paradox while imaging blackly ironic, startling "endings" to de Lauretis's question.

Condit's tapes unequivocally position us in the princess' place, Sleeping Beauty's swoon, that nightmare of Anne Sexton's poem in which the awakened princess "married the prince":

> and all went well
> except for the fear—
> the fear of sleep.
>
> Briar Rose
> was an insomniac. . . .
>
> I must not sleep
> for while asleep I'm ninety
> and think I'm dying.
> Death rattles in my throat.[18]

Unlike Freud and Sexton, Condit has no interest in either marriages to princes or thieves' viewpoints, however fascinated she is, as they are, by sleep and dream, violence and death. Her strategy, however unaware of either source, is a combination of Freud and Sexton, rewriting the "uncanny" as a fairy tale (a form which Freud absolutely and repeatedly denied was an instance of uncanny experiences) and taking Sexton's feminist revisions to different, less lonely and suicidal ends. Condit's translucent, artificial, video bodies are interrupted by recreations and documentary footage of epileptic seizures and still photographs of mummies' heads; the "classical" body is disrupted by the "grotesque" body; the private, controlled, sleeping beauty is transformed into the public, uncontrollable epileptic or the decaying body of a murderous scandal; all are instances of violent spectacle, exquisite corpses. No longer effaced or held in private spaces by "proper" discourse and decorous words, these are "undisciplined," speaking bodies—on the frontier between the modern body and the carnival body before the seventeenth century incarceration in asylums, prisons, and homes, before the ascendancy of the word over the carnal, guilty flesh and other great divides of power—adolescent rather than grown-up bodies which suggest that another interpretation of masquerade as a possibility for feminism rather than a disguise, lure, or mark of envious lack is necessary.

Via Bakhtin's work on carnival and Rabelais, Mary Russo writes in "Female Grotesques: Carnival and Theory": "The grotesque body is the open, protruding, extended, secreting body, the body of becoming, process, and change. The grotesque body is opposed to the classical body, which is monumental, static, closed, and sleek. . . ." Condit's work alternates and merges the "classical" body with the grotesque body—the latter the uncontrollable, erupting body as spectacle on public display. Russo writes of historical, female performers: "They used their bodies in public, in extravagant ways that could have only provoked wonder and ambivalence in the female viewer. . . ."[19] This image of the body and the ambivalent spectator is applicable to the "style" of Condit's work: "a body in the act of becoming. It is never finished, never completed; it is continually built, created, and builds and creates another body . . . a double body in which one link joins the other, in which the life of one body is born from the death of the preceding, older one . . . the body can merge with various natural phenomena. . . ."[20] The carnival body is an indivisible body without inner/outer, self/other polarities in which the exterior is inauthentic, merely a cover-up; it is a body of doubled surfaces rather than inner recesses which are analyzed, explained. Video is well suited to this transforming, seamless emergence of one surface from another, a fluid editing/processing capacity which Condit utilizes with skill.

"[T]his hyperbolic style, this 'overacting' can be read as double representations. . . ."[21] "Double representation" (both Bakhtin's "double body" and the "double-directed discourse" of parody)—extended to include the critique of the schizophrenic subject and the intersection of sound and image tracks—aptly describes Condit's tapes, which also demonstrate a tactic suggested by Luce Irigaray and endorsed by Russo: "to play with mimesis is thus, for a woman, to try to recover the place of her exploitation by discourse, without allowing herself simply to be reduced to it. It means to resubmit herself . . . to ideas . . . that are elaborated in/by masculine logic, but so as to make 'visible' what was supposed to remain invisible."[22] (In certain ways, this reads like a summary of Foucault's and perhaps Bakhtin's projects, which, however, were mainly about and for men.) Among the seemingly contradictory yet comparable exploitations to which Condit "resubmits" are masquerade and epilepsy, which she restages as extravagant, hyperbolic spectacle, challenging the divisions of vision and the body while escaping the confines of "discourse."

Beneath the Skin (1981) opens with Condit's conversationally intimate, incredulous voice narrating: "Let me tell you what a nightmare that *that* was. Most of the time it just feels like the news extravaganza that it was."[23] Benjamin argued that storytellers speak of the "circumstances" they have directly learned or "simply pass it off as their own experience."[24] Eliding story with the teller (raising issues of authorship), Condit's rehearsed, naive voice scales Midwest verbal registers of astonishment, stressing and elongating words like "body," and relates a lurid, first person account of her boyfriend's murder of his previous lover, whom he dismembered, "mummified, decapitated, and wrapped in plastic" and stored in his apartment during his affair with her, the storyteller "I." The film is about "this guy I had been seeing for the last four years, the police just found a body in his apartment. . . ." The passions of the body are rumors, gossip, and scandal; perhaps they are real, or not: "I'd never know if he killed her or not . . . a helluva way to continue a relationship. . . ." The audience is caught off guard by off-handed comments and laughs—*The Star* as standup comedy *and* everyday life. The details of decapitation and odorous decay on the ironic sound track—"But one of the funniest things about it . . . it came out that her head was missing"—parallels rapidly edited images of the fragmented female body, which decays in video as the corpse in the story rots. The tape goes "beneath the skin" by traversing the "inside/outside" of the body (a sack, a container) to reveal skeletons, aging, death; beneath surfaces to uncover horror or the "unconscious"; beneath the romance of relationships—of the lyrics of Frank Sinatra dreamily singing "I've got you under my skin"—to reveal beatings and murder. Perhaps these are separate but equal terrains; or they are equivalent planes of representation; or, perhaps, this is not a modern body at all which can be present only through the distance of representation but an archaic, violent, repressed body. Recurring closeups of red lips and white teeth are juxtaposed with the verbal description of the corpse's dental records. ("But the most important of all human features for the grotesque is the mouth. It dominates all else. The grotesque face is actually reduced to the gaping mouth . . . a bodily abyss": Bakhtin.[25]) Life and death, the pin-up and the coroner's report, the fetish and the fact, the beautiful and the grotesque, and the word and the image are of equal representational value.

The collision, or (in)vertical montage, of a lurid tabloid story akin to *Rear Window, Psycho,* and *Frenzy* of murder, dismemberment, and investigation (including Hitchcock's perversely comic, cannibalistic dinner-table scenes conjoined with scenes of crimes) with images of young, masquerading girls and glimpses of death, illness, and age, resembles a gyrating Möbius strip in which sound and image tracks never meet but are indissolubly connected by us in the process of enunciation—a reciprocity between author, text, and audience. As Linda Hutcheon writes in *A Theory of Parody,* parody, like Bakhtin's medieval carnival, "exists in the self-conscious borderline between art and life, making little formal distinction between actor and spectator, between author and co-creating reader."[26] For her, parody "enlists the audience in contradiction" and activates "collective participation."[27] Depending on one's gendered experiences, the collective contradictions elicited by Condit's disarming, eye-catching work are more extreme, less appetizing, hard to swallow and even harder to digest for some viewers (mainly men) than others.

Her distinctive style involves an intricate montage which spirals and loops back, intersecting the lurid narration. Studio footage alternates with processed location shots; found black and white footage is mixed by/with video in an uncanny enunciation, placing the enounced of murder in a precarious irony. Visual delicacy, like the images of the sweet young woman, disguises *and* underscores the sensational story—is this real, is this possible, is this a fable, is this serious—or not? "This" exemplifies contradiction—of response, of the structure of irony, of women's lives, crossing the "self-conscious borderline between art and life." This emphasis on process and experience in a reciprocity between speaker/listener is also central to Benjamin's valorization of the story as opposed to the novel which "neither comes from oral tradition nor goes into it. This distinguishes it from storytelling in particular. The storyteller takes what [she] tells from experience—[her] own or that reported by others. And [she] in turn makes it the experience of those who are listening to [her] tale. The novelist has isolated himself."[28] In this, the storyteller ("The first true storyteller is, and will continue to be, the teller of fairy tales"[29]) resembles the chronicler (rather than the contemporary historian) who is interested in interpretation rather than explanation, the terrain of the novel's narrative which has been divorced from "the realm of living speech." Thus, the listener has a stake not only in hearing but in remembering the story—a shared experience, a process. "A [woman] listening to a story is in the company of the storyteller; even a [woman] reading [watching] one shares this companionship."[30] It is this realm of interpretation via "living speech" forged in shared experience which is intriguing for feminism and what distinguishes the work of Condit—a telling as much as a watching.

The initial and recurring visual image is an overhead, "glamor" close-up of a young woman's face—sleeping, artifically made up and lighted. This shot is overlaid with another female face, a visual trace outlining a divided, schizophrenic subject—a complex dialogue imbricated in much feminist work. "Call them femininity and feminism, the one is made representable by the critical work of the other; the one is kept at a distance, constructed, 'framed,' to be sure, and yet 'respected,' 'loved,' 'given space' by the other."[31] (In this writing, women are "other" with/for each other rather than another, a man, and thus, a very different story.) The teller begins to identify with the murdered woman: "I always thought that she was epileptic and I, diabetic, and I identified with her." (Because Condit is epileptic, the status of "I" is complicated, biographically elided with "she.") As the tape returns to the opening shot, the dreamer/teller, self/other, voice-over/"other woman," the dead and the living merge, taking up the question of the real and fiction, the possible and the impossible, in a double denial that, like de Lauretis's Alice riddle, reaffirms women and the story's reality: "But it was never real, it was just a bizarre story . . . but I had this dream that it was so real. I dreamed that it was me, not her, that he killed two years ago."

"It is characteristic that not only a man's knowledge or wisdom, but above all his real life—and this is the stuff that stories are made of—first assumes transmissable form at the moment of his death. . . . Death is the sanction of everything that the storyteller can tell. He has borrowed his authority from death."[32] (Benjamin and Bakhtin analyze the "modern" concealment of death with arguments remarkably similar, again, to Foucault's theses.) Like the "he" of Benjamin's remarks, Condit takes her authority from death and goes public as few women storytellers do, speaking about violence through the forbidden terrain of femininity, with sacrilegious moments of gallows humor. This rewriting of Freudian bedtime stories as sensationalism concludes with "And that's another story." Like Scheherazade, Condit continues the tale two years later, this time radically revising Freud's interpretations and conclusions with a sweet-tasting vengeance and without his proper cover of "scientific discourse" which explains and contains the hysterical, spectacular body.

Possibly in Michigan (1983) is a feminist musical in which the couple doesn't, continuing the deathly, stifling scenario of *Beneath the Skin* which foreshadowed the musical style of musical voices in a chanting, childlike operetta, "gee i jo": "Talk to us about Barbie and Ken, Barbie and Men, Ken and Men. . . . Never ends." Both tapes reverse the classical text's heterosexual inevitability of Barbie and Ken, marriage or murder—both resolutions or 'endings' functioning as containments of the male fear of castration posed by the "lacking" spectacle of the female body. On the contrary, Condit gleefully realizes Freud's imaginary, anxious scenario; cannibalism, an extreme extension of dismemberment, castration, and other Freudian metaphors and/or fairy tales, is the "happy" ending.

Unlike the mainly singular storyteller of the first tape, three styles of voice alternate in this gruesomely enchanting fairy tale of female adolescence: the a cappella chorus; the sing-song dialogue/conversation between the two girl/women "stars"; and the voice-over of Condit speaking about her characters, Sharon, Janice, and Arthur, in a conspiratorial, editorial voice no longer an "I" but dispersed throughout the telling. This postmodern "once upon a time" opens in a shopping mall of diffused pastels where two young women are pursued by surreal men wearing business suits and grotesque animal heads. ("The head, ears, and nose also acquire a grotesque character when they adopt the animal form . . . the eyes have no part in these comic images; they express an individual . . . not essential to the grotesque": Bakhtin[33]) The opening lyrics of the chorus cheerily prophesy: "I bite at the hand that feeds me, slap at the face that eats me. Some kind of animal, cannibal. . . . Animal? Cannibal?" Music sweetens the scenario which equates men with animals as the frog/prince is made literal and visible. While the mundane of shopping malls and everyday life is transformed into fantasy, the second use of the voice, a sing-song dialogue, exemplifies Condit's disarming wit: "He has the head and it's the size of a wolf." A deep, echoing, male voice says: "The better to eat you with, my dear. . . . You have two choices. . . . I will cut your arms and legs off and eat them, one by one, slowly." The female chorus intones "Why?" He: "For Love." Chorus: "Why?" He: "For Love." Chorus: "But love shouldn't cost an arm and a leg."

As Sharon, the dreamer/actant, rides down the escalator, the third style of voice, Condit's voice, discusses women and violence, the complex concern beneath the veneer of fairy tales, of her work, and of women's "private" lives: "Sharon attracted violent men. She had a way of making the violence seem as if it was their idea. Her friend, Janice, was cut from the same mold." This frank, disconcerting analysis reiterates a line from *Beneath the Skin:* "I realize that if I courted violence more, I might get myself seriously hurt." In that tape she laughs, reminding me of the opening laugh of Sally Potter's 1979 film, *Thriller,* a laugh which occurs in blackness before the white of the first image, a laugh in concert with an aria of death. As Herbert Blau writes: "that seeming remembrance of/in laughter which is a mnemonic stoppage of breath. It is the mystery of the interruption which preserves something tragic in comedy, since it seems a synopsis of death. . . . Which is to say that *meaning stops for that moment,* as if in homage to more than meaning. . . ." Violence is always more or less than meaning; Condit's art and laughter are "synopses of death," stopped, as if gasping, by laughter; "when laughter comes the meaning is deadly, or there's just no meaning at all."[34]

The posing, giggling girls/women are from *Beneath the Skin,* including the raven-haired, sleeping/decaying beauty surrounded by red roses. Unlike the earlier tape, this story's violence exists more on the image track with sound as an ironic chorus or commentator: "Arthur longed for that sexual scent that smelled like home . . . he had used so many masks to disguise himself that he had forgotten who he was. He imagined himself a frog transformed into a Prince Charming. He felt the moment he kissed her, he would become the man she wanted him to be." This frog/prince inversion of Lacan's female masquerade as carnival follows the imaginary woman, Sharon, enters her home, kisses, then beats her—a startling intrusion of domestic life, reality amid the colors of fantasy. Janice, her friend, races to Sharon's house, rescues her, and shoots Arthur. These gossamer girls, together again, cook, eat, and toss Arthur's remains into the garbage after sharing Arthur with their dog, a girl's best friend. Hacking the body into stew meat is a comic parody, a shared act of intimacy, and grotesque equation of the body with food. This grizzly meal concludes with the innocent, satisfied "girls," presumably naked, made up, smoking cigarettes, and coughing in a delightfully perverse, soft-focus rendering of adolescent friendship and misbehavior. The tape concludes with the "real" garbage man and truck picking up the garbage or prince, accompanied by "natural" sound as the credits roll in this "reality."

This sensational remake of Freud, which fragments and fetishizes the female body while dismantling oedipal narratives, does indeed have conflicting effects on audiences, inverting Freud's analysis of the uncanny as an experience, a frightening effect which hinges on two figures—loss of the eyes and dismemberment—and which involves a discrepancy between the "incredible" and the "possible."[35] (It is important to "remember" that this essay depicts the dismembered, spectacular body—that "animistic" body of yore which is not fully contained by Freud's discourse, dependent as his argument is on uncertainty.) Epilepsy and the beautiful female automaton create "doubts whether an apparently animate being is really alive; or conversely, whether a lifeless object might not be in fact animate." Freud's fear of confusing the biological with the technological, the real with its simulation (a model and an essay which fits Fritz Lang's *Metropolis* like a historical glove) suggests that the "uncanny" is the precursor (or the repressed) of

Baudrillard's simulacrum which, unlike Freud, skirts the castration it fears with the loss of the real, referents, and mastery. This notion of the "double" becomes, for Freud and Condit, "a harbinger of death."[36] Condit's beautiful faces decay, dissolving into eyeless skulls; her narratives detail the dismemberment which Freud feared and analyzed: "the substitutive relation between the eye and the male organ which is seen to exist in dreams and myths and phantasies . . . the threat of being castrated is what first gives the idea of losing other organs its intense colouring."[37] Cannibalism, not only the losing but the devouring of "other organs," is an "intense colouring" of Freud's book. *Possibly in Michigan* is a serious and amusing challenge to the "relation between the eye and the male organ," a personal, historical, and recent equation certainly not "substitutive" in "women's dreams and myths and phantasies."

The fear of/defense against castration is also elicited by what Freud labels "the Medusa effect," a tactic which produces the very image which is feared for protection—yet another Freudian trope literalized in *Possibly in Michigan* in a shot of the masked man picking up a rock revealing a skull crawling with snakes which he throws through Sharon's window; it lands on her bed. The Medusa effect is reiterated in a close-up of worms/snakes crawling over a photograph of Sharon. These special effects "serve actually as a mitigation of the horror, for they replace the penis, the absence of which is the cause of the horror." Freud seriously goes on to say: "This is a confirmation of the technical rule according to which a multiplication of penis symbols signifies castration."[38] (No wonder Helene Cixous's Medusa is laughing! This reads as if Freud were writing directions for a Milton & Bradley board game, or better, a television game show. I can hear the referee's admonition: "You lose ten points on a technical rule: no multiplication of penis symbols." With the elevation of the phallus as the dominant signifier, Lacan was the big winner on "Jeopardy.")

Condit's Medusa scene, like the images of epilepsy and the automated doll-like women, takes Freud at his word; however, her Medusa effect portends violence to women and rape rather than or before castration. Because of this, she breaks Freud's crucial rule by not symbolizing disavowal but joyously "performing" dismemberment, turning the imaginary scenario of the Oedipus complex into the conclusion of cannibalism and female friendship—uniting women in an ending and relationship that classical texts have avoided and contained. It's as if the two women of *Beneath the Skin*, like Mimi and Musetta of Puccini's *La Boheme*, then Potter's *Thriller*, joined forces and refused their murder by seemingly but perversely playing by, then inverting or rewriting the rules and kicking Oedipus out of the narrative. As Benjamin suggests, "The wisest thing—so the fairytale taught mankind . . . is to meet the forces of the mythological world with cunning and high spirits." The mythological world of Freud is met by Sharon, Janice, and Cecelia, a creative trio—"with high spirits and cunning," living "happily ever after" so that Scheherazade, speaking to/with women, will continue this trilogy in *Not* a *Jealous Bone* concerning an old woman, another fairy-tale figure which Condit imagines in her off-center way.

"In every case the storyteller is a [woman] who has counsel for [her] readers. But if today 'having counsel' is beginning to have an old-fashioned ring, this is because the communicability of experience is decreasing. . . . After all, counsel is less an answer to a question than a proposal concerning the continuation of a story which is just unfolding."[39] Unlike all the recent declarations of the death of feminism because completed, old-hat, a failure, or a mistake, the public, artistic formulation of female subjects, desires, pleasures, and peculiarities continues to "unfold" fifty years after Benjamin's words; the "communicability" of women's private experiences is going massively, transgressively public. Cecilia Condit, just an "old-fashioned girl" but what a wickedly clever one, is giving us counsel, making outrageous proposals, with laughter from the audience signaling possibilities. After all, without his cloak of invisibility, the prince doesn't stand a chance.

> *Could you imagine a world of women only,*
> the interviewer asked. *Can you imagine*
>
> *a world where women are absent.* (He believed
> he was joking.) *Yet I have to imagine*
>
> *at one and the same moment, both.* Because
> I live in both. *Can you imagine,*
>
> the interviewer asked, *a world of men?*
> (He thought he was joking.) *If so, then,*
>
> *a world where men are absent?*
>
> —Adrienne Rich[40]

CHAPTER

8

LAST SCENE IN THE STREETS OF MODERNISM

In David Lodge's parody of upper-class academia and theory, appropriately titled *Small World*, Morris Zapp, the hip semiotician or postmodern critic, assesses the scholarly world as composed of cities strung together by airports, a topography of conference topics. Zapp: "Zurich is Joyce. Amsterdam is Semiotics. Vienna is Narrative. Or is it Narrative in Amsterdam and Semiotics in Vienna? . . . Anyway, Jerusalem I *do* know is about the Future of Criticism, because I'm one of the organizers. . . ." "Why Jerusalem?" "It's a draw, a novelty. It's a place people want to see, but it's not on the regular tourist circuit. Also, the Jerusalem Hilton offers very competitive rates in the summer because it's so goddam hot."[1] Funny, perhaps true, but very clever parody.

The Arthurian narrative and structure—replete with arch, jet-setting, literary clashes between doddering humanism (and sex) and philandering theory (and sex), in mise-en-scenes of identical cities and the same speakers—is Persse McGarrigle's (from Limerick) search for the ideal woman, Angelica. The book is also a parable of this young assistant professor's quest for the holy grail of tenure and his initiation into the rites of scholarly luck and fame. Along with ideal woman as lure, the prize is an expensive UNESCO chair. There are various female academics, among them the glamorous, kinky Italian, Fulvia Morgana, but they are objects not subjects of desire. The book concludes with the young Lancelot's reverie: "as on to a cinema screen, he projected his memory of Cheryl's face and figure—the blonde, shoulder-length hair, the high stepping gait, the starry, unfocused look of her blue eyes—and he wondered where in the small, narrow world he should begin to look for her?"(385). The eternal dream of woman has been an inspiration for myth and modernism; here it is the raison d'etre of conferences. Crucial, of course, is the fact that the ideal woman cannot be found; if she were, desire and motive, like the story, most international cinemas, and presumably male scholarship, would end.

When asked why he travels so much, Philip Swallow (married but looking for joy) says: "Happiness? One knows that doesn't last. Distraction, perhaps. . . . Intensity of experience is what we're looking for. We know we can't find it at home anymore, but there's always the hope that we'll find it abroad. I found it in America in 69." "With Desiree?" "Not just Desiree, although she was an important part of it." "It was the excitement, the richness of the whole experience . . ." (75–76). I wonder. Is male desire interchangeable with the object of desire, Desiree? Is this not redundant? What of the female traveler, the female academic? If told from her point of view, an actual rather than dream woman, in a claim for women's historical subjectivity and existence, the story and the theory would necessarily be different.

At a Milwaukee film theory conference, Teresa de Lauretis began with Italo Calvino's parable of the dream girl; this is a dream of history, of founding the city of Zobeide: "men of various nations had an identical dream. They saw a woman running at night through an unknown city; she was seen from behind, with long hair, and she was naked." They dreamed of pursuing her, and then constructed a city built on the memory of her. "At the spot where she had vanished, there would remain no avenue of escape. Those who had arrived first could understand what drew these people to Zobeide, this ugly city, this trap." "The City" functions as a "delusion and dream" "to keep women captive"—and it is ugly. Zobeide is a Greek maze, with the minotaur or a woman at the center, with no escape. As de Lauretis writes: "It does not come as a surprise, to us cinema people, that in that primal city built by men there are no women; or that in Calvino's seductive parable . . . woman is absent as historical subject."[2]

A detour beckons me. Lodge's "High stepping gait" has led me to a byway or blind alley—to Freud and *Delusion and Dream: Small World* is the comic remake. Like the mediocre novel which inspired him, *Gradiva: A Pompeiian Fancy* by Wilhelm Jensen (translated in 1917), Freud analyzes the male scholar's search for the classical woman. Taking his cue from Jensen, however, Freud knows that "the City," in this case Pompeii, is an excuse, a symptom; the dream girl has nothing to do with cities, science, or research but everything to do with desirous men. Norbert Hanold is an archeologist; "his interest is fixed upon a bas-relief which represents a girl walking in an unusual manner. . . . he spins a web of fantasies about her . . . transports the person created by him to Pompeii. . . . he intensifies the fantasy . . . of the girl named Gradiva [the girl splendid in walking] into a delusion which comes to influence his acts."[3] Norbert travels to Rome and Naples, grumbling about encountering so many married couples, and pursues his delusion through the ruins of Pompeii. Norbert has confused the real, a girl from his childhood, with the imaginary, her image. He is not a well man.

"There is no better reason for repression . . . than the burial which was the fate of Pompeii and from which the city was able to rise again. . . . in his imagination, the young archeologist had to transport to Pompeii the prototype of the relief which reminded him of the forgotten beloved of his youth" (61). Along with the importance of the city and childhood memory to repression (and the unconscious; Rome was another of Freud's inadvertently feminist metaphors), what intrigues me is Freud's analysis of Norbert's problem: "A psychiatrist would perhaps assign Norbert Hanold's delusion to the large group of paranoia and designate it as a 'fetishistic erotomania,' because falling in love with a bas-relief . . . the interest in the feet . . . of women must seem suspiciously like fetishism." But Freud dismisses erotomania as "awkward and useless." He goes on to hypothesize that "an old-school psychiatrist would, moreover, stamp our hero as a degenerate . . . and would investigate the heredity which has inexorably driven him to such a fate."

Freud's third and preferred analysis is the literary interpretation of Jensen, the author, who was "engrossed in the individual psychic state which can give rise to such a delusion. . . . In one important point Norbert Hanold acts quite differently from ordinary human beings. He has no interest in living women; science, which he serves, has taken this interest from him and transferred it to women of stone or bronze. Let us not consider this an unimportant peculiarity" (66–67). Indeed, let us not. Unfortunately, modernists paid scant heed to Freud. Scholastic delusions have continued to have "no interest in living women." The delusion might be more telling than the cover-up journey or scholarship—a (bas-relief) fetish. Freud's prognosis for Norbert might serve as a cure for theories of modernism and postmodernism; otherwise, the future is bleak: "The condition of continued avoidance of women results in the personal qualification . . . for the formation of a delusion; the development of psychic disturbance . . ." (68). A real woman, Zoe, is the end of the delusion, the end of the story, and Norbert's cure. I would argue that this might also be one cure for postmodernism, the inclusion of emergent voices as subjects rather than fantasy objects.

However tongue-in-cheek popular the novel *Small World,* or mediocre Jensen's *Gradiva,* they share a common premise with the great writers of modernism—the *myth* of the city as a woman. As Michel de Certeau argues in *The Practice of Everyday Life,* when encapsuled as myth, "the City" works to contain specificity and repress all differences or pollution; it is a myth which creates "a universal and anonymous subject" coterminous with "the city" itself;[4] the subject is male and the myth totalizing (albeit more poetic than the concept generated by city planners) and functions to "eliminate and reject" waste products which, like poverty, homelessness, and presumably women, can be reintroduced outside the myth, e.g., in welfare discourses. De Certeau's acute assessment of this "concept-city" points to "its forgetting of space, the condition of any city's possibility." "The City" is neither place nor space but a universal figure of history, "the machinery and hero of modernity" (95). To his critique, I must add contours: as this figure comes into focus, it is a shapely female image, de Certeau's blind spot, a telling oversight.

Before arriving at the movie theater, I want to stroll through *Reflections* with Walter Benjamin. "A Berlin Chronicle" sketches a topography of childhood memory—a provocative map of his youth drawn from the streets of

Berlin and Paris. "Now let me call back those who introduced me to the city."[5] Like medieval chronicles, this vivid, spatial map of "moments and discontinuities" (unlike the temporal sequence of autobiography which "has to do with time . . . and the continuous flow of life") (28) begins with a nursemaid, a trip to the zoo, mother and shopping, wanders through adolescent encounters, fancies sex and love, is guided by poets, essayists (particularly Baudelaire), and friendship, meanders to finances, father, and hated school discipline, and concludes with a paternal tale of death and an ominous warning, "syphilis." As enchanted as I am by Benjamin, I will focus on two recurring, interrelated and troubling figures, representative of the city, which are superimposed over his oedipal walk: the labyrinth and the prostitute.

Childhood is a "period of impotence before the city" due to "a poor sense of direction" (4) blamed on his mother; adolescence is "a crossing of frontiers not only social but topographical—a voluptuous hovering on the brink in the sense that whole networks of streets were opened up under the auspices of prostitution" (11). His political awareness of what the city hides, the poor, and his social awakening are equated with sexual awakening: "crossing the threshold of one's class for the first time had a part in the almost un-equaled fascination of publicly accosting a whore in the street." Behind the facades of the city architecture, its public image, hidden in the center was either a prostitute or Ariadne to lead him safely through the labyrinth of sex—eroticism initially curtailed by his nursemaid or his censoring mother. No matter. "Nor is it to be denied that I penetrated to its innermost place, the Minotaur's chamber, with the only difference being that *this* mythologi-cal monster had three heads: those of the occupants of the same brothel. . . . Paris thus answered my most uneasy expectations" (9). (On his quest, Theseus had an earlier encounter with Medea, who, after her separa-tion from Jason, had become the wife of Aegeus, the father of Theseus. She convinced her husband to try and poison Theseus, whose sword identified him to his father. Bulfinch [an outdated source on Greek myths who con-flates Media with the country of the Medes who occupied northern Iran before the Persians, much later than the presumed time frame of the Medea myth] writes: "Medea, detected in her arts, fled once more . . . and arrived in Asia, where the country afterwards, called Media, received its name from her."[6] The shift from Medea to Media, from woman to country, intrigues me.) In Benjamin's account, Medea is the figure on a ring purchased with friends and destined for his fiancee—"you only entered its secret by taking it off and contemplating the head against the light" (33).

Benjamin sees Berlin through the streets of Paris and the eyes of Baude-laire: "What is unique in Baudelaire's poetry is that the images of women and death are permeated by a third, that of Paris."[7] In the city, the oldest technology, sex, combines with the newest technology, mass culture, cele-brated as mass transit, skyscrapers, or decried as commodity fetishism. In his wonderful portrait of arcades and shopping, "Paris, Capital of the Nineteenth Century," Benjamin writes: "Such an image is presented by the pure commodity: as fetish. Such an image are the arcades, which are both house and stars. Such an image is the prostitute, who is saleswoman and wares in one" (157).

The city existed paradoxically as the exemplar of art and creativity and as the symptom of commodity culture—resolutely linked to the figure of woman. As Patrice Petro so decisively argues in *Joyless Streets*, "Berlin also served as the decisive metaphor for modernity, and modernity was almost invariably represented as a woman."[8] In "Mass Culture as Woman: Modernism's Other," Andreas Huyssen argues that modernism's fascination with imaginary femininity "goes hand in hand with the exclusion of real women from the literary enterprise and with the misogyny of bourgeois patriarchy itself."[9] Mass culture, site of the contemptible, is equated with women; real, authentic culture "remains the perogative of men" (191). The city is the turf of both, although in mythology, one serves the other.

The modernist art *and* commodity, cinema, picked up this division of the fetish woman. And if Benjamin is right that "only film commands optical approaches to the essence of the city . . . like conducting the motorist into the new center,"[10] then cinema, like modernism's city, is also built on a boyhood dream of woman, a dream arrested in adolescence, endlessly repeated. Benjamin's chronicle of modernity is also an old story, a Bildungsroman in which the young boy conquers the city and woman via desire, on his way to manhood and mastery; in the end, he casts his lot with his father in a shared secret, syphilis. This old story and the need to retell it might explain why the image of "the city" is such a totalizing figure. If Oedipus is our repeated narrative, then the modern city is its site. However, as Petro says, modernism is not the same as modernity, just as women and their experiences of modernity can never be captured in accounts of male modernists. As Sally Potter demonstrates in *The Gold Diggers*, the city also contains historical women who reject scenarios of male desire.

That the image of the central city of modernism is built from male desire analogous with "woman" is not, of course, new or surprising. That the city streets are not safe for women is frightening. That the feminist project in, for example, *Born in Flames* and *The Man Who Envied Women*, involves reclamation of city streets, taking on the historical weight of this modernist construction, makes their actions more culturally radical than initially imagined. That this unreconstructed myth has persisted in postmodernist claims for decentralization, pluralism, and the vernacular is rather surprising. A desirous cartography of Berlin and Paris of the 1920s, along with the visage of the male modernist author, hovers over London, Chicago, New York, and indeed cultural studies everywhere in the 1980s. While the specificity of war, recession, and industrialism have vanished, the eternal, naked woman has been transported around the world and back. What is missing from most accounts is that historical women comprised a significant part of the crowds of modernity; they went to the cities, to work, and to the movies. And we still do.

If told from the point of view of the naked woman of Zobeide, the story might be different. She must have been very frightened and cold. Was she from Zobeide? Or a visitor? Why was she naked? What had happened to her clothes? Why was she running away? Where had she been? Where were her friends? Did she make it home? Or was she murdered in a dark alley? Why didn't anyone help her? What was her name?

Or, perhaps she was more clever than imagined. Rather than guiding Theseus through the labyrinth, or believing his false promises that they would have a long-term relationship, did this Ariadne, like Collette Laffont in *The Gold Diggers*, take him on a wild goose chase? Instead of being abandoned, in need of redemption by Dionysus, she has led modernist and postmodernist alike astray, down ever narrowing argumentative paths of their own repetitive making. Everything, for them, now, is simulation or vague and constant pleasure; all the streets look alike, all their names sound alike. Her lovers are trapped in an ugly city; like a video game arcade, the maze has become crowded while she has gone home, to work, to think. She can no longer be bothered (or frightened) by his desire.

Unfortunately, the Marco Polo school of critics, like Theseus, believing they have abandoned Ariadne while she was sleeping, are now casting their wandering, fickle eyes on other cultures, specifically Eastern and third world, depositing the same myths of mysterious otherness applied to women in foreign terrain, seeking answers but not really caring if anyone lives there. After their sabbatical sojourns into the wilds of "other" university cultures, somewhere in the East, scholars return with intellectual souvenirs in the form of Ph.D. persons who give talks at scholarly symposia, frequently on Western authors.

To return to Paris and the 1960s, and issues of postmodernism through Godard and the situationists, with Japan on the horizon via Oshima. Both filmmakers occupied the streets and populated them with youth, drugs, transients, bars, rock 'n' roll, pop culture, and philosophy—celebrating the vernacular, sometimes the inarticulate, emphasizing the sexual. Godard's central characters are women, discontent with home and marriage. However, his metaphor for capitalism is prostitution, played out over women's bodies and lives. For me, this is yet another, albeit working (or not) class and gritty, everyday manifestation of modernism—the banal rather than glamorized dream whore.

Oshima's metaphor for imperialism and cultural struggle is rape. Although inscribed within a complex of avant-garde performance, a layering of the levels of representation, a revelation and interrogation of the cinematic apparatus's complicity and complexity (not unlike Godard's project), a rewriting of narrative conventions and enunciation, along with an almost parodic inquisition of the intellectual's or artist's connivance or role in dissecting capitalist exploitation, the sexual metaphor and enactment is again on woman's body. In both cases, with cultural specificity and difference in mind, woman (and her victimization) is the central myth. For me, neither prostitution nor rape will do in 1988. While these "liberated" or "radical" films posit woman as victim, she is still an object of pursuit, without subjectivity of her own.

There is a strange similarity between the concerns of Godard and Oshima then and the writers of cultural studies now, a similarity suggested to me by a passage in an essay by Morris, "At Henry Parkes Motel": "as an account primarily (and avowedly) based on the emblematic street experience of un- or under-employed males in European or American cities . . . it restricts the scope of enquiry. . . . Perhaps this is one reason why women . . . still appear in apologetic parentheses or as 'catching up' on the streets when they're not left looking out the window. The ways that economic and technological changes in the 1980s . . . have been transforming women's lives simply cannot be considered—leaving them not so much neglected in cultural studies as anachronistically mis-placed."[11] Remember the conversation scenes in various Godard films where famous philosophers either appear, are directly quoted, or whose words are embedded in dialogue. Oshima also quotes great, sometimes scandalous, male modernists, his films, like *Diary of a Shinjuku Thief*, peppered with meaningful, enigmatic citations, primarily from literature but also, like Godard, from pop culture and trash references. Citation and quotation are favored tactics for both. 1988 cultural studies might entail the sublation of 1960s politics, with Marx dropped out and postmodernism or cultural studies plugged in. If the 1960s have returned intellectually, vanquishing the gains of the women's movement and feminism by jumping over them, this might explain the anachronism. If I am right, the appropriation is depleted, divorced from Godard's and Oshima's political concern with the means of production. In the end, I prefer the modernist image of woman out front, leading a merry and dangerous chase, rather than pathetically tagging along behind.

However, there are other ways of thinking the city, other ways of charting postmodernism—the first being locating it earlier, in postwar nuclear rhetoric and realities and mass culture artifacts. Another locale might be that of Marguerite Duras's script for *Hiroshima Mon Amour* and Michel de Certeau's metaphor of the pedestrian, a guide highly recommended by Morris. To a degree, de Certeau's "Walking in the City" is a postmodern rendering of Benjamin (read through Foucault and linguistics). Later on in "A Berlin Chronicle," Benjamin imagines the labyrinth in another way. Rather than what is installed "in the chamber at its enigmatic center," he is concerned with "the many entrances leading into the interior—primal relationships, so many entrances to the maze, with men drawn on the right and women on the left."[12] This maze of stories, of books, of wandering through the city as a place of unpredicted events, while rigidly gendered, is entrancing to Benjamin and to me. The outline of the labyrinth has shifted—from the Greek model with its central chamber in which "terror is born" (according to Umberto Eco in *Postscript*) to the mannerist model, "a structure of many blind alleys . . . a model of the trial and error process," and perhaps on to the "rhizome" of Deleuze and Guattari, a labyrinth with no exit because it is potentially infinite.[13]

Benjamin calls this way of thinking the city "the art of straying." "Not to find one's way in a city may well be uninteresting and banal. It requires ignorance—nothing more. But to lose oneself in a city—as one loses oneself in a forest—that calls for quite a different schooling. Then, signboards and street names, passers-by, roofs, kiosks, or bars must speak to the wanderer like a cracking twig under his feet in the forest. . . ."[14] The wanderer, the strayer from the path, listens, gathers clues, pays attention to the details of the city, without mastery or a system, yet with knowledge. The wanderer does not have a grand theory, or central image, but learns (rather than proves) along the way; the adventure does not have a predetermined destination. For me, this is the inventive, scholarly path of discovery.

The "art of straying" is the way of the lovers in *Hiroshima Mon Amour*, wandering through the cafe streets of Hiroshima and the paths of their mutual desires. The French woman is the traveler, making a peace film; the Japanese man is an inhabitant of Hiroshima; trying to find each other/avoid each other, they speak of history, of person, of otherness. In the famous opening scene, their bodies form a topography of desire, of glistening catastrophe. "Who are you? You destroy me. How could I have known that this city was made to the size of love? How could I have known that you were made to the size of my body?"[15] Newsreels of the atomic bomb's victims, tourist monuments, Peace Square, and a busload of Japanese tourists are intercut; place and history are personal and impersonal. She has seen the tourists' view of Hiroshima and catastrophe; he insists that she has seen nothing, that she knows nothing. "No, you don't have a memory" (23). Knowledge is inextricable from memory, from lived experience, as is history. The film then precipitates the memory of her history, France's cultural history, women's history—her humiliation, her victimization for desire, loving a German soldier, in Nevers. It concludes with these remarks in the screenplay: "He looks at her, she at him, as she would look at the city . . ." "Hi-ro-shi-ma . . . that's your name." He: "That's my name. Yes. Your name is Nevers. Ne-vers in France" (83). Cities, proper names and sites of enunciation, are lived places of memory, spaces for history, love, and desire—for women travelers as well as men.

In an uncannily direct way, the film documents de Certeau's claim that "the Concept-city is decaying. . . . The ministers of knowledge have always assumed that the whole universe was threatened by the very changes that affected their . . . positions. They transmute the misfortune of their theories into theories of misfortune . . . they transform their bewilderment into 'catastrophes' . . . they seek to enclose the people in the 'panic' of their discourses" (96). De Certeau suggests a way out of castastrophe; his Diogenes is Michel Foucault: "one can analyze the microbe-like, singular and plural practices which an urbanistic system was supposed to administer or suppress . . . follow[ing] the swarming activity . . . of everyday regulations and surreptitious creativities that are . . . concealed by the . . . discourses of . . . organization" (96). For him, in the footsteps of Foucault, who was looking for a "theory of everyday practices, of lived space," and like Benjamin strolling and remembering history in the present, the scholarly and creative act is that of passing by, the operation of walking, wandering—the art of the strayer.

(I question de Certeau's tinge of nostalgia, as well as a politics of space which doesn't emphasize the twentieth-century determinant of time. Some of us might be driving rapidly in cities, on crowded freeways, or flying from airport to airport, vague and similar networks without borders or difference, a distillation of cultural differences into the mass, institutional international airport style of bland sameness depicted in *Small World*.)

In *Hiroshima Mon Amour*, the lovers walk away and toward each other, their wandering the enunciation of desire. De Certeau might assess that the museum, Peace Square, the newsreel footage, and the guided tourists have the status of the "proper meaning of grammar . . . it is a produced fiction. Theirs [urbanists and architects] is the image of a coherent and totalizing space—spaces in this view are both singular and separate" (101–103). Against this official rendering is the space and memory of the lovers: "the pedestrian walker" tells a "story jerry built . . . from common sayings, an allusive and fragmentary story whose gaps mesh with the social practices it symbolizes" (102). As if analyzing the film, he writes: "To walk is to lack a place." As if writing an epigram for the film: "Memory is a sort of anti-museum; it is not localizable."

For de Certeau, like the woman from Nevers and perhaps Norbert Hanhold, travel "produces an exploration of the deserted places of my memory, the return to nearby exoticism by way of a detour through distant places and the discovery of relics and legends. . . ." "Haunted places are the only ones people can live in." Like Benjamin, travel involves a return to childhood—"to be other and to move toward the other." Unfortunately, for both writers, "walking" is moving away from the mother, a game of *Fort da!* De Certeau's conclusion (the royal road named Lacan), like Benjamin's "syphilis" and jabbing denigrations of his mother, was unexpected, a letdown. While women travelers have come at least some distance—just before the end, de Certeau says that this experience will be different for "the female foetus introduced into another relationship to space"—Barthes might be right: to write, for men, involves the body of "the Mother."[16] If they can live through this separation (Barthes could not), then they come out siding with the father, like Benjamin. In de Certeau's account, women are still unborn.

However, there are other ways to think the city and its inhabitants: *The Gold Diggers* is one; Yvonne Rainer's *The Man Who Envied Women* is another.

CHAPTER
9

TAKING A CUE FROM ARIADNE

One fictions history starting from a political
reality that renders it true; one fictions a politics that doesn't as yet exist starting from a
historical truth.

—Michel Foucault[1]

Re-vision—the act of looking back, seeing
with fresh eyes, of entering an old text from a
new critical direction is, for women, more
than a chapter in cultural history; it is an act
of cultural survival.

—Adrienne Rich[2]

Thriller (1979) and *The Gold Diggers* (1983) by Sally Potter and *The Man
Who Envied Women* (1986) by Yvonne Rainer "fiction politics" within the
"historical truth" of personal experience and the "political reality" of feminist film theory. Unlike the makers of much of the previous work I have
analyzed, these artists—dancers, performers turned directors—influenced
by the history of avant-garde work, grappled directly with contemporary
theory, one overt frame for their films. Their participation in the theory debates was literal: for personal example, *Thriller* was shown and discussed by
Potter in 1980 at "Cinema and Film: Conditions of Presence"; Rainer delivered a version of the script for *The Man Who Envied Women* at "Cinema
Histories, Cinema Practices II."
    While the styles of these films are different, they are united through the
common thread of female subjectivity invoked by enunciation which is theoretical, personal, multiple. Unlike the simple binarism which sets avant-
garde films against commercial narrative films, these films weave the tenets
of avant-garde into a dialectic with classical and modernist conventions of
representation. Because this work is simultaneously highly theoretical and
deeply personal, I will digress to the biographical.

On an Aeroflot flight from Tblisi to Moscow, Potter and I discovered a common history in avant-garde film, performance, and the movies.[3] In different contexts, across the theory-practice divide and two continents, we had been influenced by the same work—an eclectic, asystematic mix of mass culture, art, and theory, from the Marx Brothers to Snow, Godard, and Freud.

Potter left school at fifteen, having known at fourteen, through making super 8mm films, that she wanted to be a film director. With her mother and grandmother, a music hall performer, she had attended films at a revival house, Everyman's Cinema, seeing hundreds of films ranging from *Duck Soup* to *Last Year at Marienbad*. (An aside: at this point in our conversation, Delphine Seyrig, who had also attended the congress and was sitting across the aisle, looked over, materializing the signifier, the imaginary woman as real activist.) Potter attended St. Martins for one year, studying performance, not film, where she was influenced by Tom Osborne's Group Event, a "happenings" group which was improvisational, minimalist. She took classes in dance at night, "learning to be, think, act, synchronously, in the present," learning to recognize the difference between truth and artifice in performance, learning, in essence, how to direct as well as perform. When she was eighteen, she saw the films of Snow, Warhol, Wieland, and others made by the U.S. and Canadian avant-garde at the Drury Lane, a tiny theater with mattresses and a movie screen. At a Cine-Club in Bristol, she saw early Soviet cinema and surrealist films, and particularly remembers her first screening of *Un Chien Andalou*.

She joined the London Filmmaker's Cooperative; although there were very few women, she was not then conscious of its "male-centeredness." She was interested in "expanded cinema" with multiple projections and live performance. Along with seeing classical opera, ballet, and theatre, she attended the National Film Theatre and Underground Film Festivals, watching German pornography on the same bill with Kubelka's films (pornography and avant-garde were strangely elided in the 1960s). Two of her performances which included film, live action, and split screens were *The Building* and *Play;* she also performed in others' work and toured.

Potter continued to study dance and choreography—appreciating the discipline, the physical labor, the absolute standards after the previous chaos of her life. For her, dance was about gaining strength, learning to take risks, exposing oneself to humiliation, embarrassment. To be exposed, one needed strength and flexibility, of mind and body. The means of production were simple, and she could produce much work. However, she pointed out that London was not as supportive of dance performance as New York; there were no critics like Jill Johnston and few funding sources, to say nothing of artistic respectability. The conditions of performers or musicians like Meredith Monk in New York were missing in London. Emergent from this conversation were Potter's resourcefulness, her self-taught determination, her physical and intellectual strength—refusing the position of victim or defeatism. For her, anything is possible; there is great pleasure in making something from limited resources, in circumventing constraints.

In 1970, she attended her first women's meeting at the Institute of Contemporary Arts and became "totally excited" about reading Germaine Greer, *The Second Sex*, and Freud, "which all, immediately, made sense." During this time, she also performed and toured with FIG, a Feminist Improvising Group which was "very professional, playing major jazz festivals around Europe" with Lindsay Cooper, her collaborator. She continued to stage performances, and began her collaboration with Rose English. In 1976, she attended weekend film conferences which had begun to engage issues of theory: Brecht and realism, psychoanalysis, ideology, and feminism. Although having read psychoanalysis sporadically, she was an active and resourceful participant. Her knowledge and study of theory were eclectic, self-taught, her motto being "the primacy of thought rather than theory," discovering ideas through work rather than the work merely replicating theory.

One significant means of discovery for Potter is what she calls "political psychotherapy"; "psychotherapeutic counseling" is peer counseling, informed by psychoanalysis, in which the roles of analyst and analysand continue to reverse and function without hierarchy. In her group, they paid attention to emotions, gender, race, class, as well as the politics of family—very different concerns from classical Freudian psychoanalysis (in practice and in film theory), a hierarchically structured one-way street. Perhaps because of this group logic of shared expertise, *Thriller* outruns even feminist theory in 1979. The rhetorical strategy of *Thriller*, its shifting enunciation in which participants are both analyst and analysand, critic and performer, is rather like group therapy, which is a collective process of role traversals and mutual identifications. Another explanation for the acuity of the film's insight is Potter's intense and constant scrutiny of herself and her experiences, looking within the "personal historical" for social answers.

In 1976 and 1977, she became involved in the politics of housing. She had moved to a building in Holburn that was formerly a sweat shop, and had received a grant of three thousand pounds from the British Arts Council for her on-site, ambitious, spectacular performances, which attracted quite a following. Potter has lived on her art since 1974, holding no other jobs but struggling with many separate roles, a plethora of talents—musician, dancer, choreographer, director, activist, entertainer, and theorist. *Thriller* brought all the strands together. In many ways, it summarizes her intellectual and artistic concerns—avant-garde film, commercial cinema, classical ballet and modern dance, classical and "new" music, acting and performance, psychoanalysis in film theory and in group therapy, and, critically, the women's movement and feminist theory. While Potter's history is linked to the avant-garde, she also sees herself as an entertainer, identifying with the history and forms of show business. As she says, "nothing less than everything will do."

Thriller was funded with an Arts Council grant for one thousand pounds; it was shot in the Holburn attic while she lived on the floor below, illegally—

the building was the site of history and of her present politics. Potter did everything, with her friends and collaborators, Rose English, Lindsay Cooper, and Collette Laffont, shooting on odd days over a two-week period and editing for six months on what she describes as a chaotic system that would have baffled a professional. The voice-over was added near the end; after the initial screening in London, the film was substantially re-edited for Edinburgh, where it was a huge success.

Thriller, informed by "Visual Pleasure and Narrative Cinema," Claire Johnston's writing, and other feminist texts, begins where *Meshes* and *La Boheme* end: the screen is black, Mimi is already dead, and we hear the deathly, beautiful aria from *La Boheme; Thriller* opens with the opera's climax. After a shot of Collette Laffont in a loft, reading a book and laughing, she sits in medium to close-up in front of a mirror in freeze frame—two recurring scenes which question the validity of theory for women—and poses the critical question in voice-over—a voice which is, however, with and for the audience, in a dialogue: "I'm trying to remember, to understand. There were some bodies on the floor. One of them is mine. Did I die? Was I murdered? If so . . . who killed me and why?" Like Ariadne, Potter gently and archly lays out a guiding thread, or better, takes our hand, leading us through the film's meticulously crafted argument. Laffont looks in the mirror, at herself, at other women, at *La Boheme,* and at women's history for an answer.

Like de Lauretis in "Desire in Narrative," Potter investigates Oedipus—the myth of romanticism, the story of art staged by various classic texts: opera, ballet, cinema. The film breaks into that sacred narrative by interrupting the smooth flow of representation—halting it, freezing it, repeating it, returning to the scene of the crime. Potter creates an alternate memory, one that is not criminal or self-serving, by inscribing in the present what was missing from the past—women's voice and point of view. She revises and then rewrites the classical text.

There are two scenes of the crime—one is classical, the other avant-garde; the first is staged and sung, the second improvised (performed) and danced: *La Boheme* is represented by still photographs of a London performance of the opera, with snatches of the score on the sound track; the remake or revision is a modern performance in a barren loft which shifts from freeze frames to briefly moving images of the modern performers, with bits of new music by Cooper and Bernard Herrmann's score from *Psycho.* The voice-over of Laffont, as if looking at the scenes with us, interrogates the still photographs, wondering what went on in the artist's garret of *La Boheme,* while the avant-garde restaging and historical photographs of old seamstresses are intercut in a dialectic of reconstruction. The avant-garde derails the classical in a tale told from Mimi's point of view, which becomes ours. The dominant terms of vision and voice, of active and passive, of subject and object are reversed, granting another pleasure, forging another subjectivity—a tale told by, about, for, and with women. "What if I had been the hero?" is the central question.

Fiction and history merge. Representation and the real are intertwined. History is not divorced from the present, neither dead nor over but relevant and alive; and fiction has everything to do with history, including the history of the unconscious. The historical dilemmas of the old seamstress in *Thriller* or of Mimi in *La Boheme* are not unlike women's struggles today in life or representation.

Laffont tells us the story of *La Boheme*, not presuming knowledge of art. The first telling is in the third person, a synopsis: "Act 1. Four male artists: Rudolpho the poet, Schaunard, the musician, Marcello, the painter, and Colline, the philosopher. . . . There is a knock at the door; it is Mimi, the seamstress and flower maker whose candle has gone out on the way up to her room. She comes in. They fall in love. . . . Act 3. Rudolpho has abandoned Mimi . . . because he cannot bear to see her ill." This line elicits laughter from women in the audience. After recounting Mimi's death, so many Camilles sacrificed to men's desire and the great star turn for actresses, the voice shifts its pronominal register, transforming into "I" as Laffont merges with Mimi and wonders, "Is this the story of my life? Was that the story of my death?" The sounds of the screeching violins from *Psycho* (in the shower scene, Arbogast climbing the stairs, and the discovery of the skeletal mother, that oedipal nightmare) intermingle with the score of the opera. Freeze frames of the fragmented bodies of the performers suggest Hitchcock's fragmented editing in murder scenes and avant-garde films like *Tom, Tom, the Piper's Son*.

As Laffont searches for clues in the mirror (including an impossible reverse shot from the mirror, a doubled look out or away from the mirror), an investigation of that Lacanian stage which refuses Lacan's interpretation and the negative linkage of women to mirrors and vanity, she gradually begins to identify not only with Mimi, the good girl, but with Musetta, the other woman in both the opera and the modern performance. "Sitting in front of the mirror, she waits for a clue. . . . When she first looked, she recognized her self, as the other." Rose English (as Musetta and sometimes Mimi), her collaborator, is held in arabesque, carried about by men, the female dancer limited in classical ballet space, immobile, dependent on men for movement. "For centuries, she has been jumping into his arms, over and over again." In the opera, as the bad girl, she is outside the law of proper patriarchy, and not the heroine of the story; thus, her death would not have been the tragedy Mimi's is.

The story is told again. The enunciation, which has already shifted from the third to the first person, now transforms into group identification, a process of discovery moving from "she" to "I" to "we" which incorporates the audience. The speaker, the voice-over, the investigator within the frame, Laffont, identifies with Mimi, Musetta, and seamstresses. The "ideal woman" transforms into "historical women"; primary, or narcissistic, identification becomes collective identification. This time, not only is the story told from Mimi's point of view, but Mimi has been politicized and reveals what the history of art has repressed, the conditions of production, the conditions of industrial labor concealed by the commodity fetish—art and the romantic image of woman. History provides clues, erupts into the present; the past is inscribed in the loft, formerly a garment factory. "Somehow the cold and poverty they endure is different from mine. . . . Do they really suffer to create in the way I must suffer to produce? . . . Did they take part in my death?"

Like the good story *Thriller* is, it delays the answer. *La Boheme's* narrative contract, which demands a woman's death, is still baffling—as is our pity for the suffering hero and his anguish. "Would I have preferred to be the hero?" (The answer to this simple question seems so obviously "yes." However, the few examples of female heroes suggest how arduous this assumption is.) And a bit later, "What if I had been the subject of this scenario, instead of its object?" (This is precisely what Laffont plays in *The Gold Diggers*.)

"Searching for an answer which would explain my life, my death," Laffont again reads theory in French and English, from *Tel Quel*—Freud, Marx, Mallarme—three modern theories of revolution: "Was the truth of my death written in their texts? . . . by reading, she hoped to understand. Meanwhile that other woman was watching and listening." She laughs. Then she looks for answers elsewhere, in the "other woman"—Musetta. "She was the eternal grisette, the bad girl, the one who didn't die." Only then, after positioning herself with rather than against women, does she unlock the mystery of the classical text, discover the answer, and solve women's hermeneutic question.

She tells us the story of the opera for the third time. "Act 1. There is a knock at the door. It is Mimi, the seamstress and flower maker, sewing stale flowers that didn't smell. . . . Often until the early hours working with the cold and a candle as companion. They produce stories to disguise how I must produce their goods." She skips to Act 4, her death, the necessity of her death for story: "Perhaps being young, single and vulnerable, with a death that serves their desire to become heroes in the display of their grief. . . . We were set up as opposites, as complementary characters, and kept apart to serve our roles. . . . Yes. It was murder."

In the end of *Thriller,* a genre called *film noir* dependent on women's death and guilt whose style is a reference point and memory, the two women (Mimi and Musetta/Laffont and English) survive and embrace in a thrilling and logical conclusion. By shifting the point of view to the imaginary woman, the historical object of male desire, and by incorporating history, including the history of seamstresses and representation, the story has been radically revised. Oedipus, like the two men freeze-framed at the end, poised to leave the room, has been kicked out of the narrative.

By altering enunciation and enounced, granting women the intelligence of the voice along with the power of the look, in a shared, nonhierarchical process of collective and multiple rather than divisive (or masochistic) identification, the film unravels romanticism, the tales of singular men sacrificing themselves for their own desire (called art), a destructive sadism for which women, merely obstacles, often dead objects, must be grateful.

(Whoever thought this up was a genius! I imagine two con artists, looking guilty: "But we'll never get away with this! They'll never believe this, will they?")

For Potter, the answer or solution does not lie in men, or in men's texts—leading us to the same dead ends. The answer lies within, between, and among women, Mimi and Musetta and "I," white and black, historical and representational, social and personal—at the same time. The destructive division of women against each other and against themselves just will not do; neither shrew nor victim is acceptable. Thus, along with the investigation of the murder mystery of the Oedipus scenario, a triadic structure of jealousy which catches women in contradiction, Potter also challenges the dyad of envy—a structure and emotion used to keep woman apart and isolated, a tactic ironically overlooked by much feminist analysis. Rather than repudiate the mirror stage, the imaginary to which Lacanian theory holds women, outside language and the symbolic, Laffont/Potter take their stand in front of the mirror, looking to themselves and other women rather than male theorists for answers. The look is not one of narcissistic rage, directed against the self; nor is it a look of envy at other women. The divided subject is a white woman and a black woman who unite, in the end, crossing the barrier of race along with gender, history, class, and age, to which I return in the last chapter.[4] Potter fashions and addresses a film *spectatrix*, not an unconscious labeled male, a spectator.

Spectator, derived from the Latin *spectare*, "to behold," "one who sees or beholds a given thing or event without taking an active part," has the same etymology as *spectacle*: "something to look at usually . . . presented to view as extraordinary." Taken together, as, for example, do Mulvey, de Lauretis, and Mary Ann Doane, these terms shift in a mutual tension between subject and object, between actant and object (obstacle or goal). In *Webster's*, after *spectatorship*, "the act of spectating," gender appears in the form of *spectatress* or *spectatrix*, defined as "a woman spectator," a term which, as volumes of feminist textual and theoretical deconstructions have argued, reveals that *spectator* is a masculine construct, in need of an adjective to instate difference. I wonder why *spectatrix* has never been adopted—perhaps it suggests SM (as does the Freudian model); perhaps *spectatress* is too close to the subservience of *mistress*. Perhaps it would solidify a bipolarity which notions like audience or spectator cover up, smoothing over social, historical, racial, chronological, economic, cultural, and sexual differences which we hope will change. I rather like the thought of being a spectatrix; as Virginia Woolf, older and angrier, ironically and insistently wrote in *Three Guineas*, trained differently in mind and spirit as we are from men, we see the same world, but we see it with different eyes. (*Spectacle* also means "a pair of lenses . . . worn in front of the eyes to improve the sight or correct errors of refraction." It would be nice if we could correct the refracted errors of male theorists with new optical prescriptions; at the least, I would urge women to take off their rose-colored glasses.)

While the film crosses many artificial divides—classical/avant-garde, narrative/experimental, still photograph/moving image, image track/sound track, dance/music, visual pleasure/aural pleasure, the past/the present, history/theory—the most enlightening and usually unnoticed division is that between women. Think of Lina Lamont and Kathy Selden in *Singin' in the Rain* set against each other as good/bad, with Lamont's public humiliation (at the hands of men raising the stage curtain revealing her bad voice) as the price of Selden's fame and happiness—man and marriage. Imagine the feminist remake of *Singin' in the Rain* in which Lamont and Selden form their own production company, hiring the asexual comic and idea man, Cosmo Brown, as their cohort. Or, perhaps the women go it alone, sharing top billing, and make a big (but modest) budget, feminist film on location with an all-female crew; this scenario would be *The Gold Diggers*.

Thriller chooses love, multiplicity, and unity over envy, division, and self-sacrifice. The film's last words are "We never got to know each other. Perhaps we could have loved each other." This last scene is the beginning and end of her feature length film, *The Gold Diggers*.

A digression: At a conference on feminism in Milwaukee, titled "The Reconstruction of Knowledge," I led a discussion (if 150 passionate people can constitute a discussion) of Lizzie Borden's *Born in Flames* for an audience including women of color and older women.[5] For me, the film joyously represented women within a matrix of differences which were cultural, linguistic, racial, and chronological as well as sexual. Difference emerged as a political promise and a pleasure for feminism rather than as a sexual, historical standard against which women have been measured and failed. I laughed and identified with the women in the film as they sang, worked, and talked together. There is no room in this film, as there is no room in our future, for tolerant patriarchy, even of the liberal, sensitive, Marxist kind. Thus, I was flabbergasted by the outcry against the film. Black women in the audience severely objected to the film's representation of black women as anarchists and lesbians.

While the film's embrace of lesbianism and violent action—blowing up the tower on top of the World Trade Center, bombing the bastion and trademark of capitalism and broadcasting and a symbolic explosion of the phallus—upset many viewers, I suspect that anger was also directed to what I and the two other panelists, Judith Mayne and Valie Export, seemed to represent—middle-class, white, intellectual feminism, a "branch" of feminism lampooned and "corrected" in the film. Moving from the film's critique to us was rhetorically logical. We represented the theoretical model of feminism that has developed in film studies over the past fifteen years—a critical project influenced in the United States by continental philosophy and the film criticism of Johnston and Mulvey (in turn influenced by Mitchell). This work deconstructed (1) the representation of woman as fetishized object on her way to heterosexuality, marriage, or murder at the film's ending, with woman as object of both the voyeuristic male gaze and narrative and

(2) the spectatorial mechanisms operative in the audience; it was predicated on the conventions of classical Hollywood cinema and Freudian/Lacanian psychoanalysis.

While it is true that this critique picked up Freud's obsession with sexual difference at the cost of differences of race, class, and age (making it a young white women's project both on and off screen), and disdained experience as "essentialism" due to its linkages with biology, this was not true of my position or the film, a virtual carnival of heterogeneity—of characters, materials, and arguments. No matter; what I thought was not the critical issue. And while interpretation of the film was also at issue, this, too, was secondary. It was clear to me that evening that new social, vocal subjects of feminism were publicly at stake, that prescriptions from positions of privilege and safety—white heterosexuality, whether feminist or not—would no longer, like great theoretical models, suffice.

I will briefly digress from the public scene. The radical impetus of Johnston's and Mulvey's work, with real linkages to the politics of the women's movement in Britain in the 1970s and real opposition to humanistic literary criticism, has almost vanished in the United States. Split from life, void of political commitment to action, the insights of these critics have become generic truisms, repeated ad nauseum, like the weather on TV, by symposia speakers and "art" critics. It staggers the mind to imagine the number of films which have been submitted to Mulvey's principles by virtuous scholars. Using her now formulaic "system" *means* that the writer or speaker is a feminist sympathizer. While the political depletion of this work as it has migrated over time and cultural difference is depressing, the evacuation also suggests the pitfalls of ignoring context, including personal political experience, and specificity. Without history, pure, eternal theory can be extracted; the descent into cliched platitudes is not far behind. As Trisha Brown says in *The Man Who Envied Woman* regarding the displacement of the poor in Soho by artists' lofts: "We saw the enemy and it was us."

To return to the "discussion": this moment, directed at me, was conducted in the gap between representation and experience—between the film and the audience, image and spectator, belief and action—that chasm which Eisenstein tried to cross via conflict, shock. Paradoxically, like the film which upset so many speakers, differences among (and within) women in the audience were additive, combative, and positive; *difference* was not to be feared; *differences* were productive.

Sally Potter's *The Gold Diggers* is poised on the edge of this shift within feminism: informed by psychoanalytic theory *and* alternative versions of difference and heterogeneity. Potter endorses what she calls "the paradoxical advantages of our situation"—the contradiction between women as historical subjects and "woman" as the ground of representation, between "fiction as it is lived and fiction as fiction . . . that fictive space has formed and shaped our unconscious. . . ."[6] The film pushes the Freudian unconscious, taken into representation and "fictive space," as far as these notions can be taken for women; the film is either the culmination or the conclusion of 1970s feminist film theory, a model stamped, for me (and the film), by the work of Metz, Comolli, and Heath, as well as Johnston and Mulvey.

The Gold Diggers embraces female desire by remaking film history, locating the heroic quest for female subjectivity in "primitive" and modernist cinema. The primal Freudian scene separating the daughter from the mother which structures the film is staged as "primitive" cinema, with allusions to its forebears—burlesque, music hall, vaudeville, and staged melodrama. Set within and alongside this turn-of-the-century classical history are formal concerns of avant-garde—performance art, new music, and narrative. The initiating female moment—the film's trauma and memory—and its return repeat the narrative pattern of classical cinema which often posits a tragic, originary, male moment, as in *Citizen Kane,* which the film then remembers for us: for example, the boarding house Rosebud scene in the snow separating son and Pieta mother which haunts that film. The tragedy of Charles Foster Kane is that he never forgot—he never resolved this moment, he never made it to the warehouse where his mother's Colorado possessions were stored; for Leland as an old, infirm man, formerly Kane's superego, memory is man's greatest curse. For the cinematic apparatus, memory is a blessing but a mixed one for women. *The Gold Diggers* could be interpreted as a feminist remake of *Citizen Kane,* a film which combined the oldest story of loss with the modernist special effects technology of RKO; eventually it might occupy a comparable place in the history of films by and for women and female subjectivity.

The film argues that women's subjectivity is bound up with the history of representation in narrative which, like a man, exploits women, and like a melodrama takes daughters away from mothers and other women. These historical fictions, in which women are figured as sexual objects of the male gaze and desire and conscripted into "compulsive" heterosexuality, dwell in our unconscious. (And, I would argue, our real, everyday experiences.) This sexist (racist and ageist) "inevitability" of the classical or early twentieth-century text neatly meshes with psychoanalysis' story. Like a dream (and the unconscious) or psychoanalysis, cinema is an apparatus of memories; unlike dreams, cinema's remembrances are rarely our own. Thus, the struggle for women, like the pleasure of the spectatrix at the movies, is to remember. And our history—in cinema and psychoanalysis—must be revised after being remembered.

Potter uncovers memory and locates history in two general periods: (1) in primitive cinema—well before the 1927 coming of sound, or synchronized speech, to cinema (like women for theory, film's accession to language and the symbolic was a problem of art and economics), and (2) after the "classical period" dated and analyzed by Metz, from around 1933 to 1955 (following Metz, the period invoked as the "base" of much feminist criticism and theory without acknowledgement of historical specificity),[7] resulting in an intriguing move between "primitive" and "modern" or "art house" cinema—literally enacting the primitive as the "rupture" of modernism.[8] That the development of early cinema as a discourse and narrative of the family is coincident with the writings of Freud, the family historian who deconstructed its sexual dynamics, and the ascendance of Marx, who critiqued the family's economic base, is critical to the film's structure: Julie Christie is linked to psychoanalysis, Collette Laffont to Marxism. The film's "modern" scenes of women walking and being pursued in the city resemble "art" cinema of the late 1950s and 1960s—narratives which are coincident with Lacan's and Althusser's rereadings of Freud and Marx—a critical couple via, for example, the fetish, which was so central to film theory in the 1970s. Thus, Potter locates modernist theory in historical context, focusing on two periods which feminists and theorists usually ignore.

Potter: "It's a cinematic pun, which means deep play with the language of film—a sort of semiotic shuffle."[9] Theory is literalized, concept becomes representation: for example, the landscape of Iceland is "woman" as the ground of representation, "virgin territory," or "figure versus ground" distinctions of painting. The "subject" is really divided—a black woman and a white woman; and "she" is not lacking. The gold diggers are Klondike prospectors or modern accountants rather than the chorus girls of the 1933 film. "Formalism" is familiar to women: the gleeful women wear taffeta/net, ruffled formals at the ball; Christie wears her formal gown through much of the film. "When you're trying to represent a system of representation, you're dealing with this tantalising, just out of your grasp, phenomenon."[10]

Freud's fetish and Marx's commodity fetish are conjoined through the figuration of the star. The symbolic *as representation* is made literal by depicting the star, Julie Christie, as a religious icon and carrying her in a procession to the deserted, cathedral/bank and depositing her along with the gold bars. Gender as masquerade is revealed as commodity fetishism; we see the labor of the actress, not merely the "star image." "The star is often a manifestation of an ideal type and the part of Ruby, designed for Julie Christie, plays with these ideas." Later in the interview: "The Julie Christie part has to do . . . with a certain kind of glamour and blondness and beauty. . . . In the process of the film she sheds that to an extent, it becomes evidently a form of disguise. What that does is open up a space somehow, a gap, which separates the accepted stereotype from the woman. That's perhaps the kind of space in which the female can appear without colluding with voyeuristic abuse."[11] Gender is both disguise and declaration, a costume which can be worn or shed, splitting person from actor, star, and character, producing a gap rather than creating a seamless movement among these various times and positions of identification. "So the costume changes are about the theme of disguise and also a comment on acting. The actress is not the same as her part . . . and it takes a great deal of skill. It's part of the hidden labour of the actress."[12]

"The star phenomenon is an actual form of investment . . . a circulation of the face. . . . Ruby herself is being circulated and displayed, and Celeste is helping to circulate money."[13] The film embodies the contradictions of celebrity and economics, exchange and use value. The female star becomes cinema itself as Ruby says: "I can project, I can repeat, I am repeated. . . . Investors take their place and I play my part."[14] And more specifically addressing the female spectator: "I must have been kept in the dark." "Why?" "Because of the condition." "Which condition?" "The necessary conditions of my existence." "Only in the darkness are you visible. I know you intimately and you know me not at all." "I can also remember very little." "Why?" "Because I've been kept in the dark." "Why?"[15] To answer this question, Potter denaturalizes *and* materializes the gap between signfier and referent "which separates the accepted stereotype from the woman."

By inscribing a formal system of women's rather than men's "looks," the film denies the much analyzed male gaze any validity or potency; as a result, cinema's (and theory's) perpetuation of a visual system of sexual difference serving as the sign of male power and desire becomes irrelevant. The ludicrousness then of Freud's (and other theorists') uncanny linkage of vision with the "male organ" and fear of castration and/or death is exposed as the flash in the pan it has always been from women's point of view. Our experience has little or nothing to do with fearing castration, after all. Thus, vision given over as the special prerogative of male characters is a catastrophe of the film, as are spectatorial mechanisms of sexual disavowal—the fetishist's gap between belief and knowledge—and the distanced perversion, voyeurism. Among other things, women gain the power of looking.

Potter, Rose English, Lindsay Cooper, Babette Mangolte, and the production's all-female crew thereby drop out Freud's and cinema's heterosexual contract which is at the base of all this "theory," as well as upsetting the singular determinance of "sex" to difference and cinema. If the heterosexual contract—operated and legalized by the male gaze and male desire—is shattered, Oedipus is no longer the story against which all other tales of subjectivity are measured. Female subjectivity is dramatized, revealing that, indeed, one is not, as Freud declared, and Monique Wittig, after Simone de Beauvoir, inverted, a woman born, a biological explanation which "assumes that the basis of society . . . lies in heterosexuality."[16] By incorporating women's relationships and by changing both subject and object of the gaze, women are presented as active subjects. Thus is the story of psychoanalysis reimagined, for women, by women. Yet, we do not escape it; the film remains *within* its parameters, as if it wanted to salvage psychoanalysis for women.

This relatively conservative stance might explain why this film was received with silence, at least to my knowledge[17] when compared to the whoopla generated by Potter's 1979 *Thriller*—a dissembling of the classical texts of cinema, opera, and ballet. The interview with Potter by Pam Cook in *Framework* suggests that debates within feminism might account for this academically cool reception.[18]

Just a general reminder of two divergent strains: in 1972–1973, Claire Johnston called for a reclamation of the terrain and pleasures of entertainment cinema; in 1975, Mulvey advocated that the "look" be freed into avant-garde practices. While Potter considers herself part of the tradition of narrative filmmaking, she is on the aesthetic side of the avant-garde. The film's formalism, its reliance on performance art, particularly dance and music, might have troubled the receptive waters. Cook: "The film has a formal asceticism, some might say puritanism, reminiscent of avant garde minimalism." Potter: "Where is the puritanism? . . . For me, there's great passion in austerity . . . there's everything right about wanting to make pleasure that isn't causing somebody else pain. If that's called puritanism, then I think puritanism is having a great time . . . there are a lot of scenes . . . which do a lot of playing and are about cinematic pleasure—that's why I was a bit surprised when you said it was puritanical."[19] Film theory, as I have reiterated, has preferred the pleasure of classical texts. Like me, Potter seems defensive; Cook suggests the old opposition between formal, avant-garde films and narrative pleasure.

The film is rigorously formal and deeply pleasurable, aurally and visually. Julie Christie's performance is austere, her presence quietly minimal, denying voyeurism, instituting distantiation rather than fetishization. (I must confess to desiring more of Christie; perhaps the female pleasure associated with female stars is too minimal.) In addition, it almost demands intellectual agreement. "The identificatory thread [I think of Ariadne and the labyrinth] is not along the lines of the human being providing a model that one can live vicariously through and with, but rather an identification with certain processes . . . arguments and ideas that run through the film that . . . provide an intellectual identification. . . ."[20] The film runs the risk of being rejected as argument.

Along with the problem (for me, a pleasure) of "intellectual identification" (or disagreement), and the distancing of Christie, auditory pleasure is a complex dilemma. Audiences have been historically less receptive to innovation with sound. In *Thriller,* the music from Puccini's *La Boheme* and Bernard Herrmann's score for *Psycho* provide substantial, familiar pleasure. *The Gold Diggers'* musical score by Lindsay Cooper is minimal, experimental, without the usual hierarchy of intelligibility of voice over music, of words over instrumentation or effects. In addition, there is little "presence" track, fewer "fill" sounds, little familiarity, and virtually no climactic crescendoes.

Sound serves as an experimental treatise, declaring the authors' intentions—with few clues to character, feelings, or mood, usually ascribed to music but equally applicable to the intonation of speech. Speech is analytical rather than emotive. Identification does not function through star or character or even narrative; nor do we identify with the "voice" of the artist as individual; we identify (or not) with ideas and situations. Thus, we don't need to match our theoretical wits to the film, conquering it with knowledge, demonstrating our creative prowess and granting the artists more than their due. We don't deconstruct this film—as Paul Willemen analyzes deconstruction: "The real or claimed value of the reader's competence was transmuted into the film's value . . . the 'high art' value which is only the value of the consumer's educational status delegated to the object."[21] Theory, like history and sexual politics, is *in* the film; the film is not *about* theory, nor is theory outside, waiting to be laid on; the film, including "the conditions of its production," *is* theory informed by the history of representation.

We are asked to partake in a dialogical endeavor; the filmmakers presume our knowledge and virtually sit in the enunciative laps of the audience. There are no divisions between us and them; the pronouns shift—"I" becomes "you," which turns into "we." Ruby: "I'm born in a beam of light. I move continuously yet I'm still. I am larger than life yet do not breathe. Only in the darkness am I visible. You can see me but never touch me. I can speak to you but never hear you. You know me intimately and I know you not at all. We are strangers and yet you take me inside of you. What am I?" This first person riddle of the Sphinx and of the cinematic apparatus initiates a quest for Ruby, led by Celeste who switches the pronouns: "You were born in a beam of light. . . . I know you intimately and you know me not at all. We are strangers yet I take you inside of me. . . ." "I" and "you"—including the characters, the filmmakers, and the members of the audience—become a "we" as Potter cues the characters, addresses, and then joins the audience: "We have ninety minutes to find each other." This simple declarative sentence has a powerful effect, signaling a collective, mutual quest: near the film's end, during the ride out of the labyrinth, we hear: "I am changing what is there." This presumption of inclusion and perhaps commonality, however, has caused irritation.

Perhaps more unsettling than "intellectual identification" might be the focus on women's desire—"I take you inside of me." While *Thriller* ends with the possibility of women loving each other as Mimi and Musetta embrace each other in freeze frame, *The Gold Diggers* begins and remains with women's desire for each other, a desire not deflected by men who are only caricatures—farcical, expressionistic bureaucrats or prospectors. The film is a love story, and the love is lesbian—the repressed of the criticism I have read. The actresses are dressed as "femme" and "butch"—Christie as the Princess and Laffont as Prince Charming. The tale can be read as Ruby's coming out, or coming into lesbian consciousness.

As Wittig argues, "woman" is a construct of "the ideology of gender": "We have been compelled in our bodies and in our minds to correspond, feature by feature, with the *idea* of nature that has been established for us . . . distorted . . . deformed. . . ."[22] Think of Christie's ball gown, worn out of context. "For what makes a woman is a specific social relation to a man. . . ."[23] In Wittig's polemical conclusion, survival "can only be accomplished by the destruction of heterosexuality as a social system which is based on the oppression of women by men and which produces the doctrine of the difference between the sexes to justify this oppression."[24] The "doctrine of difference" is under siege in the film. Thus, it treads on sacred ground. However, while avid in her commitment to women, Potter is not as absolute as Wittig. She is not a separatist: "in cinematic history most of the filming has been done by men. I think of myself as a director and want that sense of colleagueship, of history and tradition. It gets dangerous to say that because you're a woman you haven't got a cultural history. That's not true, that history is ours, too."[25] Arguing her personal history as a director informed by the work of Godard, Hitchcock, the Marx Brothers, and Tati, Potter asserts her position in and out of film history.

The Gold Diggers, like its namesakes, the Warner Brothers films of 1933 and 1934, is a musical. Potter deploys Lacanian psychoanalysis as Busby Berkeley literalized "Freudian symbolism" so in vogue in Hollywood in the 1930s. However, in the 1983 remake, the mainstay of the musical is absent—the heterosexual couple coupling in song, dance, and marriage. "I see this film as a musical describing a female quest . . . about the connection between gold, money, and women; about the illusion of female powerlessness . . . about imagery in the unconscious and its relationship to the power of cinema . . . seeing the history of cinema itself as our collective memory of how we see ourselves."[26] (I note that repression is also material and conscious. While the female unconscious needs to be reinvented, so do everyday realities. Also, we must begin to specify this "eternal" female spectator. I want to know more about her. Where does she live? How old is she? Who is she?)

Although not as severe as dropping both the male gaze and the heterosexual couple, the film inverts other conventions of the musical, including the film within the film, the relation between narrative and spectacle, the alternation of address and point of view, on and backstage performances, dream sequences, inscriptions of audiences and stages, and varieties of performance. This time the women behind the scenes, like the on-screen women in 1933 and 1934, are running the show. The film's collaborative conditions of production by an all-female crew result in enunciation which does not conflate production and consumption, what Jane Feuer argues is a function of musicals which concealed labor: "the producing and consuming functions severed by the passage of musical entertainment from folk to popular to mass status are rejoined through the genre's rhetoric."[27] Christie described the experience: "My relationship with film directors was paternalistic, completely irresponsible in the way I put myself in their hands. That's changed. . . . I've only worked with an all-women crew once, with *Gold Diggers*. . . . It was fantastic. There was almost no hierarchy. All the carpenters, sparks, and painters were women, which meant that they all had to have gone through the same political feminist struggle to get where they were. We were all paid the same. We didn't even have to go through all the inevitable tricks and behavior that one sex puts on for the other, so it was a great relief and more restful. Women understand things men don't, like Chantal Akerman with *Jeanne Dielman*. . . ."[28]

Musicals celebrate the nonwork of song and dance and the effortless professionalism of amateurs, denying the work of actor and apparatus alike, producing numbers only in the Marxist sense of commodity fetish. Potter's film inscribes the work of performers, sometimes witnessed in an awkwardness of gesture, overheard in a voice-over critique or pun, glimpsed in hesitancy that suggests a rehearsal. We think about the work of this production, the "alienated" consumption of women, ideas, and money, imagining the female crew in Iceland—although not directly inscribed in the film, their presence is almost palpable, their undertaking heroic. And, like Potter, I would call it entertainment. "But entertainment isn't inherently reaction. In fact, pleasure is a prerequisite for learning."[29] For Feuer, "to dare not to be entertaining is the ultimate transgression. . . . For to be unentertaining means to think about the base upon which mass entertainment itself is constructed."[30] *The Gold Diggers* is a critique of "the base of entertainment"—which leads to a pleasure different from that of deconstruction, secured after the fact.

References, including shifts between forms of representation—cinema, theater, "performance," and dance—create "layers in each scene" and are foregrounded. "The avant-garde's rejection of purism and ontological preoccupations in favour of an insistence on problems of reference can be understood as necessary pre-conditions for the elaboration of an artistic practice capable of representing the complexity of historical processes."[31] Willemen's analysis of "reference" (not the same as modernism's reflexivity or postmodernism's pastiche, where quotations float freely outside history, unmoored from time and context and hence without critique) is close to Potter's "seeing the history of cinema itself as our collective memory."[32] She describes the film's structure as a spiral "within which there are many genre references."[33] For her, as for the Soviet constructivists, the spiral is a sturdy form which accommodates history, allows for re-evaluation, and incorporates re-visions unlike a linear, chronological model in which "there's not a great deal of room to go back and change things that were wrong in the first place"[34]—particularly the representation of women.

The film's structure is labyrinthian—women escaping from the maze of dark city streets occupied by terrorist businessmen and bankers who chaotically run around in menacing pursuit, like corporate Keystone Cops. This cityscape—the stark counterpoint to the Iceland landscape—is negatively linked to masculine subjectivity: whether Greek, mannerist, or the modern rhizome of Deleuze and Guattari, it is a maze and challenge which women can master. The characters lead men down blind alleys of their own making. Via editing of discontiguous spaces and non-chronological times, and intricate camera movements, the film, like Celeste and Ruby, looks for a way through theoretical systems, including film history and psychoanalysis. Without discarding the past, the film refuses to be trapped in it. Equally, it refuses the position of victim.

To suggest the film's complexity of structure and theory, never mind style, I will elaborate a central section, which is a journey into and out of the imaginary. Julie Christie as Ruby, wearing a detective/critic's costume of an oversized coat, practical shoes, and hat, has left her room for the glistening, noir city streets. Collette Laffont, Potter's "investigator in the frame," the black protagonist of *Thriller*, who plays Celeste, also leaves. "Celeste and Ruby together make the "celestial ruby" or "philosopher's stone"; their unity is in the alchemical secret. . . . one can identify with that dialectical process, the friendship of opposites."[35] Both women are pursued in the shadowed darkness by squads of business-suited men and the exaggerated sound of their aggressive, echoing footsteps. As the two women lead their ominous pursuers on wild goose chases in this modern/primeval city, Cooper's agitated music accentuates the chase. But the women trick the men and escape; women have mastered the labyrinthian space, as they have language, and find their respective ways out—a strategy emblematic of the film's entire structure.

Celeste dodges her chasers via a fire escape (a spatial trick) and returns to her room, the women's room, a central location of the film like the frozen landscape; this space is enclosed, warm, personal; the other, vast, cold, heroic. She falls asleep. Her dream of women is erotic and embodies what Potter might call the pleasure of Puritanism by intercutting three scenarios: a performance by androgynous female dancers and a drummer, initiated by an old woman opening the curtain on a small stage; images of Ruby near the sleeping Celeste, finally carrying her to bed; and a brief shot which returns at the film's end, of women swimming in glistening, dark water to the bow of a huge ship, an allusion to Rosie the Riveter. Music signals that the dream is over, followed by cuts to the room, chair, and shoes of the dancing princess, rescued from the ball by her female prince on a white charger. One is reminded of Adrienne Rich's poetry and Virginia Woolf's "room of one's own"; this space is erotic because it is shared. The room is a performance space reminiscent of the attic in *Thriller,* a place where two women discover each other through history and the body, with intellect and affect. Thus, cinema is a dream and the spectator a dreamer—with a substantial difference; this is a dream of female fantasy and desire for women.

The "representation," the now more knowledgeable Christie, continues the investigation of her history. Ruby is chased into another anonymous building in the deserted cityscape. The building is a theater, and she sits, uncomfortably and self-consciously, in the balcony with the all-male audience of gazing businessmen/pursuers. This scene is a surreal, burlesque rendering of the male gaze of film theory. Behaving like automatons who turn their heads, clap, and look in unison—the male caricature of Busby Berkeley's zombied women—the voyeurs (who resemble a modern matinee audience at a porno film) are watching a melodrama, a Griffith restaging of the film's opening scene as vaudeville or "primitive" cinema. After cutting to a close-up of Ruby's look from the audience (where she clearly doesn't belong and is no safer than in the streets—a commentary on the risks of female spectatorship), she leaves, followed by the anonymous, identical men. Like Alice through the looking glass, she escapes through a door leading to the imaginary, her past as a young girl wearing a striped dress. She follows her past, her self/image through darkened corridors and doors, accompanied by sounds of faint piano music, like a child practicing a refrain of scales. Cinema refuses to allow her to age, or grow up, keeping her forever young, always an arrested image. At the same time, this is a search for mother.

This musical motif which begins the film and continually returns echoes silent cinema and its musical accompaniment, suggesting the score of the great male trauma film, *Citizen Kane,* music as the auditory clue to childhood memory and mother. In many ways, this film reverses that trauma of the little boy; Cooper's musical refrain remembers and rewrites Bernard Herrmann's score. The reference to Alice continues when Ruby encounters her reflection, her look, in a huge rehearsal mirror. A dancer is performing. Ruby watches. "Despite years of research, I reach a certain point and I freeze." "Have you forgotten? . . . Live in the present, don't dwell on the past." Ruby tries to remember; the dancer is analytical: "It's since I decided to go solo—the lifts are a little tricky." The dancer forgets her steps when she faces the audience—reminiscent of Arzner's *Dance Girl, Dance.* Abruptly, a stage manager enters, grabs Ruby with "You're on!" gives her the little girl costume, and shoves her onstage, into film history, into vaudeville, into a melodrama of separation from her mother. Her personal trauma becomes a public spectacle. Thus the double bind of women—seeing themselves *as* others see them, trapped between the gaze of the audience and the image on the screen.

Ruby is wearing heavy theatrical makeup in the Mae Marsh, Mary Pickford, Lillian Gish look-alike style of early cinema and using exaggerated, coded silent gestures of bewilderment and anguish. She is too old for the eternal part of the little girl. Her makeup has become a Kabuki mask. The all-male audience applauds the prospector with the gold and boos Ruby, now alone and bereft on the stage, garish in her makeup. The little girl's drama and the aging star are of no interest to the men in the audience just as they were of little concern to Freud. In an extreme closeup, like Laffont in *Thriller* when reading theory to explain her life and her death, Ruby silently and grotesquely laughs, mocking the hissing male audience.

The history of the silent female star, conscripted at the age of fourteen so that the slow film and harsh lights would not reveal the signs of age, the revelation of her identity and celebrity coincident with the economic rise of the film industry and the development of narrative, "feature" films, is invoked. Mary Pickford was the highest paid woman in the United States, with Adolph Zukor promising to pay her millions not to act in another studio's films. She joined with three famous men to form United Artists, and with the advice of her mother, became a very powerful woman—only to have the variables of age and stereotype force her into retirement, to be mocked in

Singin' in the Rain. She became too old, like Christie here, to play "Little Mary," and vanished from public view, enclosed in her mansion. These women were heroines, albeit melodramatic ones, enduring on-screen travails involving derring-do, including treacherous ice floe shots as Lillian Gish did in *Way Down East*. Yet, they had to remain sweet sixteen forever, a tragedy poignantly shown in Robert Altman's soft-focus shot of Gish in *The Wedding*. From behind, bathed in gauze lighting, the image of Gish is the same. She turns toward the camera, she is old, her "image" a portrait of Dora Gray. For female stars, categorically unlike male stars, aging is the greatest tragedy.

Ruby's journey through the history of representation and masquerade, from the real of film location to the imaginary of stage acting, now takes her back into the audience, watching herself—this time with critical awareness—as emblematic of cinema's representation of women. She leaves the theater, returns to the magical door (the entrance to the unconscious), enters, and like Alice, Buster Keaton in *Sherlock Junior*, a scholar doing research, or the analysand in film analysis, goes back to the hut on the rocky, Icelandic terrain. The little girl runs around the hut, growing older with each turn, finally transforming into Christie/Ruby. The music stops, the curtain comes down, the image fades to white, and the camera pans down. The little girl has grown up; yet the film, like the daughter's struggle to remember, understand, and control the terms of her own representation, is not over. In fact, this quest is just beginning; perhaps *The Gold Diggers* will become an early landmark, richly embracing the terrain of mother/daughter.

While disagreeing with Freud but still intrigued with "how, when and why does she detach herself from her mother," the film is not even slightly interested in Freud's second and, for him, most critical question: "how then does a little girl find her way to her father?"[36] Potter celebrates what for Freud would be a failure: "Indeed, one had to give due weight to the possibility that many a woman may remain arrested at the original mother-attachment and never properly achieve the change-over to men."[37] For Freud "at the end of the girl's development it is the man—the father—who must come to be the new love-object. . . ."[38] In a film which (1) transforms sexual objects into gendered subjects who love each other rather than into envious competitors, a "little woman jealous of her mother," and (2) refuses to compromise by idealizing the preoedipal fantasy of maternal plentitude and leaving it at that, "father" would be an absurd ending, more fantastic than being rescued from representation and exploitation by a female prince on a white stallion and triumphantly riding off into the sunset—the ending of this film.

Yet, Freud's prescription is the usual ending of narrative films—our accumulated history of passage into the arms of a man. Might this be why the men in the theater audience boo the little girl's story? To illustrate how unsettling this film's construction of female subjectivity is, let me cite a distinction absolutely critical to Freud: "Whereas in boys the Oedipus complex succumbs to the castration complex, in girls it is made possible and led up to by the castration complex."[39] Girls have no motive to emerge from the Oedipus complex and thus can never surmount it—it is infinite, like the "rhizome," fraught or blessed with interpretive possibilities and directions. One can delightfully imagine the entire film as an escape from women's endless Oedipus complex by making a claim for the symbolic, a claim which refuses the resolution of heterosexuality, the family, and the individual. Thus, comparable to Mia Campioni and Elizabeth Gross's brilliant critique via Foucault and feminism of Freud's analysis of Little Hans (a case study which Deleuze and Guattari lambasted), Potter, perhaps in accord with Luce Irigaray, revises the Freudian interpretation of the mother-daughter relationship.

The insistent repetition and reworking of the primal scene of separation throughout the film argues that something critically different is going on. To his bewilderment but not ours, Freud is amazed by the strength of this original attachment: "Our insight into this early, pre-Oedipus phase in the little girl's development comes to us as a surprise, comparable in another field with the effect of the discovery of the Minoan-Mycenaean civilization behind that of Greece."[40] In another passage, "Perhaps the real fact is that the attachment to the mother must inevitably perish just because it is the first and most intense, similarly to what we so often find in the first marriages of young women, entered into when they were passionately in love."[41]

The scene in the film is traumatic rather than a fantasy of preoedipal maternal plentitude; it is a painful separation in which the father is the villain. Structurally, the triangulated scene erupts just before Ruby speaks, just before her entrance into language and the symbolic, voicing and staking her claim to speaking subject status *and* desire; it is an oedipal (talking pictures) tale rather than a preoedipal scene (silent cinema)—for women not an unimportant discovery. In a prologue before titles, the film deliberately pans over the highly contrasted, black and white landscape of Iceland, uncovering ruins buried in the snow, revealing a path leading to an infinite horizon; a silent woman—historical woman?—wearing a long dress walks down the path and picks up a toy horse. This memory is accompanied by Potter singing "Seeing Red"; "Went to the pictures for a break, thought I'd put my feet up have a bit of intake, but then a man with a gun came in through a door and when he kissed her I couldn't take it anymore." The chorus repeats: "Please give me back my pleasure . . . give me back my leisure time, I've got the pleasure time blues. . . ."[42] The sound of wind amid the vast stillness of the unconquerable terrain—women's pleasure, desire, history, and memory—is heard before the titles.

The second return occurs after Christie/Ruby analyzes her role as the historical heroine: "In the early days, I was often to be seen tied to tracks, hanging from cliffs. I managed to be feverish yet cool, passionate yet pure, aloof and yet totally available. We were all stranded."[43] Christie as the history of her roles and characters in cinema also reminding us of the adventurous heroines who were her forebears, including Pauline and her perils. A granular image of mother, standing in the snow, laughing in silent, slowed motion (a "freeze" frame?) is followed by a shot of the isolated hut. This scene—intercut into the women's room—is heroic, tragic. Unlike Little Hans and the construction of Oedipus, mother is a central position, not solely maternal yet valuing motherhood. Mother is not subordinate, not devalued, not property; she is defined more by her daughter than her relationship to men. The memory returns again in the third scene in the women's room; it is spring, the blonde child is playing on the rocky land; Ruby is wearing her ball gown, standing in a corner: "I searched for the secret of transformations." That is followed by an older girl called "Ruby" by her mother. Images of Iceland break in as memory, the unconscious, the sign of production as a quest; the search for mother is a quest for history, for identity.

Celeste is another version of subjectivity. Laffont has short, dark hair, is a black woman, and is dressed either in slacks, office clothes, or her Prince Charming garb—a critique of femininity and capitalism. Her knowing gaze as "the investigator within the frame" as well as her leading questions— "Do you know your history?"—are Ariadne's threads guiding Ruby through the maze. She rescues the princess from the place of exploitation, leading her away from the imaginary into the symbolic, taking her to a new space of critical awareness. Celeste is the hero of the story: "I was born a genius. That's a fact. I knew what was what right from the start. I am concerned with re-dressing the balance." It is as if Laffont's character from *Thriller*, who was searching for a theory which would explain her life, her death, concluding with "It was murder," was fulfilling the promise of *Thriller's* ending by taking action with and for women.

Celeste critiques the Marx/Althusser commodity fetish and the circulation of money—like the image of woman, a representation: "I can see you but I can't touch you," and "To the bank with the beauty, to the bank with the gold. Both make money and neither grows old"—and language. She works for a male boss in an anonymous high tech corporation of computers. Seeking an explanation of gold and commodities, seeking "specificity," she visits the "experts"—a performance of theater of the absurd as homage and critique of the historical avant-garde—who cannot explain money to her. The "performance" summons many discourses in miniature, including classical art: the bureaucrat leans against a Greek column prop and places an icon of Christie on his Doric pedestal; war: a miniature battleship in a tank of water, a special effect, sinks; and gold: it moves, like cinema, it is "a subject which must be brought up." The constant punning, the literalism of abstract notions, renders them absurd. Men are drawn with their own ideas, they are farcical, comedic, George Grosz caricatures rather than characters. Although parodies of power, their smug pomposity is upsetting. They are dangerous in their bluff, blunder, generality, and stupidity.

Celeste's second lengthy scene begins with Laffont watching men; her arms are crossed, she is knowing if not downright smug. "In the beginning, a man gave a bank note . . ." initiates the story of the circulation of money. An economic procession and chant begins as Ruby is taken to the bank/ cathedral by the acolyte priests/bankers/street terrorists: "Freeze the assets,

cut the supply, drastic measures, it's do or die. . . ." Celeste rescues Ruby
from the vault as she had earlier rescued her from the dance, from the places
of her worship as the object of the spectacle, the commodity of exchange.
They run away, together. Ruby: "I was framed." In her song of capital performed on a small stage, Celeste connects the turn of the century gold diggers with the modern bankers: "Robbers and bandits, builders of nations,
armed with a pick and ill-will, plundering digging . . . impatient until
they've got their fill. . . . Commonwealth lies, May you crumble and sink!"[44]

The ballroom scene, which holds on the historical image of women on
staircases, is repeated, with a difference. Ruby descends, poses, smiles, and
is passed from man to man who, this time, all swoon, helplessly falling to
the floor; "Investors take their place and I play my part." After Celeste again
rescues Ruby, the other women recreate a joyous, private moment in movie
musicals—a dance of women without men, gaily playing, partnering each
other, sliding gleefully down the banister of propriety. The men awkwardly
try to dance with each other. The all-male film audience coughs in unison
(the little girl identifying with her mother's cough in Freud, or Mimi's cough
in Thriller, finally transferred to men as "male feminists"?) After shots of the
little girl, the hut, the landscape, the road, and sounds of the wind, all
"identificatory threads, ideas, arguments," the horse and rider move down a
tunnel, rescuing women's past and pointing to the future. The shot of water
and Rosie the Riveter concludes the film's visual track. The piano refrain,
however, continues; unlike the Rosebud musical motif of nostalgia, loss and
impossibility, this film concludes with history and possibility—of a new social subject. It's as if the "split" protagonists, the "attraction of opposites,"
have, by dialectically joining forces including racial differences, together
outrun Oedipus, including analysts, prospectors, male spectators, and other
concerned investors in women's lives. It's also not insignificant that Rosie
was working on a real, big battleship while the experts were only playing
with miniature, little model ships.

As is apparent, the film calls upon what Potter calls "identificatory
threads" leading to collective identification—Freud's third version of identification, dependent upon perception of shared commonality with a group
rather than with an individual. Freud's first instances of identification, being
and having, are frequently sexual—involving a desire to have an object, for
example, the mother, or be like someone, an ideal, perhaps the father—are
bound up with individual scenarios, castration, and, of course, the inevitable
Oedipus complex.[45] Thus, it is intriguing that film theory has depended primarily on the first two instances rather than developing the possibilities of
group identification—so pertinent given the ritualistic, collective conditions
of film viewing. Furthermore, the instances of having and being have been
reinforced by film critics' obsession with analyzing cinema's "gaze" in terms
of individual characters and the isolated spectator whereas little work has
been devoted to inscribing the collective audience in the text.

Unfortunately, Freud illustrated collective identification for women by citing a cough shared with mother, or hysterical jealousy transmitted in a boarding school. Potter gives this symptom to the men in the audience, displacing and parodying Freud's cough as their (and his) sign of disapproval. For other audiences of this film, group identification emerges in another way—as sound of recognition and approval signaled by laughter.

Perhaps as significant for women as invoking collective identification, and unlike Freud's (and later, Lacan's) analysis of identification which *assumes* an identity, and individuality, the film *constructs* identities which are historical, over time, which is history. In the second interchange in the women's room, Laffont looks at Christie, a bit disheveled and out of place in her formal ball gown: "I am concerned with redressing the balance." "Do you know your history?" Christie: "Tell me everything. . . . I've been kept in the dark, the conditions for my existence." Identity depends on history. Subjectivity is not unified but contradictory, addressing process and depending on knowledge which can be shared.

Potter frequently uses spatial metaphors to describe women's experience and the film suggesting an affinity with the psychoanalysis of Winnicott. For example, she refers to the "inner landscape of women," which has "internalized sexism. . . . The men in the film occupy that interior space."[46] As I mentioned, along with being this colonized, inner space which is still male, women's desire is also frequently associated with a space, a place represented in the film by the women's room and the landscape of Iceland. These frequently empty spaces suggest, as Willemen argues, that setting operates as "a text . . . where a different historical dynamic can be traced . . . with different historical rhythms and different dimensions of historical time. . . ."[47]

Within Potter's metaphysics of space is what she calls "the vast, imaginary space of mass cinema." Her move to feature-length, independent films is an attempt to capture this space and reach a larger audience. "I think the concept of 'breaking through' was an internal device to try and escape the internalised forms of marginalisation . . . it's a desire to occupy a big screen space. . . . Part of my job as a woman film-maker is to break out of the ghetto. However . . . that big screen space is occupied in such a way that my . . . desire, which is necessarily a revolutionary desire, is not quite going to fit in . . . maybe independent production meets thousands, rather than millions, but we're overly apologetic . . . it's more important . . . to acknowledge the ways in which independent film has changed things" (Cook, 28–30).

The crucial role of the space of history and subjectivity as "other texts" is accentuated by the cinematography of Babette Mangolte. In her film *The Sky on Location* (1982), she explores the American West: "*The Sky* is not about nature as backdrop, but more about the idea of wilderness, which I've discovered is so ingrained in American culture, but totally bewildering for Europeans . . . the discovery of that land was done by people like me, coming from Europe, people for whom that space was amazingly different. So I feel an element of identification with the first settlers."[48] The analogy of discovery—being an immigrant in foreign lands, like Charlie Chaplin in his early films and indeed the westward migration of the film industry, largely run by Jewish immigrants, to California in the 1900s—is operative throughout the film. For Willemen, the contrast between landscape as tourism and "land as a crucial element in the relations of production" marks the contemporary avant-garde narrative.[49] For Potter and Cooper, who "had been to Iceland in our music group," "it had all the connotations of virgin land and unexplored territory . . . the frozen self, the isolated self . . . the land is also a mutable element, a force. It's part of the alchemical subtext."[50]

Potter wants everything: "It's no good dwelling in the land of the victim . . . there's a point of view which is extremely handy, which is to see the paradoxical advantages of our situation and to see our inner strength. . . . we've got to get out of the way this idea that anything we want to do is denied us. Nothing less than everything will do. If we want to ride in on white chargers and carry off our favourite film star, we can do that. . . ."[51] While I'd rather be driving a Porsche, I'm with Potter. Nothing less than everything will do.

CHAPTER
10
IMAGES OF LANGUAGE AND INDISCREET DIALOGUES

I want to return to Casares's tale of the museum, which details an apparatus of power, driven by male desire, predicated on vision. On Casares's terms, this tale is a cultural fable, a perfect metaphor of cinema; I can see sweet and luminous analogies with most contemporary theories, for example, Lacan's male subject's overweening desire; Foucault's panopticon and "seeing machines"; or Baudrillard's hyperreal in which "the space of simulation confuses the real with the model." Casares's story, which I used earlier, intact and unquestioned, is, like the Oedipus scenario, dependent upon the familiar representation of woman as the luring temptress, the imaginary signifier inadvertently ensnaring hapless victims, albeit criminal ones, in narrative, love, marriage, or modernism.

The parable begs to be rewritten. Thus, I wonder how the beautiful woman felt when she saw the escaped convict, with ragged beard, filthy clothes, and feverish, staring eyes, pursue her, emerge from his powerful invisibility, enter her world and her bedroom. Did she also fall in love with him—or did Peeping Tom's desperate visage terrify her? Did he rape her, as he had obsessed over her image? Or did he woo her? And, did it matter? As ideal, she and we are imagined to be eternally grateful for a "real" man, no matter what his character or countenance, who surrenders to his desire for us—the penultimate martyrdom for men—and, outside subjectivity, without reciprocity of desire, to allow this tattered, dangerous fellow/felon to rule our stories and sometimes our lives.

When the "projected" woman either returns or deflects the aggressive gaze, claims her voice, controlling enunciation and address, and takes pleasure/knowledge and action with other women, on screen, in the audience, and in life, other scenarios result. *The Man Who Envied Women*, the acclaimed 1985 film by Yvonne Rainer, is a bold move toward a new scenario—women's subjectivity. In an unschematic manner, I will thresh out several of the issues which resonate or unravel in this sagacious labyrinth, specifically the debates which address theory—its now generic catch phrases rendering it tedious and apolitical in many versions—and arguments which touch, often indirectly or inadvertently, on feminist practices.

As de Lauretis argued at "Cinema Histories, Cinema Practices II" in Milwaukee in 1981: "The real task is to enact the contradictions of female desire, and of women as social subjects, in the terms of narrative."[1] As if on mutual cue, Rainer—speaking at the same conference, presenting her early script of this film's narrative dilemma—said that as her work was becoming "explicitly" feminist (an "evolution" from covert to overt operations), it was more closely aligned with narrative:

> From descriptions of individual feminine experience floating free of both social context and narrative hierarchy . . . to explicitly feminist speculations about feminine experience . . . an evolution which in becoming more explicitly feminist seems to demand a more solid anchoring in narrative conventions.[2]

With only the slightest of narratives, yet such a recognizable and important one for women that we fill in with our collective experiences, truly sharing the process of the film, Rainer enacts the contradiction of women as social subjects and reenacts (through the mouthpiece, Jack Deller) the double bind of women's desire, seduced and abandoned by modern theory.

The Man Who Envied Women is an idiosyncratic thesaurus of contemporary theory and personal response to daily life, art, and feminism, an artist's history of sexuality and politics. "This film is about the housing shortage, changing family patterns, the poor pitted against the middle class, Hispanics against Jews, artists and politics, female menopause, abortion rights. There's even a dream sequence."[3] I will sketch the film's arch, almost wicked portrayal of masculinity—particularly the linkage of theory with men, or better, power—a critique defined by feminism.

Rainer lambasts "theories of the subject" constructed by vision and imagined as the purview of a masterful male subject over a subordinate, passive female object. This critique of vision's parameters revitalizes feminist "deconstruction" of conventions of the gaze in narrative by inaugurating an investigation of that invaluable project's missing term—male representation or the means by which men represent themselves. (While volumes have been written about male subjectivity, including a surprising number of feminist analyses, little has been written about representation of the male body; the reverse is true for woman, whose body has remained the constant focus of analyses with rare emphasis on female subjectivity.) Two antagonists of *The Man Who Envied Women* are the unlikely but promising duo, Foucault and Lacan. Rainer has inverted Foucault's poles of the panoptic dyad, capturing Jack Deller, an unappealing "speaking eye," in revelatory visibility with only an initial, fleeting glimpse of the female protagonist.

Lacan writes in *The Four Fundamental Concepts of Psycho-Analysis:* "What determines me, at the most profound level, in the visible, is the gaze that is outside. It is through the gaze that I enter life and it is from the gaze that I receive its effects."[4] Rainer has postmodernized the rendering of this modernist, masculine scene. Jack Deller, held within a public visibility of the gaze of the camera and the spectator (rather than safe in the privacy of Lacan's imaginary mirror involving the confirmation of male identity by mother/other) is not only determined but undone, receiving satiric effects of this encounter.

I will briefly detail one lesson from Lacan's paradigm of vision and subjectivity in which seeing involves observing and knowing, blindness and ignorance, and is both punctual and durational. His reading of Poe's "The Purloined Letter" cogently maps out these parameters of vision, knowledge, time, and story:

> The first is a glance that sees nothing: The King and the Police [the time of seeing or its converse, blindness]. The second, a glance which sees that the first sees nothing and deludes itself as to the secrecy of what it hides: the Queen, then the Minister [the time of interpreting or misinterpreting]. The third sees that the first two glances leave what should be hidden exposed to whomever would seize it: the Minister, and finally Dupin [the time of knowing or denying, refusing to know].[5]

This hierarchy from seeing through interpreting and on to knowing, via the glance, is an important schema for cinema—an elaboration of the seeing into the telling glance which extends the look *in time,* through the hermeneutic staging and sets up a powerful chain of glances of knowledge which propel the story. Clearly this is a lovely model for cinema's drama of vision which includes the spectator. After reiterating Lacan's nice system, most criticism ceases; the graph is clear and satiating.[6] However, along with charting this insightful analysis, Lacan is intrigued by the fact that the letter's contents are never revealed: "The letter was able to produce its effects *within* the story: on the actors in the tale (including the narrator), as well as *outside* the story: on us, the readers, and also on its author, without anyone bothering to worry about what it meant."[7]

I must "bother" and "worry" about "what the letter meant." First, it is not irrelevant that the powerless, blackmailed Queen is trapped between male glances which accelerate the story, and is assumed guilty. This common, tainted presumption of women's guilt, embodied by the letter, is the reason for the story. Yet, like the imaginary woman in Casares's tale, the Queen is without meaning, without identity. Second, Lacan salaciously equates this letter with the feminine; for him, both are signifiers without meaning. The feminine is a "phase he [the Minister] had to pass through out of a natural affinity of the signifier." This signifier/letter is linked to narcissism, the imaginary, "more appropriate to what might concern women." The letter also "exudes the oddest *odor de feminina*." And, to top this all off, "it is known that ladies detest calling principles into question, for their charms owe much to the mystery of the signifier"—which is all the "ladies" are to Lacan, a mystery, Poe's tale retold by a real ladies' man.[8] Like the letter/ signifier, the female is an empty vessel; to be a self, to be full, "of plenitude of meaning and the security of (self) possession," means to be male, to be "we" who needn't "bother."[9]

I offer Lacan's almost lurid scene of Dupin's discovery: "Just so does the purloined letter, like an immense female body, stretch out across the Minister's office . . . but just so does he already expect to find it, and has only, with his eyes veiled by green lenses, to undress that huge body. . . . He will go straight to the spot in which lies and lives what the body is designed to hide, in a gorgeous center caught in a glimpse. . . . Look! between the cheeks of the fireplace, there's the object already in reach of a hand the ravisher has but to extend. . . ."[10] (Imagine this scene in a film co-directed by Chantal Ackerman and Alain Robbe-Grillet.) The move of the seer/ravisher—yet another dangerous felon who traps women "in a glimpse"—from his highly sexed, visual encounter with the signifier to rape is only a matter of gradation.

Jack Deller (Tell Her?), encased or embalmed in theoretical language which he uses in hot but laid-back pursuit of various women, is the unflappable, U.S. embodiment of continental theory, a transcultural mutant. This New York, left-wing professor of theory—literally a divided, speaking subject, a parody of both Lacan's other/Other and Foucault's "speaking eye"—gradually makes a fool of himself. In convoluted dialogue with himself, he is language made visible—comically and frighteningly familiar to the women in the audience, the voice-off protagonist, Trisha Brown, and Rainer. Jack is confined within his barren politics of theory rather than life. Like Lacan, he is a real "ladies' man" wearing the verbal garb of Foucault, a wolf in sheep's clothing. Like the wolf and Red Riding Hood, Jack uses this modern language to entice and lure women. Also stultifying and oblivious, he is the droning voice of theory as unrelenting patriarchy.

Jack, the analysand in film analysis, also postures as Lacan the analyst, another "man who envied women." During one session, pathetic Jack, claiming validity by fidelity to a lengthy marriage with a now dead wife, says, "I knew so little about women then. I almost know too much now."[11] (Women in the audience erupt with laughter on this line.) At least for Freud, woman was a problem and for Lacan was *the* question to which there was no answer. All-knowing Jack reiterates the contemporary spectre of the sensitive, caring man as the reluctant, adoring lover of many women—the modernist credo parodied by comparison to the several Humphrey Bogart clips and critiqued by Rainer and Martha Rosler in verbal analyses of the journalism pinned up on the wall, specifically the article expressing concern for this reputedly new man.

The film is "about this man you see and this woman you hear? He has been given a name . . . she hasn't been given a name."[12] The female body is absent except as hyperbolic interruption—intercut in short takes of multiple women and the excessive style of the dream sequences, a parody of the Oedipus scenario. This scene concluded Rainer's 1981 sketch of the film: "What? What is going *on* here? That's me in the bed. He and I shouldn't be making love. Jack and *Mama* are supposed to be married in this dream, not Jack and me. But there's my mother standing by the door. Mama, get out of there. . . . And no, I don't believe it. Mama is watching. . . ."[13] This stylistic eruption of the grotesque body, the carnival body, plays back over the film as a travesty, *and* as a question.

The film's opening and always shocking sequence of Bunuel neatly slitting the woman's eye in *Un Chien Andalou* is accompanied by a woman's matter-of-fact voice which intimately, conversationally details her difficult week.

> It was a hard week. I split up with my husband and moved into my studio. The hot water heater broke. . . . I bloodied up my white linen pants; the Senate voted for nerve gas; and my gynecologist went down in Korean Airlines Flight 007. The worst of it was the gynecologist. He was a nice man. He used to put booties on the stirrups and his speculum was always warm.

Art and the everyday intersect; image and voice collide, setting up the strategies of this film of reversals. Daily irritants, a hint of story, and an airline tragedy are disconcertingly funny in their incongruity because so true, so familiar. Caught off-guard by hearing of our experience, we recognize and laugh.

Alerted to the art historical attack on female vision, the far from blinded spectators watch Jack, the nimble and quick academic and uncaring husband, try to jump over various candlesticks. As the object of our public scrutiny, he should be squirming, although his absolute self-absorption precludes any glimmer of self-awareness. Jack is his own best lover. To our perverse delight, this character (portrayed by two actors as the schizophrenic, postmodern subject) endlessly mumbles Lacan's and Casares's self-congratulatory fantasy: that grateful women massively desire this dull creature, walking in place, going nowhere on his exercise machines, who has sacrificed himself to his own smug, indiscriminate desire. For two hours of intense bricolage, this delusory argument is enacted as the joke that it is, yet an infuriating, serious delusion which is predicated on woman being simultaneously everything and nothing, and a self-serving obsession (his language reeks of the most banal narcissism) which precludes political thought or action.

Jack is a catalogue of so many male poses and assumptions about women and politics that he becomes hilarious and repugnant. For me, he is a perfect caricature masquerading as a feminist—in theoretical drag which cannot conceal his powerful patriarchy. As Stephen Heath archly writes: "As far as male critics are concerned, indeed, the meshing in the academy of some feminist criticism with French theory, deconstruction et al, has greatly helped, especially in the United States: I can do post-structuralism, Derrideanism, Lacanianism, and feminism in a guaranteed 'radical' cocktail, theory til the cows come home or don't." For Jack, the cows never left the barn.

Heath asks: "To what extent do men use feminism for the assurance of an identity, now asking to belong as a way of at least ensuring their rightness, a position that gets her with me once more?" Regarding the notion of "woman" as the question for Freud and Lacan, he proposes: "maybe for as long as we ask the question . . . it's too easy to know, maybe we're missing the point that the question has been taken away from us, maybe if we really listened that's what we'd hear, the end of our question, of our question. . . . Feminism has decentered men. . . ."[14] By being placed in the constant visibility usually reserved for women, Jack is decentered in the act of "getting" women.

On one level, Jack's jargon is very funny. As Blau writes, "It is still hard to read that still self-consuming discourse, which offers no proof but rhetorical pleasures, without thinking of it as comic thought, thought as comedy. . . ."[15] Unfortunately, humorless Jack, without a single ironic bone in his bland body, is not funny; he deploys language as a strategic weapon of subjugation through unremitting boredom/monotony and seduction—means of power which sometimes merge. Subjection rather than subjectivity is the effect of his knowledge.

For example, in the wonderful classroom scene, while Jack the lecturer drones on, the camera, like the zombied, berserkly bored, aggressively frustrated students, becomes restless, rudely leaves the room, and explores the modern and fashionable loft/classroom, tracking from the all-white, perfectly stylish kitchen to the bathroom of glass-block decor. Along with subjection, discourses of fashion (as symptoms of class and property) permeate the film (just as fashion has become confused with and sometimes inextricable from art and academia, Barthes's notion of the new as "the stereotype of novelty"). Labels—Husserl, Heidegger, and Chomsky—are dropped into the hodgepodge of Jack's canned lecture of theory or language as obfuscation, a lazy referral without meaning yet replete with power and tedium. When Jack speaks, language is hyperreal, without referent. During this scene, which provoked intense, personal anxiety in my pedagogical soul, a woman's clear voice recounts a tragic story, a politics of the real—the poor, displaced, and homeless in the United States and violence in Central America. Meaning occurs at this intersection.

Linked to subjection and fashion, seduction propels and halts the narrative. Like classical cinema's on-screen seduction, the literal seduction of and by theory occurs: Jackie Raynal (quoting Meaghan Morris) and Deller—sensuously swaying back and forth outside the door of the liberal cocktail party talk—carry on a sexed discourse via dualing monologues. Theory is made physical, the verbal lure embodying academics' tantalizing suspicion, the underside of conferences: what if all of this discourse of sexuality as linguistic foreplay were to become real? Like participants at symposia, Jack and Jackie remain unswayed by each other's intellectual "positions."

Raynal's is an ambiguous and transgressive masquerade: her sensuous voice speaks Morris's horror show of theory, extravagant, caustic metaphors masked by Raynal's heavy French accent and breathy, arduous intonation. Morris's nightmare scene emphatically depicts one hyperbolic case of the film; Raynals's undulating body and gaping dress suggest an equivalently lusty or scandalous interpretation. Voice, body, and text figure an intricate, contradictory and literal discourse of seduction, sexuality interrupted and punctuated by the politics behind the door of the party of disembodied words. Morris's wonderful text operates with a sarcastic, witty bludgeon rather than a satiric scalpel. She is no fool and rushes in where angels fear to tread:

> What is happening when women must work so hard in distinguishing the penis and the phallus? . . . Passing from the realm of the theory of the subject to the shifty spaces of feminine writing is like emerging from a horror show to a costume ball. The world of "theorization" is a grim one, haunted by mad scientists breeding monsters through hybridization, by the haunted ghosts of a hundred isms. . . . Only overalls are distinctly out of place . . . this is the world of "style." Women are not welcome here garbed in the durable gear of men; men, instead get up in drag. . . . If a girl takes her eyes off Lacan and Derrida long enough to look, she may discover she is the invisible man.[16]

Raynal's very feminine body and French voice, speaking through these clever, Australian words, traverse national debates of feminism/femininity— issues of voice and writing—and cross the censored divides between word and image, mind and body, public and private. This marvelous scene illustrates Mary Russo's "carnival of theory," including "semiotic deliquency, parody, teasing, flirting, masquerade, seduction, counter-seduction, tightrope walking and verbal aerialisms of all kinds," what she calls a "poetics of postmodernism."[17]

Cinema has always involved a flirtatious, triple seduction: of the women in the films, of the dating couples in the movie theater, and of the theorist by the movies—a classical text without intercourse (or, for women, recourse) which is then provided by theoretical discourse which legitimates and eroticizes cinema.[18] The history of seduction/destruction is remembered in the film clips incorporated from particularly 1940s movies (e.g., *Dark Victory*, *Gilda*, and *In a Lonely Place*) but including avant-garde films and *Night of the Living Dead*, the latter a wonderful parody of Jack, unruly audiences, and family romance.[19] Strong female stars dramatize women's double bind, sacrificing their desire and grateful to "real" men—an endless retelling of Casares's and Lacan's fables as cinema's classical model of pleasure. Jack sits onstage in psycho/cinema/analysis, in front of the movie screen which for so many years has investigated and punished women. This staging, a very apt materialization of contemporary film theory (Cinema/Psychoanalysis/Subjectivity, merging the audience/critic with the psychoanalyst) is defined as male territory.

There is a fourth, usually unremarked, seduction—of female scholars by male theorists, a hazardous fall-in diagnosed by Morris. While many presumably feminist writers have, with painstaking propriety (the good daughter approach) or outrageous (dis)respect (the sassy, semi-bad girl tactic), sought for instances of women's subjectivity in modern theory by meticulously translating or producing either "ruptures" or "readings" of deconstruction, Morris works with a concise and playful sledgehammer, suggesting that we "take our eyes off theorists long enough to look," and issuing warnings that our modern, scholastic lovers are anti-heroes: "Yet we may . . . wonder whether the fascination of television enthusiasts for Baudrillard is not like that of feminists for Lacan. The great seducer, says Baudrillard, is the one who knows how to capture and to immolate the desire of the other."[20]

Regarding Foucault and women, Morris wrote in an earlier essay (in a dossier or set of working papers on/about Foucault): "In fact, the nicest thing about Foucault . . . is that not only do the offers of a philosopher to self-destruct appear to be positively serious . . . but that any feminist drawn into sending love letters to Foucault would be in no danger of reciprocation. Foucault's work is not that of a ladies' man."[21] These acute remarks, very wise cracks, explain why this film both harshly mocks Jack's posturing as the voice of Foucault (a lifeless impersonation and a charade of knowledge deployed solely as power) and employs Foucault's method: the film is an archeology (in Bakhtin's terms, an anthropology) of discourses of art, the city, politics, daily life, and jokes. For Rainer, Foucault is valuable; coming from Jack's mouth, his ideas are garbled and twisted. Although with Jack it is tempting, Rainer refuses to throw this baby out with the bathwater.

It is exactly the theoretical language which has irritated rather than amused or unsettled many critics, perhaps unsure of its paradoxical status as critique. For example, in a perceptive analysis, Helen de Michel writes: "Theories of feminism and language take up an inordinate amount of time in this film . . . the audience must sit through an interminable lecture by Jack on Foucaultian theoretical analysis [perhaps "interminable" is exactly the point of this scene]. . . . What may be important ideas to those who read Foucault become an exaggerated and frustrating parody for the general audience."[22] It is a mistaken impression that theory, or ideology, has nothing to do with everyday life; theory is not alien, outside, a hobby that can be done, but rather is imbricated with daily life. Parody is a major point of the film; however, in order to assess its work, one must know the object being parodied, or, as Bakhtin argues, share common "social horizons." It's not enough to merely recognize parody, which de Michel does, and it's not sufficient to denigrate or dismiss the parodied texts which are integral rather than peripheral. Knowledge, like boredom, is self-inflicted and in this scene leads, like the camera, away from "theory" to its comparison with political actions—which catapults parody into satire, if not straightforward critique.

In *A Theory of Parody*, Linda Hutcheon's assessment that parody involves "another work of art or coded discourse in a stylistic confrontation, a modern recoding, which establishes difference at the heart of similarity,"[23] relates to feminist strategies of "rewriting" and "revising" as well as to debates regarding postmodernism. However, unlike the negative emphasis in many postmodernist critiques which inscribe a passive audience, her model of parody ("difference at the heart of similarity") involves not only a relationship between two texts but stresses an audience capable of understanding the parodied text: "pleasure comes from the degree of engagement of the reader in the intertextual bouncing. . . ." (Cross-culturally, parody thus presents certain difficulties—of intelligibility and interpretation; unless the texts and positions are carefully noted, it might come across as elitist, as in-group, or, worst of all, as boring and irrelevant; rather than gaily bouncing, parody runs the risk of dully thudding.)

Like *The Man Who Envied Women*, parody "exists in the self-conscious borderline between art and life, making little formal distinction between actor and spectator, between author and co-creating reader."[24] Hutcheon's emphasis on enunciation which "enlists the audience in contradiction" further reiterates feminist theory, although the close affinity is not noted: parody is a form which activates "in the viewer that collective participation that enables something close to active performance." This shared, close encounter between audience and author, "the intersection of creation and re-creation, of invention and critique,"[25] is "a way to come to terms with the past." "Paradoxically, perhaps, it is parody that implies this need to 'situate' art in both the acts of enunciation and the broader historical and ideological contexts implied by that art."[26] Rainer accomplishes exactly this dual task of invention and critique, coming to terms with the theoretical/personal past. The film exists in the "self-conscious borderline between life and art," a space of contradiction and collective identifications.

Judy Stone reiterates de Michel's unease with the film's level of enunciation: "Rainer's sly visual and verbal wit refreshingly undercuts the theorizing that may be comprehensible only to sado-masochists who have digested thoroughly *The New York Review of Books*, *The Village Voice* and all the works of Michel Foucault, the French philosophe. Even so, Rainer could have done with less of it. . . ."[27] While Rainer's wily wit does undercut theory, and aside from lumping unlikely magazines together (the rigidly anti-theoretical, anti-feminist *New York Review of Books* with the populist theory/feminism of the *Voice*), this enthusiastic review, like the first, posits a "we" (the critics and the audience, albeit a specialized one) against a "they"—those who read theory, mainly in New York.

However, as Rainer so wisely knows, theory—which in context and history is political, sometimes with radical effects—is migrating and being

commodified as fodder for the art world as well as academia, in both overlapping contexts often depoliticized, turned into undergraduate gimmicks,
fashionable passwords for exchange and seduction—a situation brilliantly
portrayed in the cocktail party scene and the many diverse representations
of gentrification taking place, literally, in New York. In this depleted passage,
primary sources, along with politics and integrity, are lost; tertiary derivations by venture ventriloquists like Deller and born-again (male) feminists
promulgate empty catchwords frothing with inflated currency or righteous
hype, while boutiques and artists' lofts displace the working class. Theory, or
art, becomes a hobby that is "done" (I "do" theory). This selling of generic
theory also appropriates feminism as a singular, apolitical plaint or whine
which can be incorporated (like poor, small countries, the aged, the homeless) by the official culture of art, academia, and journalism and then declared solved, old-hat, or dead.

Rather than trashing "theory," Rainer is witnessing and judging migrating
discourses of power as a politics of defusion. This is not an anti-theoretical
film, although it is archly anti-patriarchal; rather it is insistently theoretical,
historical, and personal. It is precisely and allusively located in the context
of the New York, intellectual, art scene (its specificity and presumption of
audiences "in the know" perhaps creating problems of intelligibility when
seen in other contexts and countries). By a friendly and deadly inquisition of
the story of male subjectivity (theory's constant focus) as it bleeds into U.S.
foreign and local policy and women's lives, the film examines masculinity as
a house built of precariously yet effectively stacked words.

Because lifeless theory is yoked to the male body and voice and not to
the lively variety of succinct women's voices and feminist theory which
thread political lucidity, compassion, and wit through the film, the real irri-
tant and object of boredom might be man as well as monolithic "theory,"
who, like the historical theory of the subject, when radically dissected
rather than decorously deconstructed, is not interesting or helpful to women.
The cluttered male monotone is infinitely less fascinating and knowledgeable
than the wise kaleidoscope of women's voices, images, and issues which
swirl like a whirligig through the film. Running through the projector and
our minds like a Möbius strip, the thoroughly feminist film has two parallel
tracks which share the same terrain but can never intersect.

Mikhail Bakhtin's provocative concept of dialogical culture provides a
model for the film's double-directed discourse—toward men, for women.
Although as far as I can discern not directly mentioned, Bakhtin's favored
devices uncannily parallel Rainer's tactics—"hybridization," "heterology,"
a series of discourses and counter discourses that intertwine without either fusing or splitting. Like parody, Bakhtin's dialogical involves a trio of
voices—author, text, and listener—with personal and historical "images
of language," with shared "social horizons." Against the centripetal notion of "common language," Bakhtin prefers dispersion, plurality, and decentering, without closure or identification.[28] "The productivity of the event

does not lie in the fusion of all into one, but in . . . my nonfusion, in the reliance upon the privilege afforded me by my unique position, outside other men."[29] Although the language is not breezy like Rainer's, Bakhtin's remark—rather outrageously lifted from its Soviet time and context—reads like a working premise for the film.

Popular culture, which is "free, full of ambivalent laughter . . . disparagement and unseemly behavior, familiar contact with everybody and everything," with respect for the intimate, the familiar, "the repertory of small, everyday genres"—women's culture—is preferred to official culture, which is monologic: "monolithically serious and somber, beholden to strict hierarchical order, filled with fear, dogmatism, devotion, and pretense"—Jack's culture and sometimes Art.[30]

Bakhtin's valuation of intonation—which is "always at the boundary between the verbal and the nonverbal, the said and the unsaid. . . . Intonation is the *sound expression of social evaluation*"—is impeccably pertinent.[31] Like the film and dialogical culture, intonation is directed toward life and the listener, in his or her capacity as ally or witness, and toward the object of the utterance as if it were a third participant: "the intonation abuses it or flatters it, belittles it or elevates."[32] Women in the film and audience are allies or witnesses as the theoretical discourse of Jack is abused and belittled—although the gendered distinctions might not be this clear-cut.

Thus, enunciation—"the presence of social entities that translate the *voice* of the sender and the horizon of the receiver"—engages us in a dialogue with the film and its interpretation.[33] For Bakhtin, the "other" is not located in the unconscious as it is for Freud and Lacan but in the social, in language. I suspect that the same is true for Rainer. Thus, expression organizes experience rather than the other way around. Linked with these notions is the idea of "character zones": "from the irruption of alien expressive elements into authorial discourses—ellipsis, questions, exclamations—characters' voices intermingle with authors' voices."[34] Rainer runs the gamut of voices and grammars, throwing down a gauntlet of language by breaking and entering men's stories with abandon. Famous discourses are estranged, alien, and not very good listeners. Jack frequently wears earphones while street talk, conversation, and jokes surround him. He rarely listens to anyone other than himself. A technically brilliant and casual orchestration of bits of synched (and non) image and dialogue are picked up from performing passersby on New York streets, restaurants, and other public places in a tour-de-force cacophony of Manhattan commentary and friends.

As Bakhtin argues and the film produces, "Understanding is in search of a counter-discourse to the discourse of the utterer."[35] The film is a dialogue in search of counter discourses, not resolved or closed in the end by the analysis of "a-womanliness": "I can't live without men, but I can live without a man. . . . But I know something is different now. . . . Not a new woman. . . . A-woman is closer. A-womanly. A-womanliness." The double use of the prefix *a* is not insignificant—being not woman and being a single woman, at the same time. Like other quotations in the film, this discussion is an engagement with Morris's "The Pirate's Fiancee." Her conclusion asserts that the history of women can involve both a "strategic *specification*, a real one, in fiction and in truth," and at the same time, "a history of that in women which *defies* specification, which escapes its hold: the positively *not* specific, the unwomanly in history," with "unwomanly" the key word and clincher to her argument. The film's lack of aural credits initially creates problems of attribution and raises issues of the migration of theory. For example, in her essay on the film, de Lauretis, presumably in dialogue with Rainer, returns, in her conclusion, to Morris's formulation. I suspect that Morris must feel a bit left out.

Rainer's heterogeneous women—including the women of Lizzie Borden's *Born in Flames* in the poster about which no one speaks—are heard and, when seen, multiple, or they occupy that powerful place of invisibility and authorship behind the scenes into which they can enter at will, as Rainer does. Women—articulate, politically astute, and friends—are everywhere in this film, speaking with each other, interrupting Jack, and posing difficult questions: the relation of the artist to local and international politics; personal quandaries of the body, aging, race, and class. To echo Heath's earlier remark, the (no longer singular) question has been taken away from men; the film is the end of *their* question, of their *question*. It is also the end of woman as the question.

The film also raises the question of postmodernism (and men envious of women), and charges this belabored, portmanteau word with new meanings. Postmodernism—so rapid a commonplace in the United States—has become an art historical, pejorative label which provides entrance into fashionable discourse (much like "The Password" routine in *Horsefeathers*) as a sign of mutual knowledge often with only the vaguest notion of what it delineates; the shibboleth emits prepackaged, dismissive, or "with-it" connotations. Yet, this neologism is paradoxical and promising: while postmodernism devours everything, is stuffed full of art and interpretation like a Roman orgy or Harpo's baggy coat, it is also an emptied byword, without definition or limits. (In uncanny ways, this "all *and* nothing" is eerily akin to the representation of women in "master narratives.")

However, as the film so lucidly suggests, "all and nothing" can portend possibilities rather than liabilities—neither to drain nor fill the peremptory idea but to let it vacillate, unlocatable, traversing boundaries, advancing neither polarities nor masterful answers. In addition, the scavenging mentality of postmodernism in search of the new also reconnoiters with the past, resulting in a hybrid straddling "the old and the new" which, like Eisenstein's theories of art and montage, can involve radical (and humorous) collisions producing an art of conflict and dialectic or unsettling synthesis.

Through counter visual and verbal dialogues (an overtonal and vertical montage of sound and image tracks), *The Man Who Envied Women* prefigures the attributes of postmodernism described earlier. Intricately and abruptly shifting levels and "quality" of representation—super-8mm, shaky video, granular images shot from the TV screen, and advertisements—and like Godard's films and videotapes, which mix commercials, translations, quotations, parables, monologues and dialogues, lectures and essays, the film is a mesh of artificial and official with political and personal discourses: "With satire, however, you have free rein . . . you can turn pedagogical, dissertational, narrative, conversational, lyrical, epic. . . . In satire, genres are mixed because the persons speaking are mixed."[36] Lyotard's remark, applied earlier to Wegman, suggests the juxtapositions and derailments which don't always shock us as Eisenstein advocated, but insistently shake us into politics and knowledge through collisions which equate "discourses" of theory with policies of power—e.g., urban displacement of the aging and working class by art and academia, as well as by "urban renewal," and U.S. aggression in Central America.

The duplicities of modern life and theory, instituted as Foucault has demonstrated after the seventeenth-century confinements in homes, prisons, and asylums, have been updated: hiding the aging and homeless in drab institutions, out of sight; covering up military actions, and concealing urban land takeovers with slick boutiques and cafes are concrete manifestations of the reality beneath the veneer of the public sphere which grabs and protects precious property by camouflaging material conditions. Perhaps because of the public intrusion of the second term, many theorists of postmodernism have diagnosed a bleak, if not wretched, subject terminally awash amid the pastiche objects of art, a cultural stagnation nostalgically ascribed in literary theory to "loss"—of narrative, the dominance or mastery of vision, personal stories of authors, and history—the latter an agglutination of the first three traumas.[37] Against this pessimistic grain, *The Man Who Envied Women*, like so much recent feminist art, is culturally (even locally) and historically grounded, troubling the negative account of postmodernism.

While Rainer's male antagonist is a singular collage of (1) Casares's modern criminal, (2) the ahistorical fragmented schizophrenic and (3) sleazy verbalists everywhere, her women are witty, intelligent, sometimes middle-aged, heterogeneous subjects, in command of personal, political language laced with wit and perception. The speech of women is not like the classical cinema's dialogues; it is not sacrificial but is frequently ironic ("Sometimes, fresh from reading Fredric Jameson, I could play his game . . ."), deeply serious and moving, as in Rosler's two analyses of the photographs; interruptive and intimate—Rainer bending over into the film when Jack is reading *Playboy* with "Will all menstruating women please leave the theater"; and joking. By relating the personal of women's lives, the film risks the hue and cry of "essentialism." As Heath writes, "Anatomy isn't destiny, but neither is it irrelevant."[38] Sound does not come at us nor is it over, as truth or power, but is with us and reciprocal, laughter from the audience signaling comedy and recognition. As Russo writes, "What Rainer stages is a dialogical laughter, the laughter of intertext and multiple identifications. It is the conflictual laughter of social subjects in a classist, racist, ageist, sexist society. It is the laughter we have now: other laughter for other times. Carnival and carnival laughter remain on the horizon with a new social subjectivity."[39]

Like the metaphor of the gravel path in *A Room of One's Own,* in *Three Guineas* Virginia Woolf—then over fifty, angrier, archly ironic, and *insistent,* ruthlessly and brilliantly so—invokes metaphors of connection as division: the first is a "bridge over the Thames, an admirable vantage ground" for her scathing analysis of women and the university. Woolf's second metaphor is punctuation's ellipsis, what cannot be written or what is omitted: "But . . . those three dots mark a precipice, a gulf so deeply cut between us that . . . I have been sitting on my side of it wondering whether it is any use to try to speak across it." In addition to the bridge and the ellipsis, personal pronouns accentuate the breach between men and women's experience: " 'we' . . . still differ in some essential respects from 'you,' whose body, brain and spirit have been so differently trained and are so differently influenced by memory and tradition. Though we see the same world, we see it through different eyes."[40]

Woolf documents the exclusion of women from universities with an inquisition wielded by statistics and precise argumentation, giving the facts of social contradiction from the daughters' point of view. In 1938, almost forty years before *Discipline and Punish,* Woolf dissects the institutions of the military, the state, the corporation, the family, and the university. She calls for a new university which will be "young and poor. . . . It must be built of . . . combustible material which does not hoard dust and perpetuate traditions." When she asks what will be taught: "Not the arts of dominating other people; not the arts of ruling, of killing, of acquiring land and capital. They require too many overhead expenses; salaries and uniforms and ceremonies" (34). Her myriad, unstoppable, and impeccably logical argument assesses the exclusion of "the educated man's daughter" from the various "priest-hoods"—of medicine, of science, of the church, of the university. She presents women's point of view which Foucault ignored or repressed in his work—a telling oversight, perhaps a structuring blind spot. Marshaling many comparable terms, her appeal is to and from "facts" and experience rather than "dangerous theories of psychologists or biologists" (17), or in Foucault's case, history. Wondering "what possible satisfaction can dominance give to the dominator?"—the critical question circumvented by Foucault—she suggests that we assess "our fear" and "your anger" (129).

Three Guineas, a belated answer to a letter, begins with a politics of difference, a critique of women's inequity within patriarchy and the family, and ends by exhorting us to become outsiders, adopting a strategy of indifference which "must be given a firm footing upon fact" (107). Woolf urges us to compare the testimony of the ruled with the rulers, concluding that after all these comparisons, by way of reason, "the outsider will find herself in possession of very good reasons for indifference" (108). Outsiders will "shut the bright eyes that rain influence, or let those eyes look elsewhere" (109).

Woolf's complex rhetorical move, which I have simplified, from a critique of difference to a practice of indifference, is a double one of standing inside and outside patriarchy at the same time, with enough distance and knowledgeable investment to perceive contradictions.

Like many women of the 1980s, particularly middle-aged women, Rainer is acutely aware that Woolf's great social divide still exists. While speaking to men, she is talking with women. And, if seen through our eyes, as Woolf was arguing regarding war, the world will not remain the same. The women of *The Gold Diggers* "shut the bright eyes that rain influence" and "look elsewhere."

CHAPTER
11

THE AVANT-GARDE, THE EVERYDAY, AND THE UNDERGROUND

In *Movie Journal,* bits and pieces from a twelve-year period of writing for the *Village Voice* (1959–1971), Jonas Mekas views New York as a lively site for avant-garde, its theaters, basements, and lofts replete with antagonists—U.S. reviewers, police, and European critics.[1] The underground city spaces are scenes of discovery and confrontation, with artists and their films always on the horizon, forming what Bakhtin calls a heterology. The enunciation is conversational, a celebratory dialogue more than a monologue or tome, with the invocation of cohorts and nemeses. The collection is an impressionistic micropolitics of the 1960s underground, what Foucault might call an archeology, albeit unlike Foucault, concerned with person and authorship; or what Deleuze and Guattari might call a map as opposed to a tracing. Mekas, a Lithuanian immigrant, poet, journalist, filmmaker, and diarist was charting an artistic geography set within the peace movement and the generational revolt of the counterculture.

Although much simpler and even chatty, his manner is akin to de Certeau's in his European city of theory and daily life, and reminiscent of Benjamin's strolls through Berlin seen from the riverbanks of Paris. Like de Certeau, he has no great unifying system of artistic (like urban) planning; like Benjamin, Mekas's presence is inscribed—he inhabits the city about which he writes. More importantly, he strays from the path, absorbing experiences, listening. One significant difference in the 1980s is that theory, like Jack Deller, rarely listens, particularly to art or women, speaking out of context or in any context only to allies who aren't listening anyway—like the cocktail party scene behind closed doors in Rainer's film.

(The story would be different in Los Angeles, the city of freeways and drivers. Because Manhattan is an island, the theorist can still be a pedestrian. And while Mekas speaks of and praises women artists, they are on the periphery, although not cordoned off or qualified.)

On Mekas's forays into the city as a series of underground art events, he tells us about his friends, how Brakhage is feeling, and Baillie's concern about pollution. Or when describing the third New York Film Festival symposium, which included Pauline Kael and Hollis Alpert: "I was glad when Gregory Markopoulos stood up and, trembling with rage, told him that he was a soulless moron" (205). History is personal, anecdotal, a series of fragments, always in relation to the present, rather like Rainer, whose work is personal, satirical, political—concerned with the everyday. The immediacy is comparable to "thisness, hereness, nowness," what Deleuze and Guattari call haecceity (remember high school Latin and hic, haec, hoc—that tested litany?): "Nor do I put my stakes in the future: I am now and here" (vii); *So Is This* is another experience of haecceity.

Although the heart of this Lithuanian poet was in New York ("I am a regionalist. . . . No abstract internationalism for me"[vii]), avant-garde had few spatial, temporal, stylistic, economic, or intellectual boundaries—neither media, nor technology, nor nation. The only delimitations were personal and cultural blind spots, refusals to see. Although his criticism evokes Art and Beauty, the view is anti-establishment—anti-institutional, nonhierarchical, and anti-money—the inverse of intellectual values of the 1980s. Avant-garde, elided with a commitment to experimentation and personal-social change, had everything to do with everyday life, including radical politics. Mekas fervently believed that we could only change the world after we changed ourselves, the way we thought—perhaps comparable to Deleuze and Guattari's advocacy.

"Rhizome" and other chapters from *A Thousand Plateaus* reminded me of Mekas, like an echo from another period.[2] The analogy is not literal, more like an overtonal montage which, as Eisenstein described it, is almost a fourth dimension superseding, or in spite of, Deleuze's brief mentions of "experimental" film in *Cinema 1: The Movement-Image* which he describes as molecular (rather than molar), genetic, gaseous perception, the latter an unfortunate coinage.[3] However minimal and exceptional the references to Snow, Brakhage, or Land, it could be argued that like feminism and television, appropriated as theoretical objects for models of postmodernism, avant-garde cinema is a model of time and movement more central than Deleuze acknowledges. His theory of cinema—predicated on Bergson along with Peirce (following in the late 1960s footsteps of Peter Wollen in *Signs and Meaning in the Cinema* and de Lauretis in 1984 in *Alice Doesn't*)—is presented through a division between classical narrative and the modern European narrative. Mekas sees little difference between the two. *The Gold Diggers* crosses Deleuze's rather unbreachable distinction between classical and modern cinemas, also overturning the narrative/experimental bipolarity by instantiating politics: female subjectivity.

In *On the Line* (1983) and *A Thousand Plateaus*, D and G describe their book as an *agencement*, an arrangement, with neither subject nor object, with "lines of articulation or segmentation, strata, territorialities; but also lines of flight, movements of deterritorialization and of destratification."[4] *Movie Journal* is in line with the pantheon of Sitney and Michelson (or they with Mekas)—Brakhage, Smith, Markopoulos, Anger, Land, Snow, Frampton, and Jacobs. However, the significance accorded Warhol's films and temporality signals one crucial difference. Mekas's quarrels with the European, narrative avant-garde or the nouvelle vague, and with U.S. film reviewers and festival organizers, are constant binary oppositions or lines of segmentation to which I will return. However, unlike Sitney, his inclination is that of D and G's rhizomatic structure, spreading out in many and unpredictable directions, taking off in lines of flight. "We speak of nothing but multiplicities, lines, strata and segmentations, lines of flight and intensities . . . and their selection. . . . Writing has nothing to do with signifying [a brazen remark], but with land-surveying and map-making" (5).

In one of his longest pieces, Mekas, walking with Ken and Flo, talking about walking with Stan, arrives at Jack Smith's loft, at 11:30 P.M. "One slowly began to perceive that this was not just a set for some kind of theatre piece that was coming up, a background, a crutch for it: No, this set, this arrangement [a concept central to D and G] was already the content . . . of the evening, of the play, it was there and it spoke already at us, and acted upon us . . . around 1:30 or thereabout . . . it was no longer essential what would come or should come . . . and Jack walking there . . . picking up this and that, and whatever he did or didn't do, and whatever his actors did, by almost doing nothing, or by doing something . . . all the theatres had been closed and over, long ago . . . all the ugly, banal, stupid theatres of the world, and that only here, . . . was this huge junk set . . . the final burial rites of the capitalist civilization . . . only Jack Smith was still alive, a madman . . . we knew we had seen one of the greatest and purest theatre evenings of our lives . . . as we walked, silently" (397). This arrangement (and Mekas's response), a series of middles and their connections, which had no discernible plan, no beginning, ending, or set time, is, for me, a perfect emblem of rhizomatic criticism or thought, what D and G call a "multiplicity." Ken Jacobs's 1963 *Blonde Cobra* is also structured like a rhizome, an arrangement of bits and pieces of Smith's performances and characters, abandoned footage filmed by Bob Fleischer and Smith which Jacobs later edited.

For D and G, binary logic, dualisms, and even great structures are limits: "Each time a multiplicity is caught up in a structure, its growth is offset by a reduction in the laws of combination" (8). Smith, like Joseph Cornell, two artists treasured by Mekas, deals with arts of combination, multiplicities (for Smith, transsexualities and identities) which Mekas does not reduce by catching them "up in a structure." For D and G, like the avant-garde in the 1960s, the multiple must be made and it will be a rhizome, "absolutely distinct from roots and radicals" (10). The mundane examples of rhizomes are rats which "move by sliding over and under each other. There is the best and the worst in the rhizome: the potato, the weed" (11). The tree structure embodies order, hierarchy, a beginning and an end. The "rhizome can be connected with any other without radical separation . . . between regimes of signs" (11). D and G's botanical analogy is echoed by Mekas: "Drop me anywhere, into a dry . . . stone place . . . and I'll begin to grow" (vii). Or, Mekas as the farmer, midwife, mother hen: "So I kept running about my chickens, cackling, look how beautiful my chickens are . . . and everybody thinks they are ugly ducklings!" (ix).

While Mekas can be taken as an early theorist of postmodernism, endorsing Warhol, Burroughs (as do D and G), and Godard comparable to Wollen's model, he might better be taken as a theorist of arts of the everyday—like de Certeau, with rhizomatic roots in the anarchistic everyday of the historical avant-garde which in the 1960s had migrated to New York art galleries as surrealism, transformed in Europe into "the situationists." A poetic emblem of Mekas's valuation of the everyday is Joseph Cornell, "the real poet of dailiness, of the unpretentious, of the anti-art film" (110). Warhol is another, as is George Landow with his early loop film. "What Cornell's movies are is an essence of the home movie. They deal with things very close to us, every day and everywhere. Small things, not the big things. Not wars, not stormy emotions, dramatic clashes or situations. His images are much simpler" (407). Like the "anti-art" film, D and G claim to write the "anti-cultural book" ("The rhizome is an anti-genealogy" [21]). The similarities between phraseology are many and uncanny.

Mekas's description of a visit to Cornell's basement is comparable to the theater event in Smith's loft: "I looked in amazement at all kinds of little things in incredible number— frames, boxes, reels, little piles of mysterious objects and parts of objects, on walls, on tables, on boxes, and on the floor, in paper bags, and benches and chairs—wherever I looked I saw mysterious things growing, little by little. And there was Joseph Cornell himself, walking kindly among them, touching one, touching another, adding some detail, or just looking at them, or dusting them off—the Gardener—so they grow into their fragile, sensitive, sublime, and all-encompassing perfections." Perhaps nothing could better describe D and G's rhizome—this beautiful scene even replicating the plant metaphor. The films of Cornell are "invisible cathedrals . . . almost invisible, unless you look for them" (410).

In addition to his style of thought and value, Mekas depicts 1960s avant-garde cinema in its entirety as a line of flight: "The medium of cinema is breaking out and taking over and is going blindly and by itself. Where to— nobody knows. I am glad about both: That it's going somewhere, and that nobody knows where it's going. I like things out of control. . . . The currents that are moving within us, and are externalized by the artists, are ripe with new impulses and they spurt out in uncontrollable and unfamiliar gushes. So the avant-garde artists themselves sit in the audience, surprised, repeating, 'What the hell is happening?' " (209).

For me, *On the Line* is a model of avant-garde which advocates the overthrow of ontology (unlike the arguments of romanticism or the revelation of the signifier), the dismissal of foundations, the nullification of beginnings and endings. The logic of connections, of "and . . . ," is exemplary as a model for the political and artistic counterculture—from the mid-1960s to mid-1970s, a series of shifting, intersecting alliances, connecting in the middle. For D and G, the "middle is not at all an average—far from it—but the area where things take on speed" (58). "A rhizome . . . is always in the middle, between things. . . . The tree is filiation, but the rhizome is alliance, exclusively alliance" (57). "A rhizome never ceases to connect semiotic chains, organizations of power, and events in the arts, sciences, and social struggles" (12).

I think of volatile, mobile, eclectic, counterculture formations, including cooperatives like Ant Farm and their crazy-quilt participants and diverse projects, the intersection of political allegiances—from civil rights to Vietnam to ecology to women to freedom of speech, the connections sought between the local and the global, networking together and imagined as linked in the future by electronic technologies of immediacy. (The 1960s concept of the global and the local, which gained currency through McLuhan and video visionaries, is again in style; this strategy of radical action has been recently rediscovered by Stuart Hall, Donna Haraway, and de Lauretis, however, as a new tactic.) If the international "middle" (like women, blacks, youth, local actions, and wars of liberation) could connect in a new constellation of multiplicity, the structures of power with clear boundaries (and what D and G call "faciality," which I will not develop) of beginnings and endings could be bypassed. The cross-country traversal of the United States by mutual actions like civil rights and end the war movements are examples of geographical decentering. Like politics, art also involved a nomadic entering and leaving by traveling filmmakers.

D and G's structure describes the impulse and reality behind the filmmaker's cooperatives and distribution centers, "a-centered systems," the way the thing worked: "networks of finite automata, where communication occurs between any two neighbors, where channels or links do not pre-exist, where individuals are all interchangeable, and are defined only by their state at a given moment, and in such a way that local operations are co-ordinated and the final overall result is synchronized independently of any central authority" (38). This is also a perfect description of the international workings of AA;[5] avant-garde functioned in a comparable manner, at least for a while, before it solidified in one version into a historical Great Artist, hierarchical, segmented system.

D and G's emphasis on the middle reiterates many films' strategy —without titles or closing credits (usually taken as opposition to ownership and star authorship, the denial of either film or maker as commodities), without clearly demarked beginnings and often with only tails out endings. Conner's *A Movie* is a series of middles and connections, a film without a beginning, with titles and credits broken up and interspersed in the middle; rather than an ending, there is a respite—the film runs down, exhausted. The orchestration of chase scenes and disasters is a rhizome, or to use another of D and G's metaphors, a river or a stream, without beginning or ending, racing along, picking up speed in the middle and chipping away at the banks which try to contain it. That D and G invoke U.S. pragmatism is apparent in this metaphor, reminiscent of William James, who argues in 1894 that consciousness (or time) was not a series of discrete events but that it flowed—like a river or a stream, a "stream of consciousness." Mekas's references to James Joyce, like Smith's invocation of Baudelaire (in *Blonde Cobra*), are signals of modernism's pragmatism.

D and G's method is "pragmatism [which] . . . puts together multiplicities or aggregates of intensities" (32). "Aggregates of intensities" resembles the sublimity that Lyotard seeks to retain in events, and perhaps the passion and structure of the counterculture, remembered in the 1980s by postmodern critics as the lost intensity provided by live events, direct action, and binary oppositions—the visible and palpable clarity of "Which side are you on?" Unlike much postmodern negativity—a disdain for the present, fear of the future, and desire for the past—D and G, like Mekas, are looking for the "truly beautiful, loving, or political" (33). For Mekas, "evil and ugliness will take care of themselves; it is the beautiful and good that need our care. It is easier to criticize than to care; why choose the easy way" (59). About Ken Jacobs's films: "All things that are clear make us more radiant. These films do not want our soul; these films do not want our money; these films do not want our votes. . . . Jacobs' . . . shapes and forms transmit to us, evoke in us, or rather produce in us the states and forms of radiance . . . a happiness of one who is totally awake, in full consciousness. That's the difference between art and LSD" (351). Like Brakhage, Mekas's stance on drugs was very different from, for example, romanticism and video visionaries.

The rhizomatic structure is set against arborescent structures—the geneological, hierarchical model of the tree, the search for roots, a structure branching down akin to linguistics, information theory, communication schema, and most scholarship. The tree model, like corporate hierarchies, doesn't suggest a popular methodology for D and G. Mekas: "You see, I search for nothing, absolutely nothing. Search means nothing to me, it's meaningless. All I want is to celebrate a few things, a few very beautiful, unique, simple things. . . . It has to do with energy that sustains life and makes it more luminous" (406). For D and G, the U.S. avant-garde, the underground, are "lateral shoots in immediate connection with an outside" (43). This outside is not what Bergstrom calls for; rather, "we shall never ask what a . . . signifier or signified means . . . instead we shall wonder with what it functions, with what it transmits intensities or doesn't" (3). D and G., like Mekas, like Lyotard, seek "luminous energy," the "transmission of intensities," the "evocation of radiance." Like Lyotard's sublimity, this resembles Eisenstein's "ecstasy" which was an awakening. In all these accounts, pathos, affect are valued as transformative. During the 1970s and 1980s, the emotions were out of fashion.

Mekas endorses what Deleuze, drawing on particle physics and quantum mechanics, might describe as image-time, not the image as consciousness of something but the image as consciousness in which "the reality seems to be transformed into a . . . field of energy, aesthetic energy"; in *Serene Velocity* by Ernie Gehr or *Wavelength*, "we react kinestically to the movements of the light. But through the form we reach deeper, into the indescribable, into the invisible: we reach into the area of relationships, proportions. You can't put your finger on it . . . like the atom, splitting. . . . All architecture, I am told, is a question of relationships. . . . When two things are put together in right relationships, they sing . . . ninety-nine percent [of the under and above ground films] do not sing at all. They do not even hum. They puff, they squeak, they honk—but they don't sing" (347).

As I stated earlier, Mekas espoused, as perhaps D and G do in the 1980s, that change must occur from within, "that the real work must be done inside; that others can be reached only through the beauty of your own self" (155). Mekas represents the peace and love aspect of the counterculture, inflected by Eastern, meditative (Buddhist) thought: "Goodness . . . is boring to most of us. . . . Evil is exciting. . . . We go to movies to get the taste of the seven sins. . . . But goodness bores us; quietness bores us; simplicity bores us. Even love bores us, unless it is perverted. . . . The words 'amateur' (from 'love') and 'home' are used to describe something bad" (131). His belief in the goodness of amateur and 8mm film (against commercial cinema) is an endorsement of technology and availability comparable to the video guerrillas' faith in home video (with their opposition to commercial television). "Films . . . will be made everywhere and by everybody. The empires of professionalism and big budgets are crumbling. Every day I meet young men and women who sneak into town . . . with reels of film under their coats. . . . They screen them at some friend's loft . . . and then disappear. . . . They are the real film troubadours. This is about the best thing that has happened to cinema since Griffith shot his first close-up" (20). (Brakhage published *A Moving Picture Giving and Taking BOOK* in 1971, reprinted from *Film Culture*.)

This belief in rhizomatic multiplicity is consistent with D and G's "magic formula": "PLURALISM = MONISM" in which one passes "through all the dualisms which are the enemy, but the altogether necessary enemy, the furniture we never stop moving around" (47). Or as Mekas writes, "The old banalized culture keeps looking at the new in oppositions, in negations, while in truth the process is that of deepening, cleansing, expanding, widening, adding. The question is how much can one widen or add without upsetting people's balance so much that they see it as 'opposed' to what they know already" (400).

Comparable to the difference between rhizomatic and arborescent structures, D and G set the map against the tracing, again as an allegory of the rhizome: "Contrary to a tracing, which always returns to the 'same,' a map has multiple entrances. A map is a matter of performance, whereas the tracing always refers to an alleged competence" (26). The visit to Smith's loft is a matter of performance rather than alleged competency—the lack of which has been a constant criticism of avant-garde films. Mekas: "Even the mistakes, the out-of-focus shots, the shaky shots . . . the overexposed and underexposed bits are part of the vocabularly. The doors to the spontaneous are opening. . . . What the old, smart generation thinks important the new artist finds unimportant. . . . It is the insignificant, the fleeting, the spontaneous, the passing that reveals life and has all the excitement and beauty" (40). "The passing" is comparable to Heath's distinction between preconstruction, construction, and passage—the latter, his key to the reception of avantgarde films. Mekas's is a philosophy of everyday life, experienced in the present, in the moment, in the here and now, haeceity, while not forgetting the past.

The Gold Diggers is a map, with multiple entrances and exits for women. So is *The Man Who Envied Women*, which is an update of Mekas's New York. The cardboard cut-out figures or silhouettes of Snow's earlier *New York Eye and Ear Control (A Walking Woman Work)* (1964), a film version of Jensen's *Gradiva* without either Jensen's or Freud's diagnoses, have, in these two films, become women rather than artistic or scholastic delusions.

A structure of segmentation, the "furniture we never stop moving around," threads through Mekas's writing: the "altogether necessary enemies" are newspaper reviewers who ignore or disparage avant-garde films, most commercial cinema (with constant exceptions, for example, Hawks, Welles, Rosselini, and Marilyn Monroe), and European critics. Like critics' endless charges of the technical ineptness and unprofessionalism of the films and events, the second repeated criticism (in addition to boredom—a quality inherent in the viewer rather than the work; boredom is self-inflicted, like knowledge) has been the lack of politics. Mekas's running dispute with the European narrative cinema anticipates virtually all of the late 1970s critiques except feminism (which restates these positions for feminism with newer theories and terminology), a debate outlined by divergent definitions of politics.

In a "talk" with Louis Marcorelles, a French critic: "I personally feel that cinema should be highly socially responsible, in the Brechtian line. Cinema has to be located in a given time . . . a given purpose." Mekas: "But that's what we are doing. In Brazil they have hunger problems. But here we have hunger of the soul. . . . If you'd think deeper about the underground cinema you'd find that it reflects the American man as deeply as the Brazilian cinema reflects the Brazilian man." Marcorelles: "I feel that the underground cinema is completely divorced from America." Mekas: ". . . For the essence of the American man was beginning to die, he was becoming like a machine and like money." That Mekas shares the belief that pluralism = monism, the result of rhizomatic thought, is clear in this remark: "It may seem to you that we're all mixed up. But that's part of what we are doing. This mixup, this confusion is part of the New American Cinema. We don't like separations.

The cinema is one." Marcorelles: "It's not realistic." Mekas: "It's unrealistic to separate" (237–241). The infinite variety of styles, times, and qualities of films *as one* makes sense within this construct. That Marcorelles and Mekas are on very different wavelengths is also apparent.

In 1966, Mekas reported the following comments, the first by Carlos Saura: " 'The conception of this type of cinema is extremely amateurish, elementary.' He walked out of Andy Warhol's *The Chelsea Girls,* commenting: 'This underground cinema is disastrous and a disgrace.' " "Agnes Varda commented on the films . . . of Stan Vanderbeek, Robert Breer. . . . 'They are useless.' " "Pasolini commented on *Scorpio Rising,* 'This is an easy way of making films' " (257–258). Responding in 1969 to a comment in "a Paris film monthly" that "the American film avant-garde is totally apolitical," he replied: "The Old Establishment, the capitalists, and the New Left all miss the true meaning, and they all hate it. The capitalist hates . . . [it] because, if he be exposed to it, his very heart would be transformed, the beast would be killed. Those of the New Left who hate it are latent capitalists. My God, apolitical! . . . How strange, and how corrupt it is to think of politics only in terms of films (or actions) of destruction. . . . Our home movies are manifestoes of the politics of truth and beauty. Our films will help to sustain man, spiritually . . ." (351–352). (Claire Johnston also took European art cinema and particularly Varda to task, preferring John Ford's representation of women; Johnston sided with auteur criticism's appeal to and valuation of popular culture.)

One European narrative filmmaker was acknowledged as an intellectual ally. In 1968, Mekas wrote: "*Weekend* reconfirms my belief that Godard . . . is coming closer and closer to the techniques and aesthetics of the New American cinema. It's interesting . . . how Ron Rice . . . in *The Flower Thief,* in one big stroke managed to liberate himself from most of the restricting conventions of the cinema and the society, while it took Godard six years and ten movies to do the same, and he still hasn't made the final plunge into freedom . . . privately he still plays games with the capitalist cinema, with the Daddy's Cinema . . . (324). In June 1970: "*Pravda* is Godard's best film to date. With *Pravda* Godard finally abandons commercial cinema and joins the underground . . . we have much higher and stricter standards in the underground. A commercial film can never be discussed in terms of the perfection we have in the underground film" (385).

Mekas's definition of politics, including the war in Vietnam, which circles throughout his reviews, emerges in his referrals to Warhol's films which reveal the bleak underside of commodity culture, the tedium and destruction of values of capitalist exchange performed on bodies; sex is a commodity of exchange (neither hetero nor homosexual, perhaps Barthes's "multiplicity of homosexualities" but taken to bleak rather than "glittering" ends), not an erotics but a monotony, its unpleasurable banality another addiction, like drugs, leading nowhere except to more sex, just something to do. "The terror and hardness that we see in *The Chelsea Girls* is the same terror and hardness that is burning Vietnam; and it's the essence and blood of our culture, of our ways of living: This is the Great Society. . . . These works, once understood and embraced . . . would exorcise us from terror" (257). The art historical interpretations of Warhol as the critic/celebrator of the pleasures of consumer culture become ludicrous in front of many of his films. While his silk screens might be about the surface of franchise and celebrity culture, many of his films are all about the relentless passage of time, of deathly repetition. Freud's *Beyond The Pleasure Principle* and the death drive signaled by repetition are taken literally, with anxiety rather than pleasure the spectatorial affect.

Warhol's films also fit with Mekas's Eastern metaphysic: "As Buddha says, the more personal you are the more universal you are" (377). Regarding *Eat, Empire, Sleep:* "It is a cinema that reveals the emergence of meditation and happiness. . . . If all people could sit and watch the Empire State Building for eight hours and meditate upon it, there would be no more wars, no hate, no terror . . ." (155). And, in 1966 regarding *Eat:* "We are beginning to see ourselves in a different perspective, or in no perspective, at all, perhaps, but in the simultaneity of distances—like looking at ourselves from outside and inside at the same time, out of our own body" (247). This simultaneity of distances, the collapse of perspective and distinctions between outside and inside, is sophisticated theory—perhaps of D and G's simulacrum.

It is the countercultural stance against money, against commerce that clearly drives the period and differentiates the avant-garde from postmodernism. For Mekas, "we shouldn't give in even an inch to the commercial temptations" (278). And earlier, "Let's keep our art free of any sponsorship, whoever the sponsor may be" (114). Making films with the artists' own unfettered money was the only hope for personal creation. I suspect that artists might view this position as sacrificially ideal.

The title of a 1964 piece, "Report from Jail," and other items chart the decade's struggle over censorship, particularly *Flaming Creatures:* "A verdict was passed in the New York Criminal Court last Friday that Jack Smith's film *Flaming Creatures* is obscene. A similar decision was passed by the Los Angeles court on Kenneth Anger's film *Scorpio Rising . . .* if . . . Anger or . . . Smith were to be caught watching his own film, he could be prosecuted. The projector and the screen, seized along with the film . . . will be likewise disposed as tools of crime." The apparatus as criminal is an interesting metaphor, a modern version of Apollinaire's story of a crime in which a real murder was filmed and then incorporated into the narrative. The difference between the two is the shift from realism to modernism, from the signified to the signifier. Willard Van Dyke, Susan Sontag, Allen Ginsberg, and Shirley Clarke were among those who explained, in court, "some of the meanings of *Flaming Creatures*" (142). The battle over confiscation of prints and equipment reminds us of another political context—of governmental surveillance and imprisonment. Little details during court appearances like being threatened with a contempt citation for not wearing a necktie describe real repression by real state apparati.

At the film festival in Knokke-le Zoute in 1964, they "smuggled *Flaming Creatures* into the projection room in the can of *Dog Star Man*," storming the Crystal Room and fighting "over the projector, how the lights were cut off, and how I [tried] to push off the house detective" (110). As always, he is not alone: "Barbara Rubin shouted from the projector platform, fighting like a brave general. . . ." P. Adams Sitney was there, along with the "flaming Barbara." He describes an encounter with Agnes Varda, there with her daughter: "Only slowly did it dawn on me that she took me for a sex maniac. After all, I am showing that dirty, transvestite movie in my room. . . . No wonder a State Department man was sitting next to our table wherever we went" (114–115). This was power that could be seen, like FBI infiltrators at protest rallies (detectable by their giveaway brown laced shoes worn with blue jeans and third-world shirt), power that had overt effects. However, as Foucault argues, power is operative not only within various state apparati and is not only repressive; power, like the various machines of the visible on which much of Foucault's writing rests, produces pleasures—of evasion, the risk of protest.

When rereading these columns ("I am not a reviewer. I write, I comment only on those aspects that interest me. I never review the films" [334]), I was reminded of how much I had forgotten. "Short term memory understands forgetting as a process; it . . . merge[s] . . . with the collective rhizome which is temporal and nervous [like Mekas's fragments]. Long-term memory (family, race, society, or civilization) traces and translates . . . at a distance . . . it is 'untimely' and not instantaneous [like scholarship, including this book]" (D & G, 35). It is precisely Mekas's belief that art is linked with everyday life, the ordinary, the detail, the present, combined with his willingness for a variety of experiences, all propelled by a radical impulse that avoids binary, hierarchical systems that most attracts me.

Yet, there is something missing. While Mekas values women artists, praising Shirley Clarke, Marie Menken, Storm de Hirsch, Elaine Summers, Yoko Ono, Barbara Rubin, Joyce Wieland, along with Yvonne Rainer, it's not enough. It does not do justice to the contradictions experienced by women avant-garde artists—albeit prior for most of these women, including Rainer, to engaging feminism. Thus, I want to stray from the path, onto another source, Scott MacDonald's late-1970s interview with Hollis Frampton—with the caution that Frampton had the great advantage of hindsight.

Rainer, included in Mekas's list of the greats in U.S. theater, has become one filmmaker Framptom "pays attention to" (along with Snow and Brakhage, although the latter is a strained, double-edged influence). Frampton remembers "the first thing I ever saw Yvonne Rainer do. I was in some loft— was it Brooklyn? I don't remember. There were not many people—a small, word-of-mouth crowd. In the middle of it she started making *Noises*, little mewing sounds, squeaks, bleats. I was electrified. . . . Is this the moment? Are we witnessing it? Are we going crazy? Dance had been mute. . . . What was memorable was a violent disruption of, a transgression against, the culturally expected . . . that single gesture broke open the whole decorum of dance."[6] Avant-garde film, a transgression against the expected, also struggled with sound. Many believed, with Brakhage, that film had to be silent.

Many pages later, like an unforgettable memory, Frampton returns to "Yvonne's leaving off performance," a shift of media remarkably similar to Potter. "She has shifted from a posture of visibility to one of invisibility. What is visible about her now is what can be decoded from the work" (74–75). Increasingly, like Potter, Rainer collaborates with women and investigates the terms of vision—a doubled shift of interest (to women, to film and collaboration), a strategy derived from the women's movement which has altered the structure of avant-grade, "redressing the balance" of power whereas in the 1960s, crossdressing was the unsettling tactic.

Frampton's memory of Rainer triggers a comparison of "two modes of visibility," of the difference between Rainer and Brakhage, who "also came out of performance": "he'd like to be on both ends; he'd like to be seen and at the same time he would like to be in control of the way in which he is seen. Yvonne seems to perceive the pivot between those two modes of visibility uniquely" (75)—a prophecy of one structure of *The Man Who Envied Women*. The two poles also have everything to do with Foucault's panoptic dyad and "speaking eye," with Mulvey and the active male/passive female division of labor, and with power; Frampton's memories overlap nicely with contemporary theory.

In the (sexual) difference between Brakhage and Rainer—which might have something to do with the status of language, of speech, of sound—Frampton positions himself with Rainer: "She and I share some sympathies . . . she's involved with language, though in a different way from me. Yvonne has adopted a confessional rhetoric, an overt one of personal material. . . . While the material is personal . . . it also has a specific formal weight . . ." (74). (Since our theories of narrative are inextricably linked with linguistics, the founding Saussurean moment in film studies, in spite of Wollen's very early exegesis of Peirce, language, perhaps more than narrative, is the real debate.)

The Man Who Envied Women takes us on another journey through New York in which warehouses have become upscale boutiques, art galleries, and lofts, a film which reminds us that Rainer was there all along, performing, dancing, as was Potter, slightly later, in London. Both films are remakes of *Wavelength*—Jack's droning theory lecture to the bored students and cinematographer with their panoptic spotlight stages the endlessness of that film, made in an artist's loft. *Thriller* (and the classical artists' garret of *La Boheme*) was also performed in a loft which was formerly a garment factory; the incidental murder of *Wavelength* and the necessary death of *La Boheme* become the focus of *Thriller*.

Alice Jardine assesses D and G's awkward position "on a complex and changing epistemological and political field of battle" (reiterating the military metaphors of the avant-garde, Mekas, and D and G.) She assesses that (1) they are "ignored and dismissed by the majority of academics," except a male "student minority"; (2) their "posture towards the U.S." is "idealistic": "they are the only writers in France who have consistently taken American literature and culture as their model"; and (3) they are "publicly supportive of the feminist movement" with, however, few women disciples.[7]

I must add awkwardness, more of an embarrassment, to this list of wary avoidance. D and G's rhizomatic versus arborescent thought—established through botany and the central example of the rooted tree versus tuber plants like tiger lilies (my more glamorous example), crabgrass, or potatoes, on first and perhaps second glance seems vague, anarchic, ahistorical, downright *silly*. On initial encounter I wanted specificity, concreteness; I was bewildered and bemused but fascinated.

Then I remembered reading *S/Z* in the early 1970s: haecceity, like faciality, is no stranger a coinage or vaguer a concept than the proaretic and hermeneutic codes, and the Doxa. While the Doxa reeked of jargon, Barthes's readerly/writerly distinction bespoke the vague banality of cliche. Both devices—the commonplace and the obscure—were simultaneously empty and confusing until I could provide my own examples to fill them, to clarify them; by doing this, of course, I changed the way I thought. This switch of intellectual gears is not easy. It involves throwing out, or momentarily setting aside, a great deal of time, effort, and conviction, becoming uncomfortable with the new, struggling with ideas and terms rather than dismissing them with "I've already heard this before." As Meaghan Morris argues, the first line of dismissal of new theoretical constructs is "I cannot act with this theory." The second rebuttal is "This theory eliminates agency," in the 1980s accompanied by a plea for the psychoanalytic theory of the subject.[8]

This conservative response of knowing disregard is often invoked against avant-garde work; like dominoes, the same argument has been applied in recent years to Freud/Lacan, Althusser, Foucault, and now D and G. For example, in his recent review of Deleuze's *Foucault,* Dana Polan cautions us to retain a theory of the subject which, he suggests, these theorists lack (although he pinpoints Foucault).[9] That Deleuze *and* Foucault specifically critique psychoanalysis—D and G for its binarism (with which I, to a degree, disagree, preferring to read Freud as also functioning within a model of contradiction, both/and rather than either/or) and Foucault for its faulty major premise of sexual repression—is not mentioned. That new models have other, different, theories of the subject is not acknowledged, until later.

That theory, like avant-garde, initially struggles with academic conservatism, as I argued in earlier pages, is not so surprising within the cultural and political context of the 1980s, resulting in a determined repetition of the same as difference—like the 1988 presidential campaign. As Morris noted, deconstruction dismantles binarisms only to prove, in the end, that they do function, like the snake devouring its own tail. The ploy conserves and defends stasis, the intellectual's invested time and labor; it resists change and maintains power. (Theory converts forget their initial resistance if not mockery which eventually turns to denial as opponents become enthusiasts, but always late. As Godard said, being ahead is only possible because the rest of the world is behind.)

These gambits within the academy and the reception of avant-garde work paradoxically suggest D and G's distinction between "arborescent systems" and "rhizomatic systems": "Arborescent systems are hierarchical systems comprised of centers of significance and subjectivization . . . a subjective affect only from pre-established connections" (36). These centers are comforting, safe. Universities are arborescent—with a chain of pre-established command: from the Chancellor on top, to a few Vices, then more Deans and many disciplined Chairs, along with professors who are Full, Associate, or Assistant. At my university, the principle of "faculty governance," a rhizomatic ideal traversing discipline and rank, covers up the reality that the faculty are governed; the student protest in the 1960s was aimed at unraveling this hierarchical structure.

Commercial narrative films are on the side of arborescent—a series of "subjective affects from pre-established connections" labeled continuity style. The absense of "pre-established connections" like story and character, in many avant-garde works, initially triggers an almost painful unease in viewers; as long as the desire for the familiarity of classical film conventions remains intact, avant-garde work can only be lacking, estranged, discomforting. For, like the conventions of narrative cinema, "The arborescent structure pre-exists the individual, who is integrated into a specific position within it" (37). We know the rules of the game and our place on the story board and take comfort in this repetition and our knowledge; it's not so much what we can learn but the verification of what we already know. The opposition, commercial cinema versus avant-garde, can be simply written as arborescent versus rhizomatic.

However, this is too pat, ahistorical, and, to be fancy, binaristic. Avant-garde can also become an arborescent structure, hierarchizing artists within "significance and subjectivization," taking place *from within* in Toronto in 1989: avant-garde becomes Art. Cooptation (arborescence) *from the outside* is something else: avant-garde becomes Style (or Fashion, as Poggioli argues). Mekas described the latter process: "In 1964, film-makers left the underground and came into the light, where they immediately clashed with the outmoded tastes and morals of the Establishment, the police, and the critics. During the later months, the absence of screenings resulted in a series of articles in national magazines written mostly by people who had never seen any of the films. . . . By autumn, however, the tone of the press, the snides, began to change into fatherly friendliness. The fashion was about to be born. The magazines and the uptown decided to join the underground and make it part of the Establishment . . . which brought an obvious confusion into the ranks of the underground." Like a general, he maps three options: (1) "to be swallowed by the Establishment," (2) to "retreat further into the under- ground," and (3) the rhizomatic tactic, to "smash through the lines of the Establishment to the other side of it (or above it), thus surrounding it" (371). Or, as D and G fancifully put it, "only underground stems and aerial roots are truly . . . political."

When the underground becomes the establishment, becomes Art, only the last action is possible, as the protestors against Toronto know so well. I will briefly describe the protest. The "International Experimental Film Congress" included "practicum" sessions taught by David Rimmer, Robert Breer, Stan Brakhage, and Pat O'Neill—critiqued as perhaps fetishizing the technologi- cal; "special presentations" of curated films included sessions on abstract films, collage films, Latin American films, and women filmmakers— challenged as merely a bone to women, and as fetishizing the past, a very different era; recent films from Canada, Britain and the Continent, West Ger- many, the Philippines, and Eastern Europe—accused of a "tepid internation- alism," a leveling of differences.

The circulated protest letter was signed by seventy-six artists, including Peggy Ahwesh, Barbara Broughel, Abigail Child, Steve Fagin, Su Friedrich, Joe Gibbons, Barbara Lattanzi, Rainer, Keith Sanborn, and Leslie Thornton (to name only the film and video makers whose work I have studied and plan to write about—it takes me a very long time to figure out *how* to write about each separate avant-garde work).[10] The impassioned petition chal- lenges "the official History promoted" by the Congress: "The time is long overdue to unwrite the Institutional Canon of Masterworks of the Avant- Garde." The Congress is accused of tokenism to women, feminist film the- ory, and new work by younger artists: "the overwhelming majority of participants consists of representatives of the 60s Avant-Garde and its decay- ing power base. Only one or two younger filmmakers have been made part of the official program. Workshops are dominated by technological values and are led exclusively by older men."

The stance against canon-formation is critical, in many ways a return to the original principles of inclusion rather than exclusion, of equality rather than stars, of multiplicity rather than hierarchy of artist or films. At the same time, the emphasis on women filmmakers, feminism, and theory *is* radically different—a real avant-garde maneuver, as is the critique of the presumed internationalism of this cinema, always dominated by the United States, in turn dominated by men's films.

I want to stray from the law of this letter, taking a side journey, and detail another critical difference which the letter invokes between the historical conditions of the 1960s and 1980s avant-gardes by looking at two emblem- atic works. While both avant-garde periods endorsed multiplicity, the 1960s version was clearly defined by opposition, by the binarisms I have described, rhetorical and political tactics employed by feminism today, although that is changing. In this for or against stance of either/or options, variety came only after and within the terms of the initial big choice (for or against the war, hetero- or homosexual—the latter, broken down by Warhol in the 1960s and perhaps by Abigail Childs in *Mayhem*). A botanical example would be a garden of random and exotic wildflowers bordered by a fence. The letter partakes of the older ethos while advocating a different version of multiplicity, one without a fence. More difficult for many critics is unchecked multiplicity not clarified or defined or impassioned by binarist opposition, including mass culture versus art—the perplexing aspect of postmodernism for its theorists, many of whom are bothered, as were critics troubled by Warhol, by artists' sorties and forays with commercial artifacts and tactics, including making money, female fantasy, and narrative.

There are significant differences between then and now which I will metaphorically sketch by an analysis of two works, *Four More Years* (a videotape) and *On the Marriage Broker Joke as Cited by Sigmund Freud in Wit and Its Relation to the Unconscious, or Can the Avant-Garde Artist Be Wholed?* (a film). The first is by a collective, TVTV, or Top Value Television, taped in Miami, Florida, the site of the Republican presidential convention in 1972; the second is by Owen Land, a.k.a. George Landow, in 1978.

Four More Years was taped and broadcast as an alternative to network coverage of the conventions. Watching the tape is an unsettling experience of historical, almost cultural, displacement. While our memories view the decade as yesterday, 1972 poignantly feels light years away. Like politics and theory in the late 1960s and 1970s, carried on loudly in the margins, outside official institutions and buildings, the tape's verite, hand-held, meanderingly casual style of off the beaten track wandering is also, and rigidly, bounded by binary logic, a series of oppositions—including the networks' style of stable cameras, anchored by star reporters in the control booth above the proceedings and on the floor interviewing famous politicians. TVTV interviews the famous reporters—Walter Cronkite, who worries about the influence of TV news; Roger Mudd, who coyly refuses to speak to the TVTV roving, hippy reporters; Mike Wallace, ponderous and officious; and Cassy Macklin, who is smart, direct. They all agree that the convention is boring, an anti-event of staged enthusiasm. Opening with a rehearsal of college-aged GOP singers, "More than ever we need Nixon now," the sound of chanting protestors outside the convention walls is heard: "Tricky Dickie's Got to Go!" The hand-held camera, like the sound and editing, positioned amid "the people" as a participant, tracks the dividing lines: the anti-war protestors outside of the hall and at Flamingo Park and the conventioneers inside.

While the Vietnam War is the critical divide, the struggle is also over the student movement and reality: Youth for Nixon claim that their cheers are spontaneous, that their enthusiasm is not being coached; while they do have team leaders, they assure the reporters that their exuberance is genuine. At cocktail party headquarters, a middle-aged matron praises the sorority girls playing Nixonettes who are, in fact, paying the GOP for the privilege of hostessing at the convention. Tricia Nixon and Julie Eisenhower, uttering daughterly banalities, claim that more youth support Nixon than the end the war movement.

The visible opposition is declared by clothing—the GOP men are wearing suits and ties, the protestors wear jeans and beards; the GOP women have bouffont hairdos and wear dresses and makeup; the protesting women, albeit fewer, have long, straight hair, wear jeans, and no makeup. The GOP is the party of wealth and middle age, of cocktail parties on yachts hosted by Ron and Nancy Reagan, where corporate donors accuse the protestors of disloyalty to the United States. "If these people liked our country, they'd fight for it . . . anyone can get a job. . . . I don't mind colored people living near me if they are clean. . . ." In opposition to these scenes in the Miami harbor, the Vietnam vets, scruffy, bearded, in wheelchairs, stage a street theater of death in the parking lots outside the convention hall. The protestors play harmonicas; the Ray Bloch orchestra, in formal attire, plays show tunes.

While Nixon accepts the nomination, shots of veterans shouting "Stop the Bombing" are intercut; balloons are released on the convention floor and exuberantly popped, metaphors of the bombing, as shouts of "Four More Years"—Nixon's slogan—are intercut. The camera rapidly tracks back, revealing an empty convention floor, while the sounds of the delegates chanting continue, oddly predictive of the 1980s—the shift to the political right. Arguments which sounded ludicrous then and during the tape were right—youth did eventually support GOP politics. The unimaginable, even to Republicans, a Reagan presidency, turned into an eight-year reality.

As the black and white, verite style also reveals, these were not the good old days. The security and surveillance surrounding the convention are just hints of the violence and hatred between the factions argued as patriotism. Along with the battle for youth, another issue was at stake—reality. Was the enthusiasm of Youth for Nixon real or engineered? Were the Vietnam vets really soldiers or just impersonators? Thus, two issues which plague cultural studies scholars emerge here: oppositional practices (good) and simulacra (bad).

The transformation of culture—including the revision of the Vietnam vets against the war and the GOP, transformed into alliance in the 1980s—is extraordinary, a radical difference revealed by the tape. A politics of opposition, with clearly demarked borders—"Which side are you on?"—no longer structures our politics. Furthermore, the lines of segmentation and the tactics of opposition are not secure, not for all time, but can traverse sides. Strategies of the left have been taken up by the right, for example, anti-abortion protests, along with specific programs like day care, disarmament, and peace. The borders have shifted while left-cultural studies still adhere to the old oppositions, bemoaning their loss. However, unlike D and G's assertion, binary structures serve strategic, historical purposes. Binarism might be a left-over from the 1960s when opposition to racism, the draft, and the war was a matter of survival in an era when the world was polarized into two

Cold War camps. While duality can result in exclusion, for feminism, binary opposition was, and continues to be, a feminist claim for inclusion.

In "Politics Now (Anxieties of a Petty Bourgeois Intellectual)," Morris acutely assesses the functioning of this historical image of the left, an image preserved in *Four More Years*. She charts the differences between 1975 and 1985. "In 1975, cultural politics were the concern of the *full-time radical*. It was a matter of taking politics *to* various cultural activities. . . . By 1985, the full-time radical has in many cases become the *radical professional* . . . with 'politics' increasingly defined by . . . (usually institutional) activity."[11] She argues that in the "era of full time radicalism" the same "personnel" appeared everywhere, a "sort of familial alliance system," (a buddy network so aptly described by Stanley Aronowitz and Fredric Jameson[12]), which led to "exhaustion, paranoia and burn-out" (177), portrayed in the 1989 obituaries of Abbie Hoffman's drug overdose.

Perhaps more damaging is Morris's assessment that the life-style left had an "incapacity . . . to perceive its own cultural functioning": "We hear a lot these days about superficial style-obsessed postmoderns; but the smart young things about town have little indeed to teach the Left about the politics of authoritarian control through style. We're the ones, after all, who installed a ruthless surveillance system monitoring every aspect of style . . . a surveillance system so absolute that in the name of the personal-political, everyday life became a site of pure semiosis" (178), with activities divided into either good or bad, keeping others out.

She then suggests several problems with the left: (1) the lack of interest in the products of cultural work which, she argues, do exist; (2) the insistence on repetition; and (3) the "displacement of criticism by diagnoses of personal motivation" (183). To her list, I would add the avoidance of women's writing, art, and feminism, amid brief but categorical declarations of the critical centrality of the women's movement to the protest movement. In their assessments of that period, both Aronowitz and Jameson drop in quick references to feminism's starring role, and then proceed with their long lists of male participants and theorists. As I argued regarding avant-garde texts, cultural objects do exist—it is their distribution and criticism that is diminishing, along with their ossification into fixed and rigid interpretations, what Morris argues is a problem of *use*. Her position restates Benjamin's emphasis on exhibition, taking work into new contexts, new situations; it suggests Barthes's call to "Change the Object Itself" which feminist film theory has done to the classical Hollywood film, inscribing female subjectivity along the way.

Regarding the "radical professional" and one context: universities are rarely sites of radical activism in arts, politics, pedagogy, and everyday life as they were in the mid to late 1960s and 1970s, and, in fact, partake of the new right, supply side, careerist conservatism, a gold standard/materialist ethics operative on many levels in the culture. Like corporations, universities proclaim rather than conceal their status as marketplaces, head-hunting for

hot, famous thinkers, competing with big-buck offers, deals more than salaries, complete family packages including spousal jobs, day-care facilities,
along with household moving expenses, terms which intellectuals (unlike
the Marx Brothers in the anarchic contract scene from A Night at the Opera)
negotiate with economic savvy down to mortgage points, a travel budget,
tech equipment for personal use, and private, academic valets. Negotiating
contracts has become "Let's Make a Deal." Administrators are businessmen
rather than scholars.

Like the cultural hot commodity—time (and speed), the big bonus prize,
and paradoxically the ultimate sign of intellectual worth, is bartered time
for not teaching; in a strange inversion, the less time spent at a university
via course reductions and sabbaticals, combined with more time spent at
home or in international, scholastic tourism, the higher the salary and the
more prized the catch; the tales of the University of California's offers
are becoming legend. Like the many skewed inversions of late 1960s precepts occurring during the 1980s (some of which are terrific for white
women and women of color), many of our former values, including time and
duration, along with money, are topsy-turvy and unremarked. (If a husband
receives an offer as a condition of his spouse's acceptance, he, in turn, while
being offered a simulated position, a term of another's contract, can negotiate for a higher salary at his original university and be pretty certain of receiving it. Desire, even if feigned, is better than no offer at all.) Academic
horse trading reveals an uneasy compatibility between Lacanian desire and
raw, capitalist competition.

Theories of "traveling theory" are being proposed with no mention of this
new reality of scholastic, timeless tourism as intellectual upward mobility.
With this profitable "nomadology" of fashionable theorists (and the increasing discrepancy between superstar and yeoman faculty replicating the social
schism between rich and poor, white and "of color"), the formation of local,
intellectual communities has changed. Universities are becoming transient
marketplaces, way stations we pass through or visit, rarely places we live,
rarely repositories of personal history and collaborative work. The highest
bidder and entrepreneurial familialism distantiate this nomadology from the
treks of film and video makers. The shift in practice and theory, in the academy, from military metaphors of opposition (still functional in Deleuze and
Guattari, like Mekas) to capitalist coinage of incorporation is not coincidental or trivial. I will return to this critical notion later.

Baudrillard's urging to Forget Foucault! might be perverse when we most
need an assessment of academic politics. The beauty of teaching Foucault is
that his work concerns the practice of knowledge, the institutions we are
in—it is simultaneously theory and local practice, a history of the present.
The irony of "teaching" Foucault is that we often don't practice what he
preaches, resulting in the belief that theory has nothing to do with everyday
life. Still, for better or worse, richer or poorer, which will change anyway,
universities are one scene of avant-garde, and, for me, my daily life.

Six years after *Four More Years,* Owen Land's *On the Marriage Broker Joke* (1978) was wildly and oddly predictive of the 1980s; the film resonated D and G's critique of psychoanalysis. Printed over the beginning and end are two texts of religious ecstasy (the first by John Milton told by a character in a seventeenth-century Puritan costume)—the resurgence of religious fundamentalism in the 1980s. The film parodies avant-garde film, recent theories of the film apparatus and language, pedagogy, and Freudian psychoanalysis, the jokes more than the analysis. Panderers become costumed, talking panda bears, sitting in armchairs and conversing in their pop art living room: "We each have to tell one marriage broker joke, and then pretend that we are avant-garde filmmakers making a film about marriage broker jokes." "My film is going to be introduced by a fake panda, and it's going to be about Japanese salted plums, among other things." Psychoanalysis becomes a line of flight, careening from panderer, to panda, to salted plums, from Freud to Linnaeus to commerce—a crazy rhizome of thought set within a meticulous visual style of radiant colors, spectacular studio scenes, including a jungle with a movie screen and Liberace and Little Richard impersonators. While this mimicry (prior to Eddie Murphy on "Saturday Night Live") is of the black rock singer, Little Richard was also an infant patient of Melanie Klein.

D and G view psychoanalysis as a delimited binarism—with Little Hans as one case in point. They argue that each time Little Hans tries to get outside patriarchy, outside Freud's theory, to move to the street outside his house, to become-horse, Freud brings him back to the parental bedroom, to Oedipus. Hans wants to be like the horse, but he is brought back within psychoanalysis, his line of flight curtailed. "They kept on *smashing his rhizome and messing up his map* . . . blocking every outlet until what he desired was his own guilt and shame. . . . Freud takes explicit account of Little Hans' map-making, but always and only to reduce it back onto a family photo" (29). Here, the affinity of D and G with feminism is apparent. The paternal Oedipus and its restrictive system worked over Dora as well as Hans, two case studies which feminists and filmmakers have revisioned, arguing that Freud wasn't listening to women and children. Little Hans's father mediates the analysis, as does Dora's father.

Most critically, "The important thing is never to reduce the unconscious, to interpret it or make it signify following the tree model, but rather to *produce the unconscious* and, along with it, new utterances and other desires [precisely the goal of feminist critique, along with unbalancing the poles of power]. The rhizome is precisely this production of the unconscious" (40). For D and G, psychoanalysis like linguistics "draws only the tracings . . . of the unconscious . . . the second, the tracings . . . of language, with all the betrayals that that implies (it's not surprising that psychoanalysis has hitched its star to that of linguistics)" (29).

Two ironies of film scholarship become apparent: while many avant-garde films, including *Bleu Shut,* Land's films, and *Critical Mass,* directly explore language, and in fact could be analyzed through various models of linguistics, film theory, historically predicated on linguistics linked to psychoanalysis, explores the *visual* conventions of classical narrative, in the main, ignoring the sound track. And while the charges of being apolitical, or merely arts of the signifier, are leveled at avant-garde films, considered here as theory, we do not accuse our linguistic or semiotic theories of the same apoliticism or emphasis on signifiers. (At the same time, these avant-garde films are, in many ways, rhizomatic analyses of linguistics.)

However, using their own system, one can take D and G's anti-Freudianism to more positive ends. "But dead ends should always be re-situated on the map, and in that way opened up to possible lines of flight" (31). This is what Mitchell, Johnston, Mulvey, Campioni and Gross, and de Lauretis, for example, did with that formerly dead-end Freud. Yet, "binary logic and bi-univocal relations still dominate psychoanalysis . . . linguistics, and structuralism, even information theory" (7). When either the oedipal structure of romanticism or the binary logic of feminist sexual difference is repeated and conserved beyond its useful or political context, a gradual reduction of thought does occur.

Land's parody of avant-garde and theory is conducted by Morgan Fisher, the filmmaker as corporate, suited pedagogue standing in front of a blackboard, monotonously lecturing about film and theory. The first of his lectures concerns the apparatus: "There is no motion in a motion picture; Only the projector moves the strip. Pulled along by wheels called sprockets, With protruding teeth to get a grip." There is more of this sing-song rhyming, followed by applause, and then the film's intertitle. "What's a structural film?" inquires the first panda. "It's when engineers design an airplane or a bridge, and they build a model to find out if it will fall apart too soon. The film shows where all the stresses are," answers the second.

Fisher reappears later, with his second lecture, a disquisition on theory's logic: "Of the many theories which have been propounded there are few which merit serious consideration. Of the more credible hypotheses, the following stand out: The marriage broker is merely a pander and the so-called prospective brides are prostitutes. Textural corruption has, in some versions, changed the word pander to panda. . . . Thus, two opposing schools have developed. One claims that the panda referred to is ailurus fulgens, the Himalayan panda. . . . The other school insists that the panda referred to is ailuropa melanoleuca of Tibet and southern China. . . . Another interpretation has it that the entire situation is in fact really an allegory. . . ." Imagine Land's next film parodying Deleuze and Guattari, which he might already have done, including their notions of "becoming animal" and "faciality"—the filmmaking panda bears and the impersonators.

In an earlier scene with Japanese performers, the take-over of the U.S. economy by Japan and the shift from a culture of difference and opposition to one of differentiation and dispersion are staged. Capitalism becomes theater of the absurd. Two Japanese performers in intercut medium shots, sitting behind desks, play petty executives debating the label, the packaging of their new product, salted plums: "Now all that needs to be decided is the number of jar sizes which we will offer. I'd say extra small, small, medium, small large, and extra large." "No. There should be small, large small, small large, large, extra large, and jumbo." "But you've left out medium!" "That's right, and for a good reason. Think of the state of the economy. People want to buy a large jar, but they feel guilty; so small large satisfies both their guilt and their gluttony. Whereas people who can only afford a small feel consoled by the availability of a large small, thus giving them a sense of superiority over their neighbor who can only afford a small." This goes on until "Wait a minute, we're not talking about small large plums, medium plums and large plums. We're talking about large small jars, medium jars and small large jars; the size of the jars only, not the size of the plums!" More of this and "Extra small, small, large small, medium, small large, large, extra large, and jumbo. Are you sure we are offering enough choices?" "What do you mean?" "Well, if we limit the customer's choice too much, we are denying his free will—and he might suspect that he is being manipulated." "Good point. And don't forget we are only talking about the size of the jar and not about the number of salted plums contained within." "Precisely. The size of the jar has absolutely no relationship to the number of salted plums contained in it." A perfect description of the state of contemporary culture, including the endless repetition of the same trivia. Language's arbitrariness in advertising is comic *and,* like his earlier work, a theoretical issue.

After this film, Land began his attempts to escape universities (as D and G would put it, a rhizomatic line of flight from the arborescent structure of the Art Institute), seeking a disability discharge for health reasons. Along the way, he orchestrated musical operettas, extravaganzas with his students at the Art Institute, staging them as performances, composed music, and played in a band. From there, he went to Japan and shortly after or before began to make videotapes, a medium which he liked right away. Then to the Philippines for their hands-in healing/anti-surgery and spiritual cures. The last I heard, he was living in Los Angeles, studying the techniques of the Renaissance master painters. If you turn to the endnotes, you will be able to take an Owen Land multiple-choice film quiz—he could have done stand-up film comedy although he laughs at his own jokes.[13]

In a book review in the *Village Voice,* Doug Henwood, who should have seen this film, writes that "not even Jeane Dixon could tell in 1979 that the U.S. would find itself in hock to Japan 10 years later. Who knows what 1999 will bring?" I suggest the Live Elvis. He points out that "the Japanese experience has hardly entered into the debate over the virtues of market socialism . . . the Japanese system offers plenty of hints on how a state-led planning system can be decentralized . . . and offers living proof that low military spending is a potent economic tonic."[14] This inversion of a cold war premise of the U.S. economy, the prosperity granted by militarism, is one of the significant revisions of the late 1980s. The other, which is a condition of the first, is the end of the cold war.

Along with these two significant shifts is the multiplication of economic powers other than the United States, now a debtor nation selling off its assets through corporate takeovers to other nations, including Japan. In *The Decline of the American Economy*, Betrand Bellon and Jorge Niosi argue that economically speaking, the dominance of the United States during the postwar period was a historical fluke, that the normal state of the economy is one of multiplicity, witnessed by the rise of not only Japan but Korea and Brazil, involving a world of competition.[15] Literary theories of heterogeneity (Barthes), dispersion (Foucault), or multiplicity (D and G) oddly predicted the change in global economics. Like the state economy, however, these models don't take into consideration the bipolarity between rich and poor, male and female, white and of color, which are international, vertical divisions set against, or over and above, the horizontal dispersion model.

Rather than nuclear wars, there will be trade wars. We need to remember that fearing a nuclear war, while fighting wars of containment around the globe, had little to do with pleasure; and that tactics of opposition also instantiated hierarchy, and exclusion.

This dispersion of economic power among several nations is accompanied by what I have called franchise culture, a culture of international monopolies leased as the local, resulting in a national and international sameness, sold, however, as difference—the small large model of the world. For example, choosing a video recorder among the literally hundreds of models is a salted plum experience of trying to discern quality and difference, only to learn that the product name, the trademark guarantee, means nothing. Whether American or Japanese, most models are now made by the same companies, with, presumably, the same components. We frantically choose between McDonald's, Burger King, and Wendy's, sold as different yet relentlessly the same. Maintaining the contradictions of difference may be a critical task as it continues to be for feminism. I suspect that cultural difference will be as central to rethinking Western postmodernism as sexual difference was to redefining classical film theory.

With rare exceptions, our screens feature U.S. films, while television has a limited internationalism, no matter how many channels are added to the spectrum. We imagine that our exported cultural representations are still dominantly desired and influential, and shake our heads at the sad influence of bad-faith U.S. mass culture on other cultures. While U.S. television programs, like films, are being internationally traded for great profit in the recently deregulated markets, we forget that in that transmission they are transformed, rewritten, used differently, framed by cultural and historical conditions of reception. As Woolf noted regarding women, and as D and G view the simulacrum, we see the same world, but we see it with different eyes. However, like automobiles and electronics, this process of cultural exportation will transform to importation. The decline of the United States as a dominant representation will truly alter the face of Hollywood and Soho.

During an event at the 1989 Honolulu Film Festival, an interesting exchange occurred. Seated on the left of a long table were three U.S. filmmakers who had shown their films about Vietnam; seated on the right were a critic and two Vietnamese directors who also had shown their films about the Vietnam War. Although their sizes were glaringly different, all the participants were men. Yet, it was an auspicious, conciliatory moment. In solemn and polite turn, each side critiqued the other's films. Both sides agreed on one thing: that neither side knew how to represent the other. U.S. soldiers in the Vietnamese films were bad, macho, whiskey-swilling parodies; and the Viet Cong in U.S. films were slippery caricatures. The participants laughed at this realization, as they had guffawed during the screenings. The Vietnamese critic said that if we had known each other, there would not have been a war. Wonderful thought.

However, when I asked the directors on both sides about the difference in the representations of women, the U.S. directors became rudely defensive, interrupting my question, and citing *Coming Home* to countermand my implied critique. Morris, from the audience, silenced the interruptor. The Vietnamese directors asserted that because men were taught to worship women, it was their duty to show ideal women, accounting for the perfect makeup and eyeliner of their female characters during combat. Absent or ideal— there was, in the discussion and in the films, little difference for women, white or of color.

I want to return to the letter of protest. The conclusion endorses avant-garde as a "revolutionary frame of mind" and, as I have argued, always/ already historical, contextual (the notion of the historical avant-garde is like female woman, or better, male man): "The issues which galvanized the Cinema Avant-Gardes of earlier decades arose from different conditions than [from] those which confront us today. . . . The Avant-Garde is dead; long live the avant-garde." The switch to the humble lower case, the impressive list of signers which brilliantly illustrates the sheer number of women making films today, along with the critique of the old internationalism as a univocal, male pluralism in favor of a model which views differences—sex, race, culture— as productive of knowledge, are signs of new times.

The argument is also pitched along generational lines—age and youth, older men versus younger artists. For Mekas, avant-garde is viewed as a generational struggle: "Each generation redefines art—and not in books or essays but through the works of art" (206). "The independent cinema is not . . . a 'primitive movement,' but . . . the . . . changing frontier, the Vietnam of cinema. Thank God it is not a movement—it is a generation" (68). For Harold Bloom also, art was quintessentially a generational battle of sons against the fathers.

Yet, like the rest of life, the generational struggle is different for women. There is a double standard of chronological difference; the same standards applied to men do not apply to women, measured by a ten-year differential.

As women age, rather than achieving centrality and power, they are marginalized. As Freud writes: "I once succeeded in freeing an unmarried woman, no longer young, from the complex of symptoms which . . . had excluded her from any participation in life. She . . . plunged into eager activity, in order to develop her by no means small talent and to snatch a little recognition, enjoyment, and success *late though the moment was* [my emphasis]. But every one of her attempts ended either with people letting her know or with herself recognizing that she was too old to accomplish anything in that field." Social conditions are mistaken for symptoms; the "unmarried woman, no longer young" had continual accidents "till at last she made up her mind to resign her attempts and the whole agitation came to an end."[16] Her resignation is Freud's success, the happy ending, and women's tragedy. Rather than railing against social conditions, her anger was directed against her body (think of cosmetic surgery today). Thus, the "unmarried woman, no longer young" joins Little Hans and Dora, turning her rage inward, against herself.

Equally disheartening is the realization that conscious conventions of chronological, generational difference reiterate unconscious Freudian desires and taboos: men's desire for their mothers and women's desire to possess their sons are unconscious prohibitions restaged in the spectacle of the older woman with the younger man. Cher aside, this rare scenario is not as readily accepted as is the operative and sanctioned reverse—the older man and the younger woman, often with a twenty-year age gap, the retro-high fashion couple of the 1980s who usually have a child. For, within the Freudian scenario, it is proper that the girl pass on to her father, who in turn will care for his daughter. Thus, men traverse or can cross the generational divide—while women are rigidly held to their prescribed, chronological role and place.

It is significant that Potter, Rainer, and Condit (in *Not a Jealous Bone*) all deal with the question of age for women. It is symptomatic that few critiques, with the exception of Condit's piece, which is all about an old woman, even mention this issue, a silence suggesting that differences of age, like sexual difference earlier and "the unmarried woman, no longer young," have been internalized as prohibitions rather than being challenged as social constructions of inequality. Potter critiques the romanticism which forever holds women to youth in both *Thriller* and *The Gold Diggers*, in the latter, analyzing the mother-daughter relationship and the youthful star system. As Collette Laffont's voice-over discovers in *Thriller*: "And what if I hadn't died? I would have become a mother. . . . But the heroine of such a story doesn't just labor day and night to feed her children. And if they had let me live, I would have become an old woman. And an old seamstress would not be considered the proper subject of a love story." In *The Man Who Envied Women*, Rainer asks all women in the audience who are still menstruating to leave the room. In *Not a Jealous Bone*, Condit's star is an eighty-year-old woman, Sophie, with her wrinkled skin a sagging sack, struggling with an image of the youthful ideal body—her mother remembered as young and beautiful. On the beach, Sophie's old and flabby body is in contrast to the sleek, classical body of youth. Sophie survives the violence of city streets, takes the bone of life from the dead ideal woman, dons a party dress, and joyously dances in the last scene, singing "You are dead and I am still alive."

Potter concludes the end of *Thriller* with "We were set up as opposites, as complementary characters, and kept apart to serve our roles. . . . We never got to know each other. . . . Perhaps we could have loved each other." Mimi, "who was searching for a theory that could explain" her life, wonders whether the "key to her death was written in their texts." Laffont/Mimi laughs a mocking, hearty laugh: "Suddenly I understand. There was me in the opera. And there was me in the attic. . . . It was murder." One critical difference is that between imaginary and real women—of all ages, mothers and daughters, and the now archaic "sisters." The real avant-garde move would be, at last, to centrally include women. If told from their points of view, even the desired dream girls and imaginary women would tell very different stories—which just might be mayhem. But that's another story.

NOTES

PROLOGUE

1. Roland Barthes, *Roland Barthes*, trans. Richard Howard (New York: Hill and Wang, 1977), p. 90.
2. Ibid.
3. Meaghan Morris, "Postmodernity and Lyotard's Sublime," *Art and Text* 16 (1984–1985), p. 45; this essay is reprinted in *The Pirate's Fiancee* (New York: Verso, 1988).
4. Walter Benjamin, "The Work of Art in the Age of Mechanical Reproduction," *Illuminations* (New York: Schocken Books, 1969), p. 234.

1. HISTORICALLY SPEAKING

1. Michel Foucault, *Discipline and Punish: The Birth of the Prison*, trans. Alan Sheridan (New York: Vintage Books, 1979), p. 207.
2. "The First Statement of the New American Cinema Group" was first published in *Film Culture*, nos. 22–23 (Summer 1961). It was reprinted in P. Adams Sitney, ed., *Film Culture Reader* (New York: Praeger, 1970), from which I quote this passage (p. 83). Sitney's writing on "visionary film" has contributed not only careful analyses of hundreds of films, providing a stylistic model and a formal history; it has also served a pedagogical function. Like so many of the artists, he came to criticism at an extraordinarily young age (14?)—perhaps explaining why, like Brakhage, he has written so much at a relatively young age. The participants at the meeting included Lionel Rogosin, Peter Bogdanovich, Robert Frank, Alfred Leslie, Edouard de Laurot, Ben Carruthers and Argus Speare Julliard, Adolfas Mekas, Gregory Markopoulos, Daniel Talbot, Guy Thomajan, Louis Brigante, Harold Humes, Bert Stert, Don Gillin, Walter Gutman, Jack Perlman, David C. Stone, Sheldon Rochlin.
3. Annette Michelson, "Film and the Radical Aspiration," in Sitney, ed., *Film Culture Reader*, reprinted from *Film Culture*, no. 42 (Fall 1966).
4. Michel Foucault, *Power/Knowledge: Selected Interviews and Other Writings, 1972–1977*, ed. Colin Young (New York: Pantheon, 1980), p. 114.
5. Foucault, *Discipline and Punish*, p. 193.
6. Roland Barthes, *The Pleasure of the Text*, trans. Richard Miller (New York: Hill and Wang, 1975), p. 40.
7. Barthes, *Pleasure of the Text*, pp. 20, 14.
8. Barthes, *Roland Barthes*, p. 69.
9. *Metaphors on Vision* by Stan Brakhage was a special, beautifully printed issue of *Film Culture*, no. 30 (Fall 1963). This quotation is from the first section. We are to "imagine the eye." Other segments are titled "The Camera Eye" and "My Eye"—which might have influenced Snow's *Wavelength*: "My eye, turning toward the imaginary, will go to any wave-lengths for its sights." Later passages are titled "Move Meant" and "State Meant." Like so many avant-garde filmmakers, Brakhage is fascinated with language, and like other avant-garde filmmakers, his films are silent. The influence of the man, his films, and his teaching has been incalculable. This issue also begins another practice so central to criticism of this work: the interview with the artist. The recent University of California book by Scott MacDonald, *A Critical Cinema*, carries on this tradition of oral history and interpretation, including a significant number of women filmmakers.
10. I raised the funds for this endeavor through the Center for Twentieth Century Studies. Public performances had audiences of mainly students, with only two or

three faculty in attendance. The interesting, awkward, and inadvertently funny tapes (Paik is so bemusedly bored and sleepy that he completely bewilders the interviewer; unwittingly, the interviewer imitates Baillie's body gestures, like a monkey/mirror effect) include clips and interviews with Baillie, Paik, Bartlett, Hindle, Brakhage, Sitney, Clarke, Beck, and Mekas.

11. Stephen Heath, "Repetition Time: Notes around 'Structural/Materialist Films,' " *Wide Angle*, 2, no. 3 (1978), p. 11. This important essay is more intricate than my extraction; I analyze his argument in greater detail in chapter 5.

12. "The First Statement of the New American Cinema Group," pp. 81, 83.

13. Yvonne Rainer, "Working Title: Journeys from Berlin/1971," *October* 9 (Summer 1979), p. 90.

14. Laura Mulvey, "Visual Pleasure and Narrative Cinema," *Screen* 16, no. 3 (Autumn 1975), p. 18.

15. Roland Barthes, "Lecture in Inauguration of the Chair of Literary Semiology, College de France," *October* 8 (Spring 1979), p. 12.

16. Barthes, *Roland Barthes*, p. 103.

17. Neil Hertz, "Two Extravagant Teachings," *Yale French Studies*, no. 63 (1982), p. 67.

18. Shoshana Felman, "Psychoanalysis and Education: Teaching Terminable and Interminable," *Yale French Studies*, no. 63 (1982), p. 33.

19. Quoted in Felman, "Psychoanalysis," p. 35.

20. Barthes, "Lecture," p. 15.

21. Barthes, *Roland Barthes*, p. 121. This fragment is titled "Marriage" and speaks of the connections of that institution to narrative. His example is adultery as a source of expectations. In addition, in *The Pleasure of the Text* he wrote: "Death of the father would deprive literature of many of its pleasures. . . . As fiction, Oedipus was at least good for something . . ." (47). The central figuration of his marriage and children is proclaimed over and over again by Brakhage, with Sitney documenting his career by his marriage date in his brief introduction to *Metaphors on Vision*. Within the counterculture mentality, this makes Brakhage perhaps a bit of an anomaly—at least verbally argued if not in actuality, making him a family man.

22. Dick Hebdige, *Subculture: The Meaning of Style* (London: Methuen, 1979), pp. 2, 84. I am using *style* in Hebdige's larger sense as a resistance, a refusal that exists in moments of conjuncture. Hebdige worked on punk; in the United States, graffiti was a pertinent example.

2. VISIONARY FILM AND SEXUAL DIFFERENCE

1. Peter Wollen, " 'Ontology' and Materialism in Film," *Screen* 17, no. 1 (Spring 1976), reprinted in *Readings and Writings: Semiotic Counter-Strategies* (London: Verso, 1982). In this lucid essay, Wollen documents the shift from a Bazinian ontology, or "reproducing natural objects and events without human intervention," to an ontology of the "photo-chemical process . . . setting up an alternative to the cinema of reproduction or representation . . . a displacement of . . . 'ontology' . . . a rift between modernism and traditionalism that marked all the arts during the first decades of this century." He points to the difference, as well, between an ontology of "idealism" (Sitney) and one of materialism (Peter Gidal). Furthermore, the materialism of Godard is differentiated from the materialism of Straub, placing Godard's materialism within the purview of Brecht. This essay was a response to the U.S. avant-garde proponents' various challenges to the European narrative experimentation. Thus, it can be read in dialogue with Michelson's, detailed earlier. For both sides, Eisenstein and, to a degree, Godard, are pivotal. See also my presentation of Mekas in the last chapter, particularly regarding Godard.

2. P. Adams Sitney, *Visionary Film* (New York: Oxford University Press, 1974, 1979). My quotations are from the 1974 edition. For many years, this book has been

one of the few sources available with detailed information about these films. After an initial rush of late 1960s and early 1970s books, e.g., by Sheldon Renan, *An Introduction to the American Underground Film* (London: Studio Vista, 1968), David Curtis, *Experimental Film*, and anthologies by Sitney and Gregory Battcock, relatively few books dealt with this material. Sitney's almost had the field to itself, becoming a dominant reading. While Michelson and Sitney share, as it were, the same taste and have similar passionate commitments, their intellectual premises diverge—Michelson positions her arguments within Soviet art.

3. Mulvey's system, predicated on a textual analysis of the films of Hitchcock and Sternberg, is now being lifted off and applied to still photography and painting in explications which, along with the specificity of cinema, fail to note context, history, or the particularities of Lacanian analysis.

4. Mulvey "Visual Pleasure," p. 18.

5. Michelson, "Film and the Radical Aspiration."

6. Janet Bergstrom, "The Avant-Garde: Histories and Theories," *Screen* 19, no. 3 (Autumn 1978). Her reference, unlike Michelson's detailed analysis, is more in passing. Thus, this comparison is a bit far-fetched.

7. Teresa de Lauretis, *Alice Doesn't* (Bloomington: Indiana University Press, 1984), p. 81. This point is argued around Michael Snow's *Presents,* including his remarks in an after the film question session with Snow at the Art Institute in Chicago, which I attended with de Lauretis and Danielson.

8. Noel Burch, *A Theory of Film Practice,* trans. Helen Lane (New York: Praeger, 1973); the French edition was published in 1969. Burch maps a series of formal oppositions, including the "absence of dialectics" and "complex dialectics," the "structural use of sound," and the "two kinds of space," including off-screen space. Here, Michelson's edict that form must be raised to ideological content is a working premise. That practice was theory, as suggested in his title, was a crucial argument, again reminiscent of Soviet film; thus, using other theories to elucidate the films, already theoretical texts, was viewed as redundant, constrictive.

9. Laura Mulvey, "Changes: Thoughts on Myth, Narrative and Historical Experience," *History Workshop Journal,* no. 23 (Spring 1987), pp. 6–7.

10. De Lauretis, *Alice Doesn't,* p. 74.

11. Constance Penley, "The Avant-Garde and Its Imaginary," *Camera Obscura* 2, p. 18.

12. Ibid., p. 19.

13. Constance Penley, "The Avant-Garde: Histories and Theories," *Screen* 19, no. 3 (Autumn 1978), p. 118.

14. Ibid.

15. Renato Poggioli, *The Theory of the Avant-Garde* (New York: Harper and Row, 1968, 1971). Poggioli, speaking of the literary, historical avant-garde, discerns its connections with romanticism, but not negatively so. He charts a typology of avant-garde "attitudes," including nihilism, agonism, futurism, decadence, and alienation. His model perches somewhere between the French symbolists and Marxism, including chapters on fashion and taste along with technology. He argues that criticism of avant-garde has been primarily polemical, either for or against, and notes in his prologue that "critics have not paid much attention to its . . . manifestations," p. 1.

16. Bergstrom, "The Avant-Garde," p. 121.

17. Ibid., p. 125.

18. Ibid., pp. 126, 127.

19. As I stated earlier, Bloom's evaluation of the poets, seen as analogous to U.S. filmmakers, is Sitney's focus rather than Bloom's method, increasingly indebted to psychoanalysis. I have interpreted Freud's writing on anxiety differently from Bloom—as a model of contradiction, one in which Freud acknowledges that the subject, in this instance, might more likely be a woman—this in *Inhibitions, Symptoms,*

218 / Notes for pages 28–38

and Anxiety (1925–1926). As this text is close to *Beyond the Pleasure Principle* in time and argument, this shift to a female subject, albeit barely mentioned as an afterthought in *Inhibitions*, troubles, for me, Bloom's oedipal reading. Furthermore, in this construct, Freud's shifts from the "unconscious" to the conscious, the ego, thereby suggesting why Sitney's argument, with its premises in Bloom, stays with the conscious—so does Freud, in this instance. Thus, the debate is as much with Freud as with the U.S. phenomenology approach as ignoring Freud.

20. Helen Elam, in *Modern American Critics since 1955*, ed. Gregory Jay, 1988 (Detroit: Gale), p. 33.

21. De Lauretis, *Alice Doesn't*, p. 119.

22. Ibid., p. 120.

23. Ibid., p. 123.

24. Elam. p. 33.

25. Stan Brakhage, *Metaphors on Vision, Film Culture*, no. 30 (Fall 1963). There are no page numbers in this issue, so I will note the quotations by the (few) side-headings. This passage is from "Metaphors on Vision."

26. Brakhage, "The Camera Eye."

27. Brakhage, "My Eye."

28. Ibid.

29. Brakhage, "From a letter to a very dear friend and severe critic of *Anticipation of the Night* (1958)."

30. Brakhage, "Letter to a Friend, 1959."

31. Elam, p. 30.

32. Harold Bloom, in *The Breaking of the Vessels* (Chicago: University of Chicago Press, 1982).

33. De Lauretis, *Alice Doesn't*, p. 83.

34. VeVe A. Clark, Millicent Hodson, and Catrina Neiman, *The Legend of Maya Deren: A Documentary Biography and Collected Works, Film Culture*,, nos. 72–75. (New York: Anthology Film Archives/Film Culture, 1984), pp. xii, xiv, xxi.

35. Rudolf Arnheim, "To Maya Deren," *Film Culture*, no. 24 (Spring 1962), reprinted in *Film Culture Reader*, ed. P. Adams Sitney (New York: Praeger, 1970), pp. 84–85.

36. Phillip Drummond, "Textual Space in *Un Chien Andalou*," *Screen*, 18, no. 3 (Autumn 1977), p. 64. This is a long, extremely detailed, shot-by-shot analysis of certain sections of the film, including production history and biographical data, though Drummond says it is only a partial analysis, part of a larger project. It focuses on an avant-garde, very short film—a rare occurrence—positioning its arguments within alternate rather than dominant cinema. In many ways, Drummond employs what Foucault would call an archeology, or an analysis of discourses in and surrounding the film.

37. Rohauer has also rereleased Buster Keaton's films and withdrawn them, held up in legal battles, as the argument goes.

38. Drummond, "Textual Space," p. 57.

39. Quoted from Sitney, *Visionary Film*, p. 3.

40. Drummond, "Textual Space," p. 62.

41. Ibid., p. 65.

42. De Lauretis, *Alice Doesn't*, p. 157.

43. Drummond, "Textual Space," pp. 102–103.

44. Linda Williams, "The Prologue to *Un Chien Andalou*: A Surrealist Film Metaphor," *Screen* 17, no. 4 (Winter 1976–1977). Drummond takes issue with Williams's analysis of the opening twelve shots.

45. Sigmund Freud, "The 'Uncanny,'" *Standard Edition*, vol. 17 (London: Hogarth Press, 1964), p. 252.

46. Mulvey, "Visual Pleasure," p. 7.

47. Ibid., p. 6.

48. Drummond, "Textual Space," p. 72.

49. Ibid., p. 79. The Keaton point is made on p. 78. I didn't notice this resemblance until I read Drummond; the longer comparison with Keaton's *One Week* is mine, but it is an aftereffect of Drummond. I never would have come up with it on my own.

50. I refer to an earlier quotation and argument by Drummond. That this essay was also positioned at a turning point in the narrative–avant-garde debate in England, around the editorial board of *Screen*, a debate which would shortly thereafter travel to the United States, should be noted.

51. Michel Foucault, *The History of Sexuality* (New York: Random House, 1978, 1980).

52. Julia LeSage, "The Human Subject—You, He, or Me?" *Screen* 16, no. 2 (Summer 1975), p. 77.

53. Ellen Willis, "Radical Feminism and Feminist Radicalism," in *The 60s without Apology* (Minneapolis: University of Minnesota Press, 1984), pp. 105–106.

54. Andreas Huyssen, "The Cultural Politics of Pop," *After the Great Divide* (Bloomington: Indiana University Press, 1986), p. 143. Huyssen looks at the U.S. art scene from his German context, granting a clarity and distantiation. The differences between the reception and circulation of pop art in the United States and Germany are intriguing.

55. See note 1 to this chapter, above, and Wollen's essay. This dispute between contemporary European cinema and the U.S. avant-garde is picked up in my last chapter. See also Michelson, "Film and the Radical Aspiration."

3. VIDEO POLITICS

1. Theodore Roszak, *The Making of a Counter Culture: Reflections on the Technocratic Society and Its Youthful Opposition* (Faber, 1970). See also Alec Gordon, "Thoughts out of Season on Counter Culture," in *Contemporary Cultural Studies*, ed. David Punter (London: Hangman, 1986), pp. 185–211. Gordon's essay has directly and indirectly given me many ideas.

2. These are among the central figures for Gordon, sans communication and the cybernetic theorists, who I argue are critical.

3. Barbara London, "Video: A Selected Chronology, 1963–1983," *Art Journal* 45 no. 3 (Fall 1985), pp. 249–62. This was a special issue devoted to video, with the majority of the essays by women.

4. Walter Benjamin, *Illuminations*, ed. Hannah Arendt, trans. Harry Zohn (New York: Schocken Books, 1969).

5. Katherine Dieckmann, "Electra Myths: Video, Modernism, Postmodernism," *Art Journal* 45, no. 3 (Fall 1985), p. 195.

6. Shamberg notes these affiliations in prefatory remarks; his book contains an initial section whose pages I have numbered. The second section, called content, I have labeled with tagged numbers, such as 8a. The material becomes increasingly practical (sometimes passionate, sometimes flip; both postures become cloying, as does the repetition of labeling terms like "information" and "design" repeated ad infinitum or nauseum). The book is a how and what to do manual, which includes the suggestion of taping weddings and bar mitzvahs and selling copies as entertainment. Shamberg also recommends making "pornographic tapes. You'll find a market." It took very little thought to co-opt (shall we say reify?) such notions.

7. Jean Baudrillard, "Requiem for the Media," *For a Critique of the Political Economy of the Sign* (St. Louis: Telos Press, 1981), p. 173. The biblical invocations should not go unnoticed; along with Derrida, Baudrillard follows on the heels of the biblical catastrophists.

8. Ibid., p. 170.

9. *Domus* 522 (May 1973), p. 28.

10. *Design Quarterly* 78/79 (1979), pp. 6–18; also see *Casabella* 376 (1973), p. 30.

11. The video guerrillas' assessment of television and the general state of culture, although estranged by language—high tech talk plus low slang plus esoterica—is extraordinarily accurate, almost prophecy in reverse. Rather than "the people," corporations adopted their tactics.

12. Ant Farm participants had plans for a mobile university in a Ford truck and called themselves environmental nomads—shades of Deleuze and Guattari and traveling theory! The relation between D and G and the counterculture is examined in my last chapter, but the similarities begin here. Shamberg advocated media buses for these "cybernetic nomads," who would live in their own inflatables: "Thus, the true university is no longer anchored to one place, but free to move in all directions to enhance indigenous cybernetic activity" (92a).

13. Linda Burnham, "Ant Farm Strikes Again," *High Performance* 24 (1983), p. 27. This short piece contains a useful chronology of Ant Farm projects.

14. Shamberg argues that NASA made patriotism obsolete; who could think in terms of nations after shots of the world from space? Their "international" or "global" scope is still pertinent, taken up in arguments which depict the anonymity and evil of multinational corporations or bemoan the economic decline of the United States—actually, a monetary example of heterogeneity, a dispersal of economic centers to the East.

15. "TVTV: Video Pioneers 10 Years Later," *Send* (Summer 1983), pp. 18–23.

16. Meaghan Morris, "Room 101 or a Few Worst Things in the World," in *Seduced and Abandoned: The Baudrillard Scene*, ed. Andre Frankovits (Glebe, Australia: Stonemoss Services, 1984), pp. 91–117.

17. Fredric Jameson, "A Very Partial Chronology," in *The 60s Without Apology*, ed. Sohnya Sayres, Anders Stephanson, Stanley Aronowitz, and Fredric Jameson (Minneapolis: University of Minnesota Press, 1984), pp. 182–183. See also his "Periodizing the 60s." The difficulty of realizing a movement of *collective* protest and principles, precariously perched on the cult of individuality, and a very wealthy one at that, is apparent.

18. Jean Baudrillard, *In the Shadow of the Silent Majorities or the End of the Social*, trans. Paul Foss, Paul Patton, and John Johnston (New York: Semiotext[e], 1983), p. 84.

19. Jean Baudrillard, *Simulations*, trans. Paul Foss, Paul Patton, and Philip Baitchman (New York: Semiotext[e], 1983), p. 38.

20. Gilles Deleuze, "Plato and the Simulacrum," *October* 27 (1984), pp. 47–56.

21. Baudrillard, "Requiem," pp. 178, 179.

4. SURVEILLANCE AND SIMULATION

1. Michel Foucault, *The History of Sexuality*, vol. 1 (New York: Random House, 1978, 1980), p. 6.

2. Gene Youngblood, *Expanded Cinema* (New York: E. P. Dutton, 1970).

3. Roland Barthes, *S/Z*, trans. Richard Miller (New York: Hill and Wang, 1974), p. 188.

4. Peter Burger, *Theory of the Avant-Garde*, trans. Michael Shaw (Minneapolis: University of Minnesota Press, 1984).

5. The film consists of clips from educational, military, and corporate films from the late forties and fifties. The amateur status of film, so embraced by Mekas and Michelson, along with filmmakers' use of this degraded genre and bad style of filmmaking, is intriguing, a topic which Patricia Zimmerman has discussed.

6. Foucault, *Discipline and Punish,* p. 148.

7. The Heath passage was taken from a 1976 proseminar he conducted as a fellow of the Center for Twentieth Century Studies at the University of Wisconsin in Milwaukee; the Forrester passage is from her presentation at the 1979 conference on "Cinema and Language"; the Rose and Comolli excerpts are from the 1978 conference on "The Cinematic Apparatus." Papers and further debates from these events are to be found in *Cinema and Language,* edited by Heath and Mellencamp, and *The Cinematic Apparatus,* edited by de Lauretis and Heath. We taped all the events of the film conferences, including "Conditions of Presence" and "Cinema Histories, Cinema Practices." They would be a good source of primary information.

8. Sigmund Freud, *Beyond the Pleasure Principle,* trans. James Strachey (New York: Norton, 1961), pp. 9, 10, 11.

9. I transcribed the sound track; also, I single framed his films, the source of the written quotations. I should have asked the filmmaker for a copy of the script—this took untold hours of detailed work.

10. Deleuze, "Plato and the Simulacrum," p. 47.

11. Baudrillard, *Simulations,* p. 1.

12. Ibid., p. 53.

13. Ibid., p. 52.

14. Baudrillard, *In the Shadow of the Silent Majorities,* p. 84.

15. Ibid., p. 69.

16. Ibid., p. 39.

17. Jean Baudrillard, "The Ecstasy of Communication," in *The Anti-Aesthetic: Essays on Postmodern Culture,* ed. Hal Foster (Port Townsend, Wash.: Bay Press, 1983), pp. 126–133. I have collapsed several sentences and phrases from this essay.

18. Deleuze, "Plato and the Simulacrum," pp. 47–56. The remainder of the quotations are from this translation.

19. Baudrillard, *In the Shadow of the Silent Majorities,* pp. 99–100.

20. Roland Barthes, "Writers, Intellectuals, Teachers," *Image-Music-Text,* ed. Stephen Heath (London: Fontana/Collins, 1977), p. 191.

21. Barthes, *Roland Barthes,* p. 118. The heading of this passage, which I just now noticed, is "Readerly, writerly, and beyond."

5. THEORETICAL OBJECTS

1. Jean-Francois Lyotard, "Acinema," *Wide Angle,* 2, no. 3 (1978), pp. 53–54.

2. Meaghan Morris, "Postmodernity and Lyotard's Sublime," *Art and Text* 16 (Summer 1984–85), p. 45; reprinted in *The Pirate's Fiancee* (London: Verso, 1988).

3. Barthes, *Roland Barthes,* p. 159. "He has always regarded the (domestic) 'scene' as a pure experience of violence, to the degree that, wherever he encounters it, the scene always inspires fear, as though he were a child, panic-stricken. . . ." When I first read this passage, I thought of *Critical Mass.*

4. Roland Barthes, "Change the Object Itself," *Image-Music-Text,* p. 167.

5. Benjamin, "On Some Motifs in Baudelaire," *Illuminations,* p. 160.

6. Heath, "Repetition Time," p. 6.

7. Benjamin, "Theses on the Philosophy of History," *Illuminations,* p. 263.

8. Adrienne Rich, "When We Dead Awaken: Writing as Re-Vision," *On Lies, Secrets and Silence* (New York: Norton, 1979), p. 35.

9. Barthes, "Change the Object Itself," p. 166.

10. Philip Leider, "Bruce Conner: A New Sensibility," *Art Forum* 6 (November 1962), p. 31.

11. Peter Wollen, "Postmodernism," a talk at the Center for Twentieth Century Studies in 1984, if my memory is correct; or is that remembrance?

222 / Notes for pages 109–114

6. POSTMODERN TV

1. For example, see Andreas Huyssen, "The Hidden Dialectic: The Avant-Garde-Technology-Mass Culture," in *The Myths of Information: Technology and Postindustrial Culture,* ed. Kathleen Woodward (Bloomington: Indiana University Press, Coda Press, 1980), pp. 151–164; "The Search for Tradition: Avant-Garde and Postmodernism in the 1970s," *New German Critique* 22 (Winter 1981), pp. 23–40.

2. Andreas Huyssen, "Mapping the Postmodern," *New German Critique* 33 (Fall 1984), pp. 5–52.

3. In *The Anti-Aesthetic,* pp. 57–82.

4. Huyssen, "Mapping the Postmodern," p. 27.

5. There are comments in Huyssen's essay which disturb me. For example, "Without succumbing to the kind of feminine essentialism which is one of the more problematic sides of the feminist enterprise . . ." (p. 28). It is not essentialism which is troubling; it is "one of the more"— what are the other problems?

6. Ibid., p. 28.

7. Edited by Hal Foster for Bay Press, 1983.

8. Foster, "Postmodernism: A Preface," in *The Anti-Aesthetic,* p. xii.

9. Alice Jardine, "In the Name of the Modern: Feminist Questions d'apres *Gynesis* (a Tape Play)," delivered at a seminar series on modernism.

10. Another comment in Huyssen's "Mapping the Postmodern" is troubling: "But one might want to stop talking of postmodernism altogether, and take Barthes' writing for what it is: a theory of modernism which manages to turn the dung of post-68 disillusionment into the gold of aesthetic bliss" (p. 42).

11. Edward Said, "Opponents, Audiences, Constituencies and Community," in *The Anti-Aesthetic,* p. 158.

12. Ibid., p. 157.

13. Ibid., p. 155.

14. Baudrillard, "The Ecstasy of Communication," in *The Anti-Aesthetic,* pp. 126–133, specifically p. 130. I have collapsed several sentences and phrases from this essay—another example of Baudrillard's religious, priestly, indeed Catholic bent, also evident in "Requiem for the Media," an essay divided into the stages of the high mass. *Simulations,* for example, opens by quoting Ecclesiastes. Something more than modern art is being mourned as absent or vanishing. The religiosity is also more than decrying new and false idols.

15. Morris, "Room 101," pp. 91–117. Another quotation from this marvelous essay: "the murderous messiness of mass media culture implies something profoundly un-European; and that the lost 'reality' we mourn can sound remarkably like a declension of classical European (academic) values. The wondrous description of Disneyland . . . depends . . . on our acceptance that the American social is—really—infantile, banal, childish," p. 100.

16. Ibid., p. 98.

17. Fredric Jameson, "Postmodernism and Consumer Society," *The Anti-Aesthetic,* p. 115. This is argued amid his position on "pastiche: in a world in which stylistic innovation is no longer possible . . . and will involve the necessary failure of art and the aesthetic, the failure of the new and the imprisonment in the past."

18. Marcel Proust, *Remembrance of Things Past,* vol. 1 (New York: Random House, 1981), p. 42.

19. Tania Modleski, "The Terror of Pleasure: The Contemporary Horror Film and Postmodern Theory," *Studies in Entertainment: Critical Approaches to Mass Culture,* ed. Tania Modleski (Bloomington: Indiana University Press, 1986).

20. Jameson, "Postmodernism and Consumer Society," p. 125.

21. Ibid., p. 119.

22. Ibid., p. 125.

23. The debt of the postmodern debate to architectural works and writing is significant and perhaps as determining as television. For example, see Jameson's introduction to the recent translation of Jean-Francois Lyotard's *The Postmodern Condition*, or earlier writings by Robert Venturi, e.g., *Complexity and Contradiction in Architecture*.

24. These are the arguments made, I reiterate, by Burger in *Theory of the Avant-Garde*.

25. Sigmund Freud, *Jokes and Their Relation to the Unconscious* (New York: Norton, 1960), p. 155. I have written in greater detail on this text in "Jokes and Their Relation to the Marx Brothers," in *Cinema and Language*, ed. Stephen Heath and Patricia Mellencamp (Frederick, Md.: University Publications, 1983), pp. 63–78.

26. Barthes, *Roland Barthes*, p. 81. To refer back to Deleuze, for a caution: before any rush to embrace this decentering of flat-footed mastery, it should be noted that paternal lineage, and Plato at that, is still intact; furthermore, the theory (perhaps any model of liberation) smacks of surrealism—with its positioning of women as muse/lover.

27. Barthes, *The Pleasure of the Text*, p. 6.

28. Jean-Francois Lyotard, "Philosophy and Painting in the Age of Their Experimentation: Contribution to an Idea of Postmodernity," *Camera Obscura* 12 (1984), p. 119.

29. Freud, *Jokes and Their Relation to the Unconscious*, pp. 204, 144, 149, and 155. After writing this essay about Wegman for the Society for Cinema Studies conference, I discovered (to my research chagrin) an essay by Craig Owens on Wegman: "William Wegman's Psychoanalytic Vaudeville," *Art in America* 71 (March 1983), pp. 100–109. I recommend it, with the disclaimer that any resemblance between Owens's essay and this one is coincidental.

30. Barthes, *The Pleasure of the Text*, p. 24.

31. Ibid., p. 18.

32. Ibid., p. 30.

33. Michael Smith, "Acting/Non-Acting," *Performance Art Magazine* 2 (1979), p. 14.

34. Smith, "Acting/Non-Acting," p. 13.

35. Barthes, "Lecture," pp. 4–5.

36. Jean Baudrillard, "Requiem for the Media," *For a Critique of the Political Economy of the Sign*, p. 177. Baudrillard—picking up where Shamberg and other video visionaries, along with Paik, left off—disagrees with their dream of access, of artist producers, of pluralism: "Reversibility has nothing to do with reciprocity . . . cybernetic systems put this complex regulation and feedback to work without any 'responsibility' in exchange. This is indeed the system's surest line of defence, since it thus integrates the contingency of any such response in advance" (181). He argues against the "revolutionary" solution that "everyone becomes a manipulator": "because this revolution at bottom conserves the category of transmitter, which it is content to generalize as separated; transforming everyone into his own transmitter, it fails to place the mass media system in check" (182).

37. Huyssen, "The Hidden Dialectic," p. 155.

38. Foucault, *Discipline and Punish*, pp. 200–203.

39. This is a reference taken from the introduction to *Re-Vision: Essays in Feminist Film Criticism*, ed. Mary Ann Doane, Patricia Mellencamp, and Linda Williams (Frederick, Md.: University Publications, 1984).

7. UNCANNY FEMINISM

1. Benjamin, "The Storyteller: Reflections on the Works of Nikolai Leskov." *Illuminations*, p. 92.

2. Freud, "The 'Uncanny,' " *Standard Edition*, vol. 18, p. 252.

3. Brothers Grimm, *Grimms' Fairy Tales*, trans. Mrs. E. V. Lucas, Lucy Crane, and Marian Edwards (New York: Grosset & Dunlap, 1945), pp. 1–6.

4. Anne Sexton, "The Twelve Dancing Princesses," from *Transformations* (1971); collected in *The Complete Poems* (Boston: Houghton Mifflin, 1981), p. 281.

5. I am referring to the essays by, for example, Foster and Huyssen in *New German Critique* and Craig Owens in *The Anti-Aesthetic*.

6. Lawrence Stone, "Only Women," *New York Review of Books* 32, no. 6 (April 11, 1985), p. 21.

7. Raymond Durgnat, "Amazing Grace," *American Film* 11, no. 4 (January–February 1986), p. 35.

8. Dick Hebdige, "Posing . . . Threats, Striking . . . Poses: Youth, Surveillance, and Display," *Substance* 37/38, (1983), pp. 85, 86. I have collapsed remarks from several paragraphs in this very interesting essay concerning youth subcultures—a topic which overlaps to a vague degree Condit's concern with adolescence or moments of passage, and an area or approach which can be applied fruitfully to the "subcultures" of the art scene, including avant-garde, independent filmmaking.

9. Mary Russo, "Female Grotesques: Carnival and Theory," from her manuscript for *Feminist Studies/Critical Studies*, ed. Teresa de Lauretis (Bloomington: Indiana University Press, 1986).

10. Perhaps more than other divides, for example, between art and mass culture, the gap between men and women is the one that needs to be acknowledged, a division enhanced by sexual difference as the kingpin difference. As de Lauretis wrote in *Alice Doesn't*, "It may well be, however, that the story has to be told differently. Take Oedipus, for instance." I love the timing of the last sentence, p. 156.

11. "Postmodern TV" details a model of postmodernism as it relates to video and feminism.

12. Hal Foster, *October* 34 (1985), pp. 64, 65, 69. This last reference is comparable to other marginal allusions to feminism—for "feminists," for "minorities," for "tribal peoples." Taxonomy is not innocent, no matter how qualified by quotations.

13. Mary Ann Doane, Patricia Mellencamp, and Linda Williams, "Feminist Film Criticism: An Introduction," *Re-Vision: Essays in Feminist Film Criticism*, p. 15.

14. Teresa de Lauretis, "Aesthetic and Feminist Theory: Rethinking Women's Cinema," *New German Critique*, no. 34 (Winter 1985), pp. 164, 168.

15. Jameson, "Postmodernism and Consumer Society," in *The Anti-Aesthetic*, p. 125.

16. Roland Barthes, "Change the Object Itself: Mythology Today," *Image-Music-Text*, pp. 167–168. This short, five-page essay is an update of Barthes's earlier work on mythology—the latter, cited by Foster.

17. De Lauretis, *Alice Doesn't*, p. 186. The end of this book, like that of the classical Hollywood film, circles back to the beginning: "In the heart of Looking-Glass country, between her fifth and sixth moves across the chessboard, Alice comes to the center of the labyrinth of language," p. 1.

18. Sexton, "Briar Rose (Sleeping Beauty)," *The Complete Poems*, p. 293.

19. Russo, "Female Grotesques."

20. Mikhail Bakhtin, *Rabelais and His World*, trans. Helene Iswolsky (Bloomington: Indiana University Press, 1984), pp. 317–318.

21. Russo, "Female Grotesques."

22. Quoted from Russo.

23. I transcribed the videotapes and hope the quotations are accurate.

24. Benjamin, "The Storyteller," *Illuminations*, p. 92.

25. Bakhtin, *Rabelais and His World*, p. 317.

26. Linda Hutcheon, *A Theory of Parody* (New York: Methuen, 1985), p. 72. Her chapter "The Paradox of Parody," pp. 69–83, discusses Bakhtin's writings, taking

issue with his negative regard toward modern parody, what she calls "his rejection of the contemporary." Thus Hutcheon argues (p. 71) that "we should look to what the theories suggest, rather than what the practice denies. . . ."

27. Ibid., pp. 92, 99.
28. Benjamin "The Storyteller," *Illuminations,* p. 87.
29. Ibid., p. 102.
30. Ibid., p. 100.
31. De Lauretis, "Aesthetic and Feminist Theory," p. 160.
32. Benjamin, "The Storyteller," *Illuminations,* p. 94.
33. Bakhtin, *Rabelais and His World,* p. 316.
34. Herbert Blau, "Comedy since the Absurd," *Modern Drama* 25, no. 4 (December 1982), pp. 555, 556.
35. Freud, "The 'Uncanny,' " p. 250.
36. Ibid., p. 235.
37. Ibid., p. 231.
38. Sigmund Freud, "Medusa's Head," *Standard Edition,* vol. 18, p. 273.
39. Benjamin "The Storyteller," *Illuminations,* p. 86.
40. Adrienne Rich, "Natural Resources," *The Dream of a Common Language* (New York: Norton, 1978), p. 61.

8. LAST SCENE IN THE STREETS OF MODERNISM

1. David Lodge, *Small World* (New York: Warner Books, 1984), p. 74.
2. Teresa de Lauretis, "From a Dream of Woman," *Cinema and Language* (Frederick, Md.: University Publications, 1983), pp. 21–22.
3. Sigmund Freud, *Delusion and Dream* (Boston: Beacon Press, 1956), p. 33.
4. Michel de Certeau, *The Practice of Everyday Life,* trans. Steven Rendall (Los Angeles: University of California Press), p. 94.
5. Benjamin, "A Berlin Chronicle," *Reflections,* p. 3.
6. Thomas Bulfinch, *Mythology* (New York: Dell, 1959), p. 125.
7. Benjamin, "Paris, Capital of the Nineteenth Century," *Reflections,* p. 157.
8. Patrice Petro, *Joyless Streets: Women and Melodramatic Representation in Weimar Germany* (Princeton: Princeton University Press, 1988); the quotation is taken from her dissertation, University of Iowa, p. 69.
9. Andreas Huyssen, "Mass Culture as Woman: "Modernism's Other," *Studies in Entertainment* (Bloomington: Indiana University Press, 1986), p. 189.
10. Benjamin, "A Berlin Chronicle," *Reflections,* p. 8.
11. Meaghan Morris, "At Henry Parkes Motel," unpublished manuscript; a version is available in "Working Papers," Center for Twentieth Century Studies.
12. Benjamin, "A Berlin Chronicle," *Reflections,* p. 31.
13. Umberto Eco, *Postscript to The Name of the Rose* (New York: Harcourt Brace Jovanovich, 1983) p. 57.
14. Benjamin, "A Berlin Chronicle," *Reflections,* p. 9.
15. Marguerite Duras, *Hiroshima Mon Amour,* trans. Richard Seaver (New York: Grove Press, 1961), p. 25.
16. Barthes's "meditation" on mother culminates in *Camera Lucida.*

9. TAKING A CUE FROM ARIADNE

1. Foucault, *Power/Knowledge,* p. 193.
2. Rich, "When We Dead Awaken: Writing as Re-Vision," *On Lies, Secrets and Silence,* p. 35.
3. This was the initial meeting of KIWI, the women's international organization for film and television; it took place in Georgia, USSR, in March 1988.
4. For a detailed, shot-by-shot analysis and reading of *Thriller* in conjunction with contemporary theory, e.g., Heath, de Lauretis, and Helene Cixous, see "Mimi's

Resistance: Strategies of Refusal in Sally Potter's *Thriller*," by Sonja Rein, master's thesis, Department of Art History, University of Wisconsin-Milwaukee. Rein's transcription of the film, including her annotation of shots, is very helpful and her analysis is quite wonderful.

5. This conference was organized by de Lauretis for the Center for Twentieth Century Studies in April 1985.

6. Pam Cook, "*The Gold Diggers*: Interview with Sally Potter," *Framework* 24 (Spring 1984), p. 26. This brilliantly lucid analysis by Potter is perhaps the best critique of the film, raising most of the issues I discuss. Because all of the sections I will quote are Potter's, I will cite her name rather than Cook's. It should, however, be noted that Cook is a significant intellect, along with Johnston and Mulvey, in the feminist-theory debates in England.

7. Film history so far has largely been left up to men, who have paid scant heed to the gendered bias of its writing. Thus, a strange paradox has emerged in this discipline: feminism has pervaded film theory, while the history of women, other than as luminous objects, has been overlooked. Equally, the application of much "feminist" film theory to Hollywood films has ignored the historical context in which the films were produced. Another divide is suggestive: theory as women's work with history the domain of men. However, this, too, is rapidly changing.

8. I am referring to the essay by Hal Foster which I discussed in "Uncanny Feminism." The scene of trauma, the daughter's memory of separation, erupts into this very modern film.

9. Potter, p. 15.

10. Ibid., p. 14.

11. Ibid., p. 19.

12. Ibid., p. 25.

13. Ibid., pp. 15–16.

14. This is from the film.

15. The dialogue resembles writings from the early 1970s on "the cinematic apparatus," particularly those of Metz and Baudry, which were minus feminism, never mind gender.

16. Monique Wittig, "One Is Not Born a Woman," *Feminist Issues*, Winter 1981, p. 44.

17. At the Society for Cinema Studies annual meeting in Montreal, Kaja Silverman presented a chapter of her new book, *The Acoustic Mirror*, which contains her analysis of this film; her argument circled around a negative and positive Oedipus and female subjectivity. Because I had completed this essay four months prior to hearing this talk, I decided not to read Silverman's analysis—the negative, ostrich model of scholarship. From what I heard, our takes are very different.

18. I am thinking particularly about recent British feminist debates about pleasure—reviving pleasure for feminism. I am unsure of the terms of this debate—given that pleasure was, for me, never dead.

19. Potter, p. 18; one can feel Potter's irritation and passion regarding "formalism," usually taken to be incompatible with feminism. And, as I argue in the early chapters, feminism was largely ignored by avant-garde filmmakers. However, this is history; it can change. Potter asks the critical question here: "What is the pleasure if it's based on female pain?" This issue is also raised in the film clips which Rainer incorporates in her film.

20. Ibid., p. 20.

21. Paul Willemen, "An Avant-Garde for the Eighties," *Framework* 24 (Spring 1984), p. 62. I have not done justice to this dense argument, which positions avant-garde resolutely against modernism without, however, taking into consideration the development of the postmodern critique in the United States. Willemen, so knowl-

edgeable about avant-garde, argues through and for history and a politics of a narrative avant-garde.

22. Wittig, "One Is Not Born a Woman," p. 43.

23. Ibid., p. 53.

24. Ibid.

25. Potter, p. 27.

26. Ibid., p. 12.

27. Jane Feuer, *The Hollywood Musical* (Bloomington: Indiana University Press, 1982). This general argument runs throughout her book. See also Mellencamp, "The Spectacle and the Spectator: Looking Through the Hollywood Musical," in *Cine-Tracts*.

28. Alexander Cockburn, "Don't Look Now," *American Film* 11, no. 4, p. 19.

29. Potter, p. 29.

30. Potter would disagree with Feuer and take her pleasure in formalism, critique, and revelation. This film thinks about the base of mass entertainment—particularly the female body, largely ignored by Feuer, as are most of the musical's ramifications of gender. And, I agree with Potter: it is deeply pleasurable, as are many avant-garde films, narrative or not, which dissect the apparatus, entertaining us but in other ways.

31. Willemen, "Avant-Garde," p. 61. Given that "reference" is so critical to postmodernism, Willemen's argument *for* history might serve as a corrective to Jameson's claim that postmodernism is the loss of history.

32. Potter, p. 12.

33. Ibid., p. 16.

34. Ibid.

35. Ibid., p. 20.

36. Sigmund Freud, "Female Sexuality," *Sexuality and the Psychology of Love,* (New York: Collier Books, 1963). p. 194.

37. Ibid., p. 195.

38. Ibid., p. 197.

39. Sigmund Freud, "Some Psychological Consequences of the Anatomical Distinction between the Sexes," *Sexuality and the Psychology of Love,* p. 191.

40. Freud, "Female Sexuality," p. 195.

41. Ibid., p. 203.

42. This song is taken from the film's sound track, which is available from Arcades. Cooper's music includes twelve songs.

43. I await the publication of women writers on the history of Hollywood stars, particularly the silent film stars. I want to thank Mary Yelanjian for transcribing the sound track, which is very succinct, precisely written, like the visual track.

44. The lyrics of this performance were almost impossible for me to discern. I suspect that the sound mix was not as good as it could have been—I get the feeling that money ran out. Most critics don't realize the time, cost, and detailed effort that go into mixing sound.

45. Sigmund Freud, "Identification," *Group Psychology and the Analysis of the Ego,* trans. James Strachey (New York: Norton, 1959), pp. 37–42. Freud's opening sentences are a giveaway, linking identification, like everything else under the sun and in the universe, to the Oedipus complex: "It [identification] plays a part in the early history of the Oedipus complex. A little boy will exhibit a special interest in his father; he would like to grow like him and be like him. . . . This behaviour has nothing to do with a passive or feminine attitude towards his father (and towards males in general); it is on the contrary typically masculine." For women, identification, particularly with mothers, involves an illness or is hysterical. For men, it involves growing up.

46. Potter, p. 24.

47. Willemen, "Avant-Garde," p. 69.
48. Scott MacDonald, "Points of View: An Interview with Babette Mangolte," *Afterimage* 12, nos. 1 and 2 (Summer 1984). p. 12.
49. This is the crucial argument for Willemen, the marking of history as politics within film.
50. Potter, p. 21.
51. Potter, pp. 25–26.

10. IMAGES OF LANGUAGE AND INDISCREET DIALOGUES

1. De Lauretis, *Alice Doesn't*, p. 156.
2. Yvonne Rainer, "More Kicking and Screaming from the Narrative Front/Backwater," *Wide Angle* 7, nos. 1 and 2, p. 8. This is a sketch of the film—working thoughts and scenes as a dialogue with an imagined audience response. This special double issue of *Wide Angle*, which I edited, was the publication of the proceedings of the conference. "Cinema Histories, Cinema Practices II."
3. Rainer, "More Kicking and Screaming," p. 11.
4. Jacques Lacan, *The Four Fundamental Concepts of Psycho-Analysis*, trans. Alan Sheridan (New York: Norton, 1978), p. 106. See also Foucault, *Discipline and Punish*. This speaking eye is frequently operative in women's melodrama, particularly regarding medical discourse. For an acute analysis of the "woman's film," see Mary Ann Doane, *The Desire to Desire* (Bloomington: Indiana University Press, 1987) and her essay (as well as the introduction by Doane, Mellencamp, and Williams) in *Re-Vision: Essays in Feminist Film Criticism*.
5. Jacques Lacan, "Seminar on The Purloined Letter," in *French Freud*, ed. Jeffrey Mehlman, *Yale French Studies*, p. 44.
6. Peter Wollen's essay "The Hermeneutic Code," *Readings and Writings: Semiotic Counter Strategies* (London: Verso Editions, 1982), ferrets out this analytical schema and applies it to Hitchcock's films, with a detailed analysis of *North by Northwest*. Wollen's recent work on Hitchcock is a fine example of textual analysis applying analytical constructs to the films—critical models which Hitchcock's work can bear with little strain. Because Wollen's style of writing is so succinct, difficult arguments are presented with such ease that the unwary reader might mistakenly construe them as apparent.
7. Lacan, "Seminar." It is sometimes baffling how a simple alteration—a glance or a word—would adjust the historical terms of narrative, which repeatedly depict woman as a narrative image or empty position, a body without a soul.
8. Ibid., pp. 66, 71.
9. Ibid., pp. 66.
10. Ibid. On page 69, there is a clincher to this relation between the analyst as ravisher; Lacan's bliss of ecstastic transference is claimed for the analyst, the "we who become the emissaries of all the purloined letters which at least for a time remain in sufferance with us in the transference." In sufferance, indeed!
11. I have taken these quotations from the film, and thus they are not as accurate as they might have been if quoted from Rainer's script. Reading this text, like her other scripts, would be a pleasurable experience; Rainer is also a writer.
12. Rainer, "More Kicking and Screaming," p. 11. She appeals to the "spectator-of-my-dreams" who "has given equal attention to the fictions and the production of these fictions, to the social relations and to the representation of those relations." This ideal spectator resembles Bakhtin's "higher, *super-receiver* [I dislike this translation immensely—the Clark Kent or NFL version of wide "reception" theory] whose absolutely appropriate responsive understanding is projected either into a metaphysical distance or into a distant historical time. (A spare receiver.)" I like the imagined idea of a spare receiver—art's pinch-hitter. What an artist's and teacher's and lover's dream—an "absolutely appropriate responsive understanding." See Tzvetan Todorov,

Mikhail Bakhtin: The Dialogical Principle, trans. Wlad Godzick (Minneapolis: University of Minnesota Press, 1984), p. 110.

13. Rainer, "More Kicking and Screaming," p. 12.

14. I have taken these quotations from Stephen Heath's paper "Male Feminism," delivered at the MLA and subsequently published in a collection of essays, *Male Feminism*. This topic has been powerfully explored by Modleski in *Feminist Studies/ Critical Studies*.

15. Blau, "Comedy since the Absurd," p. 557.

16. Meaghan Morris, "The Pirate's Fiancee," in *Power, Truth, Strategy*, ed. Morris and Paul Stratton (Sydney: Feral Publications, 1980), p. 33. This essay clearly affected Rainer (as it did me when I first encountered it), who took its advice and position. Regarding Foucault's work Morris writes, "the point is to use it and not to 'apply' it." The energy and wit of her writing is contagious—like the film. The powerful women behind the scenes, pulling all the strings and making themselves heard along with Rainer, are, of course, Trisha Brown, but including Morris and Martha Rosler. Jack didn't stand a chance, although Rainer and Rosler let him off the hook at the end when they return to the "About Men" column in the *New York Times Magazine*— and Rosler's voice-over states: "It is a matter of interest whether men are or are not presented as hard surfaces . . . masculinity as uncaringness and unthinkingness. . . . It does matter. . . ." In their earlier confrontation with this essay, they harshly critiqued the attention bestowed on sensitive males as yet another example of the continual focus on male subjectivity.

17. These quotations are taken from the manuscript of Mary Russo's "Female Grotesques: Carnival and Theory," in *Feminist Studies/Critical Studies*.

18. Part of the recent history of film studies involves the legitimation of heavy-duty and constant talk about sexuality, disguised as "discourse."

19. During this terrific scene, the audience begins to fight with each other, oblivious to the escalating bloody, violent film nightmare. Dutiful onstage, Jack is also oblivious to the pandemonium of rebelling spectators; perhaps like us, they just can't stand him and his endless, platitudinous analysis anymore. This is the comically black underside of "going to the movies" akin to "going into analysis." Perhaps it is also a displaced version of the artist explicating her films to audiences on the independent traveling circuit—usually standing onstage, in front of the screen which had just shown the "new work,"—a process that has its own dynamic or inertia, pleasures and dangers. I suspect the trek and the repetition must, in the end, be boring.

20. Morris, "Room 101," p. 98. The writing is unstoppable, clever; for example, under the caption "famous last words," Morris writes about Baudrillard's conservative pessimism: "No more God, no more Subject, no more Philosophy of the Subject, no more Progress, Regress, History, Nature, Reality, Imaginary, Profit, Revolution, Repression, Representation, Power, Meaning, Production, Dialectic, Judgement, Criticism, War, Liberation, Capital, Class, Change, Exchange, Fiction, Value . . ." When read aloud, it quite makes hilarious sense, concluding with the clincher, after a pause of punctuation—the capitalized word "Death" (p. 103). This essay concludes a book in which the editor writes with comic candor about his editorship: "One immediate and widespread reaction was disbelief that it was actually I who was editing the book. Who was this Andre Frankovits and where was his curriculum vitae? Perhaps my name already sounds like a pseudonym" (p. 6).

21. Morris, "The Pirate's Fiancee," p. 152.

22. Helen de Michel, "Rainer's *Manhattan*," *Afterimage* 13, no. 5 (December 1985), p. 20.

23. Hutcheon, *Theory of Parody*, p. 8. It is disconcerting to realize the lack of acknowledgment of feminist influences on this book; for Hutcheon, feminism is merely an aside, a singular practice, a unimensional topic, albeit an interesting one; feminism, which is so apparent, is denied; I wonder why?

24. Ibid., pp. 32, 72.

25. Ibid., pp. 99, 101.

26. Ibid., pp. 101, 109.

27. Judy Stone, "Datebook," San Francisco Chronicle; this was a review of the film's opening at the Roxy Cinema in San Francisco; unlike most independent films, this feature-length film had "real" distribution and exhibition rather than the usual classroom, one-night stands of most alternative or avant-garde works.

28. For an explication of Bakhtin's writings, most of which have not been translated into English (a volume is forthcoming from the University of Minnesota Press), Todorov's compendium, Mikhail Bakhtin, was invaluable. I realize the reduction, however, of lifting quotations out of Bakhtin's Soviet time and context, from Todorov's context of fragments assembled as an argumentative whole. My ripping off this work is thus a questionable, timeless postmodern strategy of raiding—reaching back into another culture and another history—secondarily derived. This is not scholarly method and should be approached with caution.

29. Todorov quoting Bakhtin, p. 108.

30. Ibid., p. 178.

31. Ibid., p. 46.

32. Ibid.

33. Todorov, p. 39.

34. Mikhail Bakhtin, The Dialogic Imagination, ed. Michael Holquist (Austin: University of Texas Press, 1981).

35. Todorov quoting Bakhtin, p. 22.

36. Jean-Francois Lyotard, "Philosophy and Painting in the Age of Their Experimentation: Contribution to an Idea of Postmodernity," Camera Obscura 12 (Summer 1984), p. 119.

37. I refer to the comprehensive exegeses of postmodernism by Andreas Huyssen in New German Critique, Hal Foster in New German Critique and The Anti-Aesthetic, and Fredric Jameson in these and other places; I discussed their arguments in earlier chapters. The first two writers invite feminists to join this dance. Jameson and Huyssen mourn the loss of history and story. The influence of Jameson's writings on the debate has been incalculable. Ask anyone in the United States what postmodernism is and the reply will be a facile "pastiche." Ask for a definition of pastiche and the answerer will oppose it to parody. Don't pursue this line of questioning. Change the subject.

38. Heath, "Male Feminism."

39. Russo, "Female Grotesques."

40. Virginia Woolf, Three Guineas (New York: Harcourt, 1938), pp. 4, 18.

11. THE AVANT-GARDE, THE EVERYDAY, AND THE UNDERGROUND

1. Jonas Mekas, Movie Journal: The Rise of a New American Cinema, 1959–1971 (New York: Collier Books, 1972).

2. I have taken my quotations from an earlier translation/publication by Deleuze and Guattari, On the Line, trans. John Johnston (New York: Semiotext[e], 1983), which includes "Rhizome" by Deleuze and Guattari and "Politics" by Deleuze. The reason for retaining and including so many quotations from Mekas and D and G is the striking similarity between phrases and words, along with argument.

3. Gilles Deleuze, Cinema 1: The Movement-Image, trans. Hugh Tomlinson and Barbara Habberjam (Minneapolis: University of Minnesota Press, 1986).

4. Deleuze and Guattari, On the Line, p. 2.

5. There are other analogies throughout A Thousand Plateaus that suggest that this comparison is operative throughout. The organizational principles of AA are against hierarchy and leadership, cross-cutting differences of race, class, sex, economics, education, age.

6. Scott MacDonald, *A Critical Cinema: Interviews with Independent Filmmakers* (Berkeley: University of California Press, 1988), p. 30.

7. Alice A. Jardine, "Becoming a Body without Organs: Deleuze and His Brothers," *Gynesis: Configurations of Woman and Modernity* (Ithaca: Cornell University Press, 1985), pp. 208–209.

8. Meaghan Morris made these points in a graduate seminar for the Modern Studies Program, University of Wisconsin-Milwaukee, during the spring semester, 1989.

9. Dana Polan, "Powers of Vision, Visions of Power," *Camera Obscura* 18, pp. 106–119.

10. I received the protest letter in April or May 1989; the list of signers will grow, as this is also a petition, a call for action.

11. Meaghan Morris, *The Pirate's Fiancee: Feminism/Reading Postmodernism* (London: Verso, 1988), p. 176.

12. Aronowitz, in *The 60s without Apology;* Jameson, in *New German Critique* and *The Anti-Aesthetic.*

13. Examples from Land's (of course) multiple-choice exam include the following questions: "DOLLY SHOT: a) the basic technique used in filming *Un Chien Andalou,* b) Shot of a female Country and Western Singer; or c) Shot in which the camera, placed on a wheeled mount, moves closer to or away from a scene. . . . TAKE: a) What many public officials are on; b) A common name among Japanese men; or c) A run of the camera from start to finish." Note: both the correct answers are c.

14. Doug Henwood, "The Empire's New Clothes," *Village Voice,* April 18, 1989, p. 59.

15. Bertrand Bellon and Jorge Niosi, *The Decline of the American Economy,* trans. Robert Chodos and Ellen Garmaise (Black Rose Books).

16. Freud, "Anxiety and Instinctual Life," *Standard Edition,* vol. 22, p. 108.

INDEX

PATRICIA MELLENCAMP is Associate Professor of Art History at the University of Wisconsin-Milwaukee. She is the editor of *Logics of Television* and three American Film Institute monographs, including *Cinema and Language*, and the author of articles in *Screen*, *Afterimage*, *Wide Angle*, *Discourse*, and *Framework*.